Crime Prevention Policies in Comparative Perspective

Edited by

Adam Crawford

WILLAN
PUBLISHING

Published by

Willan Publishing
Culmcott House
Mill Street, Uffculme
Cullompton, Devon
EX15 3AT, UK
Tel: +44(0)1884 840337
Fax: +44(0)1884 840251
e-mail: info@willanpublishing.co.uk
Website: www.willanpublishing.co.uk

Published simultaneously in the USA and Canada by

Willan Publishing
c/o ISBS, 920 NE 58th Ave, Suite 300,
Portland, Oregon 97213-3786, USA
Tel: +001(0)503 287 3093
Fax: +001(0)503 280 8832
e-mail: info@isbs.com
Website: www.isbs.com

First published 2009

ISBN 978-1-84392-412-8 paperback
 978-1-84392-413-5 hardback

British Library Cataloguing-in-Publication Data

A catalogue record for this book is available from the British Library

FSC
Mixed Sources
Product group from well-managed
forests and other controlled sources

Cert no. SGS-COC-2482
www.fsc.org
© 1996 Forest Stewardship Council

Project management by Deer Park Productions, Tavistock, Devon
Typeset by TW Typesetting, Plymouth, Devon
Printed and bound by T J International Ltd, Trecerus Industrial Estate, Padstow, Cornwall

Contents

Figures and tables

Figures

Tables

Acknowledgements

This book arose out of an international colloquium held at the University of Leeds on 7–8 June 2007. It was organised under the framework of the CRIMPREV co-ordination action project entitled 'Assessing Crime, Deviance and Prevention' and funded by the European Commission (Contract No. 028300). The project is co-ordinated by the French *Centre National de la Recherche Scientifique* (CNRS). Further information about CRIMPREV is available from the project website: www.crimprev.eu.

All the contributors to this volume presented initial papers and arguments at the Leeds colloquium in June 2007. The resultant final versions of all the chapters benefited from the lively discussions and debates during the two-day meeting. We would like to acknowledge all those who attended and contributed to the colloquium deliberations including (in alphabetical order): Adam Crawford, Jim Dignan, Jan Van Dijk, Adam Edwards, Patrick Hebberecht, Alistair Henry, Tim Hope, Gordon Hughes, Michael Jasch, Klara Kerezsi, Hugues Lagrange, René Lévy, Stuart Lister, Livia Lucianetti, Michel Marcus, Dario Melossi, Gorazd Mesko, Margaret Shaw, Peter Traynor, Jaap De Waard and Anne Wyvekens. As ever, many thanks to Brian Willan and his team for their support and encouragement in bringing this collection to fruition.

Notes on contributors

Adam Crawford is Professor of Criminology and Criminal Justice and director of the Centre for Criminal Justice Studies at the University of Leeds. His publications include *The Local Governance of Crime* (1997), *Crime Prevention and Community Safety* (1998), *Crime and Insecurity* (2002) and *Plural Policing* (2005). He was the recipient of a Leverhulme Trust Major Research Fellowship which informed his forthcoming book *Governing the Future: The Contractual Governance of Anti-Social Behaviour*. In the past he has worked for the New Zealand government and Northern Ireland Office on matters of crime prevention and community safety and is a member of the Safer Leeds Partnership Board.

Jaap De Waard is Senior Policy Advisor at the Netherlands Ministry of Justice. He is the former secretary of the European Crime Prevention Network. He has published widely on crime prevention models, international trends in the private security industry, and international benchmark studies in the field of crime control. He is a member of the European Union Crime Experts Group, European Commission, Directorate-General for Justice, Freedom and Security. He is research fellow at the International Victimology Institute (INTERVICT), Tilburg University.

Adam Edwards is Lecturer in criminology in the School of Social Sciences, Cardiff University. His publications include *Crime Control and Community* (with Gordon Hughes, 2002). He is director of the European Governance of Public Safety Research Network, which is a working group of the European Society of Criminology that promotes comparative research into the politics of crime prevention in Europe.

Patrick Hebberecht is Professor of Criminology and Sociology of Law and director of the Research Group of Criminology and Sociology of Law at the University of Ghent. He is doing research on prevention policies in Belgium and Europe. He co-directed with Fritz Sack *La Prévention de*

Délinquance en Europe: Nouvelles Stratégies (1997) and with Dominique Duprez *The Prevention and Security Policies in Europe* (2002). His latest book is *De 'verpaarsing' van de criminaliteitsbestrijding in België: Kritische opstellen over misdaad en misdaadcontrole in de laatmoderniteit* ('The "Purple-isation" of Criminal Policy in Belgium: Critical Thoughts on Crime and Crime Control in Late Modernity').

Alistair Henry is a lecturer in criminology at the University of Edinburgh. He recently completed his doctoral research on community safety partnerships in Scotland and is currently embarking upon a knowledge transfer project on community policing funded by the Arts and Humanities Research Council. His recent publications include *Transformations of Policing* (edited with David J. Smith, 2007). He is associated with both the Scottish Institute for Policing Research and the Scottish Centre for Crime and Justice Research.

Tim Hope is Professor of Criminology at Keele University and Senior Visiting Research Fellow, Scottish Centre for Crime and Justice Research, University of Edinburgh. He has held positions at the universities of Manchester and Missouri-St Louis, and the Home Office Research and Planning Unit (1974–91). He was director of the Economic and Social Research Council's *Crime and Social Order* research programme. His research into crime prevention, community safety and victimology is published in the USA, Canada, France, Germany, Italy, Poland, the Czech Republic and Portugal.

Gordon Hughes is Professor of Criminology at the School of Social Sciences, Cardiff University. His current research interests include comparative trends in crime prevention, the politics of community safety, strategic problem-solving and the changing modes of the local governance of crime, disorder and security. Recent funded research has involved a study of the changing role and work of community safety teams and an evaluation of youth crime prevention schemes in Wales funded by the Welsh Assembly Government. His most recent monograph is *The Politics of Crime and Community* (2007). He is currently writing a book for Sage entitled *Sociology and Crime*.

Michael Jasch is a lecturer and research assistant at the Goethe-University Frankfurt/Main. His recent publications include 'The Crisis of Community Crime Prevention' (in *Monatsschrift für Kriminologie und Strafrechtsreform*, 2003), a paper on 'Criminal Law and Security' (in *Kriminologisches*, 2007) and an empirical study on the crime situation in the city of Rostock (2000). He has worked with law faculties and research institutions in Germany and with the Centre for Criminological Research at Oxford

University. Between 1996 and 2001, he was a member of the local crime prevention council in Rostock.

Klara Kerezsi is Deputy Director of the National Institute of Criminology and associate professor at Eotvos University, Hungary. She is a member of the Scientific Committee of the International Society of Criminology and vice-president of the Hungarian Society of Criminology. Her research interests are crime prevention, crime control policies and community sanctions. Her books include *Crime Prevention in Three Districts of Budapest* (2003, co-author) and *Control or Support: The Dilemma of Alternative Sanctions* (2006). She contributed a chapter to the collection *Probation in Europe* (2008). In 1996 she was commissioned to elaborate the first Hungarian national crime prevention concept and in 2002 she contributed to the elaboration of the National Crime Prevention Strategy which was approved by the parliament.

Dario Melossi is Professor of Criminology in the School of Law at the University of Bologna, to where he has returned after many years on various campuses of the University of California. His publications include *The Prison and the Factory* (with Massimo Pavarini, 1981), *The State of Social Control* (1990) and, most recently, *Controlling Crime, Controlling Society: Thinking About Crime in Europe and America* (2008). He is currently working on issues of migration and deviance, especially youth deviance, in the Italian region of Emilia-Romagna. He is also very much interested in the issue of migration in relation to the process of European unification. He has been a member of the Safe Cities project of the regional government of Emilia-Romagna.

Rossella Selmini is Director of the Department for Urban Safety and Local Police of the Italian region of Emilia-Romagna and Professor of Criminology and Sociology of Prevention at the University of Macerata. In the past she has been a researcher at the European University Institute, and then responsible for the research unit on crime and prevention in Emilia-Romagna. She has also been a consultant of local and national governments. Her recent publications include *La Sicurezza Urbana* (2004) and many articles on the local governance of crime, crime prevention and victimisation studies.

Margaret Shaw is Director of Analysis and Exchange at the International Centre for the Prevention of Crime (ICPC), based in Montreal, Canada. Since she joined ICPC in 1999 she has written and published extensively on crime prevention issues, and participated in many conferences and seminars internationally. She has worked as a consultant for UNODC, UN-HABITAT and the Inter-American Development Bank on issues of prevention and community safety. She previously taught at Concordia

University, Montreal, and was a long-time member of the Home Office Research and Planning Unit before moving to Canada. With Tim Hope she edited a first UK text on *Communities and Crime Reduction* published in 1988. She is a board member of Women in Cities International.

Jan J.M. Van Dijk holds the Pieter Van Vollenhoven Chair in Victimology, Human Security and Safety at the University of Tilburg in the Netherlands. His former posts include director of crime prevention at the Dutch Ministry of Justice and officer in charge of the United Nations crime prevention programme in Vienna. His latest book is *The World of Crime: Breaking the Silence on Issues of Security, Justice and Development* (2008). In 2003 he received the Hans von Hentig Award from the World Society of Victimology and in 2008 the Sellin-Glueck Award from the American Society of Criminology.

Anne Wyvekens is Researcher at the French National Centre for Scientific Research (CNRS/CERSA Université Paris 2) and Associate Researcher at the Facultés Universitaires Saint-Louis Brussels. Her books include *Espace Public et Sécurité* (2006) and *La Magistrature Sociale* (with Jacques Donzelot, 2004). She worked as a scientific expert for the Council of Europe's Committee on Partnerships in the Prevention of Crime and contributed to its subsequent publication *A Partnership Approach to Crime Prevention* (2004). She was director of research at the Ministry of the Interior funded Institut des Hautes Études de la Sécurité Intérieure. She is a member of the scientific committee of the International Centre for the Prevention of Crime and works with the French Forum for Urban Safety.

Introduction

The preventive turn in Europe

Adam Crawford

For the past quarter of a century or so the growth of public policies and implementation strategies advanced across diverse jurisdictions in the name of crime prevention and community safety has constituted one of the major innovations in crime control, with significant implications for the manner in which crime and safety are governed. The ensuing 'preventive turn' has been variously described as representing a 'major shift in paradigm' (Tuck 1988), an 'epistemological break' with the past (Garland 2000: 1) and 'a long-overdue recognition that the levers and causes of crime lie far from the traditional reach of the criminal justice system ... afford[ing] the potential to encourage a stronger and more participatory civil society and challenge many of the modernist assumptions about professional expertise, specialisation, state paternalism and monopoly' (Crawford 1998: 4). Others have proclaimed it as confirming the rise of 'risk' as an overarching governmental narrative (O'Malley 1992) or as ushering, and evidencing, a new era of 'networked governance' (Johnston and Shearing 2003). Despite these claims, conceptions of preventive governance are by no means new. In Britain, Patrick Colquhoun (1797) and Edwin Chadwick (1829), among others, advocated forms of crime prevention through policing aimed at reducing opportunities and temptations that resonate strikingly with contemporary trends. More broadly, classical liberal thought in the eighteenth and early nineteenth centuries promoted the governance of future life choices on the basis of rational calculations of the relative balance between risk and reward that closely echoes the logic of modern crime prevention thinking, most notably its situational variant (Clarke 1995, 2000).

Nevertheless, 'preventive partnerships' have become a defining attribute of contemporary crime control and its interface with wider social and urban policies in a way that is both novel and demands critical contextual scrutiny. As Garland noted in his assessment of shifts in contemporary crime control:

> Over the past two decades ... a whole new infrastructure has been assembled at the local level that addresses crime and disorder in a quite different manner ... The new infrastructure is strongly oriented towards a set of objectives and priorities – prevention, security, harm-reduction, loss-reduction, fear-reduction – that are quite different from the traditional goals of prosecution, punishment and 'criminal justice'. (2001: 16–17)

While Garland was writing exclusively about developments in the UK and USA, what is interesting (especially for the purposes of this book) is that novel infrastructures, technologies, mentalities and practices began to emerge, unfold and to be fashioned across different European countries from the late 1970s and early 1980s onwards. Saliently, as the contributions to this volume testify, these developments took (and continue to take) different directions, trajectories and nuances, as they were influenced by divergent political contexts and socio-cultural traditions. While crime prevention policies and practices have stimulated a wealth of commentary and analysis (too extensive to elaborate here), there have been few systematic attempts to reflect back on the varied journeys taken, the reasons that have informed particular developmental pathways and their implications, as well as possible future directions. Furthermore, while there have been some valuable exceptions (Graham 1993; Graham and Bennett 1995; Crawford 1998, 2002; Duprez and Hebberecht 2002; Hughes *et al.* 2002), much of the literature has tended to leave less space for analyses of the comparative differences and similarities between diverse models of prevention and the different routes to implementation.

By contrast to current policy deliberations, the early years of the 'preventive turn' in the 1980s were marked by a relatively stark debate concerning the merits and attractions of contrasting European models of crime prevention, its management and delivery. From the outset these models were heavily influenced by political ideology and reflected different assumptions about crime, behavioural motivations and appropriate ways of organising regulatory responses. Simply put, while the British model became coupled with a situational approach that sought directly to involve the private sector (King 1991; Hope, see Chapter 2), the French model, exemplified by the Bonnemaison commission report published in 1982, came to be seen as the archetype of a social crime prevention approach, with its emphasis on social inclusion and welfare-based interventions. Between these polarities lay the more pragmatic approach of the Dutch (and to a degree some Scandinavian countries, notably Sweden), who were recognised for their emphasis on the evaluation of new preventive interventions and a coherent strategic national focus.[1] This book traces the variable fortunes of these different models and reflects upon their impact and the lessons learnt through implementation over the subsequent years. The manner in which different models have been adopted and adapted in other European jurisdictions is a recurring theme.

Collectively, the chapters in this book attempt to take stock of, and interrogate, the nature, form and scope of contemporary crime prevention policies in a comparative perspective. In other words, they seek to chart the manner in which the general notion of a 'preventive turn' has found expression in, and been promoted through, policy developments and practice within a number of different European jurisdictions. In so doing, the metaphor of a journey, as yet incomplete, is deployed as a way of thinking about the developmental trajectories and divergent paths taken. The book seeks to explore and address a number of allied questions: How has the 'preventive turn' in crime control policies been implemented in various different countries, with what effects and with what implications? To what extent has crime prevention secured a prominent place within the governance of crime and disorder? What are the major trends influencing the direction of development? What have been the relationships between, on the one hand, crime prevention and community safety and, on the other, criminal justice and punitive responses, as against wider social and urban policies? To what extent has prevention reoriented the focus of criminal justice and/or influenced the direction of social policy? In so doing, contributors to the book explore and assess the different models adopted and the shifting emphasis accorded to differing strategies over time.

There are, however, inevitable limitations in the approach adopted in this collection and reflected in the manner in which the book is organised. By asking contributors to address a number of questions and themes with regard to a specific jurisdiction, there is an essential bias towards the nation-state and defined polities as the unit of analysis. While providing a rich understanding of national developments and experiences, as well as the role of politics and central government policy initiatives therein, by necessity less space is accorded to consideration of local differences, the role of non-state actors and the nature of sub-national comparisons. Consequently, given the approach assumed here, there is an implicit tendency to highlight and give greater priority to contrasts and comparisons between nations and to governmental programmes, legislation and policy statements.

As highlighted in this collection (notably Chapter 3), national policies must themselves be implemented and enacted. In the process, they are frequently shaped, interpreted and translated in diverse ways, influenced often by local cultures and traditions as well as by political alliances and struggles. National policies are regularly reinterpreted, resisted and revised at the local level. As a result, the expectations of central government in London, Paris or Brussels are modified and given positive and concrete form in different local contexts. This reinforces the significance of not assuming the effectiveness of central government intentions or ambitions, notably those set down in legislation. In federal constitutions, such as Belgium and Germany (Chapters 8 and 9), where legislative authority is devolved to regional structures, this disjuncture is particularly evident. However, it is also apparent in other countries, notably those with traditions of strong regional (Italy, see Chapter 7) or local government. As the British case exemplifies, the question of what constitutes a nation-state – especially in the light of the different models of devolved government in Scotland, Wales (Chapters 3 and 4) and Northern Ireland – is itself a moot subject. The constitutional arrangements, combined with the role and ambitions of the central state in organising social life and providing public safety, manifestly inform the comparative experiences of crime prevention policies and infrastructures, particularly with regard to the relations between central and local political authorities.

It is important not to ignore that much policy innovation emanates from local or regional levels, some, but not all, of which may filter 'upwards' or get appropriated by central governments. In addition, given the pivotal role of cities, towns and localities in the delivery and development of crime prevention and community safety practices, it would be wrong to discount the significance of cross-national *city-to-city* and *region-to-region* networks, policy connections and lesson-learning. The work of the European Forum for Urban Safety is a good example of city-to-city networks that transcend national boundaries and have been pivotal in the transfer and diffusion of policies across Europe.

A further limitation of the dominant focus on national experiences is an understandable prioritisation of governmental action in its diverse forms. What this tends to sideline, however, is not only the role of civil society institutions (which Margaret Shaw highlights in her contribution, see Chapter 11) but also the key role played by commercial interests and private businesses. This general overemphasis on government action is a prevalent feature of the wider criminological literature. However, Hope in his contribution (Chapter 2) provides an important corrective to this, highlighting the interplay between government action and the role of markets, the security industry and the citizenry. In this vein, a recent summary of the preventive turn in the UK concludes:

> The story of the contemporary genesis and growth of crime preven-
> tion is often written as if it was something imposed by governments
> upon the citizenry through programmes of 'responsibilisation' –
> emanating outwards from the centre – and evidenced by key policy
> initiatives. Yet, much of the credit should properly be attributed to
> small-scale, local and pragmatic developments within civil society
> and the business sector. In reality, both criminology and government
> policy were relative late-comers to a preventive way of thinking.
> (Crawford 2007: 900–1)

For example, research has highlighted the role of the insurance industry as 'agents of prevention' and its part in helping to spread actuarial logics and technologies of prediction as well as fostering networks with state agencies that have been instrumental in the ascendancy of crime prevention (Ericson *et al.* 2003). In many senses, it was only following the advent of mass consumerism and the associated growth in interest in securing property combined with the steep rise in crime risks (from the 1960s) that insurers were prompted to narrow their risk pools and foster a preventive mentality on the part of insurers. This goes some way to explaining the relatively late development of prevention in relation to crime risks as contrasted, for example, with the field of fire prevention (O'Malley and Hutchinson 2007). Nevertheless, while the insurance industry may have been relatively slow to recognise and use its potential power to influence behaviour with regard to crime risks (Litton 1982), its subsequent sway in stimulating a 'preventive mentality' is undoubted. In the ensuing years, the insurance industry has played a significant part in fostering preventive thinking and action simultaneously through networks with the police and government agencies and via diverse forms of insurance cover which have served to promote the spread and use of certain situational measures, notably forms of target-hardening.

One of the implicit aims of this collection is to highlight and explore the extent to which there has been an internationalisation and/or convergence of key ideas, strategies, technologies and practices of crime prevention and community safety. In other words, to what extent have policy ideas and practices *travelled* between different countries? Moreover, have ideas developed in one place been replicated or emulated in others? And, where this is evident, to what extent and in what ways have policies been adapted, transformed and given expression in the process of policy transfer? Where transnational diffusion has occurred, how can we explain the receptiveness within particular polities (at specific moments in time) towards given ideas, models and technologies?

To address these questions, the book brings together a collection of leading international commentators, most of whom have been intimately involved in crime prevention policy and/or researching crime prevention practices over the past two decades. A considerable number have worked either within government departments or government-based research institutes, including Jaap De Waard and Jan Van Dijk at the Dutch Ministry of Justice (the former also subsequently worked as head of the Secretariat of the European Crime Prevention Network, while the latter worked at the United Nations Centre for International Crime Prevention); Tim Hope and Margaret Shaw at the Home Office Research and Planning Unit, as it was known in the 1980s (and the latter subsequently at the International Centre for the Prevention of Crime in Montreal); Klara Kerezsi at Hungary's National Institute of Criminology; and Anne Wyvekens at the French Ministry of the Interior's Institut des Hautes

Etudes de la Sécurité Intérieure. Others have established track records of researching and commenting on the unfolding landscape of crime prevention and community safety. As such, they are all eminently well placed to reflect upon the nuances of jurisdiction-specific developmental trajectories and the direction of change over the last quarter of a century, as well as to draw out the underlying influences that have shaped events and movements.

The structure of the book is as follows. In the first chapter, Adam Crawford outlines a comparative frame of analysis for thinking about jurisdiction-specific developments in Europe, by considering a number of cross-cutting themes, issues and dynamics of change. In so doing, he highlights some challenges and insights offered by a comparative analysis, as well as drawing out areas of continuity and divergence in different national experiences. Particular attention is given to consideration of the extent to which convergence and departure are evident and to explanations for these. The chapter seeks to highlight the influence of policy transfer and the diffusion of ideas and strategies within and between nations. It questions the extent to which a common model or general direction of travel can be discerned and reflects upon future prospects.

The subsequent nine chapters present country-specific accounts of crime prevention policies and their development in a number of selected European jurisdictions. In each of these chapters, in addition to providing a descriptive overview of key events, initiatives and ideas, the authors specifically seek to explain and assess the paths taken and the factors influencing developments (both conceptual and institutional) as well as the infrastructures constructed for delivering crime prevention policies. Implicitly each chapter seeks to address a number of interrelated questions: What are the distinctive features of specific approaches to crime prevention policies across Europe? How have these changed over time and what are the dominant trajectories of development? To what extent have crime prevention policies been shaped by differences in institutional infrastructures, constitutional/legal arrangements, political ideologies, economic performance, traditions of welfare and/or cultural sensibilities? Has policy diffusion influenced development, and if so, how have policies been transformed or reshaped in the process of transfer from one context to another? What lessons have been learnt over the years and what are the possible future directions within particular countries?

This jurisdiction-specific section begins with three chapters that focus on different aspects of the British experience. In Chapter 2, Tim Hope explores the evolution of situational prevention as a 'particularly English' contribution to crime prevention technologies and practices. In so doing, he provides a situated understanding of how and why situational prevention, since the late 1970s, found a particularly favourable reception in parts of Britain. In assessing the impact of situational crime prevention in relation to the significant reduction in the number of property offences committed since the mid 1990s, Hope highlights the different modes of regulation and ways by which governmental strategies have worked through, and been constrained by, local authorities, the private sector (notably car manufacturers and the security industry) and private citizens. Importantly, he highlights both the limitations of the direct role of central government and local authorities and the pivotal influence of shifts in housing tenure (through the expansion of owner occupation), developments in the security market and the built environment, as well as the increased privatised demand for personal security. Hope's analysis underscores the important role of the market, as well as private and collective initiatives. As such, it serves as a corrective to the usual (dominant) focus on public policy delivered directly through central government. While situational prevention appears to have had a significant impact on levels of property crime, it also has served to exacerbate inequalities of security provision and potentially heighten demands for personal, domestic and parochial security. As such, the 'peculiarly British' (or should that be English?) experience, in which situational approaches have dominated implementation, may either (or both) offer a warning to, or act as a source of inspiration for, other European countries. It is clear from subsequent chapters (see particularly Chapters 5 and 8) that parts of mainland Europe have keenly felt the influence of the British approach to situational crime prevention.

By contrast, in Chapter 3 Gordon Hughes and Adam Edwards focus on the fortunes of developments elsewhere in the crime prevention field, namely the evolving contours of 'community safety' as a capacious referent for diverse preventive approaches and in the name of which an elaborate infrastructure of local partnerships has been constructed. They outline the manner in which community safety emerged in England and Wales as an alternative to the police-dominated, technologically-driven and situationally-oriented approaches that prevailed throughout much of the 1980s and 1990s in Britain. They go on to assess critically five different narratives of community safety, notably with regard to its relation with wider social and criminal justice policies and institutional practices. They advance a 'power-dependence' framework that is sensitive to the uneven distribution of resources, the contested nature of political power and the importance of local traditions and cultures – what they refer to as local 'geo-historical contexts'. From this perspective, they highlight a plurality of outcomes and (constrained) spaces for ways of governing crime under the umbrella of community safety that are not trammelled by the prevailing neo-liberal or moral authoritarian dogma, so evident in much central government policy in England and (to a lesser degree according to their analysis) Wales. They underscore the local and regional differences that prevail both within and between England and Wales. Significantly, they alert us to the importance of comparative studies within national jurisdictions in order to highlight the contested nature of implementation and the scope for political struggles over the direction and substance of governmental programmes.

This theme of differences and similarities within parts of the UK is further explored in Chapter 4. Here, Alistair Henry considers the particular experiences of, and paths taken by, Scotland in the implementation of crime prevention and community safety in both the pre- and post-devolution periods. He contrasts directly the Scottish experience with the prevailing approach in England and Wales. In this respect, the Scottish tale is one of convergence and divergence, both at different times and in different policy domains that impress upon crime prevention and community safety. Whereas in the 1980s and 1990s Scotland sought to differentiate its polity, as far as possible within the constitutional framework available, from the neo-liberal influences of Thatcherism, the last decade or so under a New Labour government saw significant policy emulation and harmonisation despite the establishment of an independent Scottish Parliament in 1999 with full competency for criminal justice and policing matters. One example of this importation of ideas and policies from England and Wales has been in regard to the anti-social behaviour agenda, although its implementation and action on the ground has taken a much more muted form (Tisdall 2006). In other areas, such as youth justice, the distinctiveness of the Scottish approach – as compared with that south of the border – has remained marked, although perversely the post-devolutionary period also saw considerable convergence in this domain. As Henry demonstrates, due to complex historical, constitutional and cultural reasons, Scotland shares certain similarities with continental European approaches to youth and urban policies, where a legacy of welfarism and social inclusion are evident. Hence, as elsewhere in mainland Europe, crime prevention and community safety have oscillated in an awkward space between criminal justice and social/urban policy, but one which, as distinct from the English experience, has seen community safety more comfortably embedded within a wider patchwork of social justice strategies rather than as an appendage to crime control.

Collectively, the three UK-focused chapters highlight the extent to which a particular model of crime prevention has become associated, particularly in the early years, with a situationally-oriented approach in Britain, albeit with a caution as to the uneven implementation and reception of situational practices and the dangers of overgeneralisations from that premise.

Chapter 5, by Anne Wyvekens, provides an account of the evolving ebb and flow of French developments, from its confident Bonnemaison origins to its present-day hesitancy and uncertain future. The social prevention model advanced by Bonnemaison, as Wyvekens shows, was rooted in the left-wing politics of the then Socialist government. It established a model of prevention organised around its defining concepts of 'solidarity', 'integration' and 'locality', which foregrounded the role of the mayor and local municipality and in which the police and judiciary remained marginal. This was part of its appeal, but as Wyvekens highlights it also limited its impact, as it became dissipated within wider urban policy over the years and the judiciary initiated their own interventions. Moreover, she notes the paradox that, having established city-level partnership structures to deliver prevention locally, the centralised nature of the French state served repeatedly to undermine their realisation by under-scoring the lack of shared competences between state and municipality. Wyvekens highlights the manner in which political fortunes have fostered a greater appetite for situational approaches, which had developed in more recent years, as well as more punitive responses. Yet, despite the close association between social prevention and the political Left, the prevention landscape in France has become more mixed: both social and situational approaches coexist within programmes and local practices managed by Left and Right administrations.

Chapter 6 provides an insider's account of Dutch developments. Jan Van Dijk and Jaap De Waard outline the particularly pragmatic and eclectic approach taken by the Dutch in their combination of situational and social prevention, as well as technological and human (people-based) interventions. This approach was initially expressed in the work of the Roethof Committee and the resultant *Society and Crime* white paper published in 1985. A central theme within the subsequent new wave of crime prevention initiatives focused on strengthening semi-formal social control and human surveillance in public and semi-public urban spaces. The best known example has been the 'city guards' (*Stadswachten*) initiative, which subsequently influenced developments in other countries including the UK (Crawford 2006). As well as an emphasis on offender-oriented projects, the Dutch also implemented significant victim-focused schemes. In addition to high-profile social prevention and youth diversion schemes such as HALT, the Dutch put significant energies into public–private partnerships between government departments and the business sector, often with a short-term situational focus. Over time, the initial, central top-down strategy has been replaced by greater autonomy on the part of local municipalities. Van Dijk and De Waard note that the strategy for implementing crime prevention in the Netherlands is relatively unique in its reliance on non-statutory collaboration structures. The effectiveness of the local partnerships has been facilitated by a corporatist tradition of regular co-ordination meetings between key local partners, notably mayors, chiefs of police and chief prosecutors. The business sector has been drawn into this framework with reasonable ease. Van Dijk and De Waard situate this experience in the Dutch cultural tradition of the Polder (as expressed in the title of their chapter), which alludes to a practice of pragmatic consensus decision-making in economic and public life. Rather than reflecting 'tolerance', they contest, the Dutch approach is marked by a pragmatism that is rooted more in identifying and evaluating 'what works' and drawing on an eclectic array of preventive techniques, than in starting from any fixed ideological premise. This, they conclude, has provided the basis not only for significant experimentation and lesson-learning, but also facilitated a considerable degree of successful implementation of crime prevention strategies and partnership infrastructures. However, given that the Dutch experience is rooted in a particular cultural tradition, they warn that its best practice lessons may be less easily transferred to other countries.

In Chapter 7, Dario Melossi and Rossella Selmini offer an account of developments in Italy which they situate within a broader canvas of the emergence and development of the 'new' crime prevention in Europe more generally. They trace the genesis of a preoccupation with extra-penal and local crime prevention to the transformations wrought by the onset of what C. Wright Mills termed 'mass society'. As a result of the spread of consumerism, they argue, the working classes, the new-found owners of commodities, became more anxious and insecure due to their potential to be victims of (property) crime. Prevention became another way of reconstituting a symbolic community in contrast to the deviant 'other', who became less the political antagonist and more the marginalised but 'common' predatory offender. It also reflected a narrowing of discourse from political relations of citizens with the nation state to the micro-management of local, mundane, everyday life and routine aspects of 'ordinary' street crime. The chapter locates the regional focus of developments in Italy in the context of the dominant prevailing models of crime prevention within Europe. It highlights the influence that French and British models of crime prevention variously exerted on Italian developments, producing a mixed model. Drawing on Italian research findings into the implementation of crime prevention strategies, Melossi and Selmini discern a mutation in traditional social crime prevention. They outline a shift away from the focus of social prevention on addressing structural factors that might influence offender motivation and towards quality of life and environmental concerns, victim protection and public reassurance, as well as social prevention increasingly serving as an auxiliary to situational crime prevention. They also highlight the emerging alliance between situational and developmental approaches. They conclude that the Italian experience reflects a wider theme of convergence across Europe with regard to crime prevention policies. This is especially notable in the light of recent national reforms that have undermined the distinctly regional focus of Italian developments by centralising greater authority.

This theme – the manner in which specific jurisdictions are influenced by prevailing models of crime prevention in other European countries – is also evident in Patrick Hebberecht's analysis of Belgian crime prevention policy. Chapter 8 presents a fascinating case of a federal country (since 1988) in which crime prevention policies have been shaped both by the political make-up of governing alliances between the established parties and the linguistic and cultural traditions of the different regions – notably the French-speaking Walloon and Brussels regions on the one hand, and on the other the Flemish region – which together constitute Belgium. The rather unusual constitutional framework whereby almost all political institutions are split into two independent Flemish and French-speaking versions of the same, has provided interesting conduits for policy transfer and emulation. In essence, Belgium has seen various waves of policy influence in ways that have sometimes belied traditional political associations with policies between the political Left and Right (as outlined in the French experience, for example, see Chapter 5). While the Anglo-Saxon model of situational prevention exerted an influence and served as a model for emulation via Dutch developments in Flemish-speaking parts of the country, the French-speaking regions more readily drew on ideas, policies and practices advanced by their French cousins. Consequently, the local implementation of national strategies has taken on very different expressions and forms in different parts of the country. Despite this uneven implementation, Hebberecht detects a significant drift over time towards more authoritarian and neo-liberal influenced policies as investments in welfare and social inclusion have waned.

In Chapter 9 Michael Jasch presents an overview of the experiences from Germany, a federal jurisdiction which like Belgium has a 'patchy picture' of crime prevention policies. The German story has certain very specific factors that have propelled and shaped developments. Reunification, for example, significantly affected perceptions of insecurity within Germany and subsequent crime prevention strategies. Despite the unevenness of practices across Germany, Jasch draws out some of the dominant trends over the last 30 years, including a move towards localisation and the reallocation of responsibilities, neither of which seems to have been fully realised. He highlights the manner in which prevention policy appears to have travelled in a full circle: from a repressive approach to crime through technical and situational prevention in the 1970s to a notion of social prevention in the 1980s, community strategies in the 1990s and back to a predominance of repressive techniques in recent years. Like Hebberecht, Jasch detects a decline in the role of social policies as a vehicle for prevention and suggests that much prevention policy has suffered from weak implementation, often due to lack of resources. It is largely in the fields of policing and surveillance that prevention has been most effectively developed, notably through forms of preventive detention and personal data collection. However, Jasch also points to the emerging influence of early intervention programmes targeting 'at risk' families and young people.

A different and more recent 'preventive turn' is highlighted by the experience of Hungary as outlined by Klara Kerezsi in Chapter 10. In common with other former Soviet-bloc countries, crime prevention policies have been closely tied with the process of political transition. The combined challenges of rising crime rates, falling perceptions of public safety and the need to transform the criminal justice system in a more democratic and open society have shaped the Hungarian experience. As Kerezsi demonstrates, the early process and direction of criminal justice reform were dominated by the requirements of so-called 'Europeanisation'. Despite much governmental activity and the establishment of a National Council of Crime Prevention and the subsequent publication of a national strategy, the continuously changing organisational structure left little clarity in terms of crime prevention definitions and responsibilities. The objectives of crime prevention practice appear to have been in a constant state of flux. Tensions between the roles of the Ministry of Justice and Ministry of the Interior served to exacerbate this. Furthermore, despite the appeals to more localised provision the strategy has predominantly been a top-down approach. Kerezsi highlights the fact that although the crime prevention strategy was oriented around the interface between criminal and social policies, in practice Hungary has seen an apparent proliferation of situational crime prevention methods. Despite the seeming lack of progress in, and resources dedicated to, embedding forms of prevention that address the social causes of crime and vulnerability and promote social cohesion, Kerezsi concludes that the aims of crime prevention remain both laudable and vital.

In the final chapter, Margaret Shaw offers a view from outside Europe. She considers the implications and relevance of European models of crime prevention and community safety for developing and third world countries, in which poverty and crime are endemic. From the *favelas* of Rio and the townships of the Cape Flats, the parameters of and resources associated with crime prevention take on very different meanings and possibilities. In situations where the state is weak, absent and/or unwelcome, safety and security are differently conceived. Local knowledge, capacity and resources take on a greater salience. So too, the role of institutions within civil society becomes crucial in realising genuinely bottom-up problem-solving that engages with key actors and agencies. In this light, Shaw highlights the central importance of context in thinking about, imagining and doing crime prevention. She advances a broad concept of crime prevention that engages with urban safety via diverse routes of community organisation, public health, urban regeneration and inclusive notions of human security. One advantage of such an approach may be to remove crime from the political agenda, to restrain the focus on policing and to de-centre criminology's narrow preoccupations.

Collectively, the chapters highlight patterns of convergence and divergence in the development of crime prevention policies and practices across (and within) different countries. They illustrate differing routes of travel, lesson-learning and institution-building in the name of crime prevention and community safety. In some senses, the various initiatives in policy formation and implementation outlined have dramatically reoriented the landscape across which crime is governed within localities, and the manner in which this is done, as well as refigured relations between local authorities and national governments and between citizens and the state. In other ways, however, the diverse reform programmes have fallen short of the lofty ambitions that many commentators held out for the modern 'preventive' turn. In sum, this collection allows a timely reflection on progress made and prospects for the future, and, in so doing, evokes a journey as yet incomplete.

Note

1 Notably, Sweden was the first country to establish a National Crime Prevention Council in 1974 to promote and co-ordinate crime prevention initiatives.

References

Chadwick, E. (1829) 'A Preventive Police', *The London Review*, 1: 252–308.

Clarke, R. V. (1995) 'Situational Crime Prevention', *Crime and Justice*, 19: 91–150.

Clarke, R. V. (2000) 'Situational Prevention, Criminology and Social Values', in A. Von Hirsch, D. Garland and A. Wakefield (eds) *Ethical and Social Perspectives on Situational Crime Prevention*. Oxford: Hart Publishing, pp. 97–112.

Colquhoun, P. (1797) *A Treatise on the Police of the Metropolis*. London: H. Fry.

Crawford, A. (1998) 'Community Safety Partnerships', *Criminal Justice Matters*, 33: 4–5.

Crawford, A. (ed.) (2002) *Crime and Insecurity: The Governance of Safety in Europe*. Cullompton: Willan Publishing.

Crawford, A. (2006) 'Fixing Broken Promises?: Neighbourhood Wardens and Social Capital', *Urban Studies*, 43(5/6): 957–76.

Crawford, A. (2007) 'Crime Prevention and Community Safety', in M. Maguire, R. Morgan and R. Reiner (eds) *The Oxford Handbook of Criminology*, 4th edn. Oxford: Oxford University Press, pp. 866–909.

Duprez, D. and Hebberecht, P. (eds) (2002) *The Prevention and Security Policies in Europe*. Brussels: VUB Press.

Ericson, R., Doyle, A. and Barry, D. (2003) *Insurance as Governance*. Toronto: University of Toronto Press.

Garland, D. (2000) 'Ideas, Institutions and Situational Crime Prevention', in A. Von Hirsch, D. Garland and A. Wakefield (eds) *Ethical and Social Perspectives on Situational Crime Prevention*. Oxford: Hart Publishing, pp. 1–16.

Garland, D. (2001) *The Culture of Control*. Oxford: Oxford University Press.

Graham, J. (1993) 'Crime Prevention Policies in Europe', *European Journal of Crime, Criminal Law and Criminal Justice*, 1(2): 126–42.

Graham, J. and Bennett, T. (1995) *Crime Prevention Strategies in Europe and North America*. Helsinki: HEUNI.

Hughes, G., McLaughlin, E. and Muncie, J. (eds) (2002) *Crime Prevention and Community Safety: New Directions*. London: Sage.

Johnston, L. and Shearing, C. (2003) *Governing Security*. London: Routledge.

King, M. (1991) 'The Political Construction of Crime Prevention', in K. Stenson and D. Cowell (eds) *The Politics of Crime Control*. London: Sage, pp. 87–108.

Litton, R. A. (1982) 'Crime Prevention and Insurance', *Howard Journal*, 21: 6–22.

O'Malley, P. (1992) 'Risk, Power and Crime Prevention', *Economy and Society*, 21(3): 252–75.

O'Malley, P. and Hutchinson, S. (2007) 'Reinventing Prevention: Why did "Crime Prevention" Develop so Late?', *British Journal of Criminology*, 47: 373–89.

Tisdall, E. K. M. (2006) 'Anti-Social Behaviour Legislation meets Children's Services: Challenging Perspectives on Children, Parents and State', *Critical Social Policy*, 26(1): 101–20.

Tuck, M. (1988) *Crime Prevention: A Shift in Concept*, Home Office Research and Planning Unit Research Bulletin, No. 24. London: Home Office.

Chapter 1

Situating crime prevention policies in comparative perspective: policy travels, transfer and translation

Adam Crawford

The aim of this chapter is threefold. First, it is intended to raise certain comparative questions and highlight challenges of comparison in order to inform and frame the subsequent country-specific accounts and trajectories of development that follow in later chapters. It poses the question, how might we understand comparative differences and similarities between jurisdictions? In this light, connections will be made with the emerging literature on comparative penal policies. Second, the chapter explores the conceptual parameters of policy convergence and divergence with regard to crime prevention. Implicitly, it poses and responds to the question, is there a common European direction of travel evidenced by the jurisdiction-specific journeys? In so doing, it explores the extent to which particular crime prevention-related policy 'ideas' may have been the subject of diffusion across Europe in recent years. Finally, it considers the extent to which the different experiences of the countries outlined in this collection corroborate or counter a number of dominant assertions that abound within the literature about the origins, nature and implications of the 'preventive turn'. Throughout, in reference to crime prevention policies, the focus deliberately seeks to include both strategies and structures: the content of policies and the mechanisms elaborated for their delivery.

Comparing crime prevention policies

What becomes clear from the collection of chapters in this volume is that some notion of crime prevention (re-)emerged in the last third of the twentieth century in diverse European countries, albeit at different moments in time, in direct response to specific stimuli and events, and following somewhat contrasting trajectories. However, at the evident risk of overgeneralisation, we can highlight the confluence of a number of similar factors and impulses that *inter alia* propelled and informed developments. These include:

- Public concerns over increased crime and the fear of crime, prompted by greater ownership of commodities vulnerable to theft and property-derived incentives to security.

- Growing acknowledgement of the limited capacity of formal institutions of criminal justice adequately to reduce crime and effect change in criminal behaviour, spurred by a recognition that the levers of crime lie beyond the reach of formal institutions of control.

- Concern that many of the traditional bonds of informal social control – that operate through families, kinship ties, communities, voluntary associations and other social networks – may be fragmenting and weakening.

- A decline in the attachments by liberal elites to social welfare-based responses to offending as captured in the 'rehabilitative ideal' and the concomitant rise in importance attributed to the role of victims of crime within public policy.

- A political desire to explore alternative means of managing crime that avoid the economic, social and human costs associated with over-reliance on traditional punitive – 'law and order' – responses.

The turn to prevention, therefore, can be seen as having emerged as an adaptation to both perceived changes in social conditions – mass consumerism, growing individualisation, high crime rates as 'a normal social fact' (Garland 2001), a culture of insecurity and the politicisation of disorder – and the acknowledged failings of the formal apparatus of criminal and penal justice, given its marginal role in regulating criminal acts (most of which never come to official attention) and its shaky assumptions about offenders and changing offending behaviour.

Brantingham and Faust's (1976) conceptual distinction, drawn from the healthcare analogy, between primary, secondary and tertiary prevention is useful in highlighting the broad shifts in contemporary understandings of prevention over recent times. They differentiate between *primary prevention*, directed at general populations to address potentially crimogenic factors before the onset of problems; *secondary prevention*, targeted at potential offenders who express or are identified by some predispositional risk factor; and *tertiary prevention* strategies that respond to known offenders in order to reduce further crimes or the harm associated with them. Van Dijk and De Waard (1991; and see Chapter 6) add a second dimension to this typology by differentiating between three targets of preventive interventions – offenders, victims and situations – to produce a ninefold categorisation. The assumption is that different types of measures will produce distinct benefits where aimed separately at preventing people from offending (often referred to as social prevention) or preventing victimisation (frequently conceived as safety advice or victim assistance), as against preventing crime opportunities in particular places (often referred to as situational prevention) and that these may be directed at the general population, at risk groups or places and those known offenders, victims and crime hot spots.

These categorisations remind us that prevention was not invented in the late twentieth century; rather it has been reconfigured and reconceptualised, previously having been disaggregated and contained within certain domains. Thus, primary prevention, where it existed, had been the stuff of social policy, but was rarely articulated or named as such. State-provided education, health, social housing and welfare, for example, for the most part were not justified in terms of their potential crime prevention effects, but rather in terms of their more direct and primary goals of an educated and productive citizenry, a healthy population, affordable housing and social security. It is only latterly that these have come to be viewed, and in some instances justified, by their ancillary crime preventive implications. Secondary prevention tended to be sidelined, given the dominant emphasis on universal social provisions. Where programmes were targeted (via means testing, more often than not) these tended to see crimogenic ends subsumed within welfarist notions of poverty prevention and alleviation. Tertiary prevention, by contrast, was the stuff of criminal justice, constituting an elaborate infrastructure designed to respond to crime (after the event) with only a limited wider primary prevention role by way of its residual deterrent effects. Thus, institutional and state bureaucratic structures tended to determine the language and location of what we now have come to define as crime prevention and community safety. A large part of the story about the 'preventive turn' is a tale of institutional reconfiguration within and between policy domains and among relations between (and responsibilities of) the state, market and citizenry.

As a distinct policy domain, crime prevention and its siblings, 'community safety' and 'urban security', emerged in an awkward policy void between criminal justice on the one hand, and social and urban policy on the other. In continental Europe, 'prevention' is commonly contrasted

3

with 'repression'. It therefore might be instructive, in considering comparative crime prevention, first to assess the insights offered by contrasts in penal policies. Before doing so, it is worth noting that just as criminal justice policies have changed and been redrawn in the last 30 years, so too social policy has been transformed. In different ways and to a greater or lesser extent in different countries, we have seen more targeting of resources (on the basis of some notion of identified need or risk) and increased conditionality.

One thing that changed with the arrival of the prevailing winds of neo-liberalism – propelled by the gulf-stream of globalisation – was that social welfarism itself became increasingly discredited as the organising governmental narrative and *raison d'être* for social policy. Not only was redistributive social welfare costly to large sections of the population in many countries, who saw little direct benefits and warmed to the politics of tax cuts, it also came to be seen as unduly paternalistic, overly interventionist, dominated by self-serving professional elites and premised on misplaced assumptions about human motivation and agency (Le Grand 2003). Marquand's evocative caricature of Fabian social policy captures well this shifting logic:

> Civil society was seen, all too often, not as an agent but as a patient: an inert body, lying on an operating table, undergoing social democratic surgery. The surgeons acted for the best, of course, but they acted on the patient from without; the patient merely received their ministrations. But in reality, of course, governments cannot behave like surgeons. Here, at any rate, Hayek was right. It is not possible to re-make society in accordance with a grand design, since no conceivable grand design can do justice to the complexity and reflexivity of human behaviour. Nor is civil society much like a patient . . . Instead of lying passively on the operating table, it insisted on arguing with the surgeon, or at least trying to do so. (1999: 17)

What is more, policies of social welfare were argued to be, themselves, crimogenic in fostering a 'culture of dependency' and loosening bonds of moral restraint (Murray 1990). From this perspective, social welfarism is envisaged as the antithesis of enterprise, autonomy, responsibility and freedom. For some, social policy came to be seen as part of the problem of crime and disorder rather than as contributing to the preventive solution.

Comparative penal policies

Analysing the comparative fortunes of penal policies in various jurisdictions might tell us something about both (i) the relative place of crime prevention within different polities and (ii) how to draw comparisons – similarities and differences – between the experiences of assorted European countries. Cavadino and Dignan's (2006a, 2006b) recent analysis of imprisonment rates, youth justice arrangements and privatisation policies in 12 western jurisdictions provides a useful reference point. Drawing upon the work of Esping-Andersen (1990), they outline a fourfold typology of criminal justice systems, situated within different kinds of political economy: the neo-liberal, conservative corporatist, oriental corporatist and social democratic. These four 'family groups' are differentiated with regard to a range of criteria including their form of economic and welfare state organisation, extent of income and status differentials, degree of protection afforded to social rights, political orientation, and scale of social inclusivity. For the purpose of a European analysis, only three of these typologies are relevant, as the oriental corporatist model seeks to explain the case of Japan (and hence will not detain us here). While neo-liberal political economies (including England and Wales) are marked by the free market and minimal welfare state provisions, as well as extreme income differentials, conservative corporatist societies (including the Netherlands, France, Germany and Italy) feature comprehensive, moderately generous, but non-egalitarian welfare states, which reflect pronounced, but not extreme income differentials (Cavadino and Dignan 2006b: 441). By contrast, social democratic regimes (notably Sweden and Finland) are marked by more universalistic, generous welfare systems and exhibit relatively limited income differentials. These 'family traits', they suggest, appear to be associated with some striking and enduring differences in terms of penal policies, notably rates of imprisonment (see Table 1.1).

According to Table 1.1, with only one exception (the Netherlands), all the neo-liberal countries have higher rates of incarceration than all the conservative corporatist regimes. Most strikingly, the Nordic social democracies, with the addition of the single oriental corporatist country (Japan), have the lowest imprisonment rate of all. Furthermore, the social democratic systems of the Nordic countries have succeeded in sustaining relatively humane and moderate penal policies in the period during which some of the neo-liberal countries – notably the United States and to a lesser extent Britain – have been moving in the direction of punitive and exclusionary policies of mass incarceration. Furthermore, Cavadino and Dignan suggest that as a society moves in the direction of neo-liberalism, its punishment tends to become harsher. The most dramatic example of this is the Netherlands, where the imprisonment rate rose exponentially between 1975 and 2006, from 17 to 128 prisoners per 100,000 population. This is a useful starting point, for our purposes, as it alerts us to the importance of differences, despite globalising pressures, in the form of variations of political economy, and also highlights sites of continuity, namely the connection between neo-liberal influences and apparent punitiveness.

5

Table 1.1 Political economy and imprisonment rates per 100,000 population

Political economy	Imprisonment rate 2005/06
Neo-liberal	
USA	736
South Africa	335
New Zealand	186
England and Wales	**148**
Australia	126
Conservative corporatist	
Netherlands	**128**
Italy	**104**
Germany	**95**
France	**85**
Social democratic	
Sweden	82
Finland	75
Oriental corporatist	
Japan	62

Source: Walmsley (2007) cited in Dignan and Cavadino (2007: 53)
Note: Countries in bold are represented in this volume.

However, the schema provided by Cavadino and Dignan offers less by way of explanation as to precisely how the variables they identify coalesce to produce particular family resemblances at the level of punishment. It takes a rather narrow interpretation of penal severity, by focusing on 'imprisonment rates', and affords less space for shifts over time as well as the role of historic institutional, constitutional and cultural factors. For our purposes, given our focus on Europe, the typology masks extensive in-group differences, some of which are considerably greater than those between groups.

The most obvious of these is evident within the neo-liberal family, where the contrasts in imprisonment rates between the USA and England, for example, are radically different, much more so than between England and the Netherlands. In many senses, American exceptionalism represents something of an outlier with imprisonment rates on a fundamentally different scale from other 'neo-liberal' countries, such as England and Australia, which are much closer to 'conservative corporatist' countries in this regard. This wide variation in indicators of penal severity raises questions about the explanatory value of 'neo-liberalism' as a coherent overarching regime type. Furthermore, if we stick with imprisonment rates for a moment and focus on a broader pool of European countries, a more muddied picture emerges.

Table 1.2 Imprisonment rates across Europe per 100,000 population (EU plus EFTA countries)

Country	Imprisonment rate 2007/08
Latvia	288
Estonia	259
Lithuania	234
Poland	222
Czech Republic	182
Spain	159
Luxembourg	155
Scotland	**155**
England and Wales	**153**
Hungary	**149**
Slovakia	148
Romania	124
Greece	109
Portugal	103
Netherlands	**100**
Austria	95
Malta	95
Belgium	**93**
Germany	**89**
Northern Ireland	87
France	**85**
Italy	**83**
Cyrus	83
Ireland	76
Switzerland	76
Sweden	74
Norway	69
Slovenia	66
Denmark	63
Finland	63
Iceland	44

Source: International Centre for Prison Studies World Prison Brief 2008
Note: Countries in bold are represented in this volume.

The Anglo-Saxon jurisdictions of the British Isles – given their association with neo-liberalism and their affinity with American-influenced penal policy – no longer stand out as significantly different from other European countries (albeit still with some of the highest rates in Europe). According to more recent data from the International Centre for Prison Studies (see Table 1.2), England and Wales imprison fewer people per 100,000 than a number of former Soviet-bloc Eastern European countries, including the Baltic nations, Poland and the Czech Republic, and sits in

7

among a group that incorporates Spain, Luxembourg and Hungary. Scotland with its welfarist traditions and distinct legal culture (see Chapter 4), has similar rates of imprisonment to England and Wales. Northern Ireland, with its evident similarities to mainland UK, nevertheless has imprisonment rates that parallel those of Belgium, Germany, France and Italy. That said, the social democratic Scandinavian countries still stand out for their low levels of imprisonment.

Nicola Lacey (2008) has argued that Cavadino and Dignan's typology accords less appreciation to the role of the labour market and the economy in both shaping penal and exclusionary responses and fostering social inclusion. In an attempt to put further explanatory flesh on their framework, Lacey distinguishes between 'liberal' and 'co-ordinated' market economies and argues that macro political-economic forces are conditioned by both cultural filters and economic, political and social institutions. In so doing, she draws attention, among other things, to the potential salience of the dynamics of different electoral systems (and the impact of electoral cycles at local as well as national levels); the nature of political decentralisation; and the relevance of education and training to a society's capacity for integration. All of these have relevance beyond the analysis of punishment and considerable implications for influencing the shape and direction of crime prevention policies. Differences between federal and non-federal constitutions, the strength of regional identities and the nature of relations between national and local government, are all strikingly evident in the accounts provided in this book.

Comparative crime prevention

There are important differences between forms of punishment and penal policies on the one hand, and crime prevention strategies and community safety policies on the other. While the former is self-evidently coercive and more often than not exclusionary – notably where imprisonment is involved – the latter fits less unambiguously into a simple or dichotomous exclusion/inclusion binary. Crime prevention and community safety can be simultaneously exclusionary and inclusionary, as well as both instrumental and moral. For example, developmental crime prevention, by targeting those 'at risk' for special attention, can be inclusionary, but also may inadvertently or otherwise stigmatise those targeted and engender forms of social exclusion. Community-based crime prevention likewise can be at the same time inclusive for some and exclusive for others. The exclusionary dynamics of the theories of 'defensible space' (Newman 1972) and 'broken windows' (Wilson and Kelling 1982) have been long recognised (Currie 1988), but this is also true of other instances where safety is a 'club good'. Tim Hope (2000) has documented the exclusive 'clubbing effects' of neighbourhood watch and situational target-hardening efforts against burglary. But these and other community-level crime prevention interventions can also foster social networks and forms of collective efficacy (Sampson *et al.* 1999). Defensive exclusivity can promote forms of *bonding* social capital between shared interest groups while undermining types of *bridging* social capital between different social groups (Putnam 2000; Crawford 2006).

Nevertheless, such conceptual modelling provides some useful insights when thinking about similarities and differences in crime prevention policies across Europe. What, then, are the potential implications for a comparative analysis of the growth and reception of crime prevention policies? Given the difficulties of quantifying and measuring prevention, we are not able to assess the degree of reception of certain types of prevention in the way that penal scholars can readily compare rough indicators of penal 'severity' through imprisonment rates. Table 1.3 presents one very limited attempt to do so using data from the European Crime and Safety Survey 2005 (Van Dijk *et al.* 2006: 116–17). It focuses not on state policies but on the reception of prevention on behalf of the public – by way of the percentage of households with a burglar alarm and special door locks. Where the data are available, they show an increase in

Table 1.3 Public reception of situational crime prevention technologies

Countries	Households with a burglar alarm (%)	Households with special door locks (%)
United Kingdom	36	61
Ireland	30	55
Italy	20	59
Belgium	15	49
Luxembourg	14	52
Portugal	13	56
Germany	12	63
Austria	12	58
Hungary	12	55
France	11	38
Netherlands	10	78
Spain	9	48
Sweden	9	46
Finland	7	43
Estonia	7	40
Greece	6	46
Denmark	6	32
Poland	3	18

Source: Van Dijk *et al.* (2006: 116–7)
Note: Countries in bold are represented in this volume.

households with a burglar alarm in recent decades. In the UK, the percentage of respondents saying that their household was fitted with a burglar alarm rose from 22 per cent in 1992 to 36 per cent in 2005. Smaller increases were evident in Belgium where the figures grew from 12 per cent to 15 per cent and in the Netherlands from 8 per cent to 10 per cent.

It is important to acknowledge the limitations of these data and the methods of their collection, as well as the manner in which the identified kinds of preventive actions are influenced by differences in residence type, security and design which find different expressions in various European countries. However, as a starting point for comparative analysis one might infer that countries where the proportion of households that have burglar alarms is high have more readily embraced the logics of situational crime prevention, whether this is through insurance-based incentives, government cajoling or autonomous action on the part of citizens. It is notable that the UK and Ireland are some way ahead of other countries in this regard and Scandinavian societies appear less attuned to the reception of these technologies.

A further indicator of the reception of situational crime prevention might be ascertained in the installation of CCTV cameras. Here the UK is a global leader, with an estimated 20 per cent of the world's CCTVs (but only less than 1 per cent of the world's population). According to the British Security Industry Association, by 2004 there were over 4.25 million CCTV cameras installed in the UK.[2] This compares markedly with France's estimated 340,000. Research confirms a higher level of public acceptance of CCTV in the UK as contrasted with other parts of Europe. The most sceptical attitudes were found in Austria and Germany (Hempel and Töpfer 2004). However, the expansion of CCTV has been strongly influenced by the very different regulatory regimes found across Europe (Gras 2004), where more robust regulatory systems have served to restrain the expansion of CCTV in public space. Hence, in Paris, for instance, while the metro and rail networks operate around 9,500 CCTV devices, there are only some 330 in operation in public spaces. However, President Nicolas Sarkozy recently announced a plan to emulate London's implementation of CCTV cameras with the programme 'A Thousand Cameras for Paris', at the launch of which he was quoted as saying: 'I am very impressed by the efficiency of the British police thanks to this network of cameras' (Samuel 2008).

In reviewing the global growth of CCTV, Norris and colleagues have identified a four-stage diffusion of CCTV that represents a 'general trend amid the messy complexity of different countries' experiences' (2004: 119). This follows a sequential path of (i) private diffusion; (ii) institutional diffusion in the public realm; (iii) limited diffusion in public space; and (iv) a final stage that they characterise as 'towards ubiquity' which 'heralds the creation of much larger systems, with hundreds of cameras providing blanket coverage of whole areas of a city' (2004: 119). If this is the case, then perhaps other European countries are less far along this path than the UK. But this suggests a rather unidirectional process of change with little sense that saturation may prompt further adaptation and questioning of the enterprise itself. Norris *et al.* are aware of the potentially deterministic nature of such a sequential path and assert that the extent to which a particular country or region will progress from one stage to another will depend on the complex interplay between socio-economic, legal, fiscal and political factors.

If neo-liberal regimes tend to exclude both those who fail in the course of economic relations in the marketplace and those who fail to abide by behavioural codes in line with their highly *individualistic* social ethos, how might this express itself in crime prevention? Might it suggest more exclusionary preventive strategies, such as those traditionally associated with 'defensible space', 'broken windows' and situational crime prevention? O'Malley (1992, 2001) has persuasively highlighted the political and ideological connections between situational approaches to crime prevention and neo-liberal assumptions about human behaviour, the limitations and perverse effects of government ambitions to provide social goods and the appropriate role of the market (Hayek 1979). Rational choice theories that inform situational prevention (Clarke 1995) resonate strongly with neo-liberal political programmes. More generally, the rise of prevention has been closely allied with the dismantling of systems of state-sponsored welfare provision that socialised risk. In their place a preventive mentality promotes individual autonomy and responsibility. Undoubtedly, situational prevention (re-)emerged at a favourable political moment and was enhanced by its connections with a neo-classical, utilitarian philosophy. Its language of economic reasoning, personal choice, responsibility and rationality fitted very well with the growing neo-liberal consensus within the British government. Its appeal to the responsibilities of people and organisations throughout civil society meshed well with the growing political will to downsize and roll back the state, in order to free up entrepreneurial initiative. In this context, situational prevention offered the promise of short-term and cost-effective, albeit small-scale, impacts, in stark contrast to the 'nothing works' pessimism connected with the grand-scale social engineering projects circulating within criminal justice and penal welfarism. A situational mentality speaks the language of the market, of supply and demand, risk and reward, opportunities and costs, while appealing to regulation beyond the state through private and quasi-private auspices. It focuses as much on potential victims as on potential offenders.

Yet, while the period of Thatcherism and Reaganism clearly coincided with the considerable expansion of situational technologies – especially in the UK – it would be an overstatement to assert that situational prevention was simply a vehicle through which a Thatcherite ideology about crime was implemented (King 1991). To do so would be to ignore the wider economic and cultural factors at play. Furthermore, it would pay insufficient attention to the tensions between neo-liberalism and neo-conservative values expressed within Thatcherism, as well as between the administrative urge to manage (and normalise) the crime problem on the one hand, and on the other hand the expressive and morally toned inclination to condemn and exclude offenders as 'other'. The instrumental logic of much situational crime prevention tends to reduce human behaviour to an economic rationale of calculative actions premised on choice and self-interest, with little or no regard for moral or cultural values. Neo-conservative influences within much recent crime control policy, with its emphasis on expressive punitiveness, by contrast have an avowedly normative agenda. They assert a notion of responsible agency that is conceived in highly moralistic tones embodying values and virtues. Here, rather than disappearing into the background and leaving the invisible hand of the market to prevail, the state's role is not merely to free autonomy but to shape it. As Cruikshank notes: 'To restore civil society back to a state of natural liberty and self-reproduction, neo-conservatives argue that it is necessary to inculcate civic virtue in the citizenry, if necessary, by force' (cited in Rose 1999: 185).

It is perhaps this ambiguous accommodation of conflicting ideologies and political forces within criminal justice policies that explains, at least in part, the manner in which CCTV technologies were so readily and extensively embraced in the UK (and possibly elsewhere). As a measure of situational crime prevention, CCTV also appeals to, and connects with, an expressive and affective dimension, reflecting a deeper cultural attraction. CCTV cameras not only evoke symbols of security by appearing to perform preventive tasks, but also facilitate the acting out of more traditional expressive and punitive sentiments provoked by the footage derived from CCTV cameras where criminal acts and disorder are captured on film. In this manner, CCTV straddles both a preventive logic and a punitive one (Norris and McCahill 2006). It enables both a governance of the present and future through surveillance and deterrence and a normative reordering of the past by witnessing and recording events and responding to them. Not only are CCTV cameras tangible reminders that something is being done to secure personal safety; they also serve to prompt moral indignation at the acts they portray.

A European model?

In thinking about comparative crime prevention across Europe (and beyond), one question prompted by the collection of essays in this book is to what extent the various country-specific experiences suggest a convergence of policies or the emergence of a common European model. Or if not, what lines of differentiation mark divergences? As we have seen, the contemporary genesis of crime prevention as a focus of public policy first emerged in Europe in the 1970s, as evidenced in early government reports and enquiries notably in France, Sweden, Britain and the Netherlands. This was followed in the 1980s by the beginnings of the institutionalisation of new infrastructures. What marked this period of development was the emergence of a number of different models of delivery. As Melossi and Selmini argue in their contribution to this collection (see Chapter 7) the two dominant models tended to associate the British with a situational approach and the French with a social approach. While something of a caricature, the following became associated with different jurisdictions, during that period:

- The Swedish model included a national strategy which sought to integrate relevant policy domains with a focus on planning, implementation and resources.

- The French model, informed by the Bonnemaison Report (1982), emphasised social crime prevention notably through inclusionary strategies targeted at alienated and marginalised young people.

- The British model, initially reflected in the Safer Cities projects, became closely associated with a situational and police-led approach to the management and modification of the physical environment to reduce opportunities for crime.

- The Dutch model was seen as a more pragmatic blend of strategies involving human agents and technology and with an emphasis on a rigorous research evidence base, reflected in the policy that 10 per cent of prevention funding should be allocated to evaluation.

- The Nordic model reflected an inclusive and non-punitive approach, with less reliance on technology and greater emphasis on human agents.

Over time other hybrid models emerged, including the regional focus of developments in Italy – notably the region of Emilia-Romagna (see Chapter 7) – and city-level developments often given practical expression through involvement in transnational networks and city-to-city alliances such as the European Forum for Urban Safety. In other jurisdictions, such as Belgium (see Chapter 8), the influence of models developed within neighbouring countries (in the Netherland and France) produced a complex mixture of approaches in different regions, reflecting different cultural traditions – notably in the separate Flemish and French-speaking parts of the country – and on account of the sway of different political parties. In former Soviet-bloc countries, such as Hungary (see Chapter 10) and Slovenia, the development of crime prevention strategies and an infrastructure to deliver them has been closely associated with the processes of transition. These countries have often seen the rapid development of policies at a national level with less emphasis on robust local delivery mechanisms.

More recent years have witnessed considerable internationalisation of crime prevention through the development of transnational and suprana-tional networks. These institutions, policy communities and forms of elite networking have generated significant flows of policy ideas across countries. This policy transfer has confused and confounded the simple association of particular jurisdictions with specific models or approaches. A number of key institutions have been instrumental in the transfer and diffusion of crime prevention ideas and practices. In so doing, they have added to the more complex picture of mixed models, as strategies devised in one country have been appropriated and adapted to other contexts. They include the European Forum for Urban Safety (EFUS); the United Nations Centre for International Crime Prevention (UN Office for Drug Control and Crime Prevention); the European Institute for Crime Preven-tion and Control, affiliated with the United Nations (HEUNI); the International Centre for the Prevention of Crime (ICPC); UN-HABITAT Safer Cities programme; and the European Crime Prevention Network (ECPN). As well as forging professional networks, these organisations disseminate models of good practice and seek to encourage their adoption (see ICPC 2008).

The establishment of the ECPN by a decision of the European Council in May 2001 (2001/427/JHA) signalled a significant institutional attempt at European-level co-ordination, lesson-learning and, by implication, harmonisation. It works to promote crime prevention activity in member states across the European Union, notably 'to provide a means through which valuable good practice in preventing crime, mainly "traditional" crime, could be shared'.[3] From the outset, its focus of attention was largely restricted to 'the fields of juvenile, urban and drug-related crime' (Art. 3(1)) and it was charged with favouring 'a multidisciplinary approach' (Art. 4(a)). A central aspect of the work of the ECPN is concerned with lesson-learning and the diffusion of apparently successful interventions. Hence, one of the criteria for the annual European Crime Prevention Award that the ECPN runs is that the projects should be 'capable of replication by organisations and groups in other Member States'.[4] Over the years, however, the ECPN's work has become mired in political difficulties, as it is required to work through government authorities. It has also been hindered by perceptions that it favours the promotion of particular approaches to crime prevention, notably those associated with situational and technological measures. In part, this perception has been fuelled by the key roles played by the Dutch and the British in running and resourcing the network.

By contrast, the European Forum for Urban Safety is a good example of a city-to-city network influenced by a different philosophy of crime prevention and community safety, notably one that emphasises the role played by municipal authorities. Established in 1987 in Barcelona, EFUS now constitutes a network of some 300 local authorities across Europe. Moreover, given its original connection with the work of Gilbert Bonnemaison – who, as well as writing the report that shaped France's model of social crime prevention (Bonnemaison 1982) also helped initiate the founding of the Forum – it has been associated with a particular social approach to prevention. It is perhaps because of this that EFUS has struggled to establish any significant presence in the UK, with only two British cities formally allied to it (Liverpool and Luton) and remains dominated by southern European cities and regions (notably in France, Italy and Spain). As Melossi and Selmini (Chapter 7) argue, the Forum played a crucial role in the diffusion of strategies allied to the 'French model' of social crime prevention within Italy and elsewhere.

The apparent distinctiveness of earlier models, and their association with particular countries and specific political affiliations over time, has given way to more mixed and varied approaches. If there is such a thing as a European model of crime prevention it would appear to coalesce around the following cluster of central themes:

- Strategies that include but extend beyond technical opportunity reduction and target-hardening.

- An emphasis upon *wider social problems*, including public perceptions and fear of crime, quality of life, broadly defined harms, incivilities and disorder.

- A focus upon modes of *informal social control* and local normative orders, as well as the manner in which they relate to, and connect with, formal systems of control.

- Implementation through decentralised, *local* arrangements – evoking the aphorism 'local problems require local solutions'.

- Delivery through co-ordinated *partnership* structures that draw together a variety of organisations and stakeholders from the public, voluntary and private sectors.

- Policies that recognise the need for social responses that reflect the multiple aetiology of crime and are aimed at producing *holistic* or 'joined-up' solutions.

- Strategies that are 'problem-oriented' rather than defined according to the bureaucratic means or organisations most readily available to respond to them.

Conceptually, the broadening out of crime prevention away from a narrow focus on crime and criminal opportunities has been reflected in the wider discursive frame in which it is frequently located. In a number of countries, the language of crime prevention has been replaced by alternative terms that reflect this shift – such as 'community safety', 'local safety', 'urban security', 'local governance'. A key theme in the institutionalisation and delivery of such policies has been the idea of local – city or regional – safety partnerships or security networks. These variously involve the co-ordination of diverse local organisations, actors and interests in multidisciplinary and interorganisational working relations. These partnerships – which might incorporate representatives from public, private and voluntary sectors – potentially mark a fundamental shift in the governance of crime and social problems. It acknowledges that there is no single agency solution to crime – it is multifaceted in both its causes and effects. In so doing, local safety partnerships challenge many bureaucratic assumptions about professional expertise, specialisation and disciplinary boundaries. In theory, it offers a de-differentiated response that is not segmented or compartmentalised but affords a generalised, non-specialist activity, built into the routines and consciousness of all citizens and organisations.

However, the experiences of all European jurisdictions show that delivering partnerships presents a considerable challenge. Often key agencies have been unwilling to get involved, while others have dominated the agenda. Tensions between central government control and local demands and interests have often stymied development such that in some countries the focus of partnerships has been compliance with national agendas or performance indicators, notwithstanding the requirement upon them to identify and pursue local priorities. Despite the rhetoric of localism and decentralisation, many national governments appear to have been unable and unwilling to adopt a more 'hands off' approach to local safety partnerships. However, where robust systems of devolution and federalism exist, the scope for local autonomy appears to have been more vibrant.

The politics of law and order has also played a significant part in undermining, or at least curtailing, the fortunes of crime prevention policies. A recurring theme from the chapters that follow is the manner in which crime prevention policies have been conditioned and influenced by wider political struggles and the alliance of particular strategies with specific political programmes. The political will and leap of faith necessary to ensure a dramatic shift in resources towards prevention have yet to transpire to the degree that most proponents would like. Given other more salient or newsworthy political demands, the focus on delivering and embedding prevention has waxed and waned. The enduring sway of 'punitive populism' and the preoccupation of politicians and the media with 'talking tough on crime', even against a background of declining aggregate crime rates (in many countries), have not provided a particularly productive environment in which to institutionalise preventive thinking in the public state sector.

Lost in translation?

Before going further, we need to sound a brief note of caution about the implied process of translation and the limitations of the comparative method. In so doing, it is valuable to differentiate two meanings of translation. The first and most obvious entails translation from one language to another. In a European context, given the rich diversity of language, this presents particularly acute challenges. Linguistic conversion implies that the same term carries the same meaning in each language. This is often a dangerous assumption. Not only do practices and institutions differ considerably but the same term can have very different meanings. One much debated example is the frequent mistranslation of 'community', a concept that has very different connotations in an Anglo-Saxon context as compared, for example, to France and Germany. The French concept of *communauté* has a very distinct and different sense (Garapon 1995; Crawford 2000; Wyvekens, Chapter 4 this volume), while 'community' in Germany has distinct authoritarian connotations (Zedner 1995). In a different but related vein, there is no French equivalent term for 'policy', which translates simply as *la politique*, the same word used for 'politics'. Bauman (1999: 5) highlights how the German term *unsicherheit* conflates experiences and sentiments conveyed by three distinct English terms: 'uncertainty', 'insecurity' and 'unsafety'. This leaves concepts such as 'community safety' and 'urban security' subject to varied interpretations, particularly where we seek to understand specific practices through such conceptual lenses. Learning not to translate both literally and figuratively, therefore, is an important aspect of comparative research. Rather, there is a need to excavate and understand the culturally specific essence of key terms and locate them within the context of wider horizons of interpretation. Nevertheless, we need also to recognise that words themselves are not static but the subject of change in which they take on new meaning, sometimes in the interplay between different languages. Notably, the terminology associated with key policy ideas may have salience and appeal that transcends linguistic traditions.

The second meaning of translation is the process by which an idea, practice or activity is translated from one place to another. This process of contextual relocation assumes that the same practices carry the same meanings in different social and cultural contexts. There is all too often a danger within comparative criminology (as in the social sciences more generally) of analysing developments in the style of a butterfly-collector, where the exhibits are plucked from the very environments that they inhabit and through which their lives make sense (Crawford 2002). We need to understand more, rather than less, about the differences and similarities in connections between responses to crime and cultures, as well as the manner in which such strategies derive their sense and meaning from their cultural ties. The limits to the transferability of crime control mechanisms or policies that advocates claim to be universal often derive from precisely such cultural and institutional connections. For this reason, as far as possible, contributors to this volume have sought to relate experiences to, and situate crime prevention policies within, the political and social conditions within each country. Comparativists need to be sensitive to the pitfalls of both linguistic conversion and contextual relocation.

As various contributors note, *context matters*. This is possibly the most valuable insight provided by situational perspectives. Situational crime prevention theory demands not merely that interventions are targeted at appropriate places rooted in an understanding of their specific crime problems but also that these should be regularly reviewed and renewed or adapted in an interactive and iterative process. As situational interventions are intended to change behaviour, they need to be continuously checked, for their ongoing effectiveness will be dependent upon how crime patterns adapt and change over time. This acknowledges that crime patterns – like the social, cultural and technological worlds – are not static. From within a situational frame of reference, new criminal opportunities are being created all the time, notably through innovations. Crime opportunities are highly specific, are concentrated in time and space, depend on everyday movements of activity and are interconnected such that one crime may produce opportunities for another (Felson and Clarke 1998). As some opportunities may be closed or restricted consequent to situational endeavours, others may be opened. Crucially, however, as Ekblom notes, continual adaptation and evolution 'makes knowledge of what works in crime prevention a wasting asset' (2005: 230). In essence, situational prevention privileges a particular kind of knowledge that is practical, empirical and reflexive.

However, the importance of context is not restricted to situational approaches. In fact, it is likely to be more salient away from technological measures and outside of interventions into the physical and built environment, in the messy world of human affairs, social relations and interpersonal dynamics where 'people matter'. This point is forcefully made by Margaret Shaw (Chapter 11), who looks beyond the confines of Europe to the very different meanings and practices of crime prevention in impoverished parts of the developing world.

The context specificity and temporal impermanence of crime prevention question the generalising claims made by many proponents of 'crime science' and 'international crime prevention'. It also challenges the transferability and replication of apparently successful prevention schemes from one country, city or locality to another. For some, the possibilities of international crime prevention offer a 'scientific' approach to the question of 'what works?' (Farrington 2000). For others, the generalisations implicit in such an approach oversimplify the interactive and constitutive relationship between crime, preventive mechanisms and the contexts in which they operate.

Convergence or divergence?

There are considerable dangers in comparative analysis in either focusing on the richness of difference and diversity of practices or – more often in criminology – rushing to hasty and misguided assumptions about the flattening of difference through policy convergence and transfer. Furthermore, transnational similarity should not automatically infer that a transnational explanation is at work. It may reflect a similar response to related structural problems. To draw a simple analogy, the wheel may well have been invented by a number of people in different places at similar times. We cannot necessarily assume the widespread use of the wheel to overcome common problems of transport was the result of diffusion from one original source. Likewise, similar policy developments may have diverse local origins in responding to similar problems. This highlights the essential dangers of functional determinism in convergence theories which often assume intentionality. Similarities may be the product of unintentionally convergent developments, whereas diffusion is an intentional and purposive activity. With this in mind, Dolowitz and Marsh define policy transfer as 'the process by which knowledge of policies, administrative arrangements, institutions and ideas in one political system (past or present) is used in the development of policies, administrative arrangements, institutions and ideas in another political system' (2000: 5). Here, convergence may be understood as not merely a response to structural forces but as a product of what we might call 'contagious diffusion' (Levi-Faur 2005: 22).

Bennett (1991: 218) distinguishes five forms of policy convergence: (i) at the level of *policy goals* where there is a similarity of intention to deal with common policy problems; (ii) in relation to a convergence of *policy content*, represented through formal expressions of government policy; (iii) by way of a coming together of *policy instruments,* namely the institutional tools available to administer policy; (iv) there may be a convergence on *policy outcomes* and impacts with regard to the consequences of policy implementation; (v) convergence may express itself in relation to *policy style*, by which he refers to a more diffuse notion of 'the process by which policy responses are formulated'. By implication, we may find examples of policy convergence in some aspects of policy coexisting with divergence on others.

In a related vein, Pollitt (2001) identifies four distinct levels of policy that allow us to differentiate between different levels of policy transfer and convergence: *policy ideas* inform or provide legitimacy for policy 'rhetoric' and 'talk'; *policy instruments* are the 'decisions' and specific programmes that constitute formal statements of policy and legislation; *policy implementation* refers to the actions of people (professionals, practitioners and 'street-level bureaucrats') given the task of implementing policy decisions on the ground in everyday practice; and *policy outcomes* represent the social consequences and impacts of policy implementation.

Both Bennett's and Pollitt's conceptualisations are useful as they allow us to explore not only the dynamics within each level or form of policy but also the interactions between them. Neither typology envisages impervious developmental stages, but rather their coexistence in a more fluid and constitutive relationship. There is, for example, an important interconnectedness between policy formation and policy implementation, which belies the idea of discrete sequential stages. As Anderson notes, 'policy is made as it is being administered and administered as it is being made' (1975: 79). The differentiation between 'talk' and 'decisions', as well as 'action', highlights the important role that ideas can play as rhetorical devices for the purposes of symbolism and legitimacy. Jones and Newburn (2007a: 25) note how the important symbolic dimension of much criminal justice policy often produces a significant dissonance between 'talk' and 'action', rhetoric and actions. Claims about convergence may be more a matter of 'talk' and symbolism than of everyday practices. In their study of the transfer of US-style policing policies and practices into the UK, Jones and Newburn (2007b) found little evidence of wholesale importation. Rather they identified elements of 'soft' policy transfer in the form of ideas, principles, symbols and rhetoric rather than 'hard' policy transfer of specific 'decisions' and 'actions'. Their research also serves as a reminder to be wary of the dangers in over-rationalising policy as both a process and a set of levels of analysis. Policy trajectories may unfold influenced as much by opportunistic and non-rational factors or affective sentiments as informed by rational deliberation. This is particularly evident in relation to matters of crime and safety, where the role of emotions can be powerful factors and where public sensibilities are volatile.

As a warning against over-interpreting policy as a mechanical process with discrete stages, Bennett highlights the 'shifting and interactive processes of feedback that shape policy content' (1991: 218). Policy convergence needs to be conceptualised in dynamic terms. The key dimension is time rather than space. In this sense, policy is in a continual process of evolution and change. To push the metaphor of travel slightly further, it is a journey with no final destination. Van Mannen (1995: 138) aptly describes policy as a 'world of continual flux, a world that is always becoming'. In a similar vein, Bennett suggests that policy convergence is 'a process of "becoming" rather than a condition of "being" more alike' (1991: 219). From this perspective, looking back over 25 years or so of developments in crime prevention allows a degree of reflection on different trajectories over time; it affords consideration of patterns of development, evolution and change. It begs the question, to what extent is there movement over time towards some identified common position? To answer this question we need to clarify further the potential causes of convergence. As suggested above, convergence may be the product of both intentional and purposive activity and the unintentional by-product of indigenous adaptations to policy dilemmas and social problems. Bennett (1991: 220–9) helpfully identifies four processes through which deliberate policy convergence might occur: emulation, elite networking, harmonisation, and penetration.

Emulation refers to the deliberate borrowing of ideas and policies from elsewhere. It constitutes a form of imitation although this may entail adapting policy innovations in a way that may not be characterised as strict replication. Emulation may occur at different stages of the policy process and may serve different purposes.

Elite networking and policy communities can play an important role as conduits in the transfer of policy innovations. Elite networking refers to the circulation of ideas within relatively coherent and stable networks of elites working within the same policy domain that engage in transnational interactions. It will often take the form of shared experience and lesson-drawing about a common problem. In the context of crime prevention, the European Forum for Urban Safety is a good example of elite networking that has significantly influenced the travel of crime prevention policies and practices across Europe. Elite networking high-lights the role that people play (especially professional groups and associations) through interactions and exchanges of ideas. It also flags the influential role played by key 'policy entrepreneurs' (Kingdon 1984) in promoting and advancing certain policy ideas, approaches and instruments.[5]

Harmonisation demands the existence of institutions and structures designed to co-ordinate, synchronise and standardise policy developments across different milieux. Unlike the informal collaboration provided through elite networking, harmonisation requires the formal existence of some overarching regime. Bennett (1991: 225) suggests that the recognition of interdependence will often provide a central *raison d'être* and driving force informing harmonisation. In the context of between-state policy transfer, this relates to the role played by intergovernmental and supra-national organisations, such as the institutions of the European Union or the United Nations (see UN 2002). Harmonisation is particularly evident with regard to transnational crime and insecurity problems where intergovernmental co-operation is prominent. In this sense, the work of the European Crime Prevention Network, given its institutional position within the European Commission, is more akin to harmonisation than elite networking, although it probably encompasses both.

By contrast, *penetration* evokes a process where policy change arises on the basis of conformity imposed by external actors or interests. In the

European context, the economic and political conditions – generally known as the Copenhagen criteria (after the Copenhagen summit in June 1993) – required before accession states can join the European Union constitute a good example of penetration. More generally, the negotiations associated with accession may impose policy prerequisites. While Bennett suggests (1991: 227) that, in contrast to the seemingly co-operative relations evident in harmonisation, penetration entails coercion or force, he also recognises that certain efforts at harmonisation can have coercive effects. At their boundaries the two shade into each other, dependent upon degrees of co-operation or coercion and perceptions about the reception of externally generated policy ideas within a given policy community. Hence, European directives and 'soft law' may be both a product of harmonisation and experienced as a form of penetration. A good example of this is the extent to which Eastern European countries and other accession states incorporated certain policy developments – including dominant ideas about crime prevention – because they perceived these as desirable and potentially necessary attributes associated with membership. The European Commission (2004) has actively promoted a preferred methodology for implementing crime prevention projects[6] – the so-called 5 Is – as well as 'essential conditions' for the prevention of crime that should prevail in all member states.[7]

As Klara Kerezsi demonstrates in Chapter 10, Hungarian reforms were heavily influenced by the (perceived) requirements of so-called 'Europeanisation'. In Hungary, diffusion via harmonisation and penetration appears to have significantly influenced the direction of development and institutionalisation of crime prevention. Given the place that prevention had secured on the European Commission's agenda, a dominant model of prevention became associated with Hungary's accession to the European Union. This appears to have occurred both as part of negotiations and as a perception that in order to join the Western European 'club' certain policy ideas needed to be formally incorporated into the domestic policy framework, with perhaps less emphasis given to how these ideas might be institutionalised and implemented in practice. From this perspective, convergence becomes something of a ritual rite of passage, imposed by an external supranational authority (in this instance the European Union), whether or not this is intentional. In the light of this blurring of self-obligation and external coercion or unwelcomed harmonisation, Dolowitz and Marsh (2000: 13) conceptualise policy transfer as lying along a continuum that runs from lesson-drawing to the direct imposition of a policy programme or institutional arrangement on one political system by another.

The detailed study of the processes through which policy transfer occurs requires the exploration of a number of allied questions. What are the key institutions through which policies are transferred? Who are the central actors engaged in policy transfer? Which policy ideas, decisions and instruments are transferred? From where are lessons learned? What facilitates or constrains transfer? How are ideas, decisions, instruments and practices transferred from one context reworked and reshaped in the process of transfer, reformulation and implementation? Various chapters in this collection highlight elements of policy transfer between European countries. In Chapter 8, for example, Patrick Hebberecht illustrates the manner in which in Belgium experienced conflicting waves of policy transfer drawn from different countries associated with various models of crime prevention policy. Policy emulation followed both ideological positions as well as different cultural and linguistic traditions. While Flemish-speaking regions were more influenced by Dutch and British developments, the French-speaking regions drew on French policy developments for inspiration.

Assessing progress

Reflecting on the past quarter of a century, there is a sense in which, to some significant degree, the preventive turn has not been fully realised and the initial optimistic aspirations have become increasingly muted. Despite the apparent proliferation of situational crime prevention in some countries, rather than celebrate its institutional successes proponents frequently bemoan the lack of influence of situational ideas and the indifference with which they have been received by many criminologists and politicians (Clarke 2000). The promise of joined-up local partnerships delivering co-ordinated prevention strategies in response to local needs remains a distant aspiration. Consequently, one question that might be asked is, why has crime prevention not taken greater hold? One response might be that the initial claims of a rupture with the past were exaggerated. A further assessment might highlight the obduracy of dominant state bureaucracies, ill-equipped at genuine problem-solving and preventive planning. Another appraisal might identify the persistence of the prevailing logic of penal sanctioning. Despite the government resources allocated to prevention, this pales in the shade of the vast amounts of money that are consumed by the traditional criminal justice estate.

To take one concrete example from England and Wales, the perceived failure to fully implement a major plank of the Crime and Disorder Act 1998 is an illustrative case in point. Section 17 imposes a duty on local authorities, in exercising their various functions, to consider the crime and disorder implications and the need to do all that they reasonably can to prevent crime and disorder in their area. This statutory duty was lobbied for and welcomed by local authority associations. According to the Home Office, the purpose of the duty was to 'give the vital work of preventing crime a new focus across a very wide range of local services ... putting crime and disorder considerations at the very heart of decision making, where they have always belonged' (1997: para. 33). Moss and Pease notably suggested that 'Section 17 is arguably the most radical part of the Act ... Because [the] "crime drivers" pervade every sphere of local authority responsibility, it is difficult to conceive of any decision which will remain untouched by s.17 considerations' (1999: 15–16). They questioned whether Section 17 might constitute 'the wolf in sheep's clothing' within the 1998 Act which itself sought to do much to advance and institutionalise crime prevention and community safety. Yet, the implementation of Section 17 has fallen considerably below expectations. One area where it might have had direct and immediate implications is the realm of planning applications, where police architectural liaison officers and crime prevention design advisors might have used it as a lever into planning decisions. As it transpired, a significant number of test cases revolved around applications for licensed premises associated with the expansion of the night-time economy. Despite the well-documented attendant crime and disorder implications of large numbers of alcohol outlets in city centres (Hadfield 2006), the Planning Inspectorate has been largely unwilling to uphold decisions to reject applications on the grounds of Section 17 where these had been made by local authorities (Moss 2006). As a branch of central government rather than the local council, the Planning Inspectorate has not felt itself bound by the legislation, which applies to local authorities alone. This illustration of implementation failure also reflects more general tensions between responsibilities of central and local government, evident in a number of European jurisdictions.

In England in late 2004, so displeased at the rate of progress was the government that it announced a major review of community safety partnership structures (see Home Office 2006), acknowledging that 'a significant number of partnerships struggle to maintain a full contribution from key agencies and even successful ones are not sufficiently visible, nor we think accountable, to the public as they should be' (Home Office 2004: 123).[8] Many partnerships have stalled due to the reluctance of some agencies to participate, the dominance of certain agendas, often policing, an unwillingness to share information, conflicting interests, priorities and cultural assumptions on the part of some partners, a lack of interorganisational trust, a desire to protect budgets and a lack of capacity and expertise. The dominance of hierarchical state bureaucracies has proved obdurate. Consequently, there was a distinct trace of *déjà vu* in the British government's latest strategy promises that 'partnership working will be strengthened' and 'Government will be more enabling, and less directive' (Home Office 2007: 5).

This rather pessimistic account of unfulfilled promises is reflected in many, although not all, contributions to this book. Yet many European countries have witnessed significant reductions in aggregate crime rates during this same period – most marked in the period since the mid 1990s.

These declines have been particularly evident in relation to domestic burglary and auto theft. Figure 1.1 presents figures on the reductions in domestic burglary where recorded by the police across all the countries represented in this collection. Figure 1.2 shows similar data in relation to theft of a motor vehicle.

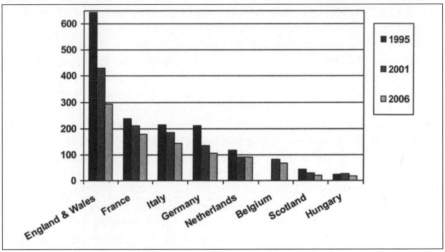

Source: Tavares and Thomas (2008: 6)

Figure 1.1 Domestic burglary recorded by the police (in thousands)

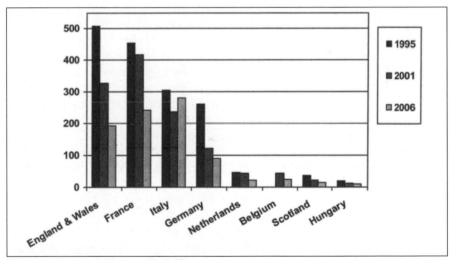

Source: Tavares and Thomas (2008: 7)

Figure 1.2 Theft of a motor vehicle recorded by the police (in thousands)

It might be expected that domestic burglary and vehicle theft would be the most susceptible to reductions due to the installation of prevention technologies, notably target-hardening devices such as burglar alarms, door and window locks regarding domestic burglary, and steering column locks and immobilisers in relation to theft of vehicles. The figures reveal significant reductions in police-recorded data in the various countries for both offence types. In England and Wales the annual number of domestic burglaries declined by 55 per cent in the 11 years between 1995 and 2006. Over the same period theft of motor cars fell by 62 per cent. France saw reductions of 25 per cent and 46 per cent respectively; Germany witnessed declines of 50 per cent and 66 per cent; Italy saw reductions of 32 per cent and 8 per cent; and the Netherlands experienced falls of 23 per cent and 52 per cent. Across Europe generally (where the data are available) there has been an *annual* 5.3 per cent decline in motor vehicle theft between 1995 and 2006. Substantial reductions in a variety of common crimes – such as burglaries, thefts, robberies and assaults – are also evidenced in the findings of the European Crime and Safety Survey, which shows significant decreases everywhere in the European Union (with the possible exceptions of Belgium and Ireland) during the period from 1995 to 2004 (Van Dijk *et al.* 2006).

Might not the shift towards greater emphasis on prevention be part of an explanation for this crime drop? There is increasing evidence that changes in the level and quality of security may have informed this momentous turnaround in the historic rise in crime rates. Using British Crime Survey data, Farrell and colleagues (2008) have put some empirical flesh on this 'securitisation' hypothesis by linking the decline in the number of vehicles without immobilisers and steering column locks in England and Wales to the decline in car thefts where the entry method was the forcing of door locks. They surmise that this is consistent with central locking as the cause of the decline 'because better locks would reduce door-forcing more than window-breaking' (Farrell *et al.* 2008: 18) with little apparent evidence of tactical displacement. Furthermore, they show how the bulk of the decline has been in relation to recovered vehicles, more likely to have been used for opportunistic purposes of joy-riding and transportation, as opposed to unrecovered vehicles which are more likely to have been stolen by professional thieves for the purpose of resale or parts (which also declined but less steeply). They suggest that this points to the conclusion that opportunistic and amateur car thieves have been 'driven out of the market by better locks and immobilisers' (2008: 18).

While there are wider issues at play, complicating any simple cause and effect relationship, and it is not clear whether this evidence is replicated in other European countries,[10] nevertheless it provides some evidence that increased security may have contributed to the overall crime drop in addition to reductions in specific crime types. This begs the question, why has prevention not been given greater credit for this apparently significant development? One answer might be that it does not accord with the prevailing politics of 'law and order' in many European countries which continues to emphasise the expressive and punitive 'criminology of the other' at the expense of the more instrumental and pragmatic 'criminology of the self' (Garland 2001: 137), with which prevention is more intimately aligned. This reflects a preoccupation in which the ambitions of governing and statecraft have been resighted in the face of uncontrollable flows of capital, goods, people and risks. Being seen to assert sovereign authority through bouts of punitive sentiments to assuage public perceptions of insecurity has become an increasingly prominent governmental *raison d'être*. This fits less comfortably with the more administrative and mundane approach to target-hardening and heightened securitisation through the actions and interventions of the private sector and ordinary citizens prompted by commercial imperatives and market-based incentives.

A further reason for the muted response to any association between the preventive turn and the historic crime drop lies in difficulties of measuring success. As it entails a 'non-event', crime prevention is intrinsically problematic to measure. There are complex issues of temporal, spatial, tactical and crime-type displacement to account for. There may also be social costs to the hardening of security around cars and domestic premises, which leaves people as the most vulnerable links in the chain of crime opportunities. Consequently, prevention does not capture the kind of simple narrative that a media-saturated world demands. We are unlikely ever to see headlines reading 'murder, rape or burglary prevented by early childhood programme'. Prevented crimes do not leave obvious traces and as such constitute what Taleb refers to as 'silent evidence', whereby the value of what we don't know – our 'known unknowns' – is downgraded: 'everybody knows that you need more prevention than treatment, but few reward acts of prevention' (Taleb 2007: xxiv).[11] This measurement difficulty and cultural salience of prevention is compounded by the problem of temporal effects. While situational prevention may produce immediate and tangible pay-offs, much social crime prevention only has effects over the long term. Furthermore, the long-term investment needed for some forms of prevention is frequently undermined by short political time horizons. Governing political alliances are more interested in effecting change that is measurable during their period of office.

In her chapter, Margaret Shaw cites Homel's analogy of crime prevention as 'a swan swimming in the surf', moving in and out of sight, and hence prominence, as it floats on the undulating waves. The point being made here is that the public salience and political fortunes of crime prevention may fluctuate, but it remains a *good idea* that is here to stay. The implication is that in the long-run crime prevention will remain an important feature of the landscape, unaffected by the swell of the choppy seas below. From the chapters in this collection, there is certainly an evident that in which in various jurisdictions crime prevention has moved in and out of favour, mirroring the swan in the surf, and it has been buffeted by changing political circumstances. Yet there is also a sense in which crime prevention and community safety are intimately bound up with, and an expression of, the wider political and cultural climate. Ultimately, crime prevention is a matter of politics, albeit not reducible to the decisions of national and local governments. It is about priorities, resource allocation, decision-making and authority.

While being aware of the dangers in overstretching an analogy, one story (and there are multiple stories to tell, as this volume testifies) of the recent experiences of state-sponsored crime prevention might be charac- terised as the 'upside-down swan'. The swan is well known for its grace and poise above the water while its legs work busily and efficiently underneath. The upside-down swan, by contrast, inverts this logic: what becomes visible is a considerable amount of activity – energy but with little to show for it by way of results. Furthermore, the frantic energy exerted is not only ineffective but can be interpreted as an end in itself as it is seen to be doing something in response to public anxieties and demands for security. The significance of governmental actions may derive as much from the symbolic messages and communicative proper- ties they express as from their instrumental capacity to control or prevent crime.

Concluding reflections

Responsibilisation strategies?

A dominant interpretation and explanation of the renaissance of crime prevention and construction of community safety partnerships is that they constitute the embodiment of 'responsibilisation strategies', whereby state authorities seek to enlist other agencies and individuals to form chains of co-ordinated action, prompting crime control endeavours on the part of 'responsibilised' actors (O'Malley 1992; Garland 1996). As Garland re- marks: 'This involves the central government seeking to act upon crime not in a direct fashion through state agencies (police, courts, prisons, social work) but instead by acting indirectly, seeking to activate action on the part of non-state agencies and organisations' (1996: 452). Through these processes of 'government at a distance', state power is extended and enhanced.

In the light of the evidence presented in this book, can we understand the rise of crime prevention and community safety as the product of a strategy on the part of central government authorities to divest themselves of direct social control roles and shift more of the burden for personal and collective safety on to individuals and groups? At one level, there is no doubt that citizens, communities and organisations are being encouraged to take on greater responsibility in matters of their own and others' safety and security. Furthermore, partnership structures have created a veneer of more co-operative and co-ordinated relations between diverse public sector organisations and between state and non-state, as well as some private sector, agencies. Yet, the nature and extent of that responsibility remains highly circumspect and ambiguous. The degree to which partnerships have been successfully implemented and to which responsibility has been embraced remains both uneven and tentative. Some 20 years (or more) on from its inception, the partnership approach remains poorly implemented across Europe, where internecine 'turf warfare' between organisations and departmentalism remain rife, often expressed in conflicts between Ministries of the Interior and Ministries of Justice in continental Europe. The intervening years have shown that realising preventive partnerships has proved stubbornly illusive. Partnerships remain dominated by public sector bodies (notably municipal authorities and the police), while the role of the voluntary sector largely has been marginalised. This is true in the UK, where the involvement of businesses was a key theme of early developments, notably through the Safer Cities programme in the 1980s and 1990s. Despite this, commercial engagement has been patchy and often unco-ordinated. In many crime-related endeavours public and private activities 'pass like ships in the night' (Crawford *et al.* 2005), as businesses frequently prefer 'to do their own thing' and manage their own affairs. There remains a deep reluctance on the part of many commercial enterprises to take on responsibilities for what they perceive as more appropriately government business. While shops, leisure outlets and licensed venues are keen to control and manage the policing and crime prevention activities within the confines of their premises, they are frequently less willing to contribute to the regulation of public spaces beyond.

Furthermore, the ever-present spectre of vigilantism and private justice, as well as concerns about 'have-a-go heroes' overstepping the bounds of acceptability, invariably constrain direct public involvement in crime control. More fundamentally, the very foundation of the modern state is intimately bound up with quests to monopolise the legitimate use of force and violence. As such, attempts to outsource crime control – to corporations as well as individuals – and enlist their active assistance raise vexed questions not just about the competency of the state but also about its essential project for governance as the prime protector of public order.

Problematically, the notion of 'responsibilisation' implies a process that emanates outwards and downwards from central government: one that is evidenced by key policy initiatives and strategies. While the chapters that follow provide corroborative evidence of and highlight such strategies, this is by no means the sole picture, nor necessarily the dominant one in all domains. The responsibilisation thesis largely downplays the crucial role that institutions – in civil society and the market place – have played and continue to play as agents of social control and prevention in the regulation of both deviant and conformist behaviour. It accepts too readily the idea of the dominant sovereign state; perversely, it seeks to highlight the mythical status of state sovereignty. It fails to connect sufficiently with wider developments and shifts in informal control, prevention and regulation outside the narrow field of crime (cf. O'Malley and Hutchinson 2007). Importantly, Braithwaite (2003) reminds us that there is a very different history of policing and prevention to be derived from the business regulatory field as distinct from the 'police-prisons' arena. One of the principal historical lessons drawn from the diverse body of regulatory agencies established in the nineteenth century is the manner in which they prioritised non-punitive modes of enforcement, preferring strategies rooted in persuasion through market-based disciplines and mentalities with a more explicit preventive orientation.

Crime and social policy

One of the recurring tensions evident in the accounts of experiences in a number of European nations concerns the porous boundaries and conceptual confusion between social crime prevention and social or urban policy more generally. There is a sense in which innovations in community safety and social crime prevention have been subsumed within, and have simultaneously refigured, social and urban policy. As a consequence of this bleeding between crime and social policy, social life is increasingly 'governed through crime and insecurity' while social policies are justified in terms of their crime reductive potential. This 'criminalisation of social policy' alerts us to the manner in which crime and insecurity have become pivotal to the exercise of authority and central organising frameworks that legitimate interventions that have other motivations (Crawford 1997: 228). The shift to prevention has accorded to crime an elevated place in the construction of social order, such that fundamental public issues may become marginalised, except in so far as they are defined in terms of their crime preventive qualities. Where social policies are justified in terms of their crime preventive potential there are real risks that the services provided will come to take on stigmatising connotations.

As the chapters in this volume testify, there certainly has been a degree of blurring of social policy and criminal justice goals, as well as mechanisms for delivering them. In their contribution, Van Dijk and De Waard warn that the integration of social crime prevention within wider policy agendas, such as urban renewal, carries evident risks: 'Funds allocated to such "crime prevention in disguise" can easily leak away to activities with little potential to reduce crime' (see page 149). However, this might also be conceptualised as the socialisation of criminal justice, whereby crime prompts social responses that target need. In the process, both social policy and criminal justice have been transformed. Social policy has become more conditional – less universal – and behaviour has become one of the key conditions attached to welfare. The danger here is that crime becomes the organising principle and vehicle for allocating and distributing social goods.

What of the future?

As befits a reflection on the journey travelled over a quarter of a century, we are left with questions over the future direction of crime prevention policies. Given the previous discussion, one possible scenario is that social crime prevention becomes increasingly lost within a more conditional, restrictive and coercive social and urban policy. Here, the dystopian logic of 'governing through crime' (Simon 2007) potentially sees an expansion of the 'penal state' (and a concomitant decline in the 'welfare state'), simultaneously through mass incarceration and exclusionary modes of prevention as mutually supportive rather than oppositional developments. Another scenario sees situational crime prevention slip into the background as part of technology, design and the routine activities of businesses and ordinary citizens as they adapt to everyday life. It becomes part of the architecture, in which the social inconveniences, erosion of civil liberties and adverse cultural implications are all sidelined as the price worth paying for managing insecurities in what Boutellier (2004) characterises as the 'safety utopia'.

Nevertheless, it is possibly in the field of developmental crime prevention that we may be witnessing the emergence of a *new orthodoxy* (Farrington 2007; Farrington and Welsh 2007). A number of chapters testify to the growing importance of what Van Dijk and De Waard term 'secondary offender-oriented crime prevention', namely early intervention programmes targeted at children and young people (and their parents) identified as 'at risk' of offending. Risk assessment and classification and actuarial profiling have become increasingly influential aspects of contemporary criminal (notably youth) justice systems. Despite the possible preventive benefits and cost savings through targeting resources at 'high-risk' groups, such early intervention schemes raise crucial normative concerns. Gatti notes the right of children and young people not to be classified as future delinquents, whether they go on to become delinquents or not, as representing 'one of the greatest ethical problems raised by early prevention programmes' (1998: 120). Furthermore, the inaccuracy of predictive knowledge prompts caution. In the conclusion to a major report for the British government on working with young people and their families to reduce risks of crime, Utting sagely warns:

[A]ny notion that better screening can enable policy makers to identify young children destined to join the 5 per cent of offenders responsible for 50–60 per cent of crime is fanciful. Even if there were no ethical objections to putting 'potential delinquent' labels round the necks of young children, there would continue to be statistical barriers . . . [Research] shows substantial flows *out of* as well as *in to* the pool of children who develop chronic conduct problems. As such [there are] dangers of assuming that anti-social five-year olds are the criminals or drug abusers of tomorrow, as well as the undoubted opportunities that exist for prevention. Since the experience of service providers suggests that labelling children would also [be] counter-productive to gaining the trust and participation of parents, there must be a strong presumption in favour of preventive services presenting and justifying themselves in terms of children's existing needs and problems, rather than future risks of criminality. (Utting 2004: 99)

Consequently, many practitioners prefer universal programmes over targeted ones, despite their obvious resource implications.

Early intervention has parallels outside of life-course and developmental criminology in forms of preventive detention and preventive exclusion, as well as a more general lowering of the threshold of intervention to incivilities, anti-social behaviour, 'quality of life' concerns and other forms of 'pre-crime' (Zedner 2007). Allied to this is the greater use of data pools, the storing of DNA records and risk profiling. Anticipating, forestalling or eliminating potential threats and risks before they present themselves is an increasing focus of concern. Yet, in governing the future, uncertainty prevails. As Utting implies, the scientific knowledge-base for prevention and pre-emption remains too ambiguous to be reliable. The limitations of knowledge serve to magnify uncertainty. Under conditions of uncertainty a pre-emptive and preventive logic implies a precautionary principle (Sunstein 2005). People are judged in terms of what they *might* do. Anticipating and forestalling potential harm in a risk-averse culture of insecurity implies erring on the side of precaution (Ericson 2007). In such circumstances, the question 'what if?' prompts action, 'just in case'. Furthermore, as Zedner highlights, 'precaution places uncertainty – not knowledge – centre stage' (2008: 37), with significant implications for traditional criminal justice principles of due process protections and proportionality. It is perhaps here, in the context of uncertainty and in the face of our lack of knowledge about future risks and harms, that the prospects for crime prevention lie, in justifying interventions as a precaution within a wider logic of (limited) predictive governance. While the future is uncertain, what is clear is that the outlook for crime prevention and community safety across Europe will be the complex outcome of local and national political and social struggles about meaning and direction, in which cultural traditions and sensibilities will inform and infuse the future routes of travel and destinations.

Notes

1 www.kcl.ac.uk/depsta/law/research/icps/worldbrief/ (accessed 18 December 2008).
2 See www.bsia.co.uk/
3 See www.eucpn.org/
4 See www.eucpn.org/eucp-award/
5 The Home Office Research and Planning Unit of the early 1980s, notably while Ron Clarke was at its helm, played an important role in the promotion of situational crime prevention ideas and practices, as did Alice Coleman with regard to 'defensible space' ideas in Britain (Coleman 1985).
6 The methodology comprises: (i) *Intelligence*: gathering and analysing information; (ii) *Intervention*: blocking, disrupting or weakening the causes of crime; (iii) *Implementation*: converting the intervention principles into practical methods; (iv) *Involvement*: mobilising other agencies, companies and individuals to play their part in implementing the intervention or acting in partnership; and (v) *Impact and process evaluation*.
7 These include the requirements to: (i) place local authorities as primarily responsible for crime prevention; (ii) promote national crime prevention policies to volume crime through formal declarations of commitment; and (iii) follow internationally agreed standards such as those set out in the United Nations Guidelines for the Prevention of Crime (UN 2002).
8 The British government had previously responded to the perceived unwillingness of some agencies to engage with statutory community safety partnerships simply by expanding the list of organisations under a legal duty to participate – a classic command-and-control solution to a complex interorganisational problem.
9 Comparable data are not available for Belgium in 1995.
10 Although Van Dijk and colleagues suggest that a similar pattern to the British experience in relation to auto theft is evident across Europe, resulting in fewer cars stolen 'thanks to improved security' (2006: 19).
11 To drive home this point, Taleb gives the hypothetical example of the courageous legislator who enacts a law that all airplane cockpits have locked, bullet-proof doors, which is put into universal effect in August 2001, thus preventing the attacks on the World Trade Center. The legislator is unlikely to be given credit for the prevented attacks and would more likely be the subject of public scorn because of the cost and the disruption to pilots and crew.

References

Anderson, J. E. (1975) *Public Policy-Making*. New York: Praeger.
Bauman, Z. (1999) *In Search of Politics*. Cambridge: Polity Press.
Bennett, C. (1991) 'What is Policy Convergence and what Causes it?', *British Journal of Political Science*, 21: 215–33.
Bonnemaison, G. (1982) *Face à la Délinquance: Prévention, Répression, Solidarité*. Commission des Maires sur la Sécurité, Paris: La Documentation Française.
Boutellier, H. (2004) *The Safety Utopia*. Dordrecht: Kluwer.

Braithwaite, J. (2003) 'What's Wrong with the Sociology of Punishment?', *Theoretical Criminology*, 7(1): 5–28.

Brantingham, P. J. and Faust, L. (1976) 'A Conceptual Model of Crime Prevention', *Crime and Delinquency*, 22: 284–96.

Cavadino, M. and Dignan, J. (2006a) *Penal Systems: A Comparative Approach.* London: Sage.

Cavadino, M. and Dignan, J. (2006b) 'Penal Policy and Political Economy', *Criminology and Criminal Justice*, 6(4): 435–56.

Clarke, R. V. (1995) 'Situational Crime Prevention', in M. Tonry and D. P. Farrington (eds) *Crime and Justice a Review of Research*, 19. Chicago: University of Chicago Press, pp. 91–50.

Clarke, R. V. (2000) 'Situational Prevention, Criminology and Social Values', in A. Von Hirsch, D. Garland and A. Wakefield (eds) *Ethical and Social Perspectives on Situational Crime Prevention*. Oxford: Hart Publishing, pp. 97–112.

Coleman, A. (1985) *Utopia on Trial*. London: Hilary Shipman.

Crawford, A. (1997) *The Local Governance of Crime: Appeals to Community and Partnerships*. Oxford: Clarendon Press.

Crawford, A. (2000) 'Contrasts in Victim/Offender Mediation and Appeals to Community in France and England', in D. Nelken (ed.) *Contrasting Criminal Justice*. Aldershot: Ashgate, pp. 205–29.

Crawford, A. (2002) 'The State, Community and Restorative Justice: Heresy, Nostalgia and Butterfly Collecting', in L. Walgrave (ed.) *Restorative Justice and the Law*. Cullompton: Willan Publishing, pp. 101–29.

Crawford, A. (2006) 'Fixing Broken Promises?: Neighbourhood Wardens and Social Capital', *Urban Studies*, 43(5/6): 957–76.

Crawford, A., Lister, S., Blackburn, S. and Burnett, J. (2005) *Plural Policing*. Bristol: Policy Press.

Currie, E. (1988) 'Two Visions of Community Crime Prevention', in T. Hope and M. Shaw (eds) *Communities and Crime Reduction*. London: HMSO, pp. 280–6.

Dignan, J. and Cavadino, M. (2007) 'Penal Policy in Comparative Perspective', in *Centre for Criminal Justice Studies Review 2006/07*. Leeds: Centre for Criminal Justice Studies, pp. 51–4. Online at: www.leeds.ac.uk/law/ccjs/an_reps/19rep.pdf

Dolowitz, D. and Marsh, D. (2000) 'Learning from Abroad: The Role of Policy Transfer in Contemporary Policy Making', *Governance*, 13(1): 5–24.

Ekblom, P. (2005) 'Designing Products Against Crime', in N. Tilley (ed.) *Handbook of Crime Prevention and Community Safety*. Cullompton: Willan Publishing, pp. 203–44.

Ericson, R. (2007) *Crime in an Insecure World*. Cambridge: Polity.

Esping-Andersen, G. (1990) *The Three Worlds of Welfare Capitalism*. Cambridge: Polity Press.

European Commission (2004) *Crime Prevention in the European Union: Communication from the Commission to the Council and the European Parliament*. Brussels: Commission of the European Communities.

Farrell, G., Tilley, N., Tseloni, A. and Mailley, J. (2008) 'The Crime Drop and the Security Hypothesis', *British Society of Criminology Newsletter*, 62:, 17–21.

Farrington, D. (2000) 'Explaining and Preventing Crime: The Globalisation of Knowledge', *Criminology*, 38(1): 1–24.

Farrington, D. P. (2007) 'Childhood Risk Factors and Risk-Focused Prevention', in M. Maguire, R. Morgan and R. Reiner (eds) *The Oxford Handbook of Criminology*, 4th edn. Oxford: Oxford University Press, pp. 602–40.

Farrington, D. P, and Welsh, B. C. (2007) *Saving Children from a Life of Crime: Early Risk Factors and Effective Intervention*. Oxford: Oxford University Press.

Felson, M. and Clarke, R. V. (1998) *Opportunity Makes the Thief: Practical Theory for Crime Prevention*. London: Home Office.

Garapon, A. (1995) 'French Legal Culture and the Shock of Globalisation', *Social & Legal Studies*, 4: 493–506.

Garland, D. (1996) 'The Limits of the Sovereign State: Strategies of Crime Control in Contemporary Society', *British Journal of Criminology*, 36(4): 445–71.

Garland, D. (2001) *The Culture of Control*. Oxford: Oxford University Press.

Gatti, U. (1998) 'Ethical Issues Raised When Early Intervention is Used to Prevent Crime', *European Journal on Criminal Policy and Research*, 6: 113–32.

Gras, M. L. (2004) 'The Legal Regulation of CCTV in Europe', *Surveillance & Society*, 2(2/3): 216–29.

Hadfield, P. (2006) *Bar Wars*. Oxford: Oxford University Press.

Hayek, F. A. (1979) *Law, Legislation and Liberty, Vol. III: The Political Order of a Free People*. London: Routledge and Kegan Paul.

Hempel, L. and Töpfer, E. (2004) *CCTV in Europe: Final Report*, Urban Eye Working Paper No. 15. Berlin: Centre for Technology and Society. Online at: www.urbaneye.net/results/ue_wp15.pdf

Home Office (1997) *Getting to Grips with Crime: A New Framework for Local Action*. London: Home Office.

Home Office (2004) *Building Communities, Beating Crime*. London: Home Office.

Home Office (2006) *Review of Partnership Provisions of the Crime and Disorder Act 1998, Report of Findings*. London: Home Office.

Home Office (2007) *Cutting Crime: A New Partnership, 2008–11*. London: Home Office.

Hope, T. (2000) 'Inequality and the Clubbing of Private Security', in T. Hope and R. Sparks (eds) *Crime, Risk and Insecurity*. London: Routledge, pp. 83–106.

International Centre for the Prevention of Crime (2008) *International Report on Crime Prevention and Community Safety: Trends and Perspectives*. Montreal: ICPC.

Jones, T. and Newburn, T. (2002) 'Policy Convergence and Crime Control in the USA and UK: Streams of Influence and Levels of Impact', *Criminal Justice*, 2: 173–203.

Jones, T. and Newburn, T. (2007a) *Policy Transfer and Criminal Justice*. Open University Press.

Jones, T. and Newburn, T. (2007b) 'Symbolizing Crime Control: Reflections on Zero Tolerance', *Theoretical Criminology*, 11(2): 221–43.

King, M. (1991) 'The Political Construction of Crime Prevention', in K. Stenson and D. Cowell (eds) *The Politics of Crime Control*. London: Sage, pp. 87–108.

Kingdon, J. (1984) *Agendas, Alternatives and Public Policies*. Boston: Little, Brown.

Lacey, N. (2008) *The Prisoner's Dilemma*. Cambridge: Cambridge University Press.

Le Grand, J. (2003) *Motivation, Agency and Public Policy*. Oxford: Oxford University Press.

Levi-Faur, D. (2005) 'The Global Diffusion of Regulatory Capitalism', *Annals of the American Academy of Political and Social Science*, 598: 12–32.

Marquand, D. (1999) 'Premature Obsequies: Social Democracy Comes in from the Cold', *Political Quarterly*, 70(1): 10–18.

Moss, K. (2006) 'Crime Prevention as Law', in K. Moss and M. Stephens (eds) *Crime Reduction and the Law*. London: Routledge, pp. 1–13.

Moss, K. and Pease, K. (1999) 'Crime and Disorder Act 1998: Section 17 A Wolf in Sheep's Clothing?', *Crime Prevention and Community Safety*, 1(4): 15–19.

Murray, C. (1990) *The Emerging British Underclass*. London: Institute for Economic Affairs.

Newman, O. (1972) *Defensible Space: People and Design in the Violent City*. London: Architectural Press.

Norris, C. and McCahill, M. (2006) 'CCTV: Beyond Penal Modernism', *British Journal of Criminology*, 46(1): 97–118.

Norris, C., McCahill, M. and Wood, D. (2004) 'The Growth of CCTV: A Global Perspective on the International Diffusion of Video Surveillance in Publicly Accessible Space', *Surveillance & Society*, 2(2/3): 110–35.

O'Malley, P. (1992) 'Risk, Power and Crime Prevention', *Economy and Society*, 21(3): 252–75.

O'Malley, P. (2001) 'Policing Crime Risks in the Neo-Liberal Era', in K. Stenson and R. Sullivan (eds) *Crime, Risk and Justice: The Politics of Crime Control in Liberal Democracies*. Cullompton: Willan Publishing, pp. 89–103.

O'Malley, P. and Hutchinson, S. (2007) 'Reinventing Prevention: Why Did "Crime Prevention" Develop So Late?' *British Journal of Criminology*, 47(3): 373–89.

Pollitt, C. (2001) 'Convergence: The Useful Myth?', *Public Administration*, 79(4): 933–47.

Putnam, R. (2000) *Bowling Alone*. New York: Touchstone.

Rose, N. (1999) *Powers of Freedom*. Cambridge: Cambridge University Press.

Sampson, R. J., Morenoff, J. and Earls, F. (1999) 'Beyond Social Capital: Spatial Dynamics of Collective Efficacy for Children', *American Sociological Review*, 64(5): 633–60.

Samuel, H. (2008) 'Paris to Quadruple Number of CCTV Cameras', *Daily Telegraph*, 16 October.

Simon, J. (2007) *Governing Through Crime*. Oxford: Oxford University Press.

Sunstein, C. (2005) *Laws of Fear: Beyond the Precautionary Principle*. Cambridge: Cambridge University Press.

Taleb, N. N. (2007) *The Black Swan: The Impact of the Highly Improbable*. London: Penguin.

Tavares, C. and Thomas, G. (2008) *Crime and Criminal Justice*. Luxembourg: Eurostat.

United Nations (2002) *Commission on Crime Prevention and Criminal Justice, Report on the Eleventh Session (16–25 April 2002)*, Economic and Social Council, Official Records, Supplement No. 10.

Utting, D. (2004) 'Overview and Conclusion', in C. Sutton, D. Utting and D. Farrington (eds) *Support from the Start: Working with Young Children and their Families to Reduce the Risks of Crime and Anti-Social Behaviour*. London: DfES.

Van Dijk, J. and De Waard, J. (1991) 'A Two-dimensional Typology of Crime Prevention Projects: With a Bibliography', *Criminal Justice Abstracts*, 23(3): 483–503.

Van Dijk, J., Manchin, R., Van Kesteren, J., Nevala, S. and Hideg, G. (2006) *The Burden of Crime in the EU, Research Report: A Comparative Analysis of the European Crime and Safety Survey (EU ICS) 2005*. Turin: UNICRI.

Van Mannen, J. (1995) 'Style as Theory', *Organisational Science*, 6: 132–44.

Walmsley, R. (2007) *World Prison Population List*, 7th edn. London: International Centre for Prison Studies, King's College London.

Wilson, J. Q. and Kelling, G. (1982) 'Broken Windows: The Police and Neighbour-hood Safety', *Atlantic Monthly*, March: 29–37.

Zedner, L. (1995) 'In Pursuit of the Vernacular: Comparing Law and Order Discourse in Britain and Germany', *Social & Legal Studies*, 4: 517–34.

Zedner, L. (2007) 'Pre-Crime and Post-Criminology', *Theoretical Criminology*, 11(2): 261–81.

Zedner, L. (2008) 'Fixing the Future? The Pre-emptive Turn in Criminal Justice', in B. McSherry, A. Norrie and S. Bronitt (eds) *Regulating Deviance: The Redirection of Criminalisation and the Futures of Criminal Law*. Oxford: Hart Publishing, pp. 35–58.

Chapter 2

The political evolution of situational crime prevention in England and Wales

Tim Hope

How do we account for a country's crime prevention practice to an international audience; and why should particular institutional forms and agency practices appear to be more successful or popular at certain times and places, both within and between jurisdictions, than at others? The intention of this book is to take these questions forward; the purpose of this chapter is to provide an account of a particularly English experience – the growth of *situational crime prevention* as a governmental crime prevention programme – in a way that provides some points of contact with other country's experience (Hope and Sparks 2000).

The United Kingdom, particularly the jurisdiction of England and Wales, has seen two major transformations in the governance of crime control since the 1970s (see Chapter 4 in relation to the Scottish experience). The first has been the emergence of 'new' techniques of crime prevention (Hope and Karstedt 2003) and the second has been an apparent transformation in the mode of governance of crime. With regard to the latter, it has become something of a *doxa* among commentators to see the signs of such transformation as archetypical of a globally pervasive *neo-liberalism*. In turn, this neo-liberalism in criminology is defined idealistically; its institutional and practical manifestations are seen as symptomatic of a pervasive culture of crime control (Garland 2001), or an ideological stratagem of government (Simon 2007), that somehow speak to the deep-rooted anxieties of late-modernity (Young 2007). In this general view, both institutional form and agency practice appear largely as *echt* exemplars of this culture, with more than a hint of historicism about their provenance (Hope and Sparks 2000). Crime prevention practices, such as 'situational crime prevention' (SCP) are distinguished as a 'new criminology of everyday life', brought into being as a collective sentiment by the preoccupations, fears and anxieties of high-crime society, coterminous with a 'new criminology of the other', again reflecting social anxiety. Both are held to be functionally equivalent phenomena of the same 'punitive turn' (Garland 2001). Finally, the economic transformations of neo-liberalism are also seen as primarily cultural in their consequences (Lash and Urry 1994), producing new needs for social discipline that drive emergent governance strategies of crime control (Rose 1999).

Yet compelling as these kinds of explanations are (apparently), purely cultural interpretations of the crime control patterns of late-modernity tend, in the main, towards attenuated explanation of specific institutional forms and manifestations (cf. Bauman 2000). As Rose remarks: 'There appears to be no overarching "post-disciplinary" logic, but rather a multiplication of possibilities and strategies deployed around different problematisations [*sic*] in different sites and with different objectives' (1999: 240).

While this does not seem to cause too many problems for his account of a new governmentality (signalling the end of grand narratives generally), something nevertheless seems to be missing as an explanation of crime prevention in its *specific institutional manifestations and agency practices*, especially the rise of SCP in late twentieth-century Britain. What has not been much discussed is:

> The apparent *disparity* in the degree to which SCP has penetrated the language and practice of crime prevention in distinct national settings ... What then explains the apparent enthusiasm – or at least preparedness – of actors in some settings to follow the situational route as compared say, with the hesitancy, lack of interest, scepticism or outright hostility of others? If SCP is the characteristic crime control apparatus of late modernity, why has it taken root more deeply in certain (political, institutional) contexts and not others? Why also does it seem to sit alongside other crime control approaches, in more or less coherent mixes of governmental styles and interventions? (Hope and Sparks 2000: 178, original emphasis)

Neither has the dominance of SCP been just a peculiarity of the English – or, rather, the Anglo-Saxons (*sic*) as we are known on the Continent – since that would merely revert to another, even less palatable, cultural explanation. Rather, part of the reason lies in the way in which the nature of governance in Britain over the period – its specific *conjuncture* of constitution, politics, social structure, culture and economy – has placed crime control generally, and SCP specifically, within a contest between the *Keynesian* and the *regulatory* modes of state governance (Braithwaite 2000a). Not only has SCP been the progeny of this contest, it has also been itself subject to its contending impulses; rather than a unitary practice, SCP has experienced the contentions and contradictions of the two modes *within itself*. Nor has this been simply an ideological struggle, since neither have Keynesian modes been vanquished, nor regulatory modes vindicated from within the crime control ideology of each contending party in British politics – represented on the one hand by the Conservatives, who held office during the first period of SCP's ascendancy (1979–97) and on the other by 'New' Labour, which has governed national politics since 1997. Instead, the forms and practices of SCP exemplify a contradiction and confusion in many respects similar to that which Rose (1999) sees more generally.

Even so, a *prima facie* case can be put forward that government action may have been responsible, at least in part, for a dramatic drop in volume property crime. Since 1995, the British Crime Survey has reported a 59 per cent reduction in domestic burglary and a two-thirds reduction in vehicle-related theft in England and Wales (Kershaw *et al.* 2008). Since these are the kinds of crime most amenable to situational (or opportunity-reducing) crime prevention measures, while not necessarily seeing these measures as the sole cause of the reduction, it seems plausible that governmental action of this kind may have had *some* effect on these volume crime rates. But this begs an important question: if we are to make such a case, we need to ask not only *what* it is that government thinks it has done but also *how* it thinks it might have done it. Regrettably, over the past years, British government ministers have been more vociferous in their claims than in the justification of them (Hope 2008a, 2008b). Be that as it may, a case will be made that while SCP as the preferred mode of government action over the period has had some success in reducing volume property crime, it has been much more successful when practised in its regulatory than in its Keynesian form.

The Keynesian and the regulatory modes of government in England and Wales

In his essay 'The New Regulatory State and the Transformation of Criminology', John Braithwaite (2000a) describes the mentality of the 'Keynesian' state as consisting of:

> a general belief that the state could do the job, including the job of policing . . . under the ideology of the Keynesian state, the response to every outbreak of disorder was to increase central state policing resources. Social workers, probation officers and other welfare

workers employed by the state also acquired ever more resources and powers under the same Keynesian disposition. (Braithwaite 2000a: 224)

Yet in general economic and social policy, UK Conservative governments led by Margaret Thatcher set about 'rolling back the state' during the 1980s through a large-scale privatisation of national economic enterprises, welfare institutions and public utilities. Braithwaite (2000a) seizes on these political developments as heralding the emergence of a 'new regulatory state':

The new regulatory state is qualitatively different ... in its reliance on self-regulatory organisations, enforced self-regulation and other responsive regulatory techniques that substitute for direct command and control. Responsive regulation also flows into strategies for regulating already private institutions through compliance systems, codes of practice and other self-regulatory strategies. (Braithwaite 2000a: 224)

The challenge, as his title presupposes, is to apply this model to crime and justice.

Nevertheless, Braithwaite is perhaps too ambitious in his enthusiasm, at least when applied specifically to the policies of crime control *actually practised* during this era and subsequently. In the first place, while 'Thatcherism' pursued deregulation, it was chiefly for the purpose of economic liberalisation and the reduction of public expenditure; in matters of social discipline, the ideology and governmental practice was distinctly authoritarian, if not necessarily always state-centric (Gamble 1988). Second, as he acknowledges elsewhere (Braithwaite 2000b), an adequately responsive regulatory state presupposes not a liberal, minimalist state but one based upon 'republican' principles, notably an assumption that civil society and local commonwealth are constitutive entities in their own right, *a priori* of the institutions of 'the sovereign State' (*pace* Garland 2001). Yet this republican assumption never has applied with much force to the constitution of the British state, nor features greatly in recent British constitutional theory (Loader and Walker 2007). While regulatory governance might operate in the UK in the manner envisaged by Braithwaite with regard to the 'private sector' – essentially to ensure the 'self-policing' of private institutions in the common interest (Braithwaite and Drahos 2000) – the way in which the regulatory state has developed in Britain with regard to the 'public sector', particularly local government and the police service, has been quite different, more akin to Rose's conception of 'governing-at-a-distance' (Rose 1999). But, *pace* Rose, this has come about arguably less because of a new 'governmentality' than as a consequence of a much more established constitutionality.

There are three constitutional principles of local government in England and Wales that not only define the state but also provide an important contextualisation for the current construction of crime prevention in Britain (Hope 2002). The first is the relative *lack of autonomy* of local government *vis-à-vis* the (central) state. The constitutional convention in Britain, upheld by the courts, is that local government can only take actions that are permitted or justifiable by legal statute or statutory instrument by virtue of Acts of Parliament. If local authorities do something that is not permitted or justifiable by reference to a specific statute they may be held to be acting *ultra vires*.[1] Thus, the framework of statutory law is the essential, permissive precondition for local government – constituted as a system of administration – and specific laws (e.g. Section 17 of the Crime and Disorder Act 1998, referred to later) need to be enacted to enable, as much as to compel, local government to perform particular functions. Arguably a consequence of this principle is that local government is effectively the administrator of public policy. From the central government perspective, local government in Britain exists to administer national policy locally. While elected officials have leeway to interpret national policy or allocate local revenue in ways appropriate to their constituencies, they can neither raise additional revenue nor dispose of central revenues outside the framework that is determined centrally. While they may innovate with practice, over much of their recent history, local authorities rarely have had the confidence or legitimacy to innovate with policy.

The second, relevant principle is that of the *fiduciary duty* of local authorities – that is, that they must be able to demonstrate that they have discharged their financial responsibilities in the public interest. This principle is the primary constitutional justification for local government accountability in the UK and provides the justification also for the external, public auditing of local government operations, carried out by statutory audit bodies (such as the Audit Commission). The third, relevant constitutional principle (following the other two) is that of *central government control* over local government revenue and expenditure. Much of the political history of central–local government relations over the past three decades has been a struggle for the control of public expenditure – much of it in the form of public services administered by local authorities (for example in delivering education, housing, personal social services, recreational and environmental services, and also of criminal justice). Nowadays, less than a quarter of local government income required to finance these services is raised through local taxation and charges (Chandler 2001). Not only does central government control the amount of tax revenue that is allocated each year to local government for service provision, but also successive Conservative governments of the period 1979–97 passed legislation (preserved by their successors) enabling central government to 'cap' local government expenditure by imposing limits on the amount that individual local authorities could raise through local taxation.[2]

A corollary of the fiduciary duty and the paucity of local revenue is that central governments have needed to institute regimes of expenditure control on local government if public sector spending and borrowing is not to unbalance central economic management. And, in the wake of such financial controls, government has been able to institute *performance accountability regimes*, not only to make public services accountable to their 'customers' but also to make them more efficient in the delivery of their services. Where governments have differed is not so much in having such regimes but in their purposes: for past Conservative governments, such regimes would provide a transparent basis for consumer choice and 'quasi-market' competition; for Labour, their purpose has been more that of providing the electorate with feedback (validated by general elections) that the 'challenges' and 'targets' the government has set for local government performance on the public's behalf have been achieved. The significance of these constitutional issues is that they demonstrate the basis for the powers of control and influence that central government (the sovereign state) is able to wield over the local administration of public services in Britain, including policing services and local government community safety practice.[3] In other words, even though the state within the UK may now increasingly govern at a distance, it retains most of the levers for ensuring compliance within the public sector through top-down policy, and to that extent, remains sovereign over public matters of crime control.

In contrast, no such central control operates over the private enterprise and civil society sectors of British society. The widespread denationalisation of formerly publicly owned services and utilities initiated by the Thatcher governments occasioned a need to replace the direct governance of public expenditure with a new mode of regulation than that which had been practised hitherto within the public sector. Since the substitution of direct, central government intervention by at-a-distance regulation was part of a more general reaction (literally) to Keynesian economic management, it is hardly surprisingly that there has been some convergence in the mode of governance applied generally to all sectors – public, private and voluntary. In this respect, Braithwaite's (2000a) 'new, regulatory state', incorporates much of Osborne and Gaebler's (1992) 'new public management' which itself incorporates orthodoxies of private sector management. Similarly, as the Conservatives' privatising impulses extended to local welfare policy, to be delivered more by the 'voluntary' or charitable sector and less by local government, so these civil society agencies too have come under similar financial and contractual regimes.

The strategy of central government has been to use regulatory instruments to engineer *voluntary compliance* with public policy objectives within the distribution of constituted power.[4] So, although a new governmentality may underlie the emergence of the idea of a regulatory state, an unchanged constitutionality concerning state–local government relations has preserved many of the institutions and government practices of the Keynesian welfare state within the public sector in Britain. The ideological impulse of the Thatcher governments was to look for ways of circumventing local government in order to reach citizens directly, using performance regimes (such as the publication of state schools' examination results) as a way of providing market information to enable citizens to exercise consumer choice (such as deciding which school their children should attend). In contrast, New Labour governments post 1997 have been much more inclined to work with the grain of local government institutions. Yet the expenditure of public revenue still provides the decisive tool of governance for the sovereign state. To a much greater degree than their predecessors, New Labour governments have sought to use performance criteria as a means of engineering the *implementation of centrally determined public policy* measures – a process it has called 'delivery' – via a regime of target setting and auditing. And central government has further imposed such targets upon itself as declared 'contracts' with the electorate in the form of public service agreements.

These differences have lead to a *bifurcation* in regulatory practice as it has affected the implementation of crime prevention policy. On the one hand, the privatising and liberalising tendencies of past Conservative governments have created capacities and opportunities for regulatory governance applicable to the private sector and civil society at large. In contrast, local government, including the police, were effectively bypassed as the principal agencies of crime prevention, which was seen to lie in the hands of private and civil bodies. As noted below, in terms of crime prevention, these have been relatively successful, though their collateral effects may have been less so overall. On the other hand, New Labour governments have placed local government and the police in a more central role as agents of crime prevention. Within existing constitutional arrangements, they have instituted new administrative machinery – notably crime and disorder reduction partnerships (CDRPs) between local government and the police (set up by the Crime and Disorder Act 1998) – and used performance regimes to ensure compliance to national objectives.[5] In effect, these latter reforms have revived Keynesian modes of the governance of crime; though they have also replicated some of the endemic failures associated with them.

Police failure and the emergence of 'partnership'

During the 1970s, the central government of the British state was faced with a crescendo of *systemic* difficulties in the administration of criminal justice (Windlesham 1987). The bottom-line cost to the state – growth in the size of the prison population – seemed inexorable, relatively unrelated to short-term changes in crime rates, and easier to increase by legislation and sentencing practice than to reduce by policing, crime prevention or alternatives to custody. Moreover, the rate of crime recorded by the police, already growing, was showing signs of increasing dramatically (which it did during the 1980s). Not least of these systemic failures had been that of the police service – evidently failing to meet public expectations in reducing the crime rate, detecting offenders or reassuring the public. Echoing public disquiet about rising crime, research had failed to find much in the way of conclusive evidence of police operational effectiveness (Bowling and Foster 2002). Further, the period saw increasing conflict over the governance of policing, particularly a set of political struggles involving local authorities, mainly representing inner-city and large metropolitan areas and controlled by a 'municipal left' within the Labour Party. Following defeat of this move for a local government of policing (largely achieved by the Thatcher government's abolition of the big city metropolitan county councils, where the movement had been most vociferous), central government turned to the idea of *partnership* as the preferred mode for delivering safety from crime (Crawford 1997; McLaughlin 2002).

The partnership idea germinated during an expert-led Home Office Working Party on Crime Prevention (Gladstone 1980), initiated under the last Labour administration of the 1970s (Crawford 1998). This early formulation, reflecting that government's 'corporatist' outlook, was to be applied primarily to local government: a better management of crime could be obtained by co-ordinating the efforts of public bodies – particularly using operational means to circumvent the constitutional division between the police and local government – and improving their consultative links with the community (Crawford 1997). This went hand in hand with an emphasis on technical expertise to inform practice (rather than political ideology or police professionalism), with the newly emerging 'situational crime prevention' promising to provide a more behaviourally sophisticated 'third way' between the crude polarity of 'physical' and 'social' crime prevention (Crawford 1998). The concept of partnership as it emerged was primarily one of ensuring governmental efficiency: it was believed that co-ordination of agencies' efforts would bring the expertise of relevant parties to the table, to focus on crime 'in the round', identifying competences and gaps in provision. The sub-text was that not only would this produce better local outcomes but also start to wrest the ownership of dealing with the crime problem away from the monopoly of the public police.[6]

By the time the Working Party had completed its deliberations, the Conservatives under Margaret Thatcher had gained power. For them, the partnership ideal was a useful and expedient way of solving the politico-administrative dilemma of crime control (Windlesham 1987). The

Conservatives' concept of partnership rested upon a notion of *voluntary association* of individual bodies, each with its own interests – in this case, protecting their own private security. It followed that no single body could have anything approaching a monopoly over the aggregate of security, least of all state agencies. And since the public good of security was thought to be produced as the sum of individual private security, then if sufficient numbers of individual agents could be brought together in mutual associations, inefficiencies and gaps in production of security could be removed. Thus, the essence of the Conservatives' approach to the partnership idea was less that of a technical, managerial blueprint for a corporatist state, as the Home Office Working Party had thought (Crawford 1998), than that of creating an infrastructure for a new, regulatory governance of crime control. Emphasis was to be placed on developing voluntary, co-operative agreements among partners based upon a common appraisal of need (Home Office 1984, 1990).

The issue of constitutionality also shaped the New Labour government's approach to crime prevention. Some while earlier, the Morgan Committee (Home Office 1991) had argued that local authorities should have 'clear statutory responsibility' for delivering the multi-agency approach (para. 6.9); something the Conservatives had refused to countenance, given their antipathy to local authorities as political institutions. Notwithstanding Labour's sentimental attachment to municipalism (which had inspired hopes that principal statutory responsibility for crime prevention might be vested in municipalities), the Crime and Disorder Act (CDA) 1998 imposed a *joint* duty falling equally upon local authorities and the police. Other than providing statutory obligation to the main partners to act as such, all other institutional arrangements and operating practices, especially for the police service, remained as they were under the Conservatives (Home Office 1998). In practice, that meant preserving the operational independence of the chief officers of police.[7]

Nevertheless, the constitutional compromise of the CDA offered a novel means for central government to shed irksome responsibilities of direct state management of crime control while also acceding to the professionally autonomous police service. Through the allocation of police resources and a legislative (steering) role in criminal justice policy-making, central government retained the possibility of taking credit for crime reduction. The CDA appeased the police by keeping their operational independence intact and headed off another bruising confrontation between Labour and the chief constables. At the same time, its statutory performance regime tied the police service into a rudimentary accounting to their local communities (Hope 2006). While it gave local government a share of the responsibility for crime control, it also widened accountability, not least creating a convenient focus (or scapegoat), if needed, for public concern. From the police perspective, the CDA offered a 'win-win' solution to their difficulties in local crime control: it would bring local authorities, and their resources, on to the police side in the 'battle against crime'; it would improve not only police effectiveness but also their image within the community; it appeared to be an easy concession to community accountability while avoiding direct accountability; and, of course, it offered some other body to take, or share, the blame, while reserving to itself the credit for crime reduction.

Partnership with private citizens

A guiding vision of the Conservatives during the 1980s had been the creation of a 'property-owning democracy'. As Margaret Thatcher said in an interview with *Time* magazine (22 June 1987), 'Far more people own their own homes now. We are nearly up to the United States – not yet quite – but now one in five of our people owns company shares. Far many more people have savings accounts. That's all extending opportunity ever more widely.'

Among the measures for doing this were the freeing up of mortgage finance and the transfer of ownership of social housing to existing tenants via preferential purchase schemes (Forrest and Murie 1988). As a consequence, between 1981 and 2007 the proportion of dwellings in owner-occupation increased by a fifth, with around three-quarters of all dwellings moving into owner-occupation.[8] Coinciding with the growth of portable, relatively high-value consumer goods, the growth of private property ownership constituted a powerful driver both of opportunities for crime and citizen demand for security, with household property crime rates growing commensurately (see Figure 2.1).

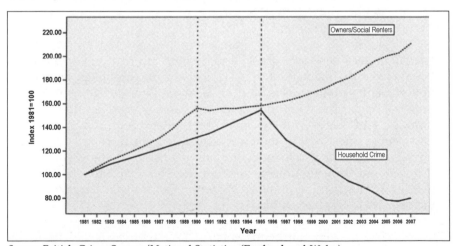

Source: British Crime Survey/National Statistics (England and Wales)

Figure 2.1   Household crime and the polarisation of tenure, 1981–2007

The 'moral vision' of situational crime prevention was in tune with the Thatcher revolution (Kleinig 2000); based upon self-interest, the ethos of situational crime prevention chimed well with the kind of property-owning, liberal democracy, inscribing the values of freedom, personal liberty and individual responsibility, to which Thatcher aspired (Duff and Marshall 2000). Hitherto, government efforts to promote crime prevention to private citizens had been in the form of 'public information' publicity backed up with free security advice, on request, from local police crime prevention officers. Reminiscent of the 'Home Front' during World War Two, this *public service* approach – whereby the state acts to exhort citizens to participate in publicly beneficial activities (such as 'digging for victory', picking up litter, crossing the road safely, sneezing into a handkerchief) – came under increasing stress in the face of private property owners' escalating demands for *private security*, that is, the protection of their persons and property, which the public police service appeared unable to meet. A Home Office survey in an affluent suburban area found that 93 per cent of dwellings had levels of home security that fell below the standard being recommended by the then police Crime Prevention Officer (CPO) service, while less than a half of 1 per cent of all households in the area were likely to receive a CPO survey each year (Winchester and Jackson 1982). Clearly, the public provision of private security, via the CPOs, was not only inimical to Conservative ideology but apparently failed to address the needs of their constituents. What was needed was to *privatise private security* by empowering the consumer.

In order to wean ordinary citizens away from their sentimental attachment to the Keynesian state and persuade them to take greater responsibility for their own security, it was necessary to convert their sense of public duty into the virtues of self-help; hence Margaret Thatcher's famous aphorism:

> I think we've been through a period where too many people have been given to understand that if they have a problem, it's the government's job to cope with it . . . And, you know, *there is no such thing as society*. There are individual men and women, and there are families. And no government can do anything except through people, and people must look to themselves first. It's our duty to look after ourselves and then also to look after our neighbour . . . there's no such thing as entitlement, unless someone has first met an obligation. (Margaret Thatcher, in an interview with *Woman's Own* magazine, 31 October 1987, emphasis added)

The concept of 'neighbourhood watch' (NW) was extremely useful in effecting this transition since it encouraged individual self-help while simultaneously reinforcing the virtues of both neighbourly reciprocity *and* support of the police. During the mid 1980s, the government launched a campaign to establish NW, with local police services acting as its agents:

An advertising campaign was run at that time that suggested that the public needed to support the police in the 'fight against crime', and a series of television and newspaper campaigns were run with supporting material for distribution through police forces and other crime prevention groups, which encouraged the public to act as the 'eyes and ears of the police'. (Laycock and Tilley 1995: 550)

If NW encouraged residents to report issues to the police, implicitly the police would reciprocate by offering their protection to these 'active citizens'. Membership of NW grew, peaking in England and Wales around 1992 (Hope and Trickett 2004), coinciding with the peaking of the property crime rate (Figure 2.1). An analysis of British Crime Survey data from that period suggested that NW required both fertile social conditions (in the form of social capital based upon a sense of community reciprocity) *and* a strong and ever-present threat of crime in the minds of residents (Hope and Trickett 2004). In this respect, worry about the growth of crime galvanised the property-owning middle classes into 'doing something' (albeit in a relatively mild way) about their own risk of crime in their residential locality.

The general effect of the campaign to market NW was to reinforce a 'taste' for private security among the propertied middle classes (Hope and Trickett 2004). Analysis of data from the 1994 British Crime Survey found a distinct cluster of crime prevention activities associated with NW membership, including security marking of household property, asking neighbours to watch the home when away, and having household contents insurance (Hope and Lab 2001). These activities reinforced the private (target-hardening) security of owner-occupiers with additional *reassurance*, forming a set of 'club-goods' that could be associated with NW membership, and that added benefit to individual private security, chiefly by retaining the externality costs of individual private security activities within the 'residential club' (Hope 2000). In return, by supporting NW via networks of local voluntary co-ordinators, the police were able to establish a conduit for inculcating a security consciousness among the mass of private property owners.

Yet consistent with Conservative ideology it was not to be the role of the police, as a public body, to supply more security to private citizens. While there was a growth in private policing and security suppliers during this period, it was also necessary to increase the *demand* for private security among private citizens, and to diversify the range of security 'products', so that they would not look to the public police and their traditional services for protection; in other words, to divert the public away from its habitual demand for 'more bobbies on the beat'.

Conveniently, the growth of private security consciousness among property-owners fostered by Neighbourhood Watch gave a welcome opportunity to the British insurance industry, which began to offer discounted premiums to NW members (Laycock and Tilley 1995). It is hard now to discern the extent to which this move reflected direct government encouragement rather than a response by the insurance industry to burgeoning market opportunities. In any event, the profitability of the domestic contents insurance market, which had been relatively small before the 1970s, depended less on the accurate targeting of risk than on market growth and penetration (Litton 1997). In this respect, NW membership flagged up a profitable market for home insurance products. Because the NW 'message' to its subscribers coupled their anxieties about their property to a generalised 'fear of crime', they became an ideal market for insurers; that is, highly risk-averse consumers able and willing to pay high insurance premiums against a low actuarial risk. Moreover, the willingness of the public police to accept insurance and security industry sponsorship gave the sponsors direct access to their target markets, thereby greatly reducing their marketing costs.

According to the British Crime Survey, by 1994 some 83 per cent of households were regularly insuring their household contents against theft (Hope 2000). In the wake of the insurers has followed widespread consumption of private security products, consequential upon the insurers' interests in loss adjustment (Hope 2006). Thus, the market for private security grew extensively, with an almost fivefold increase in the turnover of British security equipment manufacturers between 1983 and 2003.[9] According to the BCS, by 1994 around 70 per cent of households had some form of security device in their dwellings, and about a fifth had an intruder alarm installed (Hope and Lab 2001). In sum, the much-vaunted strategy of 'responsibilisation' was achieved not so much by state direction as by its opposite: indirect action to stimulate a 'taste' for private security, that would then be satisfied by private enterprise. Whether or not this has been the only thing that led to the decline in household property crime after 1995 is highly arguable; but the coincidence of the trends in Figure 2.1 suggests that, whatever the overall set of reasons, the growth of domestic private security has played a part in the 'market correction' necessary to adjust better-off private property-owners to their crime risks, without the need for direct state intervention and at some profit to the private sector. As such, the role of the regulatory state in crime prevention has been to 'make the market' for private security.

Partnership with private industry

If the consumption of domestic security by private citizens has contributed to the reduction of volume property crime in England and Wales, it has not done so without some change to the supply of property itself, particularly the supply of new motor vehicles and domestic dwellings, the major classes of citizens' private property. Significant changes in vehicle security, resulting in commensurate reductions in vehicle crime, have come about as a result of two pieces of regulatory action (Webb 2005). The first was the publication by the Home Office in 1992 of a detailed Car Theft Index – a league table of the risk of theft by make and model. Hitherto, manufacturers had been reticent about incorporating security into their models, but:

> The Car Theft Index changed all that, and made security a marketing issue. By exposing those makes and models of car most at risk, customers were empowered to make informed decisions about their choice of vehicle. Coupled with the great deal of publicity generated ... the manufacturers began to design more sophisticated devices such as deadlocks and engine immobilizers into the more numerous economy vehicles. (Webb 2005: 468)

Second, this change in manufacture was reinforced by European Union legislation requiring all new cars to be fitted with electronic immobilisers from 1998 onwards. By 1999, the Labour government had established a Vehicle Crime Reduction Action Team comprising not only experts and civil servants but also representatives of the motor industry. It encouraged changes and procedures across the board, including the continuation of the Car Theft Index, under the guise of the New Car Security Rating Scheme, operated by the Motor Insurance Repair Research Centre, which is owned by the British insurance industry. Subsequent improvements to vehicle security 'are likely to be one of the main reasons for the reduction in thefts of vehicles' (National Audit Office 2005).

Nevertheless, it is important to note that mechanisms like the Car Theft Index do not operate as a direct public service to the public (as they would in a purely Keynesian mode), particularly as it seems doubtful that most consumers would consult it before choosing a new car. Rather, the goal of crime reduction among the consumers of motor vehicles has been delivered by providing a public subsidy to facilitate a private transaction with an influential third party – that is, between the consumers' interest in risk assurance, and the insurance industry's interest in loss reduction (Hope 2006). The compliance of motor manufacturers has been achieved not by direct state intervention but by affecting the nature of the consumer–insurer transaction, shaped by consumers' interest in avoiding the otherwise higher theft premium costs that the insurers could now feel justified in passing on to them by virtue of the authority of the Car Theft Index (which they now own and operate). Still, what remains unknown is whether this has resulted in net profit or loss to the motor manufacturers. We should suspect the former if the greater demand for security has added a premium to the price charged to the consumer. Arguably, this may be another success for the responsibilisation strategy, contributing in its own small way to British industrial production.[10]

A second way in which regulatory policy may have had an impact on domestic property crime is through intervention into the built environment planning and development process. A concern with 'crime prevention through environmental design' emerged during the 1970s (Poyner and Webb 1991; Crawford 1998), leading eventually to the government circulating advice about 'planning out crime' to be considered by parties to the local statutory planning process (DoE 1994). DoE Circular 5/94 was not a statutory requirement; rather, its significance lay in indirectly creating an opportunity for 'crime prevention' to be inserted into the planning system in the following ways:

- Giving 'Police Architectural Liaison Officers' (ALOs) a formal status in the planning system as expert advisors on crime risk.

- Articulating 'crime prevention' as a purpose of urban planning, and arguing for a partnership approach to complementary activities.

- Widening the concept of crime prevention, from physical security devices to environmental design. (Schneider and Kitchen 2002: 202)

The government has continued this approach by publishing guidance and advice for local planning committees, which are administered by local government autonomously from central government (ODPM 2004). On the police side, the Association of Chief Police Officers (ACPO) established the 'Secured by Design' scheme: 'a police initiative to encourage the building industry to adopt crime prevention measures in the design of developments to assist in reducing the opportunity for crime and the fear of crime, creating a safer and more secure environment'.[11] While Secured by Design is offered as a standard 'kite-mark' to the building industry, its significance is that it legitimises the advice given by police ALOs within the planning process (Schneider and Kitchen 2002). Yet even though government advice offers a broad planning perspective, and the Secured by Design standards cover a range of design principles, in its early stages at least research found that the majority of police ALOs emphasised target-hardening and one particular form of estate layout (based around culs-de-sac linked by main feeder roads) (2002: 197). A general issue identified by Schneider and Kitchen is that the Secured by Design process, in practice, has reflected an interplay between police expertise in target-hardening and the commercial considerations of the big house-building developers of the British construction industry that has resulted in a bias towards a particular kind of suburban, low-density, private estate (2002: 230). Still, in as much as these new developments have reinforced further the 'clubbing' of private security in 'exclusive' developments, while also making them affordable to middle-income households (Hope 2000), they may well have contributed not only to the reduction of burglary but also to a growth of inequality in risk between the better and the very worse off members of society (Hope 2001).

Keynesian crime reduction

Having moved swiftly to enact the CDA, the Labour government then needed to 'task' the statutory CDRPs with things to do that would 'deliver' its promise of crime reduction, setting out its stall in the *Crime Reduction Strategy* (Home Office 1999). Two actions were prominent: investment in public 'closed-circuit television' (CCTV) systems; and a mode of governance that emphasised the delivery of crime prevention via specific 'projects'.

CCTV

In many ways, the development of open-street, publicly funded CCTV surveillance systems represents perhaps the most 'Keynesian' of all crime prevention investment in Britain, resembling as some have called it the 'fifth utility' (Graham 1999). Paradoxically, it was the Conservatives who initiated the investment: between 1994 and 1997, 78 per cent of the Home Office crime prevention budget went on CCTV, with over £250 million of public money spent on CCTV between 1992 and 2002 (which includes the 'New Labour' government), making Britain one of the most highly CCTV-surveilled societies in the world (McCahill and Norris 2002). Whether CCTV has achieved a greater level of security seems unlikely (Gill and Spriggs 2005) and perhaps even immaterial, since the idea

> dovetailed neatly with ... ideological demands for privatisation of the public sector. The private sector would be fully involved in building, equipping and maintaining the systems ... private security firms were responsible for monitoring the screens in the control rooms and, as business had contributed to the setting up of the systems, it would have a say in the shape of the systems and how they were run. (McCahill and Norris 2002: 11)

New Labour has continued this investment in public goods infrastructure via financial 'partnership' with the private sector, though it has left local authorities with the ongoing burden of financing the schemes, which must come out of their hard-pressed revenue accounts and which, if anything, has left them even more in hock (via the fiduciary duty) to central government.

Crime reduction via 'projects'

The question of what the CDRPs ought to do to prevent crime has been answered by government in the form of their undertaking time-limited, *ad hoc* 'projects'.[12] The local CDRP's job is to initiate targeted crime prevention projects and initiatives, reflecting an analysis (audit) of crime patterns and priorities in their local area (Home Office 1999; Audit Commission 1999). As a consequence of the introduction of the 'new public management' into local public administration, the performance of partnerships is to be publicly auditable, conforming to 'targets' imposed centrally as a condition of future funding. The common denominator is a belief in, and a commitment to, the principle of *rational public action*. The mode in which prevention projects are enjoined to operate conforms, in most respects, to a model of rational strategic planning by 'identifying and analysing the problem, devising solutions, assessing the likely impact of solutions, reviewing progress, refining approaches and evaluating success (sic)' (Tilley *et al.* 1999: 28). Knowledge of a particular crime problem is to be ascertained *in advance* of trying to implement action, and the selection of services and measures to be delivered is then tailored to the key features of crime manifest in the specific target area or group. The ideal model is of an influential and credible government, guided by expert knowledge, 'demonstrating' by practical example that certain programmes 'work' and thereby persuading others to adopt them.[13] Laycock (2001), for example, describes the research and implementation programmes involved in the British government's development and dissemination of a policy aiming to prevent repeat victimisation. The form of adoption is also a continuation of the project-based demonstration. Thus, once persuaded, those with the authority to act are enjoined further to establish and evaluate their own 'projects' so that they too can demonstrate benefits, both to their constituents, as the recipients of prevention, and to the public purse, that value for money has been achieved.

Unfortunately, the government's own effort at demonstration-by-project – the £250 million *Crime Reduction Programme*, which ran from 1999 to 2002 – failed rather miserably to fulfil its promise, encountering massive implementation failure across the board and meagre results (Homel *et al.* 2004; Bullock and Tilley 2003; Maguire 2004; Hope *et al.* 2004). Irrespective of who was to blame – whether government ministers, central programme managers, local projects, HM Treasury, or even the independent evaluators (Homel *et al.* 2004) – the ensuing silence from government, along with its behind-the-scenes efforts to stifle and suppress critical evaluation evidence (Hope 2008b, 2008c), is perhaps testimony enough to the collapse of the project ideal, and the Keynesian assumption of rational public action that underpins it.

Governing through insecurity

The incoming New Labour government made the control of 'anti-social behaviour' its chief aim of crime control, a residue from its muncipalism during the preceding years, combined with a sedulously fostered, election-winning populism (Burney 1999). Yet the focus on local disorder and anti-social people may have heightened public anxiety – paradoxically where such people and events are not experienced directly. Far from reducing demand upon the state, the crime prevention strategy pursued by the Conservatives and bequeathed to Labour may have stoked up citizens' demands for security and contributed to inequality in its provision, without any alleviation of the burden upon the state and its agencies: 'by making antisocial behaviour into a major social policy problem, and giving it sustained high-visibility attention, Labour has made a small problem larger, thereby making people more aware of it and less satisfied with their lives and their government' (Tonry 2004: 57).

Perhaps to avoid the buck being passed by ministers, the police service, led by ACPO, have set about responding to an apparent 'reassurance gap' – that is, the inconsistency between public anxiety about crime and the reduction in the volume crime – by directing police activity towards those crimes and disorders that (they think) give ordinary citizens most cause for concern and anxiety in their localities.[14] If these local sources of anxiety in local communities can be addressed, and the police are seen to be giving priority to local concerns, then not only will the public's sense of security increase but so will their confidence in the police as an effective service organisation.

Yet there are some policy risks in this conception. First, this extension of policing into the community may increase dissatisfaction and discontent, either if it serves to heighten and dramatise local insecurities, or if, in practice, the police prove unable to deliver on their promise of efficacious action. Second, as with many other 'community policing' initiatives, there is the widespread assumption that it is specific police action – albeit in collaboration with community partners – that is the most efficacious means of preventing disorder. Indeed, in this respect, it seems there has been little change from the ethos of NW, except that in this case efforts at responsibilisation may be even more likely to backfire into public resentment.

Third, the approach tends to downplay the role of other social factors and conditions in the creation of disorder, which may be more influenced by social policy – such as neighbourhood renewal or urban regeneration – than by criminal justice actions. And finally, action is still predicated on intelligence (although now more focused on disorder than crime), and that this intelligence should determine police operational policy. In this sense, it continues the performance-based ethos of the Crime Reduction Strategy, namely that the delivery of community safety is to come from intelligence-based policing rather than, say, from the directly expressed voice of citizens in the governance of their own community safety.

Conclusion

Despite the apparent 'success' of regulatory approaches in bringing down volume property crime, the government remains saddled with the dilemma of public provision. Notwithstanding the responsibilisation that appears to have taken place, since the financial and social capital available to citizens to consume private security of all kinds is inequitably distributed (Hope and Lab 2001), the less well-off members of society face not only higher risks (Hope 2007) but also a private security deficit that still falls, if anywhere, upon the state to redress. Despite the privatisation of 'mass private property' (Kempa *et al.* 2004), there still remains a public space that falls to public bodies to secure. Yet, the penalty of inequality in private security is that it undermines public good provision. Citizens who are required to spend more of their private resources on public goods, such as health services, education and in this case their own and their neighbourhood's security, tend to have little incentive to contribute to the general public good over and above what appears to them to meet their own needs, making them less likely to support additional contributions to the cost of public policing or the criminal justice system, particularly if they see no benefit to their own immediate security.

In a strategy of private action, those who have the capital to devote to security are more likely to want to spend it upon themselves than donate it towards ameliorating the social and economic conditions of those most at risk of crime (as victims and offenders), who are more likely to be the poorer and marginalised sectors of society (Hope 2000), even if this would be an optimum 'welfare' strategy for reducing crime from the point of view of society as a whole. Although such a strategy of risk reduction might appear socially prudent, without some agreed and ultimately enforceable conception of 'the social', that would underpin compliance and redistribution, market failure is likely to prevail, at least for the 'Keynesian' ideal of providing security as a universal public good (Hope and Karstedt 2003).

The success in reducing volume property crime has come at considerable cost, notably in undermining the public (or common) good element of crime control. As a tool of governance practised by central government, it may contain the seeds of its own destruction: while the incentives produced by market interventions have brought about a responsibilisation of self-interest, they have undermined responsibility for the public interest, since the crime rate, however much reduced on average, still falls inequitably upon the poor and propertyless, who are unable to meet their own security interests through private action. It has been the greater amenability of British politics to regulatory governance over the period (as distinct from much of Europe) combined with a constitutional predisposition to centralised state power (as distinct from North America and Australasia) that has made this a uniquely British experience. But in as much as the competition between the regulatory and the Keynesian modes of governance is becoming a common experience in many polities of the European Union, then the British experience of implementing SCP as its primary mode of crime prevention articulates a dilemma (if not a warning) for Europe as a whole.

Notes

1 An *ultra vires* act is one that is outside the specified and/or implied constitutional objects and powers of the body in question. It is 'beyond the powers' and therefore illegal.

2 The principles of *ultra vires* and fiduciary duty also constitute the powers of enforcement of central government's financial control. Local elected representatives, for instance, can be individually *surcharged* at penurious levels and barred from holding office for defying such regulations in the setting of local taxation levels.

3 Although, since devolution, the UK government has had less direct control over the Scottish government (see Chapter 4 in this volume), the latter's powers *vis-à-vis* Scottish local authorities are much the same constitutionally as are the former's for England and Wales.

4 A good example of this are the local area agreements recently established for the local strategic partnerships (comprising relevant public and other bodies in local authority areas). See www.idea.gov.uk/idk/core/page.do?pageId = 1174195.

5 Again, differences have emerged within the UK post-devolution: statutory CDRPs exist only in England and Wales (compare with Chapter 4 in this volume).

6 This is not to say that government espoused such views publicly. Indeed, the Conservative governments in particular faced a quandary – of needing to give ideological support to the police in public, while despairing in private of the police service's lack of concern for its cost-effectiveness and efficiency.

7 Essentially, the battles of the previous decade had been around precisely this issue – the operational autonomy of chief officers.

8 As the proportion of dwellings in private rental has remained constant over the period at around 10 to 11 per cent, the growth of the owner-occupier sector since the late 1970s has been in proportion to the decline in the social renting sector.

9 Information available from the British Security Industry Association, see www.bsia.co.uk/

10 So, we might infer that it is the consumer who has been required to pay for the reduction in risk, either in higher insurance premiums (accompanied by higher deductibles) or in higher retail prices.

11 See www.securedbydesign.com
12 See www.crimereduction.homeoffice.gov.uk
13 For example, 'legislative mandates and publicity exhortation can be used, but the demonstration to those with authority to act that [crime prevention] measures result in cost savings may be more effective' (Laycock and Tilley 1995: 535).
14 See www.neighbourhoodpolicing.co.uk

References

Audit Commission (1999) *Safety in Numbers*. London: Audit Commission.

Bauman, Z. (2000) *Liquid Modernity*. Cambridge: Polity.

Bowling, B. and Foster, J. (2002) 'Policing and the Police', in M. Maguire, R. Morgan and R. Reiner (eds) *The Oxford Handbook of Criminology*, 3rd edn. Oxford: Clarendon Press, pp. 980–1033.

Braithwaite, J. (2000a) 'The New Regulatory State and the Transformation of Criminology', *British Journal of Criminology*, 40: 222–38.

Braithwaite, J. (2000b) 'Republican Theory and Crime Control', in S. Karstedt and K. Bussman (eds) *Social Dynamics of Crime and Control: New Theories for a World in Transition*. Oxford: Hart Publishing, pp. 85–103.

Braithwaite, J. and Drahos, P. (2000) *Global Business Regulation*. Melbourne: Cambridge University Press.

Bullock, K. and Tilley, N. (eds) (2003) *Crime Reduction and Problem-oriented Policing*. Cullompton: Willan Publishing.

Burney, E. (1999) *Crime and Banishment: Nuisance and Exclusion in Social Housing*. Winchester: Waterside Press.

Chandler, J. A. (2001) *Local Government Today*, 3rd edn. Manchester: Manchester University Press.

Crawford, A. (1997) *The Local Governance of Crime: Appeals to Community and Partnerships*. Oxford: Clarendon Press.

Crawford, A. (1998) *Crime Prevention and Community Safety: Politics, Policies and Practices*. London: Longman.

Department of the Environment (1994) *Planning Out Crime*, DoE Circular 5/94. London: HMSO.

Duff, R. A. and Marshall, S. E. (2000) 'Benefits, Burdens and Responsibilities: Some Ethical Dimensions of Situational Crime Prevention', in A. von Hirsch, D. Garland and A. Wakefield (eds) *Ethical and Social Perspectives on Situational Crime Prevention*. Oxford: Hart Publishing, pp. 17–35.

Forrest, R. and Murie, A. (1988) *Selling the Welfare State: The Privatisation of Public Housing*. London: Routledge.

Gamble, A. (1988) *The Free Economy and the Strong State: The Politics of Thatcherism*. Basingstoke: Macmillan Education.

Garland, D. (2001) *The Culture of Control: Crime and Social Order in Contemporary Society*. Oxford: Oxford University Press.

Gill, M. and Spriggs, A. (2005) *Assessing the Impact of CCTV*, Home Office Research Study 292. London: Home Office.

Gladstone, F. J. (1980) *Co-ordinating Crime Prevention Efforts*, Home Office Research Study 62. London: HMSO.

Graham, S. (1999) 'The Eyes Have It: CCTV as the "Fifth Utility"', *Environment and Planning B: Planning and Design*, 26: 639–42.

Home Office (1984) *Crime Prevention*, Home Office Circular 8/84. London: Home Office.

Home Office (1990) *Crime Prevention: The Success of the Partnership Approach*, Home Office Circular 44/90. London: Home Office.

Home Office (1991) *Safer Communities: The Local Delivery of Crime Prevention Through the Partnership Approach* (Morgan Report). London: Home Office.

Home Office (1998) *The Crime and Disorder Act Introductory Guide. Local Strategies for Reducing Crime and Disorder*. London: Home Office.

Home Office (1999) *The Government's Crime Reduction Strategy*. London: Home Office.

Homel, P., Nutley, S., Webb, B. and Tilley, N. (2004) *Investing to Deliver: Reviewing the Implementation of the UK Crime Reduction Programme*, Home Office Research Study 281. London: Home Office.

Hope, T. (2000) 'Inequality and the clubbing of private security', in T. Hope and R. Sparks (eds) *Crime, Risk and Insecurity*. London: Routledge, pp. 83–106.

Hope, T. (2001) 'Crime Victimisation and Inequality in Risk Society', in R. Matthews and J. Pitts (eds) *Crime Prevention, Disorder and Community Safety*. London: Routledge, pp. 193–218.

Hope, T. (2002) 'La riduzione della criminalità, la sicurezza locale e la nuova filosofia del management pubblico', *Dei Delitti e della Pene*, IX, n. 1-2-3: 207–329.

Hope T. (2006) 'Mass Consumption, Mass Predation – Private Versus Public Action?: The Case Of Domestic Burglary in England And Wales', in R. Lévy, L. Mucchielli and R. Zaubermann (eds) *Crime et Insécurité: Un Demi-siècle de Bouleversements – Mélanges pour et avec Philippe Robert*. Paris: Editions l'Harmattan, pp. 45–61.

Hope, T. (2007) 'The Distribution of Household Property Crime Victimization: Insights from the British Crime Survey', in M. Hough and M. Maxfield (eds) *Surveying Crime in the 21st Century*, Crime Prevention Studies Vol. 22. Monsey, NY: Criminal Justice Press, pp. 91–124.

Hope, T. (2008a) 'Dodgy Evidence – Fallacies and Facts of Crime Reduction', *Safer Communities*, 7(3): 35–8.

Hope, T. (2008b) 'The First Casualty: Evidence and Governance in a War Against Crime', in P. Carlen (ed.) *Imaginary Penalities*. Cullompton: Willan Publishing.

Hope, T. (2008c) 'A Firing Squad to Shoot the Messenger: Home Office Peer Review of Research', in W. MacMahon (ed.) *Critical Thinking about the Uses of Research*. London: Centre for Crime and Justice Studies, pp. 27–44.

Hope, T. and Karstedt, S. (2003) 'Towards a New Social Crime Prevention', in H. Kury and J. Obergfell-Fuchs (eds) *Crime Prevention: New Approaches*. Mainz: Weisse Ring Verlag-GmbH, pp. 461–89.

Hope, T. and Lab, S. P. (2001) 'Variation in Crime Prevention Participation: Evidence from the British Crime Survey', *Crime Prevention and Community Safety*, 3: 7–21.

Hope, T. and Sparks, R. (2000) 'For a Sociological Theory of Situations (Or How Useful is Pragmatic Criminology?)', in A. von Hirsch, D. Garland and A. Wakefield (eds) *Situational Crime Prevention: Ethics and Social Context*. Oxford: Hart Publishing, pp. 175–91.

Hope, T. and Trickett, A. (2004) 'Angst Essen Seele Auf . . . But it Keeps Away the Burglars! Private Security, Neighbourhood Watch and the Social Reaction to Crime', *Kölner Zeitschrift für Soziologie und Sozialpsychologie*, 43: 441–68.

Hope, T., Bryan, J., Crawley, E., Crawley, P., Russell, N. and Trickett, A. (2004) *Strategic Development Projects in the Yorkshire and the Humber, East Midlands and Eastern Regions*, Home Office Online Report 41/04. London: Home Office.

Hough, M. and Mayhew, P. (1983) *The British Crime Survey: First Report*, Home Office Research Study 76. London: HMSO.

Houghton, G. (1992) *Car Theft in England and Wales: The Home Office Car Theft Index*. London: Home Office.

Kempa, M., Stenning, P. and Wood, J. (2004) 'Policing Communal Spaces – A Reconfiguration of the "Mass Private Property" Hypothesis', *British Journal of Criminology*, 44(4): 562–81.

Kershaw, C., Nicholas, S. and Walker, A. (2008) *Crime in England and Wales 2007/08: Findings from the British Crime Survey and Police Recorded Crime*. London: Home Office.

Kleinig, J. (2000) 'The Burdens of Situational Crime Prevention: An Ethical Commentary', in A. von Hirsch, D. Garland and A. Wakefield (eds) *Situational Crime Prevention: Ethics and Social Context*. Oxford: Hart Publishing, pp. 37–58.

Lash, S. and Urry, J. (1994) *Economies of Signs and Space*. London: Sage.

Laycock, G. (2001) 'Hypothesis-based Research: The Repeat Victimisation Story', *Criminal Justice*, 1: 59–82.

Laycock, G. and Tilley, N. (1995) 'Implementing Crime Prevention', in M. Tonry and D. P. Farrington (eds) *Building a Safer Society: Strategic Approaches to Crime Prevention*. Chicago: University of Chicago Press, pp. 535–84.

Litton, R. A. (1997) 'Crime Prevention and the Insurance Industry', in M. Felson and R. V. Clarke (eds) *Business and Crime Prevention*. Monsey, NY: Criminal Justice Press, pp. 151–96.

Loader, I. and Walker, N. (2007) *Civilising Security*. Cambridge: Cambridge University Press.

McCahill, M. and Norris, C. (2002) *CCTV in Britain*, Working Paper No. 3. Online at: www.urbaneye.net

McLaughlin, E. (2002) 'The Crisis of the Social and the Political Materialization of Community Safety', in G. Hughes, E. McLaughlin and J. Muncie (eds) *Crime Prevention and Community Safety: New Directions*. London: Sage, pp. 77–99.

Maguire, M. (2004) 'The Crime Reduction Programme in England and Wales: Reflections on the Vision and the Reality', *Criminology and Criminal Justice*, 4(3): 213–37.

National Audit Office (2005) *Home Office: Reducing Vehicle Crime*, Report by the Comptroller and Auditor General, HC 183 Session 2004–2005, 28 January 2005. London: The Stationery Office.

Office of the Deputy Prime Minister (2004) *Safer Places: The Planning System and Crime Prevention*, London: HMSO. Online at: www.communities.gov.uk/documents/planningandbuilding/pdf/147627.pdf

Osborne, D. and Gaebler, T. (1992) *Reinventing Government: How the Entrepreneurial Spirit is Transforming the Public Sector*. Reading, MA: Addison-Wesley.

Poyner, B. and Webb, B. (1991) *Crime-Free Housing*. London: Architectural Association.

Rose, N. (1999) *Powers of Freedom*. Cambridge: Cambridge University Press.

Schneider, R. H. and Kitchen, T. (2002) *Planning for Crime Prevention: A Transatlantic Perspective*. London: Routledge.

Simon, J. (2007) *Governing Through Crime: How the War on Crime Transformed American Democracy and Created a Culture of Fear*. Oxford: Oxford University Press.

Tilley, N., Pease, K., Hough, M. and Brown, R. (1999) *Burglary Prevention: Early Lessons from the Crime Reduction Programme*, Policing and Reducing Crime Unit, Crime Reduction Research Series Paper 1. London: Home Office.

Tonry, M. (2004) *Punishment and Politics: Evidence and Emulation in the Making of English Crime Control Policy*. Cullompton: Willan Publishing.

Walker, A., Kershaw, C. and Nicholas, S. (eds) (2006) *Crime in England and Wales 2005/06*, Home Office Statistical Bulletin 12/06. London: Home Office.

Webb, B. (2005) 'Preventing Vehicle Crime', in N. Tilley (ed.) *Handbook of Crime Prevention and Community Safety*. Cullompton: Willan Publishing, pp. 458–85.

Winchester, S. and Jackson, H. (1982) *Residential Burglary*. London: HMSO.

Windlesham, Lord (1987) *Responses to Crime*. Oxford: Clarendon Press.

Young, J. (2007) *The Vertigo of Late Modernity*. London: Sage.

Chapter 3

The preventive turn and the promotion of safer communities in England and Wales: political inventiveness and governmental instabilities

Adam Edwards and Gordon Hughes

Introduction

The preventive turn in England and Wales and across its diverse localities has had a longer institutional history and been the subject of more empirical research and conceptual social scientific debate than is the case for most European countries. Furthermore, and more contentiously, the preventive turn and its institutionalisation as community safety partnerships (in Wales) and crime and disorder reduction partnerships (in England), is at a more 'advanced' stage than the relative latecomers over the Channel in much of mainland Europe. Such developments in England and Wales in the past three decades point to both intense (even frenzied) bouts of 'political inventiveness' and consequences which may be termed 'governmental instabilities' (Clarke 2004; Hughes 2007).

This relative maturity in terms of multi-agency partnership work in community safety across every local government locality in England and Wales may, of course, be a source of 'Anglo-Saxon' stigma (forgetting for the moment the significant Celtic nations of the UK) to some European commentators. This is especially the case when the 'British' national model of crime prevention is interpreted by some European commentators as a metaphorical launching pad or in militaristic terms, an 'aircraft carrier' floating ominously off mainland Europe for the importation of

US-inspired neo-liberal and neo-conservative governmental practices into the seemingly more social democratic polities across Europe in the international policy transfer trade. Whatever the veracity or otherwise of this thesis, there is no denying that the English and Welsh experience is 'particular' if not 'peculiar' when compared to much of mainland Europe. Accordingly, this chapter aims in part to unravel and unveil the institutional realities and uneven development of the preventive turn across England and Wales in the recent decades.

There is already a voluminous body of published work on the recent history of crime prevention and community safety in Britain, stretching back to the early 1990s (see, for example, Crawford 1997, 2007; Gilling 1997, 2007; Hughes and Edwards 2002, 2005; Hughes 1998, 2007; Hughes et al. 2002; Stenson and Edwards 2004). Readers are encouraged to refer to this body of literature for detailed descriptions of the legislative powers, national policy developments, and formal local structures and strategies that have been implemented in England and Wales over recent years.

The chapter is organised as follows. Following a brief chronicling of the career of community safety, past and present, the chapter concentrates on unravelling the competing interpretations and different histories of current trends in this policy field which, as Adam Crawford (2007: 900) has noted, has been characterised by 'hyper innovation' and 'hyper-politicisation' alongside, we would add, a lack of any settled verdict not just on the success or failure of the policy experiment but with regard to the nature of the beast itself from social scientific commentary and research.

Any 'history of the present' in a society with a well-developed criminological research base, both in government departments and universities, necessitates a critical discussion of the competing intellectual translations of 'community safety' as a floating signifier. In other words, the telling of the competing stories of community safety is not just about describing institutional developments manufactured 'out there' by the state but is also about the relationship of this preventive turn to various proponents of the contemporary criminological imagination. Accordingly we need to consider the ways in which criminologists as academic social scientists and governmental experts have conceptualised, mapped and advised 'expertly' on the work done on the ground under the signifier of community safety. In particular, in this section of this chapter we argue that social scientists – including ourselves of course – have necessarily been engaged in both representational accounts (reflecting and capturing what has happened) and performative narratives (which help constitute and reconstitute the phenomena under study) (see Edwards and Hughes 2008a).

It is important in making sense of the institution-building in the community safety sector in England and Wales that such intellectual attempts at framing and problematising both the 'plumbing' of the new institutional architecture and its 'products' receive consideration. The five non-exhaustive narratives about community safety discussed in this section suggest that it is specious to identify a single history other than an institutionally descriptive account of key laws, policy statements and agencies. Instead, when attempts are made to interpret the consequences of such institutional developments the stories become more contested, leading us to an investigation of the politics of the history of community safety as well as the contested politics of community safety. Accordingly, in this part of the chapter a reflexive interpretation of these narratives is provided.

Finally, the chapter draws on illustrative examples from the authors' own realist conceptual framework and ongoing empirical research programme on the local politics of community safety. First, this highlights the polyvalence of the concept of community safety, pointing to its qualities as a floating signifier with no fixed referent but a multiplicity of significations, capable of being aligned with a spectrum of political positions on safety. Second, this final section also highlights some of the challenges for researching the preventive turn when the national frame is unsettled and other geo-historical contexts are acknowledged.

Community safety: career of a floating signifier

The last two decades in England and Wales have seen a dramatic shift in the local governance of crime and the politics of insecurity. More fundamentally, these developments reflect a re-articulation of powers and responsibilities in and between the state, private interests and civil society. It represents simultaneously a dramatic narrowing of the horizons of state 'sovereignty' and an attempt to reassert a form of control. (Crawford 2002: 14)

[T]his network of partnership arrangements and inter-agency working agreements is designed to foster crime prevention and to enhance community safety, primarily through the cultivation of community involvement and the dissemination of crime prevention ideas and practices. (Garland 2001: 16)

Our discussion begins with a brief resume of the 'talk' and policy *pronouncements* regarding the 'preventive turn' and associated changes in governance of crime and insecurity across localities since the 1980s (highlighted in Crawford's and Garland's claims above). We then focus on the question of where we are at the different level of competing interpretations regarding the nature and consequences of policy implementation and actual practices associated with the policy mix of community safety, neighbourhood policing and local crime and disorder reduction, and the provocations that arise from these processes on the ground today. In contemporary international policy discourses on crime control and prevention, there is much similar language used, and convergent political rallying calls made, across 'Anglophone' countries for policy change and innovation, whether it be 'policing' rather than the police, and 'safer communities together' (rather than crime prevention in the narrower sense of the word). This is captured neatly in both Garland's and Crawford's above diagnoses of the 'dramatic shift' in the governance of crime and insecurity in late-modern societies. At the same time, it needs to be acknowledged that the often bland translations and appeals for a common *lingua franca* around prevention and safety in policy discourses are less easily accomplished in non-Anglophone countries across Europe (Edwards and Hughes 2005a).

Let us examine in brief the particular career of community safety in England and Wales since the 1980s based on the 'talk' and 'decisions' dimensions of the policy process, as distinguished by Pollitt (2001). This brief account will also draw on Crawford's (2002) overview of developments in the two decades up to 2000 which, like this chapter, was written with an eye to points of both convergence and divergence across European countries. Indeed, Crawford's interpretation of developments, and in particular his emphasis on the contradictions around the governmental logics of (i) managerialism, (ii) governance through partnership, and (iii) nostalgic communitarianism, bears similarities to much of the analytical framework employed by the present authors in charting these developments since the 1990s and throughout the 2000s across the UK (see, for example, Hughes and Edwards 2005).

The origins of community safety in the 1980s are suggestive of the mixed parentage of this signifier. We should note, for example, the initial appropriations by, variously, 'radical' Metropolitan Police Authorities, who formulated local community safety plans as a counterweight to police-driven notions of public safety, the charity NACRO (National Association for the Care and Rehabilitation of Offenders) and its 'bottom-up' projects in marginalised local communities, alongside central government circulars and initiatives elaborating a new approach to crime prevention in this decade. However, the real discursive turning point at the national dimension in this decade was the Home Office Circular 8/84: this 'key symbolic landmark' (Crawford 2002: 16) being the first explicit official recognition of the limits to 'go-it-alone' policing and the capacity of constabularies to effectively prevent problems of crime without drawing on the resources (including expertise) of other key statutory partners and the wider public.

The next key discursive moment in this career was the 1991 Morgan Report, *Delivering Safer Communities* (Home Office 1991), with its social democratic ambition to conceptualise and manage holistically crime and disorder and their deeper roots through creative, democratically sensitive partnership arrangements led by local authorities rather than the police.

This report reflected an emergent consensus among academics and policy-makers that the ideal approach to prevention combines a package of both precipitating factors and predisposing influences (Crawford 2002: 21). Equally importantly, it gave the new approach a nationally recognisable 'brand name': community safety.

Crawford (2002: 23) suggests that the period 1991–97 which followed the Morgan Report was a period of 'stagnation and ambivalence'. This is true when viewed from 'on high', from the national government policy dimension. However, it is not so valid when attention is paid to the local contexts in which community safety work was institutionalised and put into practice. Indeed, Crawford (2002: 23) admits as much by noting that, unlike the 1980s when 'the' government had done so much to stimulate enthusiasm in crime prevention, 'activity and innovation had clearly shifted to the local realm of local organisations in the 1990s' (see also Hughes 1998; Hughes and Edwards 2002).

Following the Morgan agenda, which was widely and influentially, if unevenly, taken up locally, the third key discursive moment was the Crime and Disorder Act (CDA) in 1998. In retrospect the CDA helped inaugurate the New Labour 'modernisation' project associated with the three appeals to managerialism, governance through partnership and communitiarianism. The effects of this central government project have continued to resonate into the late 2000s. This period witnessed both linguistic turns and policy decisions to shift the focus from 'community safety' to 'crime and (eventually) disorder reduction' made tangible as calculable, centrally defined, targeted performance measures. Again, Crawford (2002: 25) characterised the first three years of this period (1997–2000) as that of 'rebirth and renewal focused around Disorder'. This focus was further consolidated in subsequent years by the much publicised flood of further crime and anti-social behaviour legislation, alongside a communitarian-inspired crusade around 'Respect' and the drive for moral authoritarian interventions against anti-social behaviour (see Hughes 2007: 119–25).

The broad verdict among many influential commentators on the possible consequences of the post-CDA agenda was that of a guarded optimism, as expressed by Crawford:

> recent developments potentially allow a fundamental shift in the way that crime and its prevention are governed. They represent a maturing of community safety and its movement into mainstream consciousness and service delivery ... The CDA begins a long-overdue recognition that the levers and causes of crime lie far from the traditional reach of the criminal justice system ... the new politics offers more plural understandings of and social responses to crime, drawing together a variety of organisations and stakeholders, in the public, voluntary and private sectors as well as from among relevant

community groups in ways which are problem-focused rather than defined according to the means most readily available for their solution. (Crawford 2002: 31–2)

Such optimism at the beginning of the 2000s was widely shared across much of the criminological academy. However, we also need to note Crawford's own recognition of community safety as 'sites of contradiction, ambiguity and ambivalence', which we also shared at the time (McLaughlin et al. 2001; Hughes 1998, 2002; Edwards and Hughes 2002). Much of the subsequent career of community safety has confirmed the wisdom of this recognition of the contradictory and ambivalent tendencies associated with local partnership working and their narrowly targeted focus on measurable crime and disorder reduction (see Hughes 2007; Gilling 2007).

Crime control or social policy? Community safety as a 'hybrid' policy

Community safety as a policy approach sits at the intersection of attempts by the state to deliver welfare and security, *and* policing and control in local communities. We noted earlier that community safety emerged in the 1980s as a local government strategy that sought to move beyond the traditionally police-driven agenda of crime prevention. Apart from seeking to involve other 'social' agencies in crime prevention and in turn moving from single to multi-agency activities, community safety has also been associated with more aspirational claims. One particular claim has been to generate greater participation and leadership from residential communities in promoting 'quality of life', not just tackling those social harms classified as crimes. As a long-term outcome, community safety is often linked to the communitarian ambition of replacing fragile, atomised, fearful and insecure communities with ones confident enough to take responsibility for their own safety. At the same time, in the national politics of the 1990s and 2000s, 'creating safer communities' has been a crucial component of the Labour administration's promotion of policies that could be 'tough on crime, tough on the causes of crime'. In this sense, community safety straddles the fault line of repressive crime control (tough on crime) and more preventive, welfare-oriented, interventions (tough on the causes of crime).

In the discussion that follows the main features of the institutional infrastructure of community safety are sketched in brief. As will be evident from the earlier discussion, it is difficult to deny that there has been a highly prescriptive and directive central government shaping of the contemporary preventive infrastructure in England and Wales. This is indicative of a sovereign state strategy, which stresses greater central control ('steering') alongside the diffusion of responsibility for the delivery of crime control and the promotion of safer communities ('rowing') to a wide array of agencies and groups, both public and private, voluntary and statutory in character. For commentators like Rose (1999), these developments are part of a broader neo-liberal movement towards enlisting communities as the new and preferred sites of governance.

The emergence of community safety as a policy discourse is most usefully viewed as feeding off two interconnected features of government thinking, namely a political discourse of civic communitarianism and a 'modernising' public management project. To give one example, as a result of the CDA in England and Wales the aim to tackle disorder and anti-social behaviour through the establishment of exclusion orders was a central feature of this fused communitarian and public management project. It is important to note how moral or social transgressions as well as law-breaking came under the scope of the communitarian-inspired powers vested in local crime and disorder reduction partnerships (CDRPs), or community safety partnerships (CSPs) as they are known in Wales. Such developments are illustrative of the entanglements and possible contradictions associated with control and welfare in the field of community safety.

Between 1998 and 2008 all 376 statutory partnerships in England and Wales were legally obliged and empowered to:

- Carry out audits of local crime and disorder problems.

- Consult with all sections of the local community.

- Publish three-year crime and disorder reduction strategies based on the findings of the audits.

- Identify targets and performance indicators for each part of the strategy, with specified timescales.

- Publish the audit, strategy and the targets.

- Report annually on progress against the targets.

Most CDRPs and CSPs have been characterised by very similar formal organisational structures. For example, there is a formal strategic/operational division; there are usually specific thematic or geographically based 'action' teams; the key statutory partners or 'responsible' authorities are made up of public agencies ranging from the local authority, police, probation, fire, police authority and health, alongside co-opted agencies from both the statutory and the voluntary sector. The 'community' is usually presented in the local strategies as a spatial and moral concept, emphasising locality, belonging and unity (albeit across consensual diversity). However, there is also a common tendency to place certain groups outside the community due to their 'anti-social' activities, pointing to the key role of boundary and exclusion in representations of community. In turn, the community is usually 'passively' present in terms of being 'consulted' rather than an active participant in the planning and delivery of community safety (Hughes 2009).

There continue to be ongoing reforms of CDRPs/CSPs as the vehicles for community safety at the time of writing which have the stated aim to improve their performance at the local level. However, such partnership work remains substantively determined by the evolving central government agenda of targeted, evidence-based and measurable crime and disorder reduction, linked to specific negotiated local priorities.

The priorities listed below are taken from the published strategies of the 22 CSPs in Wales for 2005–08, but they also reflect the typical priorities shared across partnerships across England and Wales. Research shows that those highlighted in bold were consistently the top priorities in local CSP strategies (Edwards and Hughes 2008c).

- **Anti-social behaviour**
- Arson
- Burglary
- Domestic abuse
- **Fear of crime**
- Hate crime
- Home safety
- Prolific and persistent offenders
- Property/business crime
- Road safety
- Rural crime
- **Substance abuse**
- Vehicle crime
- Violence
- **Youth offending**

The primary focus of community safety partnerships in terms of their stated priorities since the CDA has thus been on crime and disorder reduction. On the surface this suggests that they are primarily engaged in local crime control rather than in social policy work. However, the actual outcomes of such control work may be preventive in character rather than purely repressive and enforcement-oriented, when examined in terms of problem-solving orientation and when studied empirically 'on the ground' (Edwards and Hughes 2008b).

The centrally propelled and Home Office-directed drive towards the institutionalisation of community safety remains strikingly apparent across every local government authority in England and Wales. Such processes have seen an ever-increasing number of multi-agency community safety teams – managers, officers, project workers, police secondees, drug action/substance misuse teams, anti-social behaviour units, for example – which now form an increasingly salient, if still fragile, part of local government structures and processes.

As a relatively novel set of institutions and experts, community safety work is set to remain a key feature of the local governance of crime, disorder and security in England and Wales. However, there are major challenges that lie in wait, not least those associated with innovations in the local policing of the terror threat and 'radicalisation'; additionally, tensions exist both about the nature and form of neighbourhood policing and the uneasy and unstable relations between such 'police-ing' initiatives and local community safety policy (see Hughes and Rowe 2007).

Narratives of community safety

In this section we undertake some initial steps towards a sociology of knowledge production, namely an exploration of how exponents of the criminological imagination have contributed to the development, framing and problematisation of community safety as a field of policy and practice. In what follows, we distinguish and critique four compelling narratives or histories of community safety (and their perceived consequences) before concluding with our preferred mode of conceptualising and researching built around the 'necessary' relations of power dependence in the policy field and practices of community safety.

Community safety as a progressive third way?

We begin with the uses to which the notion of community safety has been put by a range of actors who may be grouped collectively as administrative or policy criminologists: the array of central and local governmental advisors, policy-makers, practitioners and research officers and consultants. The terms 'administrative' and 'policy' are not used in a pejorative sense here (see Hughes 2007: 201–7 on the different forms of criminological labour). We would include in this important intellectual grouping such writers as Lea, Matthews and Young, often collectively known as the 'left realists', and the work of such Home Office social scientists as Tim Hope and Margaret Shaw in the 1980s, and architects of the post-1998 crime reduction guidance, Nick Tilley and Mike Hough.

Alongside the work of policy criminologists noted above, the authors of the Morgan Report (Home Office 1991 and see pp. 65 above) used the concept of community safety to retrieve the gamut of dispositional theories of crime causation that constitute the principal sociological and psychological contributions to governmental criminology. These had been eschewed during the previous decade by a national Conservative administration critical of the social determination of crime and concerned to promote neo-classical principles of deterrent penal regimes for rational offenders and situational crime prevention techniques. The unsurprising rejection of the Morgan Report's recommendations for community safety by this administration provided the Labour Party, then in opposition in Westminster, with a basis for reformulating its approach to law and order, specifically through Tony Blair's now renowned concept of being tough on crime and tough on the causes of crime. The influence of the Morgan Report and its translation into Labour Party 'third way' thinking can also be seen in the appeal made to 'joined-up' and holistic governance and the technique of partnership working, also pioneered by the social democratic-oriented 'left realist' criminologists. This partnership approach sought to unsettle and decentre the dominant assumption of a single-agency solution to crime.

The political importance of Blair's reformulation of crime control policy, during his tenure as opposition spokesperson on Home Affairs, both for his personal political career and for the subsequent electoral fortunes of the Labour Party, has been the subject of much analysis and commentary (Downes and Morgan 2002; Matthews and Young 2003; Tonry 2004). The key point about this narrative is that the concept of community safety enabled the Labour Party, at both national and municipal levels, to reassert the social democratic association of crime control *and* social policy while accommodating more immediate, palliative measures for reducing crime and addressing the needs of victims. It therefore provided a means of loosening the 'hostages to fortune' that had characterised the Labour Party's depiction, by its political opponents, of being soft on crime, tolerant of civil disorders and more concerned with the welfare of offenders than the rights of victims (Downes and Morgan 1994; Gilling 2007).

From its origins in the political dynamics of national and local government in Britain, the very imprecision of community safety as a concept proved useful in instantiating the problem of crime as a composite of social causes, to be addressed through multi-agency policies on family support, employment and training, education and youth work, situational opportunities, support for victims and so on. In these terms, the intellectual coherence and internal consistency of the concept is less important and less interesting than its capacity to outflank and out-think more reductionist narratives about crime control through either enforcement of the criminal law and punitive deterrence or social policy interventions.

Community safety as a repressive state apparatus?

Counterpoised to the admixture of criminological ideas found in official and policy-oriented narratives on community safety, some commentators working within the tradition of critical criminology have offered an altogether 'smoother' interpretation of this concept and what it signifies. Drawing inspiration from Marxist analyses of an earlier generation of critical criminologists, these commentators identify community safety as a set of particular practices that form part of a repressive state apparatus whose function is to regulate the conditions for capital accumulation via a strategy of '"lockdown" leading inexorably and inevitably to differential policing, discriminatory targeting, universal surveillance, criminalisation and escalation in the prison population' (Scraton 2003: 31; see also Coleman *et al.* 2002; Coleman 2004, 2005).

In this narrative community safety is imagined as a set of repressive, 'revanchist' policing practices aimed at retaking public space (from the 'anti-social', for example) for the purposes of capital accumulation while obviating alternative conceptions of safety, such as youth work within disadvantaged neighbourhoods. Moreover, the narrow conception of community safety among urban elites is viewed as closing off action on other threats to public health, such as toxic waste disposal and allied corporate crimes that are excluded from the vision and horizon of community safety work. Accordingly, Coleman *et al.* (2002: 96) observe that 'these inclusionary and exclusionary practices can be understood as part of a wider social ordering strategy which is legitimated by the moral and intellectual project of social and economic regeneration'.

Interest in capturing the concept of community safety and using it to signal the need for public protection against a variety of harmful activities perpetrated by corporations against vulnerable working-class communities has increased among critical criminologists (Tombs *et al.* 2007). Again, this demonstrates both the polyvalence of the concept and its focus for political contestation over the definition of 'safety' for different communities of interest. However, our particular concern here is in the relationship between the performative and representational aspects of this critical narrative. In problematising community safety as an exercise in securing the conditions for capital accumulation strategies (such as the regeneration of post-industrial cities around retail consumption during the day and alcohol consumption at night), this narrative frames community safety as a repressive apparatus and channels the vision of the social researcher on to those policing practices that fit this initial problematisation.

To what extent this imagination also provides an accurate and/or exhaustive representation of community safety in the case study area in question (Liverpool) as well as further afield is a moot point. In our view, it is questionable because of the messy, capacious and often disorganised conceptions of community safety revealed through empirical research into the dispositions of community safety workers themselves (Edwards and Hughes 2008b; Hughes and Gilling 2004) and into the practice of partnerships in other localities in England and Wales (Hallsworth 2002; Stenson 2002; Foster 2002; Hughes 2007).

Community safety as a neo-liberal political rationality?

Whereas critical criminology was, at one time, synonymous with the kind of Marxist political economy advocated by Coleman and colleagues, it now accommodates the work of those influenced by a very different intellectual tradition associated with Foucault's study of power, particularly his concept of governmentality. The latter concept examines the role of political rationalities in defining objects of control and prescribing how these objects so defined should be interpreted and acted upon (Foucault 1991; Garland 2001; Smandych 1999).

In Britain arguments about the meaning of crime prevention and community safety have provided a focal point for this tradition of thought, particularly as a result of David Garland's thesis about the contradictory political rationalities at play in late-modern strategies of control. Specifically, the episodic bouts of punitive display by sovereign states anxious to legitimate their authority through various 'wars' on crime, drugs or terror exist in tension with the *sotto voce* admission that state authorities lack the effective capacity to govern crime and disorder alone. This limit to the sovereign state and in turn the normality of high crime rates provides the real world conditions to which governing strategies must adapt by 'responsibilising' citizens and other private actors more actively and more prudentially to participate in their own governance. Central to this adaptation is the promotion of measures for identifying and reducing the opportunities for crime and disorder generated through the everyday routines of citizens (Garland 2001; see also Crawford 2006; Johnston and Shearing 2003).

In these terms, community safety is counterpoised to various forms of punitive display, such as zero tolerance policing, ASBOs, parenting orders, and is allied to a new logic of prevention and risk management that 'instead of pursuing, prosecuting and punishing individuals . . . aims to reduce the supply of criminal events by minimising criminal opportunities, enhancing situational controls, and channelling conduct away from criminogenic situations' (Garland 2001: 171). Here, as Garland goes on to note, community safety 'becomes the chief consideration and law enforcement becomes merely a means to this end' (2001: 171).

Community safety is consequently allied to a certain neo-liberal political rationality in which state intervention, even in the core competence of order maintenance, is rolled back as private citizens are required to act as individualised, responsibilised and prudential actors, better insuring themselves against future risks of criminal victimisation. What, for Garland, is eclipsed in this interplay between punitive 'criminologies of the other' and adaptive 'criminologies of the self', is the social democratic criminology that had prevailed in the mid twentieth century and which privileged collective risk management and welfare state interventions, particularly those aimed at the education, training, employment and recreation of young people.

As noted above, however, empirical research studies suggest that community safety has been regarded, notably by community safety workers themselves, as a means of resuscitating a more social democratic vision of control (Hughes and Gilling 2004). The smooth elision of community safety with neo-liberal politics has also been challenged for obscuring the increasing accommodation of punitive strategies within community safety work, most notably through the pressure put on multi-agency partnerships to use exclusion orders, such as ASBOs, which was present at the outset of the local statutory partnerships in 1999 and further intensified following the passage of the Anti-Social Behaviour Act 2003.

An arboreal vision of control?

The fourth narrative on community safety is arguably the most provocative and destabilising exercise in the criminological imagination of all those considered here. It draws its inspiration from the work of the post-structuralist philosophers Gilles Deleuze and Felix Guattari (1987), whose broader critique of western philosophical traditions challenges the common preoccupation with producing 'arboreal' knowledge, as exemplified by the historical device of genealogical or family trees. For Deleuze and Guattari this is a specious exercise which misconceives the more inchoate, protean, multi-directional and unpredictable qualities of social relationships, which are better envisaged in terms of the botanical metaphor of the 'rhizome'. This metaphor captures the heterogeneous mutation of social relationships and their osmosis into one another, creating in turn further mutations, for example in the assemblage, breakdown and reassemblage of non-nuclear families. The point of the metaphor is that it expresses the kind of thinking that is needed to apprehend the dynamic qualities of social relationships and how this thinking has been debilitated by the rigid conceptual hierarchies and categorisation associated with, for example, modern, positivist social science.

This opposition between arboreal and rhizomatic thinking has been imported into criminological thought by those interested in innovations in the control of crime and disorder often associated with community safety (see Haggerty and Ericson 2000; Hallsworth 2002, 2008). According to Hallsworth's research in London on street crime and its (attempted) control, there is a dissonance between the rational problem-solving activities which community safety workers are asked to undertake, in order to render problems of street crime and disorder intelligible and measurable for the purposes of their subsequent remediation, and the protean qualities of these problems, which escape precise definition and calibration. Arboreal visions of control are subverted by the rhizomatic qualities of both control itself and the street crime and disorder that are the focus of much control. This narrative suggests a basic contradiction in community safety work, namely the struggle to delimit the limitless.

According to this narrative, the problems of mirror imaging – by which public authorities project their own ways of thinking on to their subjects of control – can be discerned throughout the intelligence-led, problem-solving approaches that community safety officers and police crime analysts in particular are required to undertake by the statutory duty to return annual strategic assessments of their work. Despite the persistence of extant traditions of social democratic and sociological thought among community safety practitioners, as noted earlier, the predominant intellectual traditions underpinning the routine analysis of crime patterns in these strategic assessments are those of rational choice, routine activities theory and situational crime prevention. In turn, these delimit street crime in terms of discrete 'events' that can be enumerated and mapped to reveal their concentration in time and place (Clarke and Eck 2003). In doing so, the antecedent conditions and 'upstream' causes of these events are forgotten and the meaning of street violence, for its 'rational' protagonists, is bracketed off.

If the hot-spot, situational analysis of crime patterns imposes an arboreal vision of control upon inherently rhizomatic processes of crime and disorder, as Hallsworth contends, it follows that other intellectual traditions are required for the cultivation of a rhizomatic imagination. To this end, Hallsworth identifies the promise of the phenomenological methods of 'cultural criminology' (2008: 13). In place of 'voodoo statistics' (Young 2004), qualitative research methods are required that render intelligible the 'ecologies' of street crime and the rules of violence as understood by protagonists themselves. (Hallsworth 2008: 8ff.).

Deleuzian criminology as translated in our fourth narrative is essentially performative, preoccupied as it is with deconstructing the over-rationalised, patterned and structured imagery of crime and disorder and its control found in official and in much critical social science as a means of promoting an alternative rhizomatic vision of control. It is clear, however, that Hallsworth's 'violence ecologies' are also offered as *superior representations* of crime, disorder and control; superior, that is, to the official and critical criminologies they have first deconstructed and dismissed as arboreal. In our view, it is questionable if it is possible to ever escape arboreal representations of social life. Does a non-arboreal representation of the 'inherent contingent amorphous volatility of street life' or the 'rhizomatic expansion of surveillance' (Haggerty and Ericson 2000) imply an inherently contingent amorphous and volatile or rhizomatic method of inquiry and argumentation? How can the mutable, open-ended quality of the social relations signified by the idea of community safety be represented in ways that avoid the structuring devices of social science, including, ironically, those of post-structuralist thinkers?

Power-dependence

The final narrative of community safety considered here is that associated with our own research into the unfinished politics and necessarily unstable outcomes of the struggle for security and safety (Edwards and Hughes 2005b). Central to this research is the concept of 'power-dependence', developed by political scientists to build theory about changes and continuities in governance (Rhodes 1997). The concept of power-dependence identifies a central paradox of political power: those who possess the potential to govern are not powerful when they are not actually governing, but neither are they when they seek to govern because they are dependent on others to carry out their commands. The difference between the potential to govern and actually governing is always the actions of others.

It follows that 'would-be sovereigns' are necessarily in a relationship of power-dependence with those through whom they must govern and with whom they must enter into exchange relationships to win and maintain a governing coalition. This dependence is what necessitates political competition and the consequent gaps between talk, decisions and action in any particular policy field as some actors resist recruitment and/or are interested by competing coalitions. The content of this competition, however, is contingent on the political vision, acumen and resources of the competitors, which we expect to differ among particular centres of power (national administrations, local governments, supranational organisations such as the European Union, and so on). Whether the substantive content of security politics, or any other governing project, actually differs among different centres of power is also a question for empirical research. We suggest, on the basis of case study research reported on security politics in various localities in Western Europe (Hughes and Edwards 2002; Edwards and Hughes 2005b), that this proposition has yet to be falsified, although this case study research was cross-sectional and so prospective convergence in security politics cannot be ruled out. Complete convergence in actions as well as decisions and talk would, however, be remarkable, indicating the total collapse of political competition and capacities for resistance which, certainly in liberal democracies, and other 'differentiated polities' (Rhodes 1997), we suggest, is highly unlikely.

The resources associated with relations of power-dependence are unevenly distributed but no single actor is ever completely resource-less.

For example, even poverty-stricken voluntary organisations at the subnational level have the capacity for political representation to governors anxious to 'engage' them; whether this capacity is actually realised is a contingent consequence of other factors, particularly acumen in campaigning. As a consequence, the political competition to translate talk into decisions and then decisions into action is structured by asymmetrical (rather than zero-sum) relations of power-dependence. Rhodes (1997) suggests five dimensions of power-dependence, which we have found useful as a basis for building theory about the uneven outcomes of security/safety politics in different centres of power: constitutional-legal, financial, informational, organisational, and political.

When we apply this conceptual framework to the words, decisions and actions associated with the politics of community safety in England and Wales, we are able to discern better the real terrain of (delimited) political contestation and action, (constrained) plurality of outcomes and (bounded) spaces for contingency, that has characterised the history of our floating signifier.

We now consider some of the key emergent challenges facing the hybrid policy field of community safety raised in our ongoing empirical research, alongside the opening up of potentially new research agendas when the national frame of reference is unsettled and the uneven local distribution of various asymmetric governing resources is centred in sociological and political analysis of this still evolving policy terrain.

Unsettling the 'British nation' as a unit of analysis

(i) Researching community safety in the partially devolved polity of Wales

Most research studies, as well as nationwide surveys of and commentaries on the preventive turn in British criminology, have tended to take the 'British/English' national model of crime prevention and community safety as their taken-for-granted frame of reference even when discussing 'UK' developments. Alistair Henry breaks with this tradition in part by discussing the specific characteristics of the preventive turn in Scotland (see Chapter 4, this volume). It is also evident that things are different in Northern Ireland, although we lack a firm empirical research base for drawing any subtle or firm conclusions both about the recent emergence and future direction of community safety strategies in this province. It is also often assumed that the term 'England' subsumes Wales and there has been a tradition for the 'and Wales' part of the descriptor to be ignored. This was unsatisfactory in the past, but it is now seriously flawed to presume that processes of change and adaptation in the localities across Wales, in this case with regard to community safety and crime prevention, will simply reflect the tendencies of its larger neighbour (England) given the partial devolution of powers since 2000 to the Welsh Assembly Government.

Since 2000 the Welsh Assembly Government (WAG) has had a range of statutory powers relating to the policy and practice of community safety, including local government, health and social services, and education. This is one example at the national and local levels in Wales of what we term the constitutional-legal dimension of power-dependence. At present, its powers do not extend to policing and criminal justice *per se* (unlike Scotland) but issues of crime prevention – for example, through tackling substance misuse, youth crime and annoyance, and promoting 'youth inclusion' – do fall within the Assembly's constitutional-legal and financial remit. Considered as a distinct policy area, community safety was until 2007 a responsibility of the Assembly government's Department of Social Justice and Regeneration,[1] emphasising at the level of political rhetoric the Assembly government's interest in locating issues of 'crime and disorder' prevention within a problematic of *social* rather than criminal justice. That local partnerships in Wales have retained the prefix 'community safety' rather than the officially designated 'crime and disorder reduction' partnerships in England is, in the light of recent research findings (Edwards and Hughes 2008b), also more than a semantic difference. The distinction between CSPs in Wales and CDRPs in England has performed an important symbolic political function in (as one of our research respondents put it) 'dragonising'[2] the policy area as well as further emphasising – at least at the level of 'talk' and 'decision' if not as yet proven 'action' – the social policy orientation of responses to crime and disorder in Wales as distinct from the intended central government direction for CDRPs in England. Whether such symbolic differences in the naming of the organisations tasked with delivering community safety in Wales (i.e. the organisational dimension of power-dependence) translate into radically different practices of control and outcomes for communities between England and Wales remains a moot point for the kind of comparative research that we would advocate (Edwards and Hughes 2005b) but which, to our knowledge, has yet to be undertaken systematically and comparatively.

Powerful pressures for convergence across English CDRPs and Welsh CSPs (associated with financial, informational and organisational dimensions of power-dependence) clearly include the role of the Home Office in establishing certain performance targets for CDRPs and CSPs and linking the two main funding budgets hitherto dedicated to partnership work and dispensed from Whitehall (the Basic Command Unit Fund and the Building Safer Communities Fund) to success or failure in meeting these targets.

The new informational technologies from central government departments associated, for example, with the police-driven National Intelligence Model (NIM), annual strategic assessments and the establishment of annual police and community safety statements and 34 national outcome and indicator sets for community safety in 2008 are suggestive of further penetrative processes of convergence and conformity across CSPs and CDRPs in England and Wales. That noted, findings from our survey of all 22 CSPs in Wales (Edwards and Hughes 2008c) suggest, however, that the Assembly government provides the overwhelming proportion of funding received by the Welsh partnerships, accounting for between 60–80 per cent of their annual budgets. In turn this funding is allied to a very particular post-devolutionary politics in Wales that is suggestive of a potentially important break with the direction of crime and disorder reduction in England since 1998. The WAG Safer Communities Fund established in 2004, for example, is dedicated to reducing problems of youth exclusion and promoting youth inclusion through social crime prevention and diversionary interventions. These are objectives of an 'old' social democratic impulse to engineer social integration through more intensive welfare state interventions sitting somewhat uneasily alongside the risk factor prevention paradigm of the England and Wales Youth Justice Board (Hughes *et al.* forthcoming).

Indeed, broader commentaries on post-devolution government in Wales have emphasised the political goal of reasserting the importance of social democracy and creating a 'high-trust' polity in which disillusioned citizens are reconnected to more accountable and responsive public authorities through the democratisation rather than commercialisation of public services. The Beecham Inquiry into public service delivery in Wales noted the commercial conception of citizens in England (as consumers of services delivered through quasi-market competition) could not be replicated in Wales, both because of political opposition to the very idea of commercialising public services and because of its impracticality given the problems of sustaining alternative competitors in a country with a highly dispersed demography, particularly in the rural and valleys areas (Beecham 2006: para. 2.13). This broader political context is significant for a discussion of any putative British 'ASBO nation' (Squires 2008) because ASBOs have been regarded by some key elite decision-makers in the Welsh polity as the epitome of low-trust state–citizen relations, inimical to the post-devolutionary project of building a more inclusive society and thus to be used only as a last resort (Edwards and Hughes 2008b).

(ii) Researching local negotiations and contestations of anti-social behaviour control

Let us exemplify such local struggles with the example of the resistance we found among lead community safety officers in most of the 22 localities across Wales to any uncritical implementation of the anti-social behaviour agenda promulgated from the Home Office in the mid 2000s (see Edwards and Hughes 2008b). This discussion alerts us to the importance of the 'subnational' as brought to life in specific geo-historical contexts and local practices and politics *in situ*.

It became clear from this comparative, translocal research on Welsh CSPs that the occupation of community safety manager was often a tortuous process of bargaining between implacable partners, especially with regard to the political and culturally emotive issue of governing young people's use of public space. In occupying this position, community safety managers were not in a position to act as some simple interlocutor for the Home Office's 'Respect' agenda, or foot-soldier for the government's Respect unit, if they wanted to retain the involvement of those partners primarily concerned with the welfare of children and young people. As noted earlier, there has been substantial investment of resources, financial as well as political (and symbolic), in a more social democratic, welfare-oriented approach to crime and disorder in Wales, allied to the rhetoric of a citizen-centred model of public service, for which the prolific use of 'low-trust' measures such as ASBOs is anathema. As a consequence, this broader post-devolutionary project places a considerable pressure on community safety managers, reinforced by funding streams from the WAG that account for the overwhelming share of their annual budgets, to counterbalance the 'Manchester tendency' (the local authority area with by far the highest number of ASBOs in recent years) with strategies that place a premium on the social inclusion of young people. However, there is also evidence of variation in local CSPs' adherence across Wales to this social democratic project, with some notable advocates of ASBOs as an economic and highly effective means of restoring order.

Such uneven contestation emphasises the local political agency of community safety managers and the partnerships they co-ordinate, the consequences of which cannot be articulated within the smooth narratives of disorder that have predominated in both official and academic discourses. The conception and governance of anti-social behaviour is a complex and unevenly developed practice both in its 'doing' by practitioners and in its apprehension by social researchers. The greater concerns of community safety managers across many localities in Wales are focused on efforts to prevent or at best to manage disorder and local feelings of fear and insecurity. Much of this work is profoundly influenced by a social democratic ethos that belies seductive but simplistic official narratives of ASBOs as a progressive palliative for 'feral' populations.

What we have termed the 'resilient Fabianism' (or social democratic and socialist ideological orientation) of local community safety managers' accounts of their own work also disturbs narratives of social control in critical social science, which are in danger of believing the hype of the very political projects they seek to challenge. The distinction between the neo-liberal and neo-conservative impulses constituting the 'free economy, strong state' project of New Right politics has animated critical commentary on British government for too long, obfuscating the complex interdependencies between state and civil society that both necessitate political agency and enable local resistance. The incorporation of this distinction into criminological research, notably through the work of David Garland (1996, 2001) and Nikolas Rose (1999, 2000), has further obscured an understanding of social control as an emergent, necessarily contingent, product of the struggle for sovereignty over territories and populations.

As such, grand narrative themes, such as the eclipse, even death, of social democratic 'criminologies of everyday life', underestimate the complex interplay between local priorities and extant political traditions over social order and those emanating from both Whitehall and the WAG. In this way, our research suggests that it is both conceptually flawed and empirically misleading to speak of a unitary 'British model' or 'ASBO nation' that governs populations through sanctioning anti-social behaviour, particularly when the impact of the devolved polities of the UK on policy responses to crime and disorder is recognised.

A larger challenge for research and policy in this field is to explore both the broader conditions of social integration, which explain the generation of these new forms of disordering, and their anti-social consequences, as lived experiences for the populations most ravaged by the loss of old stabilities around previous divisions of labour at the workplace and in the home. To paraphrase Paul Willis (1977), what does it mean, especially for young men, to 'learn *not* to labour', given their actual and prospective ejection from stable, full-time employment?

Conclusion

Throughout the discussion in this chapter it has been argued that any adequate social scientific interpretation of both the broad trends and specific realisations of community safety must centre on the following issues:

- The distinction between security and safety talk, decisions and actions: specifically, the gap between intended governmental projects and their actual outcomes.

- The role of relations of power-dependence between (would-be) sovereign actors in causing gaps between talk, decisions and actions.

- The consequent political struggles over safety and security and their uneven outcomes in particular places and moments or geo-historical contexts.

Our discussion of current tendencies and consequences, and their interpretation, suggests that the field of community safety is marked by contradictory and unstable forces. Across England and Wales we currently lack a systematic comparative research programme into the kind of security politics produced by community safety work, at both national and subnational levels, and especially across English localities. That noted, the rediscovery of political agency implied by the concept of geo-historical context makes visible and salient the ongoing struggles to govern. The outcomes of these struggles derive from the diverse as well as comparable political, economic and cultural trajectories found in 'British' localities.

Notes

1 Following the Assembly election in May 2007 the department was restructured and renamed the Department of Social Justice and Local Government. Community safety remains within this department. The emphasis on social rather than criminal justice approaches to reducing crime and disorder is, if anything, likely to be further enhanced following the agreement, in July 2007, between the Labour Party and Plaid Cymru (the nationalist party of Wales that adopts a relatively left-wing stance on social policy issues including those of crime and disorder) to form a coalition government.
2 A reference to *Y Ddraig Goch* or the Red Dragon that is the national symbol of Wales.

References

Beecham, J. (2006) *Beyond Boundaries: A Review of Service Delivery* (Beecham Report). Cardiff: Welsh Assembly Government.

Clarke, J. (2004) *Changing Welfare, Changing States*. London: Sage.

Clarke, R. V. and Eck, J. (2003) *Become a Problem-Solving Crime Analyst in 55 Small Steps*. London: Jill Dando Institute, University College London.

Coleman, R. (2004) *Reclaiming the Streets: Surveillance, Social Control and the City*. Cullompton: Willan Publishing.

Coleman, R. (2005) 'Surveillance in the City: Primary Definition and Urban Spatial Order', *Crime, Media and Culture*, 1(2): 131–48.

Coleman, R., Sim, J. and Whyte, D. (2002) 'Power, Politics and Partnerships: The State of Crime Prevention on Merseyside', in G. Hughes and A. Edwards (eds) *Crime Control and Community: The New Politics of Public Safety*. Cullompton: Willan Publishing, pp. 86–108.

Crawford, A. (1997) *The Local Governance of Crime: Appeals to Community and Partnerships*. Oxford: Clarendon Press.

Crawford, A. (2002) 'The Governance of Crime and Insecurity in an Anxious Age: The Trans-European and the Local', in A. Crawford (ed.) *Crime and Insecurity*. Cullompton: Willian Publishing, pp. 27–51.

Crawford, A. (2006) 'Networked Governance and the Post-Regulatory State?', *Theoretical Criminology*, 10(4): 449–79.

Crawford, A. (2007) 'Crime Prevention and Community Safety', in M. Maguire, R. Morgan and R. Reiner (eds) *The Oxford Handbook of Criminology*, 4th edn. Oxford: Oxford University Press, pp. 866–909.

Deleuze, G. and Guattari, F. (1987) *A Thousand Plateaus: Capitalism and Schizopherenia*. Minnesota: University of Minnesota Press.

Downes, D. and Morgan, R. (1994) '"Hostages to Fortune"? The Politics of Law and Order in Post-War Britain', in M. Maguire, R. Morgan and R. Reiner (eds) *The Oxford Handbook of Criminology*. Oxford: Oxford University Press, pp. 183–232.

Downes, D. and Morgan, R. (2002) 'The Skeletons in the Cupboard: The Politics of Law and Order at the Turn of the Millennium', in M. Maguire, R. Morgan and R. Reiner (eds) *The Oxford Handbook of Criminology*, 3rd edn. Oxford: Oxford University Press, pp. 286–321.

Edwards, A. and Hughes, G. (2002) 'Introduction: The New Community Governance of Crime Control', in G. Hughes and A. Edwards (eds) *Crime Control and Community: The New Politics of Public Safety*. Cullompton: Willan Publishing, pp. 1–19.

Edwards, A. and Hughes, G. (2005a) 'Editorial', *Theoretical Criminology*, 9(3): 259–63.

Edwards, A. and Hughes, G. (2005b) 'Comparing the Governance of Safety in Europe: A Geo-historical Approach', *Theoretical Criminology*, 9(3): 345–63.

Edwards, A. and Hughes, G. (2008a) 'Inventing Community Safety', in P. Carlen (ed.) *Imaginary Penalities*. Cullompton: Willan Publishing.

Edwards, A. and Hughes, G. (2008b) 'Resilient Fabians? Anti-social Behaviour and Community Safety Work in Wales', in P. Squires (ed.) *ASBO Nation*. Bristol, Policy Press, pp. 57–72.

Edwards, A. and Hughes, G. (2008c) *The Changing Role of the Community Safety Officer in Wales*. Cardiff: WACSO/Cardiff University.

Foster, J. (2002) '"People Pieces": The Neglected but Essential Elements of Community Crime Prevention', in G. Hughes, and A. Edwards (eds) *Crime Control and Community: The New Politics of Public Safety*. Cullompton: Willan Publishing, pp. 167–97.

Foucault, M. (1991) 'On Governmentality', in G. Burchell, C. Gordon and P. Miller (eds) *The Foucault Effect: Studies in Governmentality*. Hemel Hempstead: Harvester Wheatsheaf, pp. 87–104.

Garland, D. (1996) 'The Limits of the Sovereign State: Strategies of Crime Control in Contemporary Society', *British Journal of Criminology*, 35(4): 445–71.

Garland, D. (2001) *The Culture of Control*. Oxford: Oxford University Press.

Gilling, D. (1997) *Crime Prevention: Theory, Policy and Politics*. London: UCL Press.

Gilling, D. (2007) *Crime Reduction and Community Safety: Labour and the Politics of Local Crime Control*. Cullompton: Willan Publishing.

Haggerty, K. and Ericson, R. (2000) 'The Surveillant Assemblage', *British Journal of Sociology*, 51(4): 605–22.

Hallsworth, S. (2002) 'Representations and Realities in Local Crime Prevention: Some Lessons from London and Lessons for Criminology', in G. Hughes and A. Edwards (eds) *Crime Control and Community: The New Politics of Public Safety*. Cullompton: Willan Publishing, pp. 197–215.

Hallsworth, S. (2008) 'Interpreting Violent Street Worlds', Inaugural lecture, Department of Applied Social Sciences, London Metropolitan University, 27th February.

Home Office (1991) *Safer Communities: The Local Delivery of Crime Prevention Through the Partnership Approach* (Morgan Report). London: Home Office.

Hughes, G. (1998) *Understanding Crime Prevention*. Buckingham: Open University Press.

Hughes, G. (2002) 'Plotting the Rise of Community Safety: Critical Reflections on Research, Theory and Practice', in G. Hughes and A. Edwards (eds) *Crime Control and Community: The New Politics of Public Safety*. Cullompton: Willan Publishing, pp. 20–45.

Hughes, G. (2007) *The Politics of Crime and Community*. London: Palgrave.

Hughes, G. (2009) 'Community Safety and the Governance of Problem Populations', in G. Mooney and S. Neal (eds) *Community*. Maidenhead: McGraw Hill, pp. 99–134.

Hughes, G. and Edwards, A. (eds) (2002) *Crime Control and Community: The New Politics of Public Safety*. Cullompton: Willan Publishing.

Hughes, G. and Edwards, A. (2005) 'Crime Prevention in Context', in N. Tilley (ed.) *Handbook of Crime Prevention and Community Safety*. Cullompton: Willan Publishing, pp. 14–34.

Hughes, G. and Gilling, D. (2004) '"Mission Impossible"': The Habitus of the Community Safety Manager', *Criminal Justice*, 4(2): 129–49.

Hughes, G. and Rowe, M. (2007) 'Neighbourhood Policing and Community Safety: Researching the Instabilities of the Local Governance of Crime, Disorder and Safety in Contemporary UK', *Criminology and Criminal Justice*, 7(4): 315–46.

Hughes, G., McLaughlin, E. and Muncie, J. (eds) (2002) *Crime Prevention and Community Safety: New Directions*, London: Sage.

Hughes, G. *et al.* (forthcoming) *Youth Crime Prevention in Wales: A National Evaluation of the Safer Communities Fund*. Cardiff: Welsh Assembly Government.

Johnston, L. and Shearing, C. (2003) *The Governance of Security*. London: Routledge.

McLaughlin, E., Muncie, J. and Hughes, G. (2001) 'The Permanent Revolution', *Criminal Justice*, 1(3): 301–18.

Matthews, R. and Young, J. (eds) (2003) *The New Politics of Crime and Punishment*. Cullompton: Willan Publishing.

Pollitt, C. (2001) 'Convergence: A Useful Myth', *Public Administration*, 79(4): 933–47.

Rhodes, R. (1997) *Understanding Governance*. Buckingham: Open University Press.

Rose, N. (1999) *Powers of Freedom: Reframing Political Thought*. Cambridge: Cambridge University Press.

Rose, N. (2000) 'Government and Control', *British Journal of Criminology*, 40: 321–39.

Scraton, P. (2003) 'Defining Power and Changing "Knowledge": Critical Analysis as Resistance in the UK', in K. Carrington and R. Hogg (eds) *Critical Criminology*. Cullompton: Willan Publishing, pp. 15–40.

Smandych, R. (ed.) (1999) *Governable Places: Readings on Governmentality and Crime Control*. Dartmouth: Ashgate.

Squires, P. (2008) *ASBO Nation*. Bristol: Policy Press.

Stenson, K. (2002) 'Community Safety in Middle England: The Local Politics of Crime Control', in G. Hughes and A. Edwards (eds) *Crime Control and Community: The New Politics of Public Safety*. Cullompton: Willan Publishing, pp. 109–39.

Stenson, K. and Edwards, A. (2004) 'Policy Transfer in Local Crime Control: Beyond Naive Emulation', in T. Newburn and R. Sparks (eds) *Criminal Justice and Political Cultures: National and International Dimensions of Crime Control.* Cullompton: Willan Publishing, pp. 209–33.

Tombs, S., Croall, H. and Whyte, D. (2007) *Safety Crimes.* Cullompton: Willan Publishing.

Tonry, M. (2004) *Punishment and Politics: Evidence and Emulation in the Making of English Crime Control Policy.* Cullompton: Willan Publishing.

Willis, P. (1977) *Learning to Labour.* Farnborough: Saxon House.

Young, J. (2004) 'Voodoo Criminology and the Numbers Game', in J. Ferrell, K. Hayward., W. Morrison and M. Presdee (eds) *Cultural Criminology Unleashed.* London: Glasshouse.

Chapter 4

The development of community safety in Scotland: a different path?

Alistair Henry

Introduction

The various contributions to this collection ably demonstrate the differences and the similarities in the ways in which community safety has developed throughout Europe. It may be surprising to some to see a separate chapter on Scotland, however. As a constituent part of the United Kingdom it might be expected that developments in Scotland would simply mimic those of its larger, and more thoroughly researched, neighbour. One of the aims of this chapter is to show that such an assumption should be treated with a degree of caution. Despite the fact that formal constitutional arrangements meant that Scotland was governed by a Westminster Parliament following the 1707 Acts of Union, the practice of government was, to an important degree, retained within Scotland. The absence of a Scottish parliament between 1707 and 1999 has thus often masked the fact that Scotland retained a substantial amount of autonomy within the Union, and with this autonomy came the *potential* that Scotland could, and would, do some things differently from its neighbour.

However, one should be wary of overstating the differences that emerged between the two countries. If one looks at the development of community safety in Scotland since the 1980s, for example, one sees much that will be familiar to those aware of developments in England and Wales over the same period. Indeed, wider developments in the field of criminal justice including, but not restricted to, community safety show strong similarities with developments in England and Wales, and elsewhere in Europe, over this period. That said, the development of community safety has not followed an identical trajectory in Scotland. The sections of the Crime and Disorder Act 1998 that established the statutory infrastructure of community safety in England and Wales were not implemented north of the border, and so marked a clear point of divergence between the systems. Although the statutory infrastructure that has subsequently evolved in Scotland does send out some contradictory messages it will be argued that, for the moment at least, it can be seen as giving some emphasis to a fairly broad social justice, rather than an unnecessarily narrow criminal justice, agenda. The chapter concludes by offering some speculations on the likely near-future development of community safety in Scotland.

The autonomy of small nations in Europe: the case of Scotland

Scotland has been the anomaly that has made an ostensibly unitary state, an archetype of 'nation state' in certain political-theoretical terms, function internally in a markedly federal way. This has been hitherto a federalism of political management and judicial separation rather than a federalism of constitutional form. (MacCormick 1999: 60)

In May 1999 a newly elected Scottish Parliament sat in Edinburgh for the first time since the 1707 Acts of Union had established Great Britain, with its single parliament based at Westminster. The setting up of a parliament in Scotland had been a manifesto pledge of the incoming New Labour administration that took power in 1997. The subsequent referendum showed strong support for this formal devolution of government to Scotland, support that had been growing since the 1960s at least, and seemed to have strengthened throughout the Thatcher and Major administrations between 1979 and 1997 (Hirst 1989; Paterson 1994; McCrone 2001). Nationalist sentiment and calls for 'home rule' were not, however, new to this period and can be spotted sporadically, albeit with different levels of support, throughout the period of the Union (Donaldson 1969; McCrone 1992). What was new was the resounding support for formal constitutional recognition of Scotland's status as a nation with the capacity to govern itself – demands that have been articulated in other nations within nation states (such as Quebec in Canada and Catalonia in Spain) over roughly the same period (Tierney 2005; MacInnes and McCrone 2001). However, the re-establishment of a Scottish Parliament should not mask the fact that Scotland retained an important degree of autonomy as a country *prior* to this recent constitutional settlement. Although the United Kingdom may have been viewed as an archetype example of the homogeneous, unitary nation-state this was, in fact, something of a myth (Midwinter *et al.* 1991; McCrone 1992; MacCormick 1999). The purpose of this section of the chapter is to provide a brief account of Scotland's long-term autonomy, as it is with this in mind that the *potential* for developments in community safety to have been distinctive from those in England and Wales can be understood.

Scotland's autonomy was enshrined within the Acts of Union from the outset. The Union was intended to be 'an incorporating but not an assimilating union' (Midwinter *et al.* 1991: 3). It was incorporating both in the sense that it formally dissolved the old Scottish and English parliaments and created the unitary sovereign Parliament of Great Britain (arguably an incorporation of the Scottish parliament into the ongoing English parliament) (Midwinter *et al.* 1991: 2; MacCormick 1999: 57–8) and in that it freed up economic exchange between the two nations, creating a single British market with a single currency (MacCormick 1999: 52). However, although the Treaty did create this new British state architecture it also explicitly retained important aspects of Scottish civil society, 'those institutions which operate in the public domain but are not part of government' and which 'include economic institutions, professions and other self-governing institutions' (Midwinter *et al.* 1991: 3). Three domains of civil society are given particular prominence in analyses of post-union Scottish autonomy, identity and politics: the legal system, the church and education (see Midwinter *et al.* 1991: 9–14; McCrone 1992, 2001; Paterson 1994; Young 1996). Where it is true that all of these institutions would come under criticism for being Anglicised at various points, it remains the case that their organisational and institutional development, and the social and professional worlds inhabited by the people within them, remained, to varying degrees, separate from those of their counterparts in England and Wales. This institutional separation, which also applied to other spheres of central and local government and administration, would allow for the survival of distinctive Scottish values and traditions among those who were, to an important degree, governing the nation (McCrone 1992: 23; Paterson 1994: 131).

> If we ask why Scotland can still be recognised as distinct at the end of the twentieth century, the answer is much the same as would be given for any small European country: the character of a society is conditioned more by the daily interactions of human beings, drawing on a common history, than by the broad sweep of enabling legislation. If the state does have an influence in this respect, it is through the direct contact which people have with it – through its professional staff such as teachers or social workers or bureaucrats . . . in Scotland, these professionals operated according to Scottish traditions and rules. (Paterson 1994: 130–1)

Thus, Scotland retained a capacity for distinctiveness because it maintained a distinctive institutional apparatus within which cadres of professionals and bureaucrats worked according to Scottish traditions and ways of doing things (Paterson 1994: chapter 3; Phillipson 1976). McCrone has gone so far as to argue that, particularly following the move of the Scottish Office to Edinburgh in 1939, Scotland had incrementally evolved its own distinctive welfare state structures and that by the 1970s it could be characterised as a 'semi-state with powerful administrative apparatus' (1992: 22). The architecture of government that had evolved was only scrutinized by Parliament at Westminster to a limited degree (Midwinter *et al.* 1991: chapter 4) as much of its work was policy implementation rather than development. Government in Scotland had become a 'technocracy' run by Scottish Office civil servants and officials, interest groups and policy networks populated by members of Scotland's separate civil society institutions, and the growing body of public sector professionals created by the welfare state, including doctors, teachers and social workers (Paterson 1994: 103). This did not mean that policy in Scotland would *necessarily* be much different from that in England and Wales, it merely created a possibility that it could be. Keating's argument that Westminster's sovereignty over setting the 'goals' of government was fundamental, because Scottish autonomy in choosing the 'means' through which policy would be implemented would ultimately be limited by the parameters of these goals (2001: 97–8), is a reminder that Scottish autonomy, though real, should not be overstated and was not without constraints. Indeed, one of the striking features of much of the twentieth century was that there was a high degree of agreement about the fundamental objectives of government among politicians and bureaucrats in both Scotland and England and Wales. The development of the welfare state was an endeavour based upon considerable political consensus about the role of the state in maintaining a healthy and active population, full employment and political emancipation and entitlements (Paterson 1994: 104–6). There are examples of different approaches to policy implementation being taken, even in this period of relative consensus over governmental goals (such as in relation to economic development, planning and housing policy, see Paterson 1994: 117–23), and studies have provided evidence of Scottish distinctiveness in relation to several important social dimensions, including national identity, voting patterns, party political affiliation, health and education (McCrone 1992, 2001); however, the welfare project underpinned similarities that would characterise Scotland and England and Wales for much of the last century.

Although difference is not a necessary outcome of autonomy it *can* provide evidence of it. It is of particular relevance to the present discussion that the Scottish legal system remained institutionally separate from the system in England and Wales, and that it retained and developed its own distinguishing features, some of which are summarised below:

- *Criminal courts.* The structure and organisation of the courts differs markedly in Scotland from England and Wales (Young 1997). Although the House of Lords acts as a court of final appeal in Scottish civil cases, it has no such jurisdiction in relation to criminal matters where the High Court of Justiciary acts in this capacity (Himsworth 2007: 35). The Constitution Reform Act 2005 established a Supreme Court of the United Kingdom as a court of last resort on constitutional matters. The consultation that preceded the Act was contentious as there were concerns that a Supreme Court could threaten the autonomy of Scots law in general, and the High Court of Justiciary in particular (Himsworth and Paterson 2004), but the long-term impact that it will have on the three independent legal systems in the UK (England and Wales, Northern Ireland and Scotland) remains to be seen (Himsworth 2007: 37–40).

- *Criminal court procedure.* Despite criminal court procedure being formally adversarial, as it is in England and Wales (Gane 1999), it also contains features, such as the intermediate diet where the judge plays an active role in assessing preparedness of council to proceed, that some commentators have considered to be more inquisitorial in nature (Young 1996; McCallum and Duff 2000).

- *Prosecution.* Scotland has long had a system of public prosecution through the independent office of the Procurator Fiscal which, even following the establishment of the Crown Prosecution Service in England and Wales, has arguably more in common with systems of prosecution on the Continent (Duff 1999).

- *Criminal justice social work.* The Social Work (Scotland) Act 1968 controversially closed down the specialist Scottish Probation Service in favour of having criminal justice social work provided through more generic social work services (McIvor and Williams 1999:199–200; Schaffer 1980: 40). Although there is evidence that criminal justice social work has become increasingly specialised within Social Work Departments (and so personnel may have rather less generic social work experience than would have been envisaged) it remains the case that personnel who undertake criminal justice social work services identify themselves as social workers, and generally espouse the outlook and penal welfare values of social workers (even in the face of alternative discourses, such as public protection, see McNeil and Whyte 2007: 21–30).

- *Children's Hearings and youth justice.* The Children's Hearing system is arguably the most distinctive feature of Scottish criminal justice process. Set up under the Social Work (Scotland) Act 1968, Children's Hearings were based on the understanding that there was no difference between young people who offended and those who were in need of social support and/or intervention. According to the report of the Kilbrandon

Committee (which informed much of the 1968 Act) offending was simply a consequence or manifestation of wider social problems in the young person's environment and so addressing these problems was central to addressing offending behaviour. Therefore, when youth courts were abolished and the Children's Hearings system established in 1971, Scotland had essentially adopted an explicitly welfarist approach to youth justice at precisely the moment that such approaches were coming under direct attack south of the border (McAra 2004: 27–32; Whyte 2003).

The distinctive features of Scottish criminal justice serve to illustrate the potential for difference between Scotland and England and Wales. It has further been argued that the period between the Kilbrandon Report (the 1960s) and the mid 1990s can be characterised as one in which divergence between the criminal justice systems of Scotland and England and Wales became particularly acute, the former retaining a much stronger commitment to the values of penal welfarism than the latter (McAra 2004, 2005). This was a period in which political sentiment in Scotland was noticeably out of kilter with the rest of the UK – the Thatcher and Major administrations never enjoyed a political mandate in Scotland (see McCrone 2001: chapter 5) – resulting in Scottish elites adopting an 'other than England' position when it came to policy development and implementation (McAra 2007). This period of divergence was not to last, however, and would swiftly be followed by a period in which there would be evidence of considerable convergence of criminal justice policy. The development of community safety in Scotland, and this complex and contradictory policy environment in which it occurred, will now be examined.

The development of community safety and partnerships in Scotland: a familiar tale?

The story of the development of community safety in Scotland since the 1980s is one that will be very familiar to those who have observed England and Wales over the same period. Although the chapter *will* move on to identify and examine some features of the organisation and structure of community safety and partnership working in Scotland that are distinctive from how things have evolved south of the border, it is the similarities between the jurisdictions that will be made apparent in this section. In fact, the story in Scotland also has striking similarities with developments throughout Europe. The 'cluster of central themes' that Crawford sees as characterising policy responses to insecurity throughout Europe (see Chapter 1, this volume) are all visible within the Scottish context.

Recent accounts of the development of crime prevention and community safety within the Scottish police often take the setting up of Juvenile Liaison Schemes in the 1950s as their starting point (Schaffer 1980; Monaghan 1997; Fyfe 2005). The first Scottish scheme was set up in Greenock in 1956 (it had been tried some years earlier in Liverpool), a force that quickly developed a reputation for innovative community policing (Schaffer 1980: 68–72; Fyfe 2005: 109–10). Further schemes were later set up in the towns of Coatbridge, Kilmarnock, Paisley and Perth (as well as in Stirling and Clackmannan police districts) (see Mack 1963: 361) and they would soon form part of the work of all Scottish police forces. The Juvenile Liaison Scheme was undoubtedly interesting as it involved police officers working closely with a range of other local social services and community members (including schools, probation officers, ministers, local businesses and families themselves) in order to supervise and monitor young people who had been identified as being engaged in what would probably be described as 'anti-social behaviour' in modern parlance – problematic and disruptive behaviour that might be a minor offence in itself, or could be viewed as evidence that the young person was out of family control and 'at risk' of engaging in future offending (Schaffer 1980: 30–1; Monaghan 1997: 25). As such, the Juvenile Liaison Scheme was both an early attempt to highlight the importance of multi-agency co-operation and an articulated recognition that the police alone did not necessarily control all of the means through which to prevent crime. It was also 'part of a wider project of crime and delinquency prevention' that, at this point, was particularly focused on the impact of urban decay on young people and crime rates (Mack 1963: 367; Monaghan 1997: 27), an area of concern that would continue to shape developments in the future.

The approach of the Juvenile Liaison Schemes would not, however, receive universal support within the Scottish police, mirroring debates about the role of the police and the meaning of 'crime prevention' that have also been documented in England and Wales (Crawford 1997). One of the aims of the Juvenile Liaison Scheme had been to keep young people out of formal criminal justice process (in this way it sat quite comfortably with the Kilbrandon philosophy discussed earlier), and there is evidence that it was quite successful in this respect (Mack 1963: 367–8). The Royal Commission on Police in Scotland (which reported in 1962) would also give some thought as to what the nature of, and priority to be given to, crime prevention ought to be – was it to be achieved through effective detection and prosecution of crimes, through better community involvement and liaison, or with reference to proactive physical and social crime prevention measures (Monaghan 1997: 27)? Basically, the Commission weighed up the relative value of proactive measures (such as juvenile liaison and community involvement) against reactive policing (law enforcement and prosecution). Monaghan observed that the Commission did not come to any clear conclusions on this matter and defined the functions of the Scottish police in broad terms that were interpretable either way (1997: 27).[1] The point is that in large part the police themselves continued to give emphasis to the reactive role of police as crime-fighters, and considered proactive and community-based work as being 'social work' and certainly not 'real' police work (Schaffer 1980: 26). Culturally this meant that the Scottish police (like their English colleagues) gave priority and status to work that produced 'results' (in the form of arrests and/or convictions) and would come to think of crime prevention in such terms. The generally low numbers of police officers involved in specialist crime prevention work, despite it becoming a focus of policy, continued into the 1990s, and it was found to be a relatively marginal activity within the organisation by Her Majesty's Inspectorate of Constabulary as late as 1995 (Monaghan 1997: 31).

Despite this internal resistance within the police there would continue to be important developments that would give emphasis to more proactive and multi-agency forms of crime prevention. For example, the Scottish Home and Health Department's 1971 circular (4/71) sought to develop community relations work through the recommendation that specialist community involvement branches be established (Schaffer 1980: 47–8). After the 1975 rationalisation of the Scottish police there were found to be community involvement branches in all eight of the newly established forces (there had previously been 22) (Monaghan 1997: 29). It remains unclear how active all of these community involvement branches actually were in practice, but there is evidence that some of them were active and took the role seriously. For example, the newly established Strathclyde police force set up a working party to develop the community involvement role (Schaffer 1980: 48). It understood 'crime prevention' in much broader terms than just 'law enforcement', distinguishing between physical measures (from target-hardening to being involved in architectural design), social measures (with a particular focus on working with young people and the Children's Hearing system, but also including working with schools and in deprived urban neighbourhoods) and community relations (which it described as being about maintaining good contacts with various local services and local government, noting, interestingly, that 'race relations present no problem in Strathclyde') (Schaffer 1980: 47–8).

Similar themes were also found within the often quite contemporary sounding report of the Scottish Council on Crime from 1975. It was possible to argue that the report rather played down the potential role of opportunity reduction and physical crime prevention to act as anything other than a short-term solution, but it was nonetheless interesting that such measures, coupled with the idea that they needed to be implemented by communities themselves (citizens, businesses and so on) were already well in evidence (see Scottish Council on Crime 1975). It was also interesting that the report gave some emphasis to the importance of 'social' causes of crime (defined as poverty, bad housing, family upbring-ing and unemployment) as key to long-term crime prevention, even if it did so with a caveat that rising crime could not easily be attributed to social factors alone (1975: 22–3). Taking such an approach again meant that the Council was inclined to conclude that crime prevention would ultimately require the co-operation of a wide range of social services, government bodies, community representatives and local people them-selves – it was not a task for any single agency (1975: 22). Even though the report did move on to give some consideration to the potential role of penal sanctions and treatment-based disposals in crime prevention (doing so with quite a critical eye as to the efficacy of the latter, chiming with the emerging 'nothing works' cynicism of this period; see para. 53 of the report), it did not take too police-centred a view of crime prevention, seeing the police as but one element of a larger network of governmental and informal social control, a view that has become much more widely accepted in recent years (Loader 2000).

By the early 1980s it would appear that there was quite a lot of multi-agency work going on in Scotland that saw the police working with schools, social workers, local businesses, churches, architects, town planners, local government and a developing network of local crime prevention panels (which were themselves populated by local interested parties) (Schaffer 1980). Some of the problems inherent in multi-agency working, such as the difficulty in getting local people involved and taking ownership of projects, and the related problem of the same faces turning up to get involved every time, were already recognised (Schaffer 1980: 74). However, despite some focused strategies in the 1980s that would continue to emphasise partnership working (which will be outlined shortly), it remained uncertain as to how much, if at all, partnership working or crime prevention initiatives were having an impact on the ground. The Central Research Unit's *Directory of Crime Prevention Initiat-ives in Scotland* (Valentin 1995) showed that there was a lot of work out there, but that it was developing sporadically, under different auspices (some were police-led initiatives, others were led by crime prevention panels, others appeared to be run by some form of partnership), and with different visions of 'crime prevention' (there was a mix of situational and social projects). Very little of it appeared to have been evaluated and so it is difficult to make anything but quite cautious claims about the extent to which crime prevention and community safety in practice in Scotland was different, if at all, from that in England and Wales. The co-ordination of these piecemeal developments would become all the more important over the 1990s as a potentially overlapping set of partnership structures evolved.

Not only did the Scottish Home and Health Department circular 6/84, much like its counterpart in England and Wales issued six months earlier, reiterate a commitment to the shared responsibility for crime prevention and the need, therefore, for a multi-agency response to it, it also indicated something of a shift in thinking about crime prevention towards the situational (Bottoms 1990). By this time the influence of the Home Office Research Unit, and the powerful research that it was producing (Clarke and Mayhew 1980), was clearly being felt in Scotland. For Monaghan this represented an example of anti-welfarist sentiment having an impact upon Scottish policy (1997: 35). That said, the conception of crime prevention that continued to be articulated in Scotland throughout the 1980s also gave emphasis to the perceived link between the socio-economic decline of urban centres and housing estates ('impossible communities'), the rising crime problem, and wider concerns about problem young people (Schaffer 1980: 78–80). The Safer Neighbourhood schemes organised by SACRO in 1986, although similar to earlier work conducted in England and Wales by NACRO (Bottoms 1990: 5, 9–10) reflected this, as did 1988's *New Life for Urban Scotland*, a partnership-based initiative which actively sought to involve local communities and the private sector in urban redevelopment. At this point in late 1980s Scotland 'crime prevention . . . was set within the wider context of urban regeneration' (Monaghan 1997: 35). The next series of multi-agency initiatives, in the form of the Safer Cities projects, would continue with this tendency to nest crime prevention within broader policy concerns, and would also see community safety emerge as a more widely used term.

The Scottish Office announced its Safer Cities programme in 1989, again following the lead of the Home Office which had announced its programme the previous year. Four Scottish projects were initially set up, in Central Edinburgh, Castlemilk (Glasgow), Greater Easterhouse (Glasgow) and North East Dundee, with a fifth project being added in Aberdeen in 1992 (see Carnie 1996). All of the projects continued to be situated within the logic of urban regeneration to the extent that one of their objectives was to 'create safer cities in which economic enterprise and community life could flourish' (Carnie 1999: 76). However, the Safer Cities programmes, on both sides of the border, were also more explicitly focused on crime and fear of crime issues than previous initiatives, and had, from the outset at least, an orientation that favoured the use of situational crime prevention measures over more social (or welfare-based) measures (Pease 1997; Carnie 1999). This orientation, despite being favoured by government officials and many Home Office researchers at the time (Ekblom 1995), would not be accepted unreservedly by the local practitioners who would end up running the projects. For example, Carnie found that the Castlemilk Safer Cities project had been able to negotiate a broad community safety agenda that understood crime prevention in social welfare terms (1999: 77–8). It had been able to do this because the multi-agency group that would develop the agenda pre-existed its Safer Cities status and was already working with this broader perspective. This was not the case with the other projects, but even there situational measures would be balanced with social initiatives (Carnie 1999: 79–82). Indeed, analyses of projects throughout Scotland and England and Wales found that there tended to be a movement towards social measures and away from purely situational measures throughout the lives of projects (Pease 1997: 982). The reason for this seemed to be that local practitioners, in both jurisdictions, favoured what they saw as more 'holistic' and 'long-term' solutions to crime prevention (i.e. social measures), and remained unconvinced that situational measures would produce much else other than displacement (Pease 1997; Gilling 1997). This was despite the fact that there was evidence that working with the less clearly defined social measures was often the source of disagreement and conflict within partnerships, whereas situational measures were more clearly defined, their effects also being more readily measurable (Gilling 1994). The Safer Cities projects certainly suggested that 'community safety' seemed to be a more politically attractive rallying call than 'crime prevention', despite its shortcomings (Gilling 1997; Carnie 1999). In any case the evaluations would prove to be sufficiently positive to ensure that the commitment to multi-agency work would not only continue, but would gather momentum.

The Scottish Office's strategy document *Preventing Crime Together in Scotland: A Strategy for the 1990s* (1992) emerged just as internal developments within central government (including the setting up of a Crime Prevention Unit within the Scottish Office in the same year) were serving to underline the increasing importance being given to crime prevention (see Monaghan 1997: 34–9). The document continued to extol the virtues of the partnership approach to problem-solving that would be taken up, or would develop, in a range of social policy areas by the end of the decade. Interestingly, the document was quite clear about the importance of local government to the development of 'holistic' crime prevention strategies, in contrast to what Monaghan had seen as active attempts to exclude it throughout the preceding decade, and in the Safer Cities experiments specifically where appointed co-ordinators came from the Scottish Office or organisations such as Crime Concern, but not from local government (1997: 39; Carnie 1996, 1999). It was also clear that the intention was that the resources to develop crime prevention partnership work would have to come from the reallocation of existing local government funds, rather than from additional streams of funding. This was just prior to a substantial reorganisation of local government structures in both Scotland and in England and Wales (McCrone 2001), so it is perhaps not surprising that developments in partnership work seem to have been piecemeal at best in this period of uncertainty (Craig and Manthorpe 1999). Partnerships would continue to receive core support through resource reallocation and 'in kind' (i.e. through local authority and police commitments to provide designated community safety officers to develop strategies) for around another decade, although additional pots of Challenge Fund monies would also be available through competitive tender competitions for specific initiatives (such as CCTV). More sustainable core annual funding for community safety partnerships was only introduced in 2002 (Scottish Executive 2002, 2003, 2005), but since the election of a new administration to Holyrood (the Scottish National Party) in May 2007 future funding arrangements for community safety have again become uncertain.

The turning point in England and Wales occurred when local authorities and the police were given statutory duties to develop local crime and disorder reduction partnerships (CDRPs) under the Crime and Disorder Act 1998, thus creating the formal 'infrastructure' within which community safety would develop over the following decade (see Crawford 2007: 893–5). These sections of the Act did not apply to Scotland, possibly because devolution was in the air and it was felt that the creation of such responsibilities should lie with a future Scottish Parliament. This is not to say, however, that the position in Scotland was necessarily so different in practice. The importance, and possible benefits, of working in partnership would be emphasised in a number of high-profile documents produced in the late 1990s. *Community Safety: A Key Council Strategy* (1997) is of particular interest in that it was published by the Convention of Scottish Local Authorities (CoSLA – a body that represents the interests of local government in Scotland), articulated a broad view of community safety partnership work (ranging from CCTV to youth cafés to intergenerational problems to fire and road safety), and, among others, gave the new administration's manifesto commitment to community safety and its affinity with the 'Best Value' agenda as key reasons for local authorities to engage with community safety. CoSLA would also, along with the Association of Chief Police Officers Scotland (ACPOS), contribute to the Scottish Executive's *Safer Communities in Scotland* (1999), designed to play a not dissimilar role to the guidance material for new CDRPs issued by the Home Office, in that it was about giving advice to the police and local authorities about how they should go about setting up partnership structures (it included sections on conducting community safety audits, monitoring programmes and evaluating initiatives). So even though partnership remained non-statutory north of the border the level of encouragement to develop such strategies was such that it is questionable whether it actually remained genuinely 'voluntary'. Certainly by the end of the decade all 32 of the Scottish local authorities were involved in some kind of community safety-related multi-agency work, even though much of it remained, disappointingly, 'at a very early stage of development' (Accounts Commission 2000a: 2; 2000b; Hewitt et al. 2000).

It should also be noted at this point that partnership working in Scotland (and England and Wales too) was being extolled as a virtue in a wide range of other, often related, policy fields. One of the first things that Donald Dewar, the incoming Secretary of State for Scotland, did upon the

election of the New Labour administration in 1997 was issue a consultation paper on the problem of social exclusion in Scotland (Scottish Office
1998). Social exclusion was defined to incorporate a wide social welfare
agenda that made explicit reference to community safety, but also
identified poor housing and urban decay, unemployment and low levels
of marketable skills, the lack of resources for children and young people,
ill health and inequitable access to transport, as means through which
citizens were effectively prevented from fully participating in public life.
As with urban regeneration before it, crime prevention and community
safety were being nested within a broader social welfare agenda. Social
Inclusion Partnerships (SIPs) emerged throughout the UK in the late 1990s
and a substantial amount of work continues to be done under its rubric
(Scottish Executive 2007), including the development of community-based
interventions that may impact on offending (see Bannister and Dillane
2005). Without entering into a larger discussion of what is a substantial
area of social policy in its own right, the central point to be made here is
that by the end of the twentieth century there was a plethora of
partnership structures in Scotland (for example, community safety, social
inclusion, partnerships for parenting, lifelong learning partnerships),
many of which could potentially overlap in various ways. If one took a
broad enough view of 'crime prevention' all of these partnerships could
be deemed to have a role to play. The desire to co-ordinate the work of
this patchwork of partnerships, and avoid overlap and duplication of
effort, would find expression in community planning, the development of
which has played an important role in shaping the infrastructure of
community safety in Scotland (see below).

The development of community safety in Scotland can thus be seen as
having followed a very similar, but not identical, trajectory to that of
England and Wales. There are arguments to be made that the size of the
jurisdiction, the rural character of much of it, and the history of officials
and community members working in partnership in other fields (such as
economic development, see Paterson 1994: 117–23) gave developments
something of a more consensual and social welfare-oriented edge than
was the case south of the border, but in the absence of rigorous evaluation
and research throughout much of this period such claims ought to be
made with some degree of caution. A picture of similarity also emerges if
one looks at broader developments in criminal justice since the mid 1990s
– the period when, according to McAra (2004, 2005), Scottish and English
divergence came to an end, and convergence became more apparent. By
the early years of the new century both jurisdictions could be characterised as articulating a complicated, and very often contradictory, set of
rationales and values ('punitive, preventative, restorative, actuarial'), all
of which were further justified on the grounds of, and underpinned by, a
commitment to 'scientific rationalism' and the value of evidence-led
policy (McAra 2004: 39–40). Realising that all of the following can be

thought of as features of the recent criminal justice landscape in Scotland gives some sense of this confusion, and the contradictory tendencies that characterise the system (see Garland 1996; Fyfe 2005; McAra 2004; Whyte 2003):

- Zero-tolerance policing
- Anti-social behaviour orders and parenting orders
- Curfews on young people
- Neighbourhood watch
- Children's Hearings
- Youth courts
- Drugs courts
- Risk-assessment and risk-management regimes
- Municipal policing
- Community Wardens Schemes
- Restorative justice programmes
- A growing prison population
- Electronic tagging
- Widespread use of CCTV in public and semi-public spaces
- Growth of the private security sector
- Multi-agency youth teams

However, despite these very apparent similarities the development of community safety in Scotland has not been identical to that in England and Wales. This is best illustrated through reference to the statutory infrastructures that have emerged in both countries, and it is to this that I now turn.

Current developments in the infrastructure of community safety in Scotland: a contradictory tale

The sections of the Crime and Disorder Act 1998 that placed a statutory duty upon local authorities and the police to set up and co-ordinate CDRPs were not implemented in Scotland. It is already clear that this did not mean that calls for partnership working and multi-agency co-operation did not preoccupy Scottish policy-makers throughout the 1990s. However, it did mean that the infrastructure within which community safety developed remained less formal for longer than it did in England and Wales. Indeed, it is only in the last few years that what might be viewed as a statutory infrastructure for community safety has been erected. There are three main pieces of legislation that are of great importance to the current and future development of community safety in Scotland. Taken together they create the infrastructure within which community safety is nested. Whether this infrastructure reflects a distinctive set of value commitments within criminal justice and social policy in Scotland is an altogether more vexed question, upon which I will conclude. The discussion will be organised around the three statutory obligations that have a bearing on the location and future development of community safety in Scotland: community planning, anti-social behaviour and community justice authorities.

Community planning

Community planning was first mooted in Labour Party policy documents on local government in the mid 1990s. The concept was closely linked with current thinking on the Best Value agenda, and the importance of improving local government efficiencies and performance through it. In Scotland five local authorities (Edinburgh, Highland, Perth and Kinross, South Lanarkshire and Stirling) voluntarily became Pathfinder projects in 1998 and developed and published their own Community Plans by December of that year. The Pathfinders were reviewed, in generally favourable terms, by a team from the University of Birmingham that identified four core components underlying the concept of community planning (see Rogers *et al.* 2000: 6–7):

1. *Strategic vision.* Community planning was to be very much about emphasising 'holistic' approaches to social policy. It saw that many of the needs of local communities were interlinked and, as we will see, would also come to be a model through which the existing patchwork of sometimes overlapping partnerships (including community safety and social inclusion as but two examples) could be subjected to increased oversight and co-ordination.

2. *Community consultation and involvement.* The views of the community itself and of local public, private and voluntary agencies were to be sought and, more importantly, they were to be actively involved in the process.

3. *Partnership.* Both planning and implementation were, unsurprisingly, to be done in partnership.

4. *Community leadership.* It was interesting that, despite the emphasis on partnership working, there was nonetheless a view that local government had an especially important role to take in terms of initiating and 'leading' the community planning process. Rogers *et al.* argue that this idea came from the fact that local authorities tapped into local democracy through their elected membership and that they also had

responsibility for the broadest range of social services, and so were best placed to take the lead (2000: 7).

The Birmingham team found that there was 'no basic dispute about the fundamental value of community planning' (Rogers *et al.* 2000: 9) and that there were high levels of goodwill towards the approach from within local government and among partners. More specifically the team found that there was strong support within local government for community planning to be given statutory backing in a manner that would underline the commitment to be given to strategic planning (2000: 19–20). It is interesting to note that local government in England and Wales had been vocal some years earlier (following the influential Morgan Report in 1991) about the need for a statutory duty to underscore partnership commitments (Crawford 1997; Hughes and Edwards 2002), but in Scotland the pressure came in relation to broad and strategic partnership working and without much specific reference to crime prevention or community safety at all (among the Pathfinders only Stirling had community safety as a priority of the community plan; see Rogers *et al.* 2000: 15).

Community planning was given statutory force in the Local Government (Scotland) Act 2003. The Act does articulate the community leadership role of local government through placing the duty to 'initiate' community planning on it (Section 15), although it also places a specific duty on a broad range of other agencies (including health boards, joint police boards, chief constables of the police, joint fire boards, and Scottish Enterprise) to 'participate in community planning' (Section 16). Since the Act, community safety has been placed within the framework of Community Planning as a strategic priority for many of the partners. It sits, therefore, nested among other partnership-based strategic priorities that vary in different community plans, but include social inclusion, partnerships for parenting, healthy communities, social justice, lifelong learning, economic development and sustainability, and environmental planning. It is, of course, the case that CDRPs in England and Wales also developed from and alongside other partnership structures that included urban regeneration and social inclusion (Hughes 2002: 31), but in Scotland the statutory duty itself has given emphasis to the more holistic community planning over the potentially more crime-focused community safety.

Antisocial behaviour

The Antisocial Behaviour (Scotland) Act 2004 largely followed the lead of its English counterpart enacted around a year earlier. There is nothing in this Act that gave a nod to any residual commitment to welfare values. The Act extended the use of anti-social behaviour orders (ASBOs) to young people between the ages of 12 and 16, gave the police increased powers to disperse groups of young people, created community reparation orders, extended the use of electronic monitoring in the community and created parenting orders for parents who were viewed as 'failing' their problematic children (see McAra 2004: 34, 38–9; Walters and Woodward 2007). Recent research has suggested that there was some resistance to the use of some of the orders provided for by the Act. Although use of ASBOs in Scotland has been on the increase since the Act, the extent to which they were actually being used for under 16s, for example, remained unclear, possibly because local authorities were viewing them as a 'last resort' for this group, and continued to favour the Children's Hearings system where possible (Zuleeg *et al.* 2007). Walters and Woodward's (2007) study of local practitioners' attitudes towards parenting orders also found there to be resistance to what was perceived as the 'punitive' language of the Act and its central government sponsors.

Returning to the preoccupations of the present discussion, the 2004 Act contributed to the community safety infrastructure in Scotland by placing a statutory duty on local authorities and chief constables to develop and publish an antisocial behaviour strategy for their areas (Section 1(1)). However, in practice it was assumed from the outset that such strategies would be written using existing community planning structures, most likely their community safety partnerships or members thereof (Scottish Executive 2004a: 6–7). In effect, the duty to draft anti-social behaviour strategies had become a means through which community safety and community planning could be required to focus on more explicitly crime-related issues (although it must be noted that much anti-social behaviour is not itself a crime, even though breach of an ASBO is). There have long been tensions between the Scottish Executive and community safety partnerships about the degree to which broad social justice agendas should form the focus of their work, the former, unsurprisingly, showing a preference for the deployment of more measurable and 'scientific' situational measures (Shiel *et al.* 2005). It is uncertain whether the focus on anti-social behaviour will generate a more 'punitive' focus of partnerships in the long term but the current series of strategies that have been published suggest that there is an ongoing resistance to placing reliance upon such rhetoric. For example, the Strategic Plan for 2005–2008 for Highlands and Islands observes:

[W]hile the Council's performance survey showed that respondents noted some concern about high spirits among young people, this was outweighed by a stronger feeling that young people are the lifeblood of our community and should not be blamed for social problems. (Highland Wellbeing Alliance 2005)

Community justice authorities

Since devolution there have been a number of long-overdue reviews of different aspects of Scottish criminal justice (see Bonomy 2002; Normand 2003; McInnes 2004) and an attempt to articulate a more co-ordinated and managerial approach to the problem of crime through, for example, publication of a criminal justice plan (Scottish Executive 2004b). The plan gave particular focus to the vexed issue of recidivism rates and would open up discussion about the management of offenders in the community. There was considerable activity over the next couple of years, including the publication of a National Strategy for the Management of Offenders (Scottish Executive 2006) and the passing of the Management of Offenders (Scotland) Act 2005. This Act established eight Community Justice Authorities (CJAs) around the country (McNeil and Whyte 2007: 8–10).

In a sense CJAs represented something of a climbdown for the previous administration because it had actually been the intention of the Scottish Labour Party to create a single-agency correctional service for Scotland instead (McNeil and Whyte 2007: 8). The climbdown is important because the creation of such an agency would have had the effect of removing criminal justice social work from generic social work practice. This connection between criminal justice and generic social work remains a distinctive characteristic of the Scottish system and so its survival is important.

However, the compromise that followed consultation on the matter – CJAs – became operational in April 2007. CJAs were designed to provide a co-ordinated and strategic approach to the management and planning of services that were available to offenders in the community and were also required to co-ordinate the work of the Scottish Prison Service and local authority/community providers to ensure continuity between them, the belief being that better co-ordination of services would serve to reduce re-offending. According to McNeil and Whyte, both the list of partners ('the police, courts, prosecution, prisons, Victim Support Scotland, Health Boards and relevant voluntary agencies') and the range of offender groups to be focused upon ('less serious/first-time offenders; offenders with mental health problems; offenders with substance misuse problems; persistent offenders, including young offenders coming through from the youth system; prisoners needing resettlement and rehabilitation services; violent, serious and sex offenders; and women offenders') are broad (2007: 9).

The creation of CJAs reflects ongoing tendencies felt around the world for there to be increased co-ordination, management and monitoring of criminal justice services (Crawford 1997: 86–92; Normand 2003). It is rather less clear how they will fit, if at all, next to Community Planning. There are undoubted differences between the objectives of the two partnership structures that are readily illustrated by reference to Brantingham and Faust's classic typology of crime prevention approaches. CJAs focus upon people who have already been identified as offenders and try to stop them re-offending (tertiary crime prevention). On the other hand, Community Planning is a much more proactive enterprise that focuses on the social welfare of the population at large (primary crime prevention) and, potentially, on needy groups within the population who might be viewed as being at risk of becoming offenders (secondary crime prevention) (Brantingham and Faust 1976). The distinctive objectives of the two structures may keep them separate, in theory at least, but partner agencies may ultimately be placed in the position of balancing resources for one off against the other and it is possible in a political environment, where anxieties about crime are politically potent, that reactive, measurable and more explicitly crime-focused partnership work will prevail. Such balancing of objectives is, of course, not a new problem for local government, or for many of the partner agencies involved, but is nonetheless likely to be important for the future of both CJAs and Community Planning and the relative emphasis in practice given to them.

Discussion

This chapter has shown that developments in community safety in Scotland have taken a similar, though not identical, trajectory to those in England and Wales over the same period. On the one hand, this should not be surprising given the long history of Scottish autonomy that belied the constitutional settlement that established the United Kingdom. On the other hand, it might be asked whether *greater* differences should have been expected, given McAra's analysis of policy divergence between Scotland and England and Wales over precisely the period in which contemporary thinking about crime prevention was developing (the 1970s to the mid 1990s). More specifically, it might be asked if crime prevention and community safety in Scotland, like its youth justice system, bore a stronger imprint of social welfare values than did developments in England and Wales.

Applying Paterson's analysis of autonomy to the first question, it is clear that the relative similarity of developments in crime prevention and community safety on both sides of the border does not undermine either the belief in Scottish autonomy or McAra's analysis of policy divergence in specific areas of criminal justice, notably youth justice. Autonomy does not necessitate difference and in the case of the 'preventative turn' in thinking about crime (Garland 1996; Hughes 2002) there is no evidence to suggest that officials and practitioners did not agree on the basic idea that prevention would be a good idea (i.e. the 'goals' of policy). There were, of course, debates in both jurisdictions about the relative merits of different approaches to crime prevention (Crawford 1997; Carnie 1999) (the 'means' of implementation) but the open-textured nature of the concepts concerned allowed them to engender broad political appeal, ensuring that 'crime prevention' did not become the site of 'other than England' politics that youth justice had. Situational crime prevention can, for example, be viewed as holding appeal for those on the political right because it assumes that individuals are rational actors (thus emphasising personal responsibility), diffuses responsibility for crime prevention to individuals rather than the state, and underplays the importance of broader 'social' causes of crime. However, it also has appeal to those on the left, albeit for different reasons – it is a pragmatic approach that can be used to quickly give help to communities that need to see that action is being taken, and can also be readily targeted at those vulnerable communities and individuals suffering the corrosive effects of repeat victimisation (Gilling 1997). In any case, local implementation also gave practitioners a degree of discretion in terms of the approach to be taken, evidenced by the drift towards being more offender-oriented over situational measures (Pease 1997: 982) despite Home Office and Scottish Office exhortations to focus on the latter. In short, the terms 'crime prevention' and 'community safety' were too politically vague and open to interpretation for them to be perceived as challenges to traditional Scottish ways of doing things – in the same way that challenges to social work and Children's Hearings were. If anything, the preventive turn that was given such impetus by Home Office research in the 1970s and 1980s found very fertile ground in Scotland where community involvement (Schaffer 1980), a belief in multi-agency co-operation (Paterson 1994) and a none too police-centred understanding of social control (Scottish Council on Crime 1975) had long histories. Far from being a challenge to Scottish sensibilities, developments in crime prevention and community safety fitted with them. Indeed, it should also be remembered that these developments were perceived as providing an alternative to the seeming rise of punitive, managerial and actuarial rhetoric within criminal justice policy in England and Wales: their *potential* to promote social justice as well as technical crime prevention was understood in both jurisdictions.

This begs the second question: does community safety in Scotland bear a stronger imprint of commitment to social justice or penal welfare values than it does in England and Wales? There are certainly concerns that work in England and Wales, despite coming from a similar background in urban regeneration, became too narrowly focused on crime-control issues throughout the 1990s (Crawford 2007; Hughes 2002), quite probably because of central government attempts to micro-manage community safety through detailed performance measurement regimes (Edwards and Hughes 2002). For the moment community safety partnerships in Scotland continue to articulate a broader commitment to social justice and welfare, despite Scottish Executive attempts to narrow the focus. The fact that the statutory duty for partnership working was tied to Community Planning in Scotland also reinforces the impression that this broader vision has a stronger foothold. Although the future of community safety in Scotland, and its social welfare character, are by no means certain, there are reasons to be cautiously optimistic. The election of the SNP to Holyrood in 2007 reconfigured the political landscape that had formed the backdrop to the period of policy convergence in the UK (New Labour held office in both Holyrood and Westminster). The 'other than England' orientation of Scottish policy-makers is likely to become more tenable again now that the elected political elites in Scotland are once more of a different (and more leftist) political hue from their colleagues in the south. This may well provide fertile ground for future divergence and the long-term entrenchment of social welfare values into community safety and partnership working in Scotland.

Note

1 The functions of the Scottish Police were defined as the prevention of crime, the protection of life and property and the detection and bringing to justice of offenders and were subsequently enshrined in the Police Scotland Act 1967.

References

Accounts Commission (2000a) *Safe and Sound: A Study of Community Safety Partnerships in Scotland*. Edinburgh: Audit Scotland.

Accounts Commission (2000b) *How Are We Doing? Measuring the Performance of Community Safety Partnerships*. Edinburgh: Audit Scotland.

Bannister, J. and Dillane, J. (2005) *Communities that Care: An Evaluation of the Scottish Pilot Programme*, Crime and Criminal Justice Research Findings, No. 79. Edinburgh: HMSO.

Bonomy (2002) *Improving Practice: 2002 Review of the Practices and Procedure of the High Court of Justiciary*. Edinburgh: HMSO.

Bottoms, A. E. (1990) 'Crime Prevention Facing the 1990s', *Policing and Society*, 1: 3–22.

Brantingham, P. J. and Faust, L. (1976) 'A Conceptual Model of Crime Prevention', *Crime and Delinquency*, 22: 284–96.

Carnie, J. (1996) *The Safer Cities Programme in Scotland: Overview Report*. Edinburgh: Scottish Office Central Research Unit.

Carnie, J. (1999) 'The Politics of Crime Prevention: The Safer Cities Experiment in Scotland', in P. Duff and N. Hutton (eds) *Criminal Justice in Scotland*. Dartmouth: Ashgate, pp. 74–93.

Clarke, R. V. and Mayhew, P. (1980) *Designing Out Crime*. London: HMSO.

Council of Scottish Local Authorities (1998) *Community Safety: A Key Council Strategy*. Edinburgh: CoSLA.

Craig, G. and Manthorpe, J. (1999) 'Unequal Partners? Local Government Reorganization and the Voluntary Sector', *Social Policy and Administration*, 33(1): 55–72.

Crawford, A. (1997) *The Local Governance of Crime: Appeals to Community and Partnerships*. Oxford: Clarendon Press.

Crawford, A. (2002) *Crime and Insecurity: The Governance of Safety in Europe*. Cullompton: Willan Publishing.

Crawford, A. (2007) 'Crime Prevention and Community Safety', in M. Maguire, R. Morgan, and R. Reiner (eds) *The Oxford Handbook of Criminology*, 4th edn. Oxford: Oxford University Press, pp. 866–909.

Donaldson, D. (1969) 'Scottish Devolution: The Historical Background', in J. N. Wolf (ed.) *Government and Nationalism in Scotland: An Enquiry by Members of the University of Edinburgh*. Edinburgh: Edinburgh University Press, pp. 4–16.

Duff, P. (1999) 'The Prosecution Service: Independence and Accountability', in P. Duff and N. Hutton (eds) *Criminal Justice in Scotland*. Dartmouth: Ashgate, pp. 115–130.

Edwards, A. and Hughes, G. (2002) 'Introduction: The Community Governance of Crime Control', in G. Hughes and A. Edwards (eds) *Crime Control and Community: The New Politics of Public Safety*. Cullompton: Willan Publishing.

Ekblom, P. (1995) 'Less Crime By Design', *The Annals AAPSS*, 539: 112–29.

Fyfe, N. (2005) 'Policing Crime and Disorder in Scotland', in D. Donnelly and K. Scott (eds) *Policing Scotland*. Cullompton: Willan Publishing, pp. 109–29.

Gane, C. (1999) 'Classifying Scottish Criminal Procedure', in P. Duff and N. Hutton (eds) *Criminal Justice in Scotland*. Dartmouth: Ashgate, pp. 56–73.

Garland, D. (1996) 'The Limits of the Sovereign State: Strategies of Crime Control in Contemporary Society', *British Journal of Criminology*, 36(4): 445–71.

Gilling, D. (1994) 'Multi-agency Crime Prevention in Britain: The Problem of Combining Situational and Social Strategies', *Crime Prevention Studies*, 3: 231–48.

Gilling, D. (1997) *Crime Prevention: Theory, Policy and Politics*. London: UCL Press.

Hewitt, J., Cryle, G. and Ballintyne, S. (2000) *Threads of Success: A Study of Community Safety Partnerships in Scotland*. Edinburgh: HMSO.

Highland Wellbeing Alliance (2005) *Highland Wellbeing Alliance: Antisocial Behaviour Strategy 2005–2008*. Inverness: Highland Wellbeing Alliance.

Himsworth, C. M. G. (2007) 'Devolution and its Jurisdictional Asymmetries', *Modern Law Review*, 70(1): 31–58.

Himsworth, C. and Paterson, A. (2004) 'A Supreme Court for the United Kingdom: Views from the Northern Kingdom', *Legal Studies*, 24(1/2): 99–118.

Hirst, P. (1989) *After Thatcher*. London: Collins.

Hughes, G. (2002) 'Plotting the Rise of Community Safety: Critical Reflections on Research, Theory and Politics', in G. Hughes and A. Edwards (eds) *Crime Control and Community: The New Politics of Public Safety*. Cullompton: Willan Publishing, pp. 20–45.

Hughes, G. and Edwards, A. (eds) (2002) *Crime Control and Community: The New Politics of Public Safety*. Cullompton: Willan Publishing.

Keating, M. (2001) 'Scottish Autonomy: Now and Then', in J. MacInnes and D. McCrone (eds) *Stateless Nations in the 21st Century: Scotland, Catalonia and Quebec*. Edinburgh: Unit for the Study of Government in Scotland, University of Edinburgh, pp. 91–103.

Loader, I. (2000) 'Plural Policing and Democratic Governance', *Social and Legal Studies*, 9(3): 323–45.

MacCormick, N. (1999) *Questioning Sovereignty: Law, State and Nation in the European Commonwealth*. Oxford: Oxford University Press.

MacInnes, J. and McCrone, D. (2001) *Stateless Nations in the 21st Century: Scotland, Catalonia and Quebec*. Edinburgh: Unit for the Study of Government in Scotland, University of Edinburgh.

McAra, L. (2004) 'The Cultural and Institutional Dynamics of Transformation: Youth Justice in Scotland and England and Wales', *Cambrian Law Review*, 35, 23–54.

McAra, L. (2005) 'Modelling Penal Transformation', *Punishment and Society*, 7: 277–302.

McAra, L. (2007) 'Welfarism in Crisis: Crime Control and Penal Practice in Post-devolution Scotland', in M. Keating (ed.) *Scottish Social Democracy: Progressive Ideals for Public Policy*. Brussels: P.I.E. Peter Lang, pp. 115–58.

McCallum, F. and Duff, P. (2000) *Intermediate Diets, First Diets and Agreement of Evidence in Criminal Cases: An Evaluation*, Central Research Unit Papers. Edinburgh: HMSO.

McCrone, D. (1992) *Understanding Scotland: The Sociology of a Stateless Nation*. London: Routledge.

McCrone, D. (2001) *Understanding Scotland: The Sociology of a Nation*, 2nd edn. London: Routledge.

McInnes, J. (2004) *The Summary Justice Review Committee: Report to Ministers*. Edinburgh: HMSO.

McIvor, G. and Williams, B. (1999) 'Community-based Disposals', in P. Duff and N. Hutton (eds) *Criminal Justice in Scotland*. Dartmouth: Ashgate, pp. 198–227.

McNeil, F. and Whyte, B. (2007) *Reducing Re-offending: Social Work and Community Justice in Scotland*. Cullompton: Willan Publishing.

Mack, J. A. (1963) 'Police Juvenile Liaison Schemes', *British Journal of Criminology*, 3(4): 361–75.

Midwinter, A., Keating, M. and Mitchell, J. (1991) *Politics and Public Policy in Scotland*. London: Palgrave Macmillan.

Monaghan, B. (1997) 'Crime Prevention in Scotland', *International Journal of the Sociology of Law*, 25: 21–44.

Normand, A. (2003) *Proposals for the Integration of Aims, Objectives and Targets in the Scottish Criminal Justice System*. Edinburgh: HMSO.

Paterson, L. (1994) *The Autonomy of Modern Scotland*. Edinburgh: Edinburgh University Press.

Pease, K. (1997) 'Crime Reduction', in M. Maguire, R. Morgan and R. Reiner (eds) *The Oxford Handbook of Criminology*, 2nd edn. Oxford: Oxford University Press, pp. 963–95.

Phillipson, N. T. (1976) 'Lawyers, Landowners and the Civic Leadership of Post-Union Scotland: An Essay on the Social Role of the Faculty of Advocates 1661–1830 in 18th Century Scottish Society', in N. MacCormick (ed.) *Lawyers in their Social Setting*. Edinburgh: W. Green and Sons, pp. 171–94.

Rogers, S., Smith, M., Sullivan, H. and Clarke, M. (2000) *Community Planning in Scotland: An Evaluation of the Pathfinder Projects Commissioned by CoSLA*. Edinburgh: CoSLA and The Scottish Executive.

Schaffer, E. B. (1980) *Community Policing*. London: Croom Helm.

Scottish Council on Crime (1975) *Crime and the Prevention of Crime: A Memorandum by the Scottish Council on Crime*. Edinburgh: HMSO.

Scottish Executive (1999) *Safer Communities in Scotland: Guidance for Community Safety Partnerships*. Edinburgh: HMSO.

Scottish Executive (2002) *Community Safety Award Programme: Application Guidance for Community Safety Partnerships, 2003–2004*. Edinburgh: HMSO.

Scottish Executive (2003) *Community Safety Award Programme: Application Guidance for Community Safety Partnerships, 2004–2005*. Edinburgh: HMSO.

Scottish Executive (2004a) *Guidance on Antisocial Behaviour Strategies*. Edinburgh: HMSO.

Scottish Executive (2004b) *Supporting Safer, Stronger Communities: Scotland's Criminal Justice Plan*. Edinburgh: HMSO.

Scottish Executive (2005) *Community Safety Partnership Award Programme 2005–2008*. Edinburgh: HMSO.

Scottish Executive (2006) *Reducing Reoffending: National Strategy for the Management of Offenders*. Edinburgh: HMSO.

Scottish Executive (2007) *Social Inclusion Research Bulletin*, No. 16. Edinburgh: HMSO.

Scottish Office (1992) *Preventing Crime Together in Scotland: A Strategy for the 1990s*. Edinburgh: HMSO.

Scottish Office (1998) *Social Exclusion in Scotland: A Consultation Paper*. Edinburgh: HMSO.

Shiel, L., Clark, I. and Richards, F. (2005) *Approaches to Community Safety and Anti-Social Behaviour in the Better Neighbourhood Services Programme*. Edinburgh: HMSO.

Tierney, S. (2005) 'Reframing Sovereignty? Sub-state National Societies and Contemporary Challenges to Nation-state', *International and Comparative Law Quarterly*, 54(1): 161–83.

Valentin, C. (1995) *Directory of Crime Prevention Initiatives in Scotland*. Edinburgh: HMSO.

Walters, R. and Woodward, R. (2007) 'Punishing Poor Parents: "Respect", "Responsibility" and Parenting Orders in Scotland', *Youth Justice*, 7(1): 5–20.

Whyte, B. (2003) 'Young and Persistent: Recent Developments in Youth Justice Policy and Practice in Scotland', *Youth Justice*, 3: 74–85.

Young, P. (1996) 'The Peculiarities of the Scots', *Criminal Justice Matters*, 26: 22–3.

Young, P. (1997) *Crime and Criminal Justice in Scotland*. Edinburgh: HMSO.

Zuleeg, F., Boyle, J., Lees, F., Patterson, K., Pawson, H. and Davidson, E. (2007) *Use of Antisocial Behaviour Orders in Scotland*. Edinburgh: HMSO.

Chapter 5

The evolving story of crime prevention in France

Anne Wyvekens

What can be said about crime prevention in France today? It can be considered from various angles. This chapter first gives an overview, tracing the evolution of crime prevention within the broader context of other policies such as law enforcement and urban policies. Then, in a more 'prospective' view, the question of whether or not the recent emergence of situational prevention constitutes one illustration, among others, of a break with the past or a new paradigm is discussed.

From Bonnemaison to Sarkozy

The history of crime prevention in France can be seen as the history of an awkward relationship between 'prevention' and 'repression', the latter being the term used in French as a synonym for 'law enforcement'.[1] From this perspective, three main contemporary historical periods can be identified and are discussed to begin with. In the subsequent section consideration is given to the nuanced impact of political changes and their limitations.

Prevention versus repression

The 1980s: renewing crime prevention
In France, like elsewhere in Europe, crime prevention policy arose in response to the limits of the traditional penal approach. In the late 1970s, figures began to show a significant rise in recorded crime,

especially petty offences. Much of the blame for this situation fell at the feet of the police and the judiciary. Fear of crime began to infuse the political debate: polarising Right *versus* Left and repression *versus* prevention. Then, in 1981 urban riots erupted in disadvantaged urban areas, most notably in *Les Minguettes* in Venissieux, a suburb of Lyon.

The Left had recently come into power, in May 1981. It swiftly implemented the 'new crime prevention policy', based on a report prepared by a commission of city mayors led by Gilbert Bonnemaison (Commission des maires sur la sécurité 1982). The purpose was to be pragmatic and break from the sterile ideological debate on either prevention or repression. Rather they were to be seen as mutually supportive in a way that constituted a 'renewal of crime prevention'. The new policy was to be local, involving various agencies under the authority of the city mayor, and was quickly to become articulated with a more overarching policy relating to deprived neighbourhoods: the very basis for urban policy (*politique de la ville*).

Originally, French crime prevention was primarily social prevention. In this way it contrasted significantly with Anglo-American trends. The police played only a minor role in the implementation of the policy and the judiciary largely remained in the background. Moreover, the method of funding – following which the contribution of the national level was equal to the amount decided by the city in the framework of its local priorities – encouraged the tendency to favour programmes with a wider social and cultural emphasis, easier technically and politically to implement than specific crime prevention strategies.

The 1990s: rehabilitating safety

The following decade was defined by the concern to correct this lack of correspondence and connection between social measures and law enforcement. Hence, it can be characterised as 'rehabilitating safety'. In policy discourse, the word 'prevention' was replaced by the word 'safety' as exemplified in the creation of local safety contracts (*contrats locaux de sécurité* (CLS)) in 1997. These contracts were signed by the local mayor, the *préfet* (the state's representative within a department)[2] and the prosecutor. They were still based on the principle of a local partnership, but they entailed a stronger involvement of the police and the judiciary. Furthermore, the partnership was broadened to include new actors, those who were more comfortable with the concept of safety than that of prevention, namely those from the private sector or semi-private institutions (like public housing and transport companies).

In the meantime, the judiciary developed its own partnerships under the rubric of 'alternatives to prosecution' and 'proximity justice' (*justice de proximité*) (Wyvekens 2001, 2007a). In tandem with these developments, the *police de proximité* reform was launched. This was not exactly community policing, but a French way of trying to get the police closer to the population (Monjardet 1999).

Since 2002: a repression named prevention?
A third period began in 2002, when the political Right returned to office. The first important changes did not concern local safety policy. Although in 2002 local councils of safety and crime prevention (*conseils locaux de sécurité et de prévention de la délinquance* (CLSPD)) were indeed created, the primary objective was a rationalisation of the structures rather than a fundamental change in policy direction.

The first important change concerned the police, when the reform that had created the *police de proximité* was dramatically brought to a halt (Roché 2005). According to the Minister of the Interior: 'The role of the police is not to play football with young people, it is to catch criminals.' At the same time, between 2002 and 2004, four laws were passed on safety issues – two at the initiative of the Minister of the Interior,[3] and two introduced by the Minister of Justice.[4] All were understood as 'repressive'. Beyond the measures that extended the powers of the police to carry out investigations justified by the fight against terrorism, one could also find various offences in connection with the occupation and use of public space, targeted at gypsies, prostitutes, beggars or young people in the lobbies of public housing estates. Other special offences appeared that could be called 'opportunistic', in the sense that they were introduced in response to a specific problem that captured public debate, such as the new offence of insulting the national anthem. Laws relating to the judiciary contained new measures towards minors, such as the creation of 'closed educational centres' and 'educational sanctions', in particular for children under 13 years. New kinds of simplified proceedings were created in the French criminal procedure, named 'appearance on preliminary recognition of culpability' and inspired by Anglo-American criminal procedure and intended to accelerate the course of justice. In parallel, the debate on juvenile justice grew sharper, fuelled by the then Minister of the Interior (and future president) Nicolas Sarkozy who argued strongly for the weakening, and even the disappearance, of some specific legal protections for young offenders, such as reducing the age of criminal responsibility, limiting the scope of specialised jurisdiction, and abolishing the traditional priority within the youth justice system for education over repression.

Above all, over a five-year period a special 'law relating to crime prevention' was in preparation under the control of the Ministry of the Interior. This fed the debate on safety issues. It was promulgated in March 2007.[5] Its content goes far beyond mere crime prevention. One could say that this law covers everything *but* crime prevention. Thus, this period in France could be called 'a repression named prevention'. First of all, the law provides no definition of crime prevention. It contains two main series of measures. First, the central role of the mayor in the local safety policies is recognised officially, with a set of measures intended to embed this role, especially as regards information-sharing. In addition, mayors have also been given new competences. For instance, the mayor is entitled to create a 'council of the rights and duties of families' or to propose parental support (*accompagnement parental*)[6] in relation to the parents of unruly youths. Second, a set of measures reforming juvenile justice in the direction evoked above have been introduced. Furthermore, the law contains a set of new offences, including more measures related to public space, as well as some new opportunistic offences such as those relating to ambushing or 'happy-slapping'.

The emphasis on repression is conveyed by two more laws that were passed very soon after Nicolas Sarkozy was elected president in May 2007. The first one reflected an electoral promise relating to repeat offenders.[7] It instituted minimum sentences (*peines planchers*) for both juveniles and adults. It also sought to abolish the so-called 'minority excuse' (*excuse de minorité*) for young people aged between 16 and 18, which means that juveniles could only be sentenced to penalties not in excess of half of those applicable to adults for the same offence. Due to international and constitutional provisions, however, the minority excuse could only be bypassed in a limited number of cases.

The second law is called the 'law related to security detention' (*rétention de sûreté*).[8] Security detention is aimed at offenders 'for whom, following a review of their situation at the end of their sentence, it is assessed that they represent a particular danger characterised by an extremely high likelihood of re-offending because they suffer from serious personality disorders', as well as at perpetrators of particularly serious offences: 'Security detention entails placing the person concerned in a secure judicial-medical-social centre where he/she will be offered permanent medical, social and psychological treatment aimed at bringing to an end the need for detention'.[9] The measure can be renewed for as long as the person remains 'dangerous'.

Left versus Right?

France is well known for having a relatively polarised debate on safety issues. Prevention can be said to be a left-wing issue while law enforcement and 'repression' have tended to be a right-wing concern. Therefore, can we understand this intense legislative activity (outlined above) simply as a result of political change?

Political shifts do have effects, but these effects are only relative. First of all, several counter-examples can be observed. For instance, the new crime prevention policy, created by a left-wing government, focusing on social and urban aspects, has often been and is still implemented by right-wing municipalities. In other words, we must make a distinction between national and local levels of politics. Conversely, regarding juvenile justice, the idea of weakening its special protections and separate philosophy already began to appear under a left-wing administration, prior to 2002. The same is true as regards the detention of juveniles. The 'reinforced educational centres' were not actually invented by the Right, which merely renamed a structure created under a previous left-wing government. So 'the Left', or part of the Left, years ago had already realised the need to address safety issues not only from a social prevention perspective.

A second element that needs to be taken into account is the growing gap between *words* and practice. In France there are more and more examples of a phenomenon that could be called 'one problem, one law'. This was the case with the public debate about the Islamic veil, for instance. The same can be observed with regard to local safety issues. It was also the case with the laws initiated between 2002 and 2004 by the Ministries of the Interior and Justice. The preparation of the laws, and the debate around them, have had at least as much impact as has their subsequent implementation. Moreover, several implementing decrees have either never been taken or have only been initiated after some considerable delay. Some measures are – in practice – inapplicable or simply not applied, like the new offence of loitering in groups in common parts of apartment buildings. The same has happened with the law relating to repeat offenders: there is a noticeable difference between what was announced during the campaign and the eventual terms of the law. The law related to security detention gave the President the opportunity to go even further. Despite the fact that the Constitutional Court (*Conseil constitutionnel*) ruled against the article that provided for retroactive implementation, the President announced that he would nonetheless retain the power, thus contesting the decision of the highest constitutional authority in France. All of this raises a central question that demands more in-depth consideration, namely concerning the vexed relationship between safety policies and public opinion.

Another feature of French political culture leads to a specific question which appears to be common to both left- and right-wing governments: to what extent is it possible to implement a real and genuine local policy in the context of such a *centralised* state apparatus as exists in France? Importantly, the new crime prevention policy began with a 'commission of city mayors'. Today, the law on crime prevention institutionalises the core role of the mayor in local safety policies. And yet what can be observed of developments in the field? Not only are not all mayors ready to assume this role, but they are far from having the means to assume it, either financially or in terms of information tools and methodology of implementation. So we face the paradox of a state which on the one hand 'invents' or encourages local partnerships and on the other hand maintains a form of centralisation, which is incompatible with the idea of sharing competences (Marcus 2006). In other words, in France, safety remains a state business; or more precisely a police business. Initiatives that are intended to involve the police in partnerships, especially in the name of prevention, invariably end up disqualifying police work. Simply consider how France is unable – or doesn't want – to reform its police (Monjardet 2004; Roché 2005). The situation is not any better when we consider the judiciary. With the exception of a few 'atypical' prosecutors, the judiciary does not appear to be ready to share either information or even less its competences with local representatives. Thus, even if the mayor is keen to champion local safety issues, he/she remains quite powerless: missing information, missing funding, missing methodology. And it cannot be certain that the situation will improve with the new law.

Finally, questions concerning the impact of political changes should also be seen from a broader point of view, in the way safety policies are linked with *urban policies*. The safety issue is indeed closely related to urban segregation (and social (dis)integration). Hence the point is not only to consider whether there is more or less punishment or to worry about a 'penalisation of the social' (Mary 2003), we should also bear in mind the need to link safety policies with urban, employment and integration policies. Since the Right came back into power in 2002 the real change may have occurred less in the extent to which law enforcement has *increased*, than in the question of how investment in urban policy has *decreased* and evolved.

Since 2002 the funding allocated to urban policy has decreased significantly. Many NGOs working in the suburbs are facing acute financial difficulties. In this regard, the *politique de la ville* has evolved both in its contents and its organisation. A law dated 1 August 2003, relating to urban renewal,[10] set up the National Agency for Urban Renovation (ANRU). The ANRU is responsible for implementing a national programme of urban renewal that 'aims to promote the objective of social diversity (*mixité sociale*) and sustainable development, to restructure neighbourhoods classified as sensitive urban areas (*zones urbaines sensibles* (ZUS))'. It includes 'operations for urban planning, renovation, residentialisation, demolition and construction of housing, the creation, renovation and demolition of public and collective structures, or any other investment consistent with urban renewal.'[11] Within the period 2004–08 the quantitative objective of the programme is to build 200,000 new public housing units, to renovate 200,000 of them and to demolish 200,000 others. The 'social' approach that was prevalent in urban policy has tended to be replaced or even ousted by a more 'urbanistic' approach, focused on places more than people (Donzelot *et al.* 2003). Only after new urban riots had occurred, in November 2005, did attention return to the social dimension of urban policy through the creation, in January 2006, of the National Agency for Social Cohesion and Equal Opportunities (Acsé). The Agency is in charge of funding for integration issues as well as crime prevention. Currently, some 30 per cent of this budget is devoted to CCTV.

Urban policy has not been the new President's first concern. The first measures his government took were in the areas of taxation and employment. Lowering taxes for upper middle classes and 'working more to earn more' was given priority and only much later, in February 2008, was a plan entitled *Espoir banlieues* (banlieues' hope)[12] presented, whose concrete measures were detailed later in June 2008. Without entering into a detailed analysis of the plan, we can simply observe that its development has lagged considerably and the means of financing it remain to be clarified. The measures announced were aimed at fostering desegregation and enhancing 'mobility' – through schooling, training, improved job opportunities for the young or better public transport to make neighbourhoods more accessible. In the meantime, however, ANRU is continuing its work and the CCTV system is expanding. We should also note – and once again the remark applies to both the Left and the Right – that nothing in actual fact seems to point to a shift in the tendency to treat the *banlieues* as anything other than completely isolated territories.

Break with the past? New model?

Maybe a better way to frame the question of a break with the past is to talk about the effects of neo-liberalism on safety policies. What are the main shifts that can be observed in French policies? To what extent can we identify a new model of crime prevention? Let us first draw a quick parallel between past and present safety and crime prevention policies.

There are indeed several signs of a possible break. Over the past few years, we have witnessed intense legislative activity in relation to criminal issues, with a double trend. On the one hand, particularly (but not only) for serious offences, more severe measures have been introduced: new categories of crime (particularly regarding improper occupation of public areas), longer prison sentences, increased punitiveness for young delinquents, strong concerns about imprisonment of minors, the institution of minimum sentences for repeat offenders, and so on. On the other hand, the development of alternatives to prosecution for petty crime suggests an increasing emphasis on responsibility. The offender has to provide concrete compensation for the harm he/she has caused. The same trends are at work with regard to juvenile justice. Whereas traditionally the young person, even if he/she was dangerous, used to be primarily considered as 'in danger', today we are witnessing a clear desire to treat delinquent youths like adults, or at least as autonomous, responsible individuals, able to understand the meaning of what they do. Protection or education tends to be replaced by educational sanctions. These are also used as a way of punishing even very young children. Likewise, according to the 2007 law relating to prevention, parents are to be made responsible for their children's behaviour.

In addition, a form of prevention not previously widespread in France – situational prevention – is growing, with more and more CCTV and greater interest in action through environmental design and urban planning in relation to safety concerns.

The final shift lies in the kind of agencies in charge of implementing safety policies. In the past, the state was the main actor, the police and the judiciary holding almost exclusive competences to address safety issues, intervening generally in isolation from wider social and educational agencies. The state now appears to be losing its monopolistic position – at least partly. Local partnerships involve a broad range of actors – local authorities, the private sector, NGOs, the civil society – so that the state tends to 'steer' more than it 'rows' in quests to 'govern at a distance'. Meanwhile it has developed new managerial logics and technologies, albeit less than in the United Kingdom. Performance monitoring and assessment have been introduced in the police. In the judiciary, 'real time' processing is moving along the same lines.

On this basis, two kinds of interpretation or analysis may be possible. One is to say that we have finally adopted a new paradigm, and we have definitely entered a 'culture of control' as described by Garland (2001); that neo-liberalism has finally won out.[13] An even darker picture in this respect has been painted in the early stages of Nicolas Sarkozy's presidency. Another interpretation is to adopt a longer-term view, at some distance from the frenzied atmosphere of French elections, to go beyond the word 'break', aimed to reassure the middle class – but hiding the continuities between policies, beyond the Right–Left opposition. We should also bear in mind the contradictory tendencies already evoked, such as the discrepancy between words and practice, and between the national and local levels; the various ways policies can be implemented from one place to another, by one actor or another; the enduring significant remnants of welfarism; and above all the dynamism of civil society and the concern – hard going but real – to involve citizens in safety (co-)production. Possibly we are witnessing more a shift or transition rather than a complete break or rupture with the past. This could be illustrated through the issue of safety in public spaces, with some examples of the growth of situational prevention in France.

The French model of crime prevention

The French model of crime prevention, the so-called Bonnemaison model, which was designed in the early 1980s and implemented since then, has for years focused on social prevention. The purpose is to have an indirect or direct 'influence on the personality and living conditions of individuals to avoid spawning deviant behaviour and to reduce the social factors that encourage deviance' (DIV 2004). The French model focuses on the root causes of crime: poverty, lack of education, bad jobs and poor housing conditions. Acting on these causes is supposed to move people away from crime. In this view, French crime prevention has always been linked with the *politique de la ville*, targeting disadvantaged urban areas, with a twofold approach: actions of a social nature on the one hand, and urbanism, urban renewal on the other. It is interesting to note that the Bonnemaison Report focused on safety issues, was prepared in the same context as two other reports: the Dubedout Report (1983), on social development of neighbourhoods, and the Schwartz Report (1981) on professional integration of youth.

After the previously mentioned drift towards a 'generalist' kind of prevention, there was some concern about a repressive turn following the introduction of the word 'safety' as well as the reinforcement of the police and the judiciary's role in the local safety contracts (CLS) (Ferret and Mouhanna 2005). Nevertheless, social prevention remained important, with a number of actions or programmes continuing those implemented in earlier prevention action contracts (*contrats d'action de prévention*). But CLSs can be analysed primarily as aiming to 'restore social bonds' much more than improving law enforcement. *Police de proximité, justice de proximité*, hiring young people to make public spaces safer, all these measures are described as means of tackling a 'feeling of abandonment' that would be characteristic of people living in disadvantaged urban areas. Proximity is thus viewed not only as a goal in itself, but also as a way to implement a kind of 'education', teaching people their duties as well as their rights (Donzelot and Wyvekens 2004). In other words, CLSs have not put an end to French social prevention, rather they have given it a new tone, emphasising the aspect of 'responsibility'.

In that context, French prevention contrasted with what we call the Anglo-American model, which is much more focused on situational prevention. Whereas the French model aims to act on offenders, to prevent them from committing crimes by improving their living conditions, the Anglo-American model aims to act on the targets of crime – either persons or goods – by protecting them. It does not deal first with root causes of crime but rather with immediate or 'proximal' ones.

> Oriented towards the criminal act, situational prevention designates measures that aim to suppress or limit the opportunities to commit an infraction by modifying the circumstances in which they can be committed. The intention is to make crimes harder, riskier and less profitable by dissuasion and protecting potential victims, whether they are people or goods. (DIV 2004)

For a very long time France has had a quite narrow view of situational prevention, which has remained marginal in practice. Not only was it not part of the French culture of prevention, it was even associated with repressive methods of dealing with crime. In practice, situational prevention was considered as synonymous with CCTV. And the debate on CCTV focused on the threat it represented for civil liberties. On one side, CCTV was blamed and opposed because of that threat; on the other side, its use was justified as a means to achieve public safety. On both sides the public debate on CCTV was ideological, not practical; the question was not: does it work to prevent crime? Furthermore, for a long time there was no empirical research to answer that question (Ocqueteau 2004: 130). Moreover, the first study relied only on British data (Heilmann and Mornet 2003). At the same time another study, although entitled *The Impact of CCTV on Security in Public Space and Private Domains with Public Access* (Pécaud 2002),[14] was devoted more to the notion of control than to the impact of CCTV devices. The ideal pursued by the Bonnemaison Report – to combine prevention, repression and solidarity, and overall to end the opposition between prevention and repression – remained somewhat of a utopia.

The same mistrust can be observed from a theoretical point of view, when we consider the way France received some American reflections on the relationship between places and safety, such as 'broken windows' or 'defensible space' theories, which developed a broader notion of situational prevention. Both are 'broader' because they make a link between the quality of space and its safety. The objective is still to dissuade offenders by intervening on the physical, urban environment, in order to make it harder and riskier to commit a crime. But instead of implementing solely technical solutions, like CCTV, alarms, protection of entrances and anti-theft marking of goods, they include something more complex. The purpose is to facilitate a social control of places through a design that makes it possible for their users to monitor them.

Jane Jacobs (1961), in *The Death and Life of Great American Cities*, and after her Oscar Newman (1972), with his 'defensible space', explain how the street or public space can be designed so that people enjoy being in these areas and are then monitored in a way that dissuades potential offenders. In their turn, Wilson and Kelling (1982) pointed out that an abandoned space (i.e. dirty and neglected) looks like it is out of control, thus a suitable place to commit crime or disorders. On the one hand, urban studies theorists worried about safety, while on the other hand criminologists were taking space into account. Both reached the same conclusion: space belongs to its users, and they have to take care of it and are able to prevent disorders or crimes that happen there. The only area in which they differ is in relation to the role of the police. For the urban theorists, residents replace the police, whereas in criminologists' view the police have to rely on the residents to do their job.

Both theories received a less than enthusiastic welcome in France. Both were reduced to notions of control, exclusion and denunciation. Newman's work provoked polemical views more than real evaluations

(Mosser 2007). Defensible space was criticised as advocating a 'safety urbanism', leading to 'the city as a fortress' (Lemonier 1998). Broken windows theory was reduced to zero tolerance: being tough on any slight offence or incivility would be the only way to keep people from embarking on a criminal career. In both cases, the idea that citizens could take care of their neighbourhood was completely ignored, because it would mean controlling each other or informing the police, and that is definitely unthinkable for a French mentality that shuns 'social control' and does not really trust the police.

The emergence of situational prevention: 'safety urbanism' or quality of public space?

Over the past few years, it can be said that France has 'discovered' situational prevention, at the same time as it has discovered public space. Public space is not new – it has always existed, but without being a subject of either discourses or policy. For a long time, urbanists ignored public space. In the functional city of the Athens Charter public space was little more than an area for traffic, binding together various places with various functions. It had none of the social, civic or festive attributes that we are rediscovering today (Claval 2001). Derelict public spaces, often uncared for and ignored by urban planners, increasingly have attracted private sector investment (Ghorra-Gobin 2001). Businesses have invented 'private spaces open to the public', what has been termed 'private mass property' (Shearing and Stenning 1983). A public space is public through its uses much more than through its legal status. Some spaces are private but open to the public, like shopping malls; other ones are public but abandoned and left to the strongest in some disadvantaged neighbourhoods; others that were previously public have become privatised, like gated communities. Public space has become hybrid, hesitating between opening and closure, between community and individuality (Burgel 2006). As regards safety, public space may be threatened by misuse or disturbing uses. Anti-social behaviour and the sometimes disturbing control of public space by groups represent important issues for local safety policies. After the implementation of various programmes intended to foster increased 'human presence' in public spaces in the framework of local safety contracts, situational prevention is now developing under various forms, institutionalised or not, in the field of urban practices.

First of all, CCTV, which has for long been marginal, has steadily grown over the past few years. The French railway company is about to launch an ambitious installation programme in its stations. The Conservative candidate for the municipal election in Paris in 2008 intended to set up 3,000 cameras in the city. Under the March 2007 law related to crime prevention, priority is now given to CCTV funding. In 2007 central government funded 315 projects for a total amount of 13.4 million euro.

Furthermore, in the same year the private sector requested 10,000 authorisations to allow the installation of CCTV cameras, compared to only 4,000 in 2006.[15] This increase is being facilitated by a law of 23 January 2006 related to the fight against terrorism. The law allows private companies that are 'exposed to risks of terrorist attacks' to install cameras near their buildings without having to wait for the prior authorisation from the videosurveillance commission of the department (*Commission départementale de vidéosurveillance*) (Ocqueteau 2007). The French data protection authority (*Commission nationale de l'informatique et des libertés*, CNIL) expressed concern about this proliferation of CCTV cameras in its 2006 annual report (CNIL 2007). One chapter of the report is entitled 'Warning about the surveillance society' (*Alerte à la société de surveillance*). The commission sought to raise public awareness about the risks of systematic computerisation and called for more resources to help the commission play its role as a protector of freedoms. In 2007, CCTV remained 'under CNIL's watchful eye' (CNIL 2008). At the same time, it is striking to observe that, except for the CNIL, there are no other prevalent voices expressing deep concerns about possible threats to civil liberties. Public opinion, even on the Left, now views the development of CCTV without any particular emotion. For instance, pupils were interviewed for a recent poll about CCTV in high schools in the region Ile-de-France: according to the research findings, CCTV does not seem to represent any significant problem for them (Le Goff *et al.* 2007).

Situational prevention is also developing in disadvantaged urban areas. The new National Agency for Urban Renovation (ANRU) funds and manages urban renewal programmes, including what in France we call *résidentialisation*. Even if the word is used in many senses, it can be defined as a way to rearrange the landscape of these disadvantaged neighbour-hoods so that they appear more like typical residential neighbourhoods – especially in the clear distinction between public and private spaces – which is thought to foster among the inhabitants a greater sense of security (Billard *et al.* 2005).

Another form of situational prevention takes place in a decree related to urban planning actions dated 3 August 2007 and nicknamed the 'decree on situational prevention'.[16] It is the outcome of a lengthy process, in that it provides the implementation clauses of a law initially passed in 1995,[17] making public safety audits compulsory before conducting certain urban renewal works or constructing buildings that will be open to the public.[18] In the event, nothing happened before 2007, when the law related to crime prevention was passed which reiterated this obligation. Finally, the decree of 3 August 2007 detailed what kinds of programmes were targeted, how the studies would be conducted and what their effects would be. This long delay (12 years) can be explained by the resistance of urban planners and architects to an approach they considered as unacceptable because of what they called an intrusion of the police in the design of buildings.

If France seems to be converting to situational prevention, all these 'official' and visible forms have prompted emotion or raised criticism. CCTV remains the object of scepticism at least about its real effectiveness. For example, will there be a human eye behind each camera? (Anache 2004; Heilmann 2008). *Résidentialisation* has its detractors who point to risks of exclusion when certain places are privatised (Tabet 1999). As regards public safety audits, it is too early to know what their implementation will be and how they will be received.

Towards a 'successful' public space

We would now like to point out other, less spectacular, examples of care for public space and try to analyse them. Recent research describes various forms of 'production of safety or civility' that recall American community prevention: the way that inhabitants or users, along with other agencies, can take care of the places where they live or visit. This set of research is conducted on the initiative of businesses that are worried about the increase of disorder and incivilities on their premises: in post offices, railway stations, shopping malls – all public places or places open to the public where tranquillity or safety are threatened by behaviours that are not serious but sufficiently worrisome and cumulative to require some response. All these businesses face the problem in the same way: with pragmatism. They do not care about discussions on prevention versus repression. For a member of staff of the French national railway company, disorder and delinquency threaten both the clients' trust and the efficiency of the company (André 2005). In that way, they are a 'business problem', part of its activity, which has to be addressed from within its resources.

The research conducted on this issue points in the same direction. The basic idea is to invert the way disorders – 'incivilities' – are considered. What one no longer sees when trying to remove deviant behaviour is the other side of the coin: civility. In other words, we forget that in many public places a whole set of situations either do not cause any problem or are solved without the intervention of any authority, thanks simply to successful interactions between the users of the place. Civility, just like incivility, is the result of interactions. Civility constitutes 'those innumerable tiny acts which often avert conflicts' (Vidal-Naquet and Tiévant 2006). We merely have to watch the subway at rush hour: people walk past each other without colliding, just because they spontaneously find the way to walk past each other. Another example can be observed at the post office, in the queue: whereas people could quickly be irritated, many incidents are avoided thanks to a look, a word, or silence. This is what is called 'civic skills'. 'Civility' is a polite way of using public space. When one replaces a substantialist approach to incivilities – namely one that views incivility as a behaviour that is problematic in and of itself – with an interactionist view – that sees incivility as the product of an interaction – this highlights the civic skills of the users and their ability to produce civility.

The same has been observed, on a larger scale, in a large public park located just outside Paris, the Parc de la Villette (Tiévant 2006). This park is open 24 hours a day and frequented by a wide variety of people: families with young children, tourists, young people coming from the nearby *banlieue*, known as '*bobos*'. All the people come there for completely different purposes, not necessarily compatible with one another, like playing music, sleeping on the grass, playing football, walking babies, etc. Nevertheless, thanks to the way the place is designed and the way it is managed everyone can use it peacefully and in safety. How is this possible? The park is managed based on the idea of defining and implementing rules for its use that can be respected by all users, thus defined *with* the users. So not only are the needs of the users taken into account, but also their civic skills: they are trusted as people who are able to define, possibly negotiate, and then enforce rules for the use of the place they enjoy visiting. Together they build an 'order of the place'. The result is that several different uses of the park take place together and contribute to the quality of that space, in which safety is only one aspect among others.

Another body of research, conducted for the National Institute for Advanced Security Studies (*Institut national des hautes études de sécurité* (INHES)), demonstrates the same point starting from the opposite direction (Réussir l'espace public 2006). To restore safety in a space requires first considering its uses, its users, and their skills. Indeed, safety is one element, among many others, of the quality of a public space. The purpose of this set of studies was to show, on several sites in France and abroad, how the situation in different places where safety had dramatically deteriorated subsequently could be turned around. The places studied included a public school and its surroundings; a railway station (the Gare de Lyon in Paris); a shopping mall (La Part-Dieu in Lyon); a bus line in Toulouse; an African neighbourhood in Brussels (Matongé); Broad Street in Birmingham; and the Piazza Vittorio Emmanuele in Rome. In all cases, the action was based on problem-solving: in other words, dealing with the problem in a pragmatic way by involving the people more directly concerned, taking their interests into account instead of legalistic answers coming from institutional points of view, with their interests being related to the way they use the places. So, from the perspective of situational prevention, in every case, environmental management or physical improvements were combined with measures taken as a consequence of observing the way places were used by their various users. In most cases, in one way or another, involving the users in caring for the space, using their civic skills was a key element in the success of the operation.

The situation in the shopping mall was improved by physical measures like modifying the lighting or organising the movement of people, but also by finding a way to combine safety and business imperatives. Young people sometimes can cause trouble but they are also customers, which the mall managers take into account. They are concerned with safety but also with their profits. This leads to building an 'order of the place' in which everyone has a share of responsibility.

The railway station was disturbed by the presence of homeless people and drug dealers. The solution succeeded in combining safety requirements and solidarity in such a way that the station was no longer unsafe but still remained hospitable, for the homeless people as well who were invited to stay in some places and not in others, and not to have disturbing behaviours. Once again, creating an 'order of the place', in which safety is only one element of the quality of space, was the dominant approach. Furthermore, this highlights the manner in which situational prevention does not necessarily mean placing cameras everywhere.

Another research conducted in post offices (Wyvekens *et al.* 2003), showed that disorders decreased when a 'queue guide' is installed, in order to organise the queue and make the waiting quieter. But disorders and conflicts also decreased naturally, simply because customers as well as employees have regulating skills, not necessarily consciously recognised as such, but effective nevertheless.

People are never asked to 'collaborate' with authorities, with the police. They are just asked about what is important for them in the way they use the space, and also made to feel that they can be trusted as being able to participate in producing an 'order of the place'.

A final, somewhat different, example also appears to be interesting: it is the work done by a police service called *Prévention et sécurité urbaine* (Urban Prevention and Safety) in the department of Seine-Saint-Denis. A group called Safety of the Economic Sector had been created in order to advise senior company executives how to fight property crime and street crime in a developing economic and industrial area of this 'problematic' department. Public services then asked for safety audits. The scope of the group became broader, targeting public buildings like schools, city halls and hospitals. Later public housing companies conducting renovation and *résidentialisation* programmes were incorporated. In 2005, the service was renamed Urban Prevention and Safety Service, and its activities became focused on public spaces, implementing situational prevention. In an interview, one of the service's directors explains the approach:

> You can almost immediately tell if a space is safe or unsafe, manageable or unmanageable: paint, in other words, cleanliness, pleasantness, lighting, green areas. The same can be said for private spaces: a metro station for example. So we had the idea to reverse [the situation], to influence this area through recommendations on various

issues. In the realm of *coveillance*, this means having as many witnesses, observers, as possible: so large windows, openings, views, louvred fences instead of palisades, or hedges that are not too high, taking what pollutes or what's useless off the public thorough way, making public furnishing more transparent, installing billboards on the sides of buildings instead of perpendicular ... We try to put into practice the idea of positive occupation of space: so that the space protects itself ... When a space is offered to everyone they protect it. Do things so that, without police presence, the people feel safe in a public space – that's situational prevention.

Conclusion

Does such a complex form of situational crime prevention announce a renewal of crime prevention in France? The answer is even more significant in the present context where social prevention is said to be ineffective and where law enforcement seems to be a priority. In other words, if we consider the reality on the ground, do local agents and agencies just blindly follow national trends and discourses? Even though American theories have been criticised, some approaches like those I have described are along the lines of the 'broken windows' or 'defensible space' approaches. As in 'broken windows', we find the idea that local safety is linked to the material quality of space as much as to the absence of deviant behaviour. And as in 'defensible space', we can observe attempts to create a space that would be shared, thus better controlled. Of course this is a long step from Anglo-American community prevention. After all, the French abhor the concept of community!

But in these times when everyone deplores the lack of resident participation (Estèbe 2002; Bacqué *et al.* 2005; Donzelot and Epstein 2006), what seems promising is a bottom-up approach to problems and a concern with making people responsible for the places they use. Safety production becomes less specialised: everyone has a role to play in it. It is an interesting way to move from the French trend to expect everything from the state. It looks like a new form of social control (Wyvekens 2007b), where citizens are considered as capable of being co-responsible for the public space, not as a 'club good' (Hope 2000), but as a 'common good'. The 'overly social' French model would leave some room, but not all, to a situational logic, taking into account the notion of risk and the concern for efficiency: to address problems at a level where something can be done, while relying on civil skills. This could remedy the weakness of French crime prevention, without either eliminating it or reducing it to a monitoring of people and places.

Notes

1 As the weight of this term is important in understanding the French context, it will be used in this text.

2 A French *département* is an administrative unit roughly analogous with a county in the British context. The 100 French departments are grouped into 22 metropolitan and four overseas regions. The *préfet* is the state's representative in the department.

3 Law 2002-1094 of 29 August 2002 on the direction and operation of domestic security (*d'orientation et de programmation pour la sécurité intérieure*). Law 2003-239 of 18 March 2003 for domestic security (*pour la sécurité intérieure*).

4 Law 2002-1138 of 9 September 2002 on the direction and operation of the justice system (*d'orientation et de programmation pour la justice*). Law 2004-204 of 9 March 2004 on adapting the justice system to developments in crime (*portant adaptation de la justice aux évolutions de la criminalité*).

5 Law 2007-297 of 5 March 2007 relating to the prevention of crime (*relative à la prévention de la délinquance*).

6 Where local order, security and public tranquillity are threatened by lack of parental surveillance and control or parental failure to assist in their child's education, the mayor can propose parental support, consisting of an individualised programme combining counselling and educational work. The programme of support aims to help parents in parenting, but does so within a context of control and constraint as parents must have good reason to refuse the support offered.

7 Law 2007-1198 of 10 August 2007 reinforcing the fight against recidivism among adults and minors (*renforçant la lutte contre la récidive des majeurs et des mineurs*).

8 Law 2008-174 of 25 February 2008 on security detention and criminal irresponsibility due to mental disorder (*relative à la rétention de sûreté et à la déclaration d'irresponsabilité pénale pour cause de trouble mental*).

9 Article 706-53-13 of the 2008-174 law.

10 Law 2003-710 of 1 August 2003 on the direction and operation of city and urban renewal (*d'orientation et de programmation pour la ville et la rénovation urbaine*).

11 Article 6 of the 2003-710 law.

12 The *banlieues* are high-density peripheral housing estates around French cities in which low-income and disadvantaged populations tend to be concentrated, often in social housing.

13 On this question, it is useful to warn against the confusion sometimes made between close notions, such as neo-liberalism, neo-conservatism and the Americanisation of public policies (Crawford and Lewis 2007).

14 *L'impact de la vidéosurveillance sur la sécurité dans les espaces publics et les établissements privés recevant du public.*

15 Speech by Michèle Alliot-Marie, Interior Minister, at a meeting held on 20 May 2008, at the Interior Ministry, between the National Commission on videosurveillance, the chairs of the department level commissions and the *préfets* or their representative, *Maire Info*, 21 May 2008.

16 Its official title is actually the 'decree taken for the implementation of article L 111-3-1 of the code of urbanism and related to public safety studies'.

17 Law 95-73 of 21 January 1995 on the direction and operation for security (*d'orientation et de programmation relative à la sécurité*).
18 Extract from art. 11 of the law: 'Preliminary studies prior to urban renewal, collective infrastructure and building projects, undertaken by a collectivity or requiring an administrative authorisation and which, because of their scope, location or characteristics may have an impact on protection of people or goods against threats and aggressions, are subject to a public safety study to assess the consequences.'

References

Anache, M. (ed.) (2004) *Évaluation de l'impact de la vidéosurveillance sur la sécurisation des transports en commun en Région Île-de-France*. IAURIF.

André, P. (2005) 'Concilier service et sûreté. Une nouvelle exigence pour la SNCF', *Les Cahiers de la sécurité*, 57(2): 85–113.

Bacqué, M.-H., Rey, H. and Sintomer, Y. (eds) (2005) *Gestion de proximité et démocratie participative. Une perspective comparative*. Paris: La Découverte.

Billard, G., Chevalier, J. and Madoré, F. (2005) *Ville fermée, ville surveillée. La sécurisation des espaces résidentiels en France et en Amérique du Nord*. Rennes: Presses universitaires de Rennes.

Burgel, G. (2006) *La revanche des villes*. Paris: Hachette Littératures.

Claval, P. (2001) 'Clisthène, Habermas, Rawls et la privatisation de la ville', in C. Ghorra-Gobin (ed.) *Réinventer le sens de la ville, les espaces publics à l'heure globale*. Paris: L'Harmattan, pp. 23–32.

Commission des maires sur la sécurité (1982) *Face à la délinquance: prévention, répression, solidarité*. Paris: La Documentation Française.

Commission nationale informatique et libertés (CNIL) (2007) *27e rapport d'activité 2006*. Paris: La Documentation Française.

Commission nationale informatique et libertés (CNIL) (2008) *28e rapport d'activité 2007*. Paris: La Documentation Française.

Crawford, A. and Lewis, S. (2007) 'Évolutions mondiales, orientations nationales et justice locale: Les effets du néo-libéralisme sur la justice des mineurs en Angleterre et au Pays de Galles', in F. Bailleau and Y. Cartuyvels (eds) *Les évolutions de la justice pénale des mineurs en Europe. Entre modèle welfare et inflexions néo-libérales*. Paris: L'Harmattan, pp. 23–43.

Délégation interministérielle à la ville (DIV) (2004) *Politique de la ville et prévention de la délinquance. Recueil d'actions locales*. Paris: Éditions de la DIV, coll. «Repères».

Donzelot, J. and Epstein, R. (2006) 'Démocratie et participation: l'exemple de la rénovation urbaine', *Esprit*, July: 5–34.

Donzelot, J. and Wyvekens, A. (2004) *La magistrature sociale. Enquêtes sur les politiques locales de sécurité*. Paris: La Documentation Française.

Donzelot, J., Mevel, C. and Wyvekens, A. (2003) *Faire société. La politique de la ville aux Etats-Unis et en France*. Paris: Seuil.

Dubedout, H. (1983) *Ensemble, refaire la ville*. Paris: La Documentation Française.

Estèbe, P. (2002) 'L'habitant, ou le cher disparu. Disparitions, apparitions et résurgences de l'habitant comme figure de la participation politique en France', *Les Cahiers de la sécurité intérieure*, 49: 151–71.

Ferret, J. and Mouhanna, Ch. (eds) (2005) *Peurs sur les villes. Vers un populisme punitif à la française?* Paris: PUF.

Garland, D. (2001) *Culture of Control: Crime and Social Order in Contemporary Society.* Oxford: Oxford University Press.

Ghorra-Gobin, C. (2001) 'Réinvestir la dimension symbolique des espaces publics', in C. Ghorra-Gobin (ed.) *Réinventer le sens de la ville, les espaces publics à l'heure globale.* Paris: L'Harmattan, pp. 5–15.

Heilmann, E. (2008) 'La vidéosurveillance, un mirage technologique et politique', in L. Mucchielli (ed.) *La frénésie sécuritaire. Retour à l'ordre et nouveau contrôle social.* Paris: La Découverte, pp. 113–24.

Heilmann, E. and Mornet, M.-N. (2003) *Vidéosurveillance et prévention de la criminalité. L'impact des dispositifs dans les espaces urbains en Grande-Bretagne.* IHESI, coll. Etudes et Recherches.

Hope, T. (2000) 'Inequality and the Clubbing of Private Security', in T. Hope and R. Sparks (eds) *Crime, Risk and Insecurity.* London: Routledge, pp. 83–106.

Jacobs, J. (1961) *The Death and Life of Great American Cities.* New York: Random House.

Le Goff, T., Loudier-Malgouyres, C., Lavocat, Ch. and Dautheville, M. (2007) *La vidéosurveillance dans les lycées en Île-de-France. Usages et impacts.* IAURIF.

Lemonier, M. (1998) 'De l'espace défendable à la prévention situationnelle', *Diagonal*, 129.

Marcus, M. (2006) 'Le rôle du maire dans les politiques locales de prévention/sécurité', *Les Cahiers de la sécurité*, 61: 131–42.

Mary, P. (2003) *Insécurité et pénalisation du social.* Bruxelles: Labor, coll. Quartier libre.

Monjardet, D. (1999) 'La police de proximité: ce qu'elle n'est pas', *Revue française d'administration publique*, 91: 519–25.

Monjardet, D. (2004) 'L'information, l'urgence et la réforme, réflexions sur le fonctionnement de la Direction centrale de la sécurité publique', in S. Roché (ed.) *Réformer la police et la sécurité.* Paris: Odile Jacob, pp. 128–42.

Mosser, S. (2007) 'Eclairage et sécurité en ville: l'état des savoirs', *Déviance et Société*, 31(1): 77–100.

Newman, O. (1971) *Defensible Space. People and Design in the Violent City.* London: Architectural Press.

Ocqueteau, F. (2004), *Polices entre Etat et marché.* Paris, Presses de Sciences Po.

Ocqueteau, F. (2007) 'La «sécurité globale», une réponse à la menace terroriste?', *Regards sur l'actualité*, 328: 49–60.

Pécaud, D. (2002) *L'impact de la vidéosurveillance sur la sécurité dans les espaces publics et les établissements privés recevant du public.* IHESI, coll. Etudes et recherches.

Réussir l'espace public (2006) *Qualité globale de l'espace et sécurité.* Paris: Rapport d'études pour l'Institut national des hautes études de sécurité.

Roché, S. (2005) *Police de proximité. Nos politiques de sécurité.* Paris: Seuil.

Schwartz, B. (1981) *L'insertion professionnelle et sociale des jeunes.* Paris: La Documentation Française.

Shearing, C. and Stenning, P. (1983) 'Private Security: Implications for Social Control', *Social Problems*, 30(5): 493–506.

Tabet, J. (1999) 'La résidentialisation du logement social à Paris', *Annales de la recherche urbaine*, 83–84: 155–63.

Tiévant, S. (2006) 'Le parc de la Villette, îlot de civilité', *Les Cahiers de la sécurité*, 57(2): 131–52.

Vidal-Naquet, P. A. and Tiévant, S. (2006) 'Incivilités et travail de civilité', *Les Cahiers de la sécurité*, 57(2): 13–31.

Wilson, J. Q. and Kelling, G. (1982) 'Broken Windows', *The Atlantic Monthly*, March: 29–37.

Wyvekens, A. (2001) 'La justice de proximité en France. Politique judiciaire de la ville et interrogations sur la fonction de justice', in A. Wyvekens and J. Faget (eds) *La justice de proximité en Europe: Pratiques et enjeux*. Toulouse: Erès, pp. 17–36.

Wyvekens, A. (2007a) 'Proximity Justice in France: Anything but "Justice and Community"?', in J. Shapland (ed.) *Justice, Community and Civil Society*. Cullompton: Willan Publishing, pp. 30–46.

Wyvekens, A. (2007b) 'Espace public et civilité: réinventer un contrôle social? Perspectives pour la "France"', *Lien social et politiques*, 57: 35–45.

Wyvekens, A., Donzelot, J., Mével, C., Oblet, T. and Villechaise-Dupont, A. (2003) *Les incivilités à la Poste*. CEPS/La Poste.

Chapter 6

Forty years of crime prevention in the Dutch polder

Jan J. M. Van Dijk and Jaap De Waard[1]

Introduction

In 1992 a delegation of Dutch crime prevention practitioners, headed by the junior Minister of Justice, attended a major conference in Paris organised by the European Forum on Crime Prevention (later called European Forum for Urban Safety). At the end of the first day the anchorman of the conference announced a special presentation on a project to prevent bicycle theft in Groningen, the Netherlands. He added that this would be followed by a presentation from Aix en Provence on the prevention of theft of *jeu de boules* balls. His aside caused great merriment among the largely French audience but annoyed the Dutch delegates. They sensed that their carefully designed and proven project, where unemployed youngsters assisted bike owners in installing security locks and identification tags on their bikes, was out of place. This clearly was a high-level conference where mayors and other dignitaries spoke eloquently about social solidarity rather than a forum for practitioners to exchange success stories about reducing crime by mundane, non-punitive means.

In this chapter we describe developments in crime prevention policies in the Netherlands over the past 40 years. In many respects crime prevention in the Low Countries resembles that in other western countries. Its focus on surveillance and semi-social control could, for example, be understood as manifestations of an international trend towards expanded state control (Cohen 1985). Its pragmatic approach of crime problems has been critiqued as a form of risk management against the background of neo-liberalism (Hebberecht 1997). Its later, more punitive manifestations could perhaps be interpreted as yet another expression of the common trend of penal populism in the western world (Garland 2001). Clearly the Dutch experience of crime prevention can be interpreted from an international theoretical perspective. For this chapter, however, we have opted for another theoretical approach by focusing not on commonalities with trends elsewhere but on special, possibly unique features of Dutch crime prevention. We try to bring out continuities in the nature and organisation of Dutch policies that seem to stand out from an international perspective. In the final section we argue that some characteristics of Dutch crime prevention can be interpreted as a product of the Dutch Polder model, a metaphor for the Dutch tradition of consensus policies in the pragmatic pursuit of the common good.

Crime trends and victimisation surveys

Trends in anti-crime policies must, of course, be understood in relation to the public debate on crime. This public debate is at least in part a response to information on trends in crime as communicated by the media. In many countries such information is traditionally under the control of the police administration. The Netherlands has been the first European country to invest in the execution of regular victimisation surveys among the general public as a source of information on crime, independent of police administrations. The first large-scale victimisation survey was launched by the Research and Documentation Centre of the Ministry of Justice in 1973 (Van Dijk and Steinmetz 1979). In the first reports on the survey the point was made that the dark figure of crime was huge but consisted mainly of relatively minor crimes. This conclusion was reflected in the report's subtitle: *Results of a Study into the Volume and Trends in Petty Crime*. In later years, the survey results showed that various types of petty crime were increasing. In the Netherlands, reports on the results of the National Victimisation Surveys have sensitised public opinion to the need to tackle types of volume crime such as vandalism and shoplifting (around 1980), household burglary and car-related thefts (around 1985), robberies (around 1990), street violence (around 2000) and domestic violence (around 2003).

Crime trends in the Netherlands: 1950–2007

Figure 6.1 shows the development of aggregate crime, as recorded by the police, since the 1950s. The increase in crime was most marked in the period 1970–85. While until then the Netherlands was a low-crime society compared to surrounding countries, crime rates caught up quickly. The

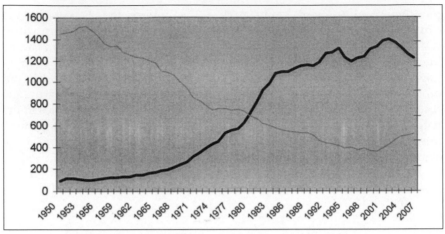

Key: Black line represents the volume of recorded crimes (in thousands).
Grey line represents the clearance rate as a percentage of recorded crimes.

Figure 6.1　Recorded crime and clearance rates in the Netherlands, 1950–2007

increase was partly a result of growing anonymity of society and the abundance of goods susceptible to theft, and partly due to social problems such as drug addiction and unemployment. With hindsight it can be argued that Dutch society and government were overtaken by events. Long-standing attitudes of tolerance and anti-authoritarianism fuelled a permissive society. In the 1980s attitudes started to change and the pressure on government to act against crime increased rapidly. The result was a fast catch-up of policies to reduce crime (Society and Crime 1985). Since 1985 the sharp annual rises in the incidence of recorded crime have tailed off. Over the last years, a sharp downward trend in crime can be observed, while clearance rates show an upward trend. The downward trend in crime is confirmed by the results from the Dutch National Victimisation Surveys.

Figure 6.2 shows the development in self-reported victimisation among the population aged 15 years and older. On the basis of victim surveys we see a gradual stabilisation of crime. When we compare the outcomes from 2007 with 2002, a major crime drop can be observed. The overall levels of victimisation have declined by 23 per cent; violence is down by 33 per cent (Berghuis and De Waard 2008). When looking at property crime, most notably household burglaries, car-related thefts and bicycle thefts show the biggest reductions in this category. These developments are not unique for the Netherlands alone. As in the United States of America and Australia, in many European countries there are indicators of a downward trend in the total level of crime. Also the results of the various crime victim surveys among the population indicate a downward trend of the general level of crime. The decline in crime can be observed in many

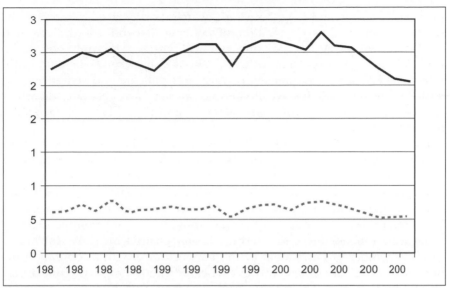

Key: Black line represents the overall victimisation rate in percentage.
Grey dotted line represents victimisation rate of violence in percentage.

Figure 6.2 Self-reported victimisation among the population aged 15 years and older, 1980–2008

countries. Starting in the USA in 1992, other countries followed in the years thereafter (Van Dijk 2008).

A combination of three major factors can be given to explain the Dutch drop in crime. First, drug-related crime has fallen sharply due to the decreasing number of heroin addicts (active heroin cohorts have partly dried up). Second, since 1993 crime preventative behaviour among the population at large and businesses is booming. Third, the criminal justice system is responding more seriously and in a stricter manner to criminal and delinquent behaviour. The permissive society of the Netherlands has come to an end.

Crime prevention as an alternative strategy

Crime prevention in the Netherlands is, as elsewhere, a relatively new phenomenon. In the late 1960s police forces started with information campaigns among the public about the importance of precautionary measures to prevent victimisation by petty crime. In 1979 a National Bureau for Crime Prevention was set up at the Dutch Ministry of Justice to promote police-based crime prevention. This national bureau mainly promoted different forms of technical crime prevention (target-hardening). In the late 1970s it also supported police-based programmes such as property-marking and neighbourhood watch. Police-based crime prevention was seen as a new technique of policing that did not attract much political attention. At the time only political parties at the right end of the political spectrum expressed concerns about rising crime rates, typically interpreted as the consequence of overly soft policing and sentencing. In leftist political circles the so-called crime problem was generally regarded as a social construction of conservative political parties, fuelled by the media (e.g. Van Dijk 1979).

In the early 1980s the steady increase in petty crime according to both police statistics and victimisation surveys gave rise to heated political debates. In 1983 the centre-right government consisting of the Christian democratic (CDA) and liberal conservative (VVD) parties established an Advisory Committee on Petty Crime (*Adviescommissie Kleine Criminaliteit*). This committee was requested to come up with a set of recommendations to address the rise in volume crime. It was chaired by Hein Roethof, a former Member of Parliament of the Labour Party with a reputation for liberal ideas about crime control. Members included experts from different political parties, including the future threefold Minister of Justice Ernst Hirsch Ballin and Jan Van Dijk, at the time head of the Research Centre of the Ministry of Justice. In the winter of 1984 the committee in its first report advised that volume crime had indeed become a serious social problem for large segments of the population but should be tackled primarily with preventive means. This recognition heralded a new consensus among the main political parties, including the Labour Party, about both diagnosis and cure. While acknowledging the seriousness of the crime problem, the report categorically rejected proposals for a mere expansion of the criminal justice system. It also questioned a further expansion of technical crime prevention measures as a viable response to the problem of volume crime. Its key message was that volume crime had grown from a weakening of informal social controls in an urbanised, consumerist society and should primarily be tackled by reintroducing modern versions of informal social control. Its main recommendations were a strengthening of the national government's commitment to crime prevention, the involvement of intermediary structures (such as schools and sports clubs) and businesses to that end and inter-agency co-operation at the central and local levels of government (Van Dijk and Junger-Tas 1988). The report specifically recommended the involvement of intermediary structures such as schools, sports clubs and churches as well as public transport companies, shopping malls and other businesses to increase natural surveillance in their semi-public domains. The report also made the recommendation to make criminal justice more victim-centred and to offer state funding for specialised support for crime victims as a means to prevent their alienation from society. The recommendations of the committee were favourably received by all main political parties and soon came to constitute the cornerstone of the government's anti-crime policies as formulated in the white paper *Society and Crime* in 1985.

Conceptualising the new crime prevention

Crime prevention in both the Roethof Report and in the *Society and Crime* white paper was conceptualised as a set of measures distinct from law enforcement that would supplement conventional criminal policies. In this vein, Van Dijk and De Waard, both involved in the design of the Dutch crime prevention policies between 1985 and 1995, defined crime prevention as: 'the total of all private initiatives and state policies, other than the enforcement of criminal law, aimed at the reduction of damage caused by acts defined as criminal by the state' (1991: 483). Dutch crime prevention has been from the outset eclectic in its orientation. According to a typology developed by Van Dijk and De Waard (1991), crime prevention measures can be distinguished by looking at the nature of the target (either the offenders, the victims or the physical environment) and the reach of the measures directed at the country or public at large, focusing on at-risk areas or groups or tackling already existing problems. The first distinction looks at the target of the measures:

- Measures aimed at preventing (potential) offenders from committing crimes or re-offending; known as *offender-oriented or social prevention*.

- Measures that attempt to reduce the opportunities to commit crime, either by changing the behaviour of potential victims (*victim-oriented prevention*) or by intervention in situations with inherent risks (*situational prevention*).

Offender-oriented measures can be seen as practical applications of conventional criminological theories on the causes of crime such as Hirschi's (1969) theory of social control. Victimological studies on vulnerabilities for criminal victimisation and victim-precipitation have laid the foundation for victim-oriented crime prevention. Recent interest in repeat victimisation underlines the relevance of this type of measures. The new brand of criminological theories regarding routine activities and criminal opportunities has informed situational crime prevention (Clarke 1995; Felson 1994; Van Dijk and Steinmetz 1979).

The second dimension, which is well known in the literature on drugs prevention, makes a distinction between the stages of development of problems determining the reach of the measures. It distinguishes:

- *Primary prevention.* This relates to general preventative activities, aimed at the public or the country at large.

- *Secondary prevention*. This relates to measures aimed at specific risk factors (on the victim or offender side) and on vulnerable neighbourhoods.

- *Tertiary prevention*. This form of prevention is aimed at people and situations actually affected by crime. Examples are rehabilitation of offenders, victim support to prevent repeat victimisation or alienation, and intensive surveillance at so-called 'hot spots' in urban environments.

If we set the two dimensions alongside each other, nine forms of crime prevention can be distinguished. In Table 6.1 we present the matrix with some examples of each type of prevention.

The typology reflects the broad Dutch conception of crime prevention policies, encompassing both social crime prevention, prevailing in France and Sweden, and environmental or situational prevention, more prevalent in England and Wales (Sutton *et al.* 2008). In the Roethof Report and the ensuing *Society and Crime* white paper, emphasis was put on secondary situational crime prevention consisting not of technologies but of semiformal surveillance, on secondary offender-oriented prevention (e.g. truancy prevention by schools) and on tertiary victim-oriented prevention (victim support). From the outset Dutch crime prevention has been multidimensional and informed by academic research about 'what works' in reducing types of crime, deemed worrying by the population (Van Noije and Wittebrood 2008).

Implementing the new crime prevention

To implement the newly announced policies, an Interdepartmental Committee for Crime Prevention was set up in 1985 comprising high-level representatives of the ministries of Justice and the Interior and several other key ministries, under the chairmanship of the secretary general of the Prime Minister's office. It administered a fund of 25 million euro to permit local authorities to mount crime prevention programmes in the period 1986–1990. Almost all larger towns appointed crime prevention co-ordinators to draft proposals for projects and oversee their implementation. During the period 1986–1990 some 200 local projects were subsidised. Central funds were supplemented with money raised locally. Ten per cent of the total budget was earmarked for independent evaluation by the Research Centre of the Ministry of Justice or university-based institutes. The secretariat of the new policies in 1990 was upgraded to a fully fledged directorate at the Ministry of Justice, with separate departments for offender-based and situational prevention. It set up a database with current projects and their first results, and launched a

Table 6.1 Matrix of types of preventative measures

Primary offender-oriented prevention	Secondary offender-oriented prevention	Tertiary offender-oriented prevention
Academic enrichment	Apprenticeships	Alternative sanctions
Advertising	Bootcamps/wilderness camps	Child care
After-school activities (latchkey children)	Communication skills	Community-based corrections
Deterrence	Education projects	Curfew
Education in the law	Employment skill-building	Diversion
Information campaigns (vandalism, tax evasion)	Foster parenting	Electronic monitoring
Normative training	Inner city empowerment	Intensive supervision probation
Parent education and training	Out-of-home placements	Restitution
Police talks in school	Scared straight programmes	Training courses for drunk drivers
Recreation and social activities	Social development	Victim–offender mediation
School discipline code	Truancy patrols (police)	Vocational training/Curriculum
Family support services	College scholarships	Conflict resolution
Health care access	Job creation/placement	Gang intervention
Literacy	Mental health screenings	Mentoring
Nutrition services	Parental involvement	Periodic drug testing
Substance abuse education	Summer jobs for youth	Anger management therapy
Intervening in biological and psychological development	Cognitive-behavioural techniques	Pharmacological managing of behaviour

Primary situational-oriented prevention	Secondary situational-oriented prevention	Tertiary situational-oriented prevention
Architectural design	Access control (entry phones)	Behavioural geography and criminal behaviour
Building safety and security	Burglar alarms	Crime analysis/crime mapping
Checklists for criminologically sound designs	Business watch/security	Closing criminogenic places
Crime impact statements	Caretakers (concierges)	Focused or saturation policing
Defensible space	Clean-ups	Hot spots/crime locations
	Closure of access points	

Table 6.1 *Continued*

Primary offender-oriented prevention	Secondary offender-oriented prevention	Tertiary offender-oriented prevention
Facility site selection	Community policing	Increased police patrols
Housing design/renovation	Employee screening	Licensing policies
Housing programmes	Extra ticket inspection staff	Micro-environments of violence
Improving domestic door and window locks	Fencing	Offender mobility
Insurance	Improved visibility	Police crackdowns
Law as situational measure	Increased staffing of facilities	Problem-oriented policing styles
Improved visibility	Landscaping	Reduce amount of cash in tills
Opportunity reducing techniques	Private security guards	Target removal
Security inspections/surveys	Rapid repair	Trouble spot clustering
Steering column locks	Surveillance by employees (formal)	Video control/CCTV
Target-hardening	Reducing weapon lethality	Public/private partnerships
Safe passages/corridors		Disruption tactics for illegal markets
Zoning		

Primary victim-oriented prevention	Secondary victim-oriented prevention	Tertiary victim-oriented prevention
Awareness of victimisation risks	Block parent programmes	Civil protection orders
Crime stoppers programmes	Citizen patrols	Crisis counselling
Leafletting	Doorstep campaigns	Police referral schemes
Mass-media campaigns/publicity	Emergency phone lines	Police–victim communication
Property marking/operation identification	Escort services	Post-trauma counselling
Public education/information	Guardian Angels	Rape Crisis centres
Public meetings	Municipal bylaw changes	Repeat victimisation prevention
Public speaking presentations	Neighbourhood watch	Self-help groups
Special information campaigns (elderly, violence)	Safe houses for children	Victim assistance (projects)
	Services to the elderly/isolated	Victim impact statement
Self-defence training	VIP-protection	Victim notification
Site surveys		

journal on crime prevention with a distribution among 20,000 practioners. It also introduced an annual award for the most successful project, the Roethof Award, which was later extended to include Belgian and British projects and eventually inspired the current Prevention Award of the European Union. In 1992, the directorate was also made responsible for the screening of companies with limited liability as a means to prevent infiltration of the legitimate economy by (associates of) organised crime groups. To this end a database was set up of all Dutch limited companies, listing their board members and owners as well as records of past bankruptcies and criminal convictions (called Vennoot) (T.M.C. Asser Instituut 2006).

As mentioned earlier, a main focus of the new wave of crime prevention was the strengthening of semi-formal social control or surveillance in the public and semi-public domain. For historical reasons, the contribution of voluntary groups of citizens to patrolling or other forms of surveillance was relatively small in the Netherlands. Neighbourhood watch, for example, brings back associations of spying on behalf of the government during the German occupation in the Nazi period. Attempts by police forces to promote such schemes were never very successful. One of the more interesting Dutch examples of crime prevention and arguably the Dutch alternative of neighbourhood watch are the 'city guards' (*Stadswachten*). *Stadswachten* are municipal security guards who patrol the inner cities and give assistance to passers-by. They are unarmed and have no special authority. In the event that they witness the commission of a crime they are bound to immediately alert the police. They are largely recruited from the long-term unemployed and are financed by the Ministry of Employment. Evaluation studies have shown that the presence of *stadswachten* is greatly appreciated by shopkeepers and passers-by and reduces feelings of unsafety and possibly (minor) crime (Hofstra and Shapland 1997). The UK took this model as an inspiration when implementing their Neighbourhood Warden Scheme in 2000.

Other examples of this type of crime prevention include the appointment of extra inspectors in public transport and the use of caretakers in crime-ridden high-rise apartment buildings (Hesseling 1995). An essential element in these projects is the joint tackling of three social problems: unemployment, volume crime, and resulting feelings of insecurity in the public domain (Willemse 1996). When unemployment rates plummeted in the Netherlands after 1995, the funding of the schemes became less generous. The policies have, however, proved their worth and could easily be revitalised when needed (Van Noije and Wittebrood 2008).

The new crime prevention of the 1980s was mainly directed at reducing the opportunities for crime. In addition, a nationwide network of victim support schemes came into being, assisting over 100,000 crime victims per year. A sizeable minority of the funded projects can be categorised as offender-oriented. Pilot projects focused on reducing truancy and improving academic achievement in secondary schools through improved record systems and early contacting of parents. Results at the experimental site were compared systematically with a control school of similar size and student composition. A final, modified programme was then implemented on a national basis (Van Dijk and Junger-Tas 1988).

Arguably one of the most successful innovations was the introduction of community service as a diversionary option for minors (the so-called HALT option). Young people arrested for minor crimes for the first time are referred to special agencies, which arrange for them to carry out an unpaid job on a free Saturday, e.g. cleaning the floor of the department store where they committed shoplifting or cleaning graffiti from buses. If the youth complies with the appointment no report is sent to the prosecutor and no record will be kept of the arrest. Formally, the community service is a condition for discontinuing the prosecution, mandated by the prosecutor to the police. Evaluation studies showed favourable reductions in recidivism rates for former clients of the HALT bureaus (Van Hees 1998). Later studies, however, have shown fewer or no effects on recidivism, probably because the young people are currently more deeply involved in criminality at their first arrest than was the case ten years ago. It has also been observed that options such as HALT have little impact upon clients from ethnic minorities (Ferwerda et al. 2006).

Van Swaaningen and Uit Beijerse (2006) point at the failure of Dutch crime prevention policies to make a significant contribution to the social integration of (marginalised) youth. In their view the policies insufficiently addressed root causes of crime and expected municipalities to solve deeply rooted social problems with minimal additional financial support. With hindsight the new crime prevention for many years has ignored the growing involvement in forms of serious delinquency at a very young age of youths from ethnic minority groups, notably Moroccans and Antilleans (Van Gemert et al. 2008).

Public–private partnerships

One special feature of the Dutch approach in preventing crime is the collaboration between government and the business world. In 1992 the government agreed to set up the National Platform of Crime Control. In this body, under the presidency of the Minister of Justice and the Chair of the Dutch Employers Federation, public institutions such as the police and prosecutors as well as the business community are represented at the highest level (for instance, board members of the largest Dutch corporations such as AMRO, ING, AHOLD and Unilever). Security and criminal justice experts are brought together in task forces under its supervision. The National Platform for Crime Control promotes the co-operation between the Ministries of Justice, the Interior, Economic Affairs, Transport, Finance and the business community (insurance companies, banking retail and so on). To inform the policy agenda of the Platform, the Directorate for Crime Prevention commissioned the International Crimes against Businesses Survey (Van Dijk and Terlouw 1996). The funding arrangement of concrete actions foresees an equally shared (50 per cent each) division of costs between the government and the business sector. This co-operation has resulted in several successful joint initiatives against specific types of crime. The number of commercial robberies and auto thefts, for example, declined in the late 1990s as a result of initiatives of the National Platform on Crime Control (Van Dijk 1997a). The programmes funded are a mixture of situational measures (such as improved security in banks and immobilisers in cars) and extra efforts of police forces and prosecutors to target crimes against the business sector.

The introduction of the Dutch version of Secured by Design has involved close co-ordination between the Ministries of Justice, the Interior and Housing and Planning with a view to influencing planners and architects to include crime prevention as one of their concerns in designs for new homes and renovating existing ones. The evaluation of projects undertaken has led to the identification and dissemination of best practice throughout the country on such issues as residential burglary, vandalism and security on public transport (De Waard 1996). The concept of certification for safety aspects was later extended to businesses in general and bars and discos specifically. The Safe Enterprises programme focuses on the safety of businesses, their customers and the physical environment in which businesses operate. In recent years, a wide range of initiatives for improving safety in the business community has been developed on the basis of public–private partnerships. At this moment the Safe Enterprises Quality Mark, the Urgent Strategy for Business Locations, and the Safe Enterprises Action Plans are implemented nationwide.[2]

The National Platform on Crime Control has proved to be one of the most stable co-operation structures in the field of crime prevention in the Netherlands and is still in full swing in 2008. In the late 1990s a dozen or so larger cities set up local Platforms for Crime Control with a similar composition and support from the National Platform. To promote public and private partnerships in the field of crime prevention a National Centre for Crime Prevention and Safety was set up on 1 July 2004. It was established as a private foundation and co-funded by the business sector and the ministries of Justice and the Interior. Its key tasks are gathering information and dissemination of best practices on tackling crime problems at local level and in specific areas of the business sector. The Centre promotes the quality mark for safe entrepreneurship and the certification marks for going out safely, tackling commercial robberies and tackling violence in the leisure industry. It also supports existing networks, such as in the areas of integrity at the workplace and the prevention of employee theft.

Further developments

In 1994 Dutch central government initiated a public safety and security policy as part of its Larger Towns policy (1995–98). The Larger Towns policy sought to address problems of urban decay through the promotion of local, integrated programmes for neighbourhoods with high concentrations of social problems, including crime. Its security component stood for the co-ordination of all parties involved in crime prevention: ministries, local and regional government and various kinds of non-governmental organisations. According to the plan, strengthening of punitive action should go hand in hand with more targeted and specialised crime prevention. It was argued that only such comprehensive criminal policies could lead to a structurally improved control of the various forms of crime.

In this framework considerable funds were placed at the disposal of the municipal authorities in the largest cities to tackle drug abuse and youth crime. This new policy resulted in action programmes for the preventive and repressive approach to youth crime, and the formulation of neighbourhood security plans. Covenants were signed with 15 cities in relation to, among other things, youth and crime and hard-core persistent offenders. Extra funds have also been made available for the police to tackle these issues. In contrast to the previous funding arrangements, municipalities were given considerable freedom in spending the funds and oversight from central government was deliberately reduced. In this political context, it was also decided to downsize the Directorate of Crime Prevention at the Ministry of Justice and to transfer some of its responsibilities to the Ministry of the Interior, which has responsibility for the Larger Town Policies. Responsibilities for project design and innovation in situational crime prevention were later partly handed over to the previously mentioned National Centre for Crime Prevention and Safety. This centre has also taken over the production of the journal on crime prevention and the organisation of the annual Roethof Award for the most successful local project.

In the course of the 1990s new types of crime began to dominate public debate. One new trend in the discourse on crime and crime prevention was the attention accorded to so-called 'hard-core juvenile delinquents'. This hard core of young offenders are supposed to commit chronically a variety of serious crimes including violent offences. As confirmed by research (Leuw 1997; Van Gemert *et al.* 2008), adolescents from certain ethnic minorities are over-represented among these groups (for example, Moroccans and Antilleans). In response to this, crime prevention underwent a gradual change. In several towns experiments were initiated with intensive probation supervision. For example, young offenders detained in a pre-trial detention centre are placed in an intensive vocational training and work experience programme as a condition for their release.

In the case of a relapse or non-compliance with the rules they are re-arrested and tried. Young people who complete the programme are offered jobs under the municipal employment schemes. The best-known project in Amsterdam, called New Perspectives, processes several hundred young offenders per year and seems to have achieved good results. In a similar project in Rotterdam drug addicts highly active in crime are given vocational training and work experience during a two-year programme as an alternative to a prison sentence of a few months. In all these projects, offenders are approached with both a 'carrot' and a 'stick'.

Other recent initiatives worth mentioning are experiments with parental support in the framework of integrated community programmes for difficult neighbourhoods (along the lines of 'communities that care') and the establishment of offices of the public prosecutor in difficult neighbourhoods (*Justitie in de Buurt*, which translates as 'Justice Nearby'). Prosecutors working in these offices deal with minor crimes on the spot through administrative fines, conditional discontinuance of prosecutions or mediation.[3] More serious cases are brought before the court in special sessions. In some offices other justice agencies such as probation, victim support and HALT are also represented. The central concept behind these front offices is that criminal justice interventions are more effective if applied 'in context', ensuring due knowledge about and consideration of the unique local circumstances of the incidents at issue. More recently, several larger cities have established integrated centres that bring together police, prosecutors and municipal agencies responsible for youth work, social work and health. These centres are called Safety Houses (*Veiligheidshuizen*). At the time of writing (November 2008) 25 Safety Houses are active. They are the shared responsibility of the Public Prosecutor's Office and the municipalities. The Ministry of Justice contributes to their funding.

These initiatives clearly signal the re-emergence of offender-oriented prevention in the Netherlands. Knowledge about the crucial influence of responsible parenting on the development of self-control has also led to the promotion and subsequent adoption of early intervention programmes that would have been a political anathema only a few years ago. Primary prevention targeted at families in difficult neighbourhoods is seen as a promising approach by the Ministry of Justice (Junger-Tas 1997). At both central and local level there is a growing interest in tertiary offender-oriented prevention. Topical programmes for young offenders and drug addicts combine punitive or coercive elements with measures aimed at reintegration through training and employment. The presence of prosecutors in Safety Houses adds a coercive edge to existing community-based crime prevention and community-based policing in difficult neighbourhoods. Mayors of the largest cities have requested new authority to impose coercive measures on families with children who are routinely in conflict with the law, under the threat of the withdrawal of social benefits (Ministries of Justice and Interior 2007).

Safety begins with prevention

In 2007, the new coalition government consisting of Christian democrats and Labour issued a new programme called Safety Begins with Prevention. In an introductory statement the new Minister of Justice Ernst Hirsch Ballin writes that crime control no longer can be regarded as the sole responsibility of police and justice and that many other government agencies at all levels have important roles to play. The programme bears the signatures of six other ministers and its overarching objective is a reduction of overall victimisation rates by 25 per cent in 2010. The programme has set targets in six different areas: violence in public places and family violence; crimes against businesses; bicycle theft; reduction of recidivism by 10 per cent through better aftercare; organised crime; and cyber crimes. It also foresees a strong emphasis on safety aspects in a new programme to upgrade a selection of run-down neighbourhoods in the largest towns.

Primary responsibility for the programme's implementation lies with a special directorate at the Ministry of Justice. For its implementation the programme will rely on an extended network of integrated Safety Centres under the national supervision of the Minister of Justice. Special centres in larger cities have also been set up to co-ordinate measures against family violence including temporary bans for abusing partners. Projects to prevent violence in public spaces, bicycle theft and crimes against businesses will be executed in co-operation with the National Platform for Crime Control and affiliated entities such as the Centre for Crime Prevention and Safety (CCV). Renewed attention is given to the screening of companies that seek (renewals of) municipal licences or public contracts for links with organised crime groups. To facilitate this preventive screening, legislation was passed in 2002 and 2006 offering public bodies access to criminal records and investigative information (Law to Facilitate Integrity Checks by Public Bodies of 2002, last amended 2006).[4] These new instruments are, for example, actively and successfully used by the city of Amsterdam (Huisman and Nelen 2007; Kleemans 2007) in its drive to clean up the red light district in the inner city.

The changing agenda of crime prevention

As in the United Kingdom and the United States of America, there are clear indicators of a downward trend in the overall level of crime. According to reports from Statistics Netherlands, crime recorded by the police has declined since 1997. Also the results of the annual Crime Victim Survey among the population indicate a downward trend in the general level of crime (see Figures 6.1 and 6.2). As in other countries, the level of

Table 6.2 Security precautions in percentage of the total number of households in the Netherlands, 1993–2008

Year	1993	1995	1997	1999	2002	2004	2006	2008	Change
Burglar alarm	6.2	6.9	7.7	8.3	8.8	9.5	10.9	12.2	97%
Special door locks	67.6	71.8	74.4	74.2	77.0	77.4	82.6	83.6	24%
Secured by design	n.a.	n.a.	n.a.	n.a.	n.a.	n.a.	15.3	16.4	
Extra lighting	51.4	64.2	66.6	68.6	70.1	70.7	77.7	80.8	57%

self-protection against property crime has risen significantly over the past ten years (Van Dijk *et al.* 2008). The recent decline in the overall crime rates – car-related thefts and household burglaries in particular – might in part be the effect of this improved self-protection (see Table 6.2). In the Netherlands, this has been actively promoted by the government's crime prevention policies (Van Dijk 2008). Dutch households are among the best secured against crime in the western world (Van Dijk *et al.* 2008). Compared to the situation 30 years ago, the extent of semi-formal surveillance, for instance in public transport, has also been greatly improved.

Statistics indicate a rise in certain forms of violent crime, in particular among adolescents. Dutch society has been deeply affected by the political assassination of the right-wing politician Pim Fortuyn and the subsequent brutal murder of film-maker Theo Van Gogh in 2004 by a Muslim fundamentalist. Over the past ten years, the crime discourse in the Netherlands has focused less on vandalism and burglary or other petty crimes and more on violent youth crime and organised criminality (Kleemans 2007). Arguably, crimes have indeed become more serious and less opportunistic in nature. Current crime problems seem to be more clearly related to problems of inhabitants of socially problematic neighbourhoods. Parallel to this shift, the focus of crime prevention has gradually moved towards 'secondary offender-oriented approaches' targeted at early invention with 'at-risk' families. As said, mayors are propagating coercive forms of early intervention in at-risk families, many of Moroccan descent. One of the most outspoken protagonists of such approaches is a former junior minister of social affairs of Moroccan descent who was recently elected as Mayor of Rotterdam.

An acclaimed innovation of the 1980s was the community service as diversionary option for minors (HALT). The newest offender-oriented preventive measures are more coercive in nature. The boundaries between offender-oriented crime prevention and probation have been blurred. Community service is one of the most frequently imposed penalties. For young offenders too there is the possibility of community service, but they can also be sentenced to follow a training course (Van der Laan 1993, 2006). Many of the new offender-oriented preventive projects, described above, rely heavily on criminal justice based coercion. On the plus side, the widespread substitution of community service for short-term prison sentences seems to pay off in fewer prison sentences. The numbers of prisoners per 100,000 have started to fall. Since 2006, the total number of prisoners in the Netherlands has declined by almost 20 per cent. If this downward trend persists, the country might once again become one of the less punitive countries in Europe.

Discussion

Looking back at 40 years of crime prevention in the Netherlands the following observations can be made. In conjunction with the types of crime dominating debate, the measures promoted have undergone important transformations. Situational crime prevention dominated the first wave of projects. It has proven its efficacy and is now widely implemented to prevent crimes against households and businesses and to increase safety in public spaces. Evaluation studies have contributed to the social acceptance of these measures and also to the international literature on crime prevention. Offender-oriented projects, especially parent–child interaction therapy, are now widely regarded to be promising responses to current problems of violent crime (Junger et al. 2007). Simulation models, relying mainly on findings from American research (Greenwood et al. 1996; Sherman et al. 1997), have shown the superior cost-effectiveness of both situational and offender-oriented prevention compared to conventional criminal justice measures (Van Dijk 1997b).

Despite these transformations in Dutch crime prevention policies over the years, certain characteristics seem to have prevailed. Policies have first of all been planned and monitored using results of national and local major victimisation surveys. In the Netherlands, as in England and Wales, national victimisation surveys have later been supplemented by local surveys focusing on police performance and the impact of crime prevention measures. Programmes and projects have been informed by criminological knowledge and many have been independently evaluated (De Waard 2004). In this respect, Dutch crime prevention policies resemble the British 'what works' approach to crime prevention (Sutton et al. 2008). In line with 'what works', Dutch crime prevention has initially been more oriented towards proven situational measures, though with a distinct preference for people-based surveillance over technical measures such as CCTV. In this respect, Dutch crime prevention can be characterised as being pragmatic and people-centred in its orientation.

The 'rationalist' approach favours a top-down implementation strategy. Evidence-based programmes are typically designed at the level of central government and local agencies are held accountable in relation to previously agreed outcomes. In the United Kingdom this centralist tendency, prevailing during the crime reduction programme in the late 1990s, has been criticised for its lack of flexibility in implementation (Homel *et al.* 2004). In the Netherlands, a similar top-down implementation strategy was practised by the police-based Crime Prevention Bureau, the Interministerial Steering Committee and the Directorate for Crime Prevention at the Ministry of Justice. Since the mid 1990s municipalities have gained greater autonomy in both design and implementation of their crime prevention policies. Several municipalities have launched well-funded and closely monitored safety programmes of their own. On the downside, projects are less often independently evaluated and outcomes are less systematically recorded and shared with others at the national level than before (Van Noije and Wittebrood 2008).

Most western countries have introduced special legislation mandating existing administrative structures or stand-alone structures such as crime prevention councils to carry out crime prevention policies. Dutch crime prevention seems to be fairly unique in its reliance on non-statutory collaboration structures. Design, funding and implementation have remained the responsibility of joined-up ministries and municipal agencies without a special statutory footing. Collaboration with local police forces and the prosecutors has been facilitated at the local level by the existing tradition of regular co-ordination meetings, called triangle meetings, between mayors, chiefs of police and chief prosecutors. The collaborative approach has been permanently adjusted to new situations, most notably by including the business sector with the establishment of the National Platform on Crime Control in 1992 and subsequent local platforms and the National Centre for Crime Prevention and Safety.

In its comparatively loose and flexible form of organisation, Dutch crime prevention can also be characterised as being pragmatic. The pragmatic nature of Dutch crime prevention and its organisational form seems to have been mutually reinforcing. For example, the successful involvement of the business sector is predicated on the 'what works' approach, including a keen interest in implementing situational measures. Dutch crime control policies have been characterised as tolerant and non-punitive by foreign observers (Downes 1988; Crawford 1989) but should in its more recent manifestations perhaps better be described as pragmatic. This raises the question as to the historical or cultural roots of such pragmatism in the face of collective problems such as the crime threat.

One of the protagonists of the National Platform on Crime Control, a former CEO of the British-Dutch multinational Unilever, once confessed to the first author that in the United Kingdom the hands-on collaboration between the ministers of justice, a prosecutor-general, a chief of police and board members of key Dutch companies would not be feasible. Such pragmatic co-operation at the highest level of government and the business world was, in his view, only possible due to the Dutch tradition of the Polder. The so-called Polder model stands for a tradition of pragmatic consensus decision-making in economics and other public domains (*The Economist*, 22 May 2002). As is widely known, large parts of the Netherlands have been reclaimed from the sea through water drainage. Ever since the Middle Ages, competing or even warring cities in the same polder were forced to set aside their differences to maintain the polders, lest they both be flooded.[5] The common fight against the sea is seen as the root cause of the Dutch tradition of pragmatism and consensual policies (Romein and Romein-Verschoor 1934). Regardless of whether or not these instances of collaboration are indeed rooted in the cultural heritage of the polder, coalition-building across religious denominations and parties have undeniably been a characteristic of Dutch politics for a long time (Lijphart 1975).

In some respects, the experience of Dutch crime prevention over the past 30 years seems to have been comparatively successful. Considering the lack of stable institutional arrangements for crime prevention in Europe, Australia and elsewhere, it would seem of great practical relevance to collect best practices in the governance of crime prevention. To the extent that Dutch crime prevention is predicated upon specific cultural traditions, the Dutch experience, however, cannot be transferred as a best practice to other countries. Attempts to copy elements of the Dutch approach in Belgium under Minister of the Interior Louis Tobback in the early 1990s have indeed been short-lived (see Chapter 8, this volume). Pioneering efforts from the Permanent Secretariat for Crime Prevention in Brussels to collaborate with Belgian companies in the funding of crime prevention projects resulted in allegations of corruption and ultimately to the resignation of the responsible administrator.

In our view the Dutch experience of crime prevention confirms some of the recommendations for sustainable crime prevention made by Adam Sutton, former director of crime prevention in South Australia, and his colleagues (Sutton *et al.* 2008). To be sustainable, besides political leadership, crime prevention requires a solid partnership between central and local government to execute a comprehensive programme of both short-term (e.g. situational) and long-term (e.g. social) prevention measures. The still weak, evolving knowledge base, and dynamic nature of crime problems call for strong research and development efforts at the central (national or European) level. We also agree with Sutton *et al.* that social crime prevention should not necessarily be implemented under the banner of crime prevention due to its stigmatising connotations. The integration of crime prevention in larger policy agendas such as urban renewal, however, is not without risks. Funds allocated to such 'crime prevention in disguise' can easily leak away to activities with little potential to reduce crime. This is not, as Sutton *et al.* seem to believe, just a question of lack of expertise that can be remedied by the deployment of more crime prevention experts. The leakage results from the inherent tendency of both bureaucratic and commercial agencies to focus activities on client groups that look promising and rewarding to work with. Effective crime prevention requires an unwavering commitment to invest in families and young persons that offer no prospects for easy gains. Such commitment can be assured only under a system of rigorous monitoring from a centre whose ultimate objective is to reduce levels of crime.

According to article 1.1 of the United Nations *Guidelines for the Prevention of Crime*, adopted on 24 July 2002 by the Economic and Social Council: 'Crime prevention offers opportunities for a humane and more cost-effective approach to the problems of crime.' To make full use of these opportunities, countries must succeed in creating organisational conditions for crime prevention that fit their specific national setting. In many countries such best-fit arrangements for crime prevention can be found only after extensive trial and error. Countries that flinch from this difficult search are doomed to continue conducting crime control policies that are unnecessarily costly in both economic and humanitarian terms.

Notes

1 We dedicate this chapter to our friend and former colleague at the Directorate of Crime Prevention at the Ministry of Justice, Hans Willemse. His intellectual merit and commitment has been important to continue 'flying the flag for crime prevention' in The Netherlands.
2 For an overview of these initiatives see www.theccv.eu/
3 There are strong similarities between the *Justitie in de Buurt* and the *Maison de Justice et du Droit* that was developed in France during the late 1980s and early 1990s and was a source of inspiration for the Dutch Ministry of Justice (Wyvekens 1997).
4 Wet Bevordering Integriteit Beoordeling door het Opembaar Bestuur van 20 Juni, 2002, laatstelijk gewijzigd op 04.08.2006.
5 A polder is a low-lying tract of land enclosed by embankments known as dikes, usually drained and reclaimed marshland, and a common feature of the Netherlands.

References

Berghuis, B. and De Waard, J. (2008) *Trends in criminaliteit en de handhaving in macroperspectief*. The Hague: Ministry of Justice.

Clarke, R. V. (1995) 'Situational Crime Prevention', in M. Tonry and D. P. Farrington (eds) *Building a Safer Society: Strategic Approaches to Crime Prevention*. Chicago: University of Chicago Press, pp. 91–150.

Cohen, S. (1985) *Visions of Social Control: Crime, Punishment and Classification*. Cambridge: Polity Press.

Crawford, A. (1989) *Crime Prevention and Community Safety: Politics, Policies and Practices*. London: Longman.

De Waard, J. (ed.) (1996) 'Crime Prevention in the Netherlands: Policies, Research, and Practice, Part 2', *Security Journal*, 7(3): 155–234.

De Waard, J. (2004) *Innovations for Crime Prevention: An Exploration Towards More Effective Crime Prevention Policies in the Netherlands*. The Hague: Ministry of Justice. Online at: www.theccv.eu/dossiers/crime-reduction/crimeprevention.html

Downes, D. (1988) *Contrasts in Tolerance: Post War Penal Policy in The Netherlands and England and Wales*. Oxford: Clarendon Press.

Felson, M. (1994) *Crime and Everyday Life: Insight and Implications for Society*. Thousand Oaks, CA: Pine Forge Press.

Ferwerda, H., Van Leiden, I. M. G. G., Arts, N. A. M. and Hauber, A. R. (2006) *Halt, het alternatief?: De effecten van Halt beschreven*. Arnhem: Boom Juridische uitgevers.

Garland, D. (2001) *The Culture of Control: Crime and Social Control in Contemporary Society*. Oxford: Oxford University Press.

Greenwood, P. W., Model, K. E., Rydell, C. P. and Chiesa, J. (1996) *Diverting Children from a Life of Crime: Measuring Costs and Benefits*. Santa Monica: RAND.

Hebberecht, P. (1997) *La prévention de la délinquance en Europe*. Paris: L'Harmattan.

Hesseling, R. (1995) 'Functional surveillance in the Netherlands: Exemplary Projects', *Security Journal*, 6(1): 21–5.

Hirschi, T. (1969) *Causes of Delinquency*. Berkeley: University of California Press.

Hofstra, B. and Shapland, J. (1997) 'Who is in Control?', *Policing and Society*, 6(4): 265–81.

Homel, P., Nutley, S. and Webb, B. (2004) *Investing to Deliver: Reviewing the Implementation of the UK Crime Reduction Programme*, Home Office Research Study 281. London: Home Office.

Huisman, W. and Nelen, H. (2007) 'Gotham unbound Dutch style: The Administrative Approach to Organized Crime in Amsterdam'. *Crime Law and Social Change*, 48: 87–103.

Junger, M., Feder, L., Clay, J., Côté, S. M., Farrington, D. P., Freiberg, K., Genovés, V. G., Homel, R., Lösel, F., Manning, M., Mazerolle, P., Santos, R., Schmuckler, M., Sullivan, C., Sutton, C., Van Yperen, T. and Tremblay, R. E. (2007) 'Preventing Violence in Seven Countries: Global Convergence in Policies', *European Journal on Criminal Policy and Research*, 13: 327–56.

Junger-Tas, J. (1997) *Jeugd en gezin II: Naar een effectief preventiebeleid*. The Hague: Ministerie van Justitie, Directoraat Generaal Preventie, Jeugd en Sancties.

Kleemans, E. (2007) 'Organized crime, transit crime, and racketeering', in M. Tonry and C. Bijleveld (eds) *Crime and Justice: A review of research*, Chicago: University of Chicago Press, pp. 163–215.

Leuw, E. (1997) *Criminaliteit en etnische minderheden: Een criminologische analyse*. The Hague: WODC.

Lijphart, A. (1975) *The Politics of Accommodation: Pluralism and Democracy in the Netherlands*, 2nd edn. Berkeley: University of California Press.

Mayhew, P. and Van Dijk, J. J. M. (1997) *Criminal Victimisation in Eleven Industrialized Countries: Key Findings from the 1996 International Victms Surveys*. The Hague: Ministry of Justice, Research and Documentation Centre.

Ministries of Justice and Interior (2007) *Safety Begins with Prevention: Continuing Building a Safer Society*. The Hague: Ministry of Justice.

Romein, J. and Romein-Verschoor, A. (1934) *De Lage Landen bij de Zee: een geïllustreerde geschiedenis van het Nederlandse Volk*. Utrecht: de Haan.

Sherman, L., Gottfredson, D., MacKenzie, D., Eck, J., Reuter, P. and Bushway, S. (1997) *Preventing Crime: What Works, What Doesn't, What's Promising*. Washington DC: National Institute of Justice.

Society and Crime (1985) *A Policy Plan for The Netherlands*. The Hague: Ministry of Justice.

Sutton, A., Cherney, A. and White, R. (2008) *Crime Prevention: Principles, Perspectives and Practices*. Cambridge: Cambridge University Press.

T. M. C. Asser Instituut (2006) *Prevention of Organised Crime: The Registration of Legal Persons and their Directors and the International Exchange of Information*. The Hague: T. M. C. Asser Instituut.

Van der Laan, P. H. (1993) *Alternative Sanctions for Juveniles in the Netherlands*. The Hague: Ministry of Justice, Research and Documentation Centre.

Van der Laan, P. H. (2006) 'Just Desert and Welfare: Juvenile Justice in the Netherlands', in J. Junger-Tas and S. H. Decker (eds) *International Handbook of Juvenile Justice*, Dordrecht: Springer, pp. 145–70.

Van Dijk, J. J. M. (1979) 'The Extent of Public Information and the Nature of Public Attitudes Towards Crime', in *Public Opinion on Crime and Criminal Justice: Reports Presented to the Thirteenth Criminological Research Conference (1978)*. Strasbourg: Council of Europe, pp. 7–42.

Van Dijk, J. J. M. (1997a) 'Towards Effective Public Private Partnerships in Crime Control: Experiences in the Netherlands', in R. V. Clarke and M. Felson (eds) *Business and Crime Prevention*. Monsey, NY: Criminal Justice Press, pp. 97–124.

Van Dijk, J. J. M. (1997b) 'Towards a Research-Based Crime Reduction Policy: Crime Prevention as a Cost-effective Policy Option', *European Journal on Criminal Policy and Research*, 5(3): 13–27.

Van Dijk, J. J. M. (2008) *The World of Crime: Breaking the Silence on Problems of Security, Justice and Development Across the World*. Thousand Oaks, Sage.

Van Dijk, J. J. M. and Junger-Tas, J. (1988) 'Trends in Crime Prevention in The Netherlands', in T. Hope and M. Shaw (eds) *Communities and Crime Reduction*. London: HMSO, pp. 260–77.

Van Dijk, J. J. M. and De Waard, J. (1991) 'A Two-dimensional Typology of Crime Prevention Projects: With a Bibliography', *Criminal Justice Abstracts*, 23(3): 483–503.

Van Dijk, J. J. M. and Steinmetz, C. H. D. (1979) *The Research and Documentation Centre Victimisation Surveys, 1974–1977: Results of a Study into the Volume and Trends in Petty Crime*. The Hague: Ministry of Justice, Research and Documentation Centre.

Van Dijk, J. J. M. and Terlouw, G.-J. (1996) 'An International Perspective of the Business Community as Victims of Fraud and Crime', *Security Journal*, 7: 157–67.

Van Dijk, J. J. M., Kesteren, J. N. and Smit, P. (2008) *Criminal Victimisation in International Perspective: Key Findings from the 2004–2005 ICVS and EU ICS*. The Hague: Boom Legal Publishers.

Van Gemert, F., Petersen, D. and Lien, I.-L. (eds) (2008) *Street Gangs, Migration and Ethnicity*. Cullompton: Willan Publishing.

Van Hees, A. (1998) 'De ontwikkeling van Halt in cijfers', *Kwartaalbericht Rechtsbescherming en Veiligheid*, 11(2): 48–50.

Van Noije, L. and Wittebrood, K. (2008) *Sociale veiligheid ontsleuteld: Veronderstelde en werkelijke effecten van veiligheidsbeleid*. The Hague: Sociaal en Cultureel Planbureau.

Van Swaaningen, R. and Uit Beijerse, J. (2006) 'The Netherlands: Penal Welfarism and Risk Management', in J. Muncie and B. Goldson (eds) *Comparative Youth Justice*. London: Sage, pp. 65–78.

Willemse, H. M. (1996) 'Overlooking Crime Prevention: Ten Years of Crime Prevention in the Netherlands', *Security Journal*, 7(3): 177–84.

Wyvekens, A. (1997) 'Mediation and Proximity', *European Journal on Criminal Policy and Research*, 5(4): 27–42.

Chapter 7

'Modernisation' of institutions of social and penal control in Italy/Europe: the 'new' crime prevention[1]

Dario Melossi and Rossella Selmini

The first part of this chapter, mainly authored by Dario Melossi, looks at the genealogy of the emergence of a preoccupation with extra-penal and local crime prevention in Europe and more specifically in Italy. The second part, mainly authored by Rossella Selmini, looks at the current situation of 'new' crime prevention policies in Europe and more specifically in Italy.

The dialectic of the criminal and the political: changes in the representation of crime and insecurity

In this first part, we would like to retrace and reconstruct developments in the field of crime prevention from an early period, after World War Two, to the current state of affairs, moving from a broader context towards the specificity of the Italian situation. In many European countries and also in North America there was a major overhaul having to do with issues of crime and crime prevention that coincided with the advent of what we could call, for want of a better term, 'mass society' (going back to the already quite old but never enough acclaimed landmark by C. Wright Mills (1956), *The Power Elite*). By 'mass society' we do not simply mean – as C. Wright Mills did not simply mean – the kind of society where the 'mass media of communication' has become so crucially important! We rather mean the society where the 'mass' of the people became less and less of an oppositional, poor and easily radicalisable 'working class', and more and more of a consumerist, opportunistic and moderate 'lower middle class' – the mass media being nothing but a very strategic articulation within this more general change.

This transition nowhere happened very suddenly and was nowhere ever complete. It happened at different times in different places. In the USA, Roosevelt's 'New Deal' was crucial but its effects were not really felt until the 1950s. In Northern Europe, this transition was connected with the coming to power of social democracies. In Germany, France and Italy it happened with the post-war 'economic miracle', between the 1950s and the 1960s. In Spain, Greece and Portugal, it occurred after the demise of those countries' dictatorships in the 1970s. Everywhere it was connected to some forms of the welfare state.[2]

The definition by David Garland of 'penal welfarism' (2001), applied to the management of penal issues during this period, is therefore very *à propos* (even if we may not completely agree on time lags and chronologies). A class perspective, such as the one adopted here, tends to emphasise in fact a few elements related to such pivotal transition. Mass employment in Fordist factories, starting in the 1920s but never really taking off until after World War Two, meant the possibility for the working class of saving money and consuming on a mass scale, and having for the first time in history a vested economic interest in the conservation of the social system (the harsh struggles that culminated in the recognition of trade unions' and therefore workers' rights – between the 1930s and the 1970s – contributed massively to such new working-class welfare). This vested interest also meant home ownership – Americans' famed post-war 'little boxes' – and the possibility of purchasing the gadgets of daily lives. For the first time in history, therefore, at least on a 'mass' scale, workers became potential victims of crime. At the same time and even more crucially, however, what in the early 1970s in France, Italy, Germany or Spain we still used to call the 'repressive state apparatuses' became less involved with class oppression, and with keeping the streets free of workers' and unions' rallies (often in crucial connection with the international necessities of the Cold War, given that in many countries the leading workers' parties had been forged in a strategic alliance with the Soviet Union). These repressive state apparatuses became increasingly involved with defending the material interests of home- and gadget-owners who were now the majority of the population. The 'two-thirds and one-third' society was born. As mentioned earlier, the true explosion of the mass media, from the cinema and radio in the 1920s and 1930s to television in the 1950s and 1960s, was certainly a crucial aspect of all this, to which corresponded an 'anthropological mutation' that cannot be expressed better than in Mills' own words:

[T]he man in the mass does not gain a transcending view from these media; instead he gets his experience stereotyped, and then he gets sunk further by that experience. He cannot detach himself in order to observe, much less to evaluate, what he is experiencing, much less what he is not experiencing. Rather than that internal discussion we call reflection, he is accompanied through his life-experience with a sort of unconscious, echoing monologue. He has no projects of his own: he fulfils the routines that exist. He does not transcend whatever he is at any moment, because he does not, he cannot, transcend his daily milieu. He is not truly aware of his own daily experience and of its actual standards: he drifts, he fulfils habits, his behaviour a result of a planless mixture of the confused standards and the uncriticized expectations that he has taken over from others whom he no longer really knows or trusts, if indeed he ever really did ... He does not formulate his desires; they are insinuated into him. And, in the mass, he loses the self-confidence of the human being – if indeed he has ever had it. For life in a society of masses implants insecurity and further impotence; it makes men uneasy and vaguely anxious. (Mills 1956: 322–3)[3]

If to such feelings of vague insecurity and anxiety one were to add that in the following period the crime rate – especially crime against property – increased manifold everywhere, even if with some time lag between countries (in the USA and the UK starting during the 1960s, in Italy in the 1970s), the whole picture becomes a bit clearer. So, this period of 'high crime societies' (Garland 2001) is essentially at the turning point between the climax of development of welfarism and the beginning of the crisis in penal welfarism. And this because the increase in the crime rate – due to the increase in the general wealth – was interpreted as a symptom of the malaise of penal welfarism and the welfare state in general, so that it became a very powerful argument in the construction not only of the whole discourse that Garland calls the 'culture of control' (that we may also want to call 'penal liberalism' in opposition to 'penal welfarism') but also of neo-liberal ideology more generally.

The dialectics of 'the political' and 'the criminal'

From another landmark work by C. Wright Mills, *The Sociological Imagination* (1959), can be derived another central image, having to do with a sort of dialectic between 'private troubles' and 'public problems'. Indeed, if 'anomie' is connected to periods of dislocation and transformation, when society becomes unable to support, so to speak, individual morality (Durkheim 1893), then periods of rationalisation are prime targets for anomie – and the sectors of the working class hardest hit by these processes are the ones destined to become most anomic. Whereas

155

the 'old' sectors of the working class vent their moral indignation against the immoral habits of the 'new' working class, the latter is certainly more likely to engage in, or anyway be perceived as engaging in, behaviour that is criminalised or defined as characterised by a lack of 'civility'. For the new working class (often the product of processes of social disorganisation of previous social groupings, such as rural workers), the transformation crisis in fact brings about the impossibility both of a decent livelihood and of understanding oneself as a dignified human being. In other words, the devalorisation of labour goes hand in hand with criminalisation, in the two senses of the term – an increasing involvement of some sectors of the 'new' working class in criminal behaviour and an increasing visibility of those same sectors by agencies of formal control.

The conflicts in which a new, emerging working class is involved are at first defined as 'criminal', and rightly so. It is only when, in turn, this 'new' working class becomes central to production, organised and socially recognised, that the root conflicts within which it dwells can be redefined as 'political' and eventually incorporated within the new structure of power. To a large degree such processes of decriminalisation and politicisation are due to the increasing importance of the new working class, which, through organising, becomes able to affirm its human and political dignity. On the contrary, the ability of the ruling class to define the main social conflicts as 'criminal' rather than 'political' – as 'private troubles' rather than as 'public issues' – is a sure sign of its hegemony; a hegemony, however, that is not only constructed ideologically through persuasion but is also deeply rooted in the 'reality' of social relationships.

Paradoxically, the victory of the working class within the New Deal – and in all the other 'new deals' that followed in many other countries between the 1930s and the 1970s – meant that what up to that point had been understood as a form of 'public issue', the misery and desperation of marginalisation being the experience of a whole social class, could become now again 'private troubles', once that experience was the experience of a minority, even if a substantial minority, of the population. It was around the time of the New Deal in the USA that a rhetoric of the 'public enemy' emerged; during the period, that is, that marked the first pioneering entry of organised labour into the establishment. In a similar way, it is only recently, with the coming to maturity of a 'respectable' and non 'anti-system' Left in Italy and other European and Latin American countries, that the spectre of 'crime' (as opposed to that of 'political violence', whether from governmental or non-governmental agencies) is appearing in these societies for the first time as a matter of public concern. It is this connection between political pacification and marginalisation of a minority that we see in the connection between mass media and moral panic. We see the mass media and moral panic as children of a society where that kind of 'new deal' was reached – a new deal that was also fed, at the representational level, by the construction of that imagery.

First in North American societies, and later in Europe, this process has unfolded together with the maturation of a democratic form of government that has put an end to very deep divisions in civil society and has emphasised at the same time the need for social unification. 'Crime' became then the rallying cry for the reunification of society, as David Matza indicated in *Becoming Deviant* (1969). The 'outsiders' are not really any longer those 'antagonists' to power but a fragmented reality of marginalised, excluded outcasts, 'deviant', 'predators' or 'suitable enemies', as Nils Christie (1986) has called them. This story was first told by Herbert Marcuse,[4] one that, we have to admit, at the time from within Continental Europe we could not comprehend, because we were not familiar with what was going on already in Southern California, which was the focus of Marcuse's perspective.

In this sense, whether the rhetorical appeal is to punishment or to social prevention, these are simply (not indifferent) variations on the same motif, namely the reconstitution of a symbolic community. This is particularly the case in Europe, where the root causes of crisis have been multifarious: from the deep transformations in state sovereignty (Garland 1996) to the crisis of the welfare state; from the emergence of a European society to what Etienne Balibar (1991) has called 'identity panic', and the consequent rise and emergence of 'localities', 'regions' and 'stateless nations' (Jauregui Bereciartu 1994; Melossi 1990, 2005). In other words, paradoxically, the very process of democratisation of European societies, in conjunction with the end of the Cold War, has facilitated the emergence of a common internal enemy. We will see the case of Italy in greater detail below. Similar reconstructions have, however, been presented for developments of the police in France (Monjardet 1999; Laurent 1999), on the transformations following Franco's death in Spain (Cid and Larrauri 1998), on Turkey (Green 2000) and on Northern Ireland (Mulcahy 1999).

The turn of the 1970s: the Italian case

Both authors of this chapter have contributed to the pioneering years of the initiative termed *Città sicure*, a project of social prevention of crime and deviance created in 1994 by the regional government of Emilia-Romagna, an Italian region that has traditionally been characterised by its progressive political and social orientation (Putnam 1993). This project is best characterised for being situated at the juncture point of two axes, or dimensions. On the one hand, the project developed, and was in part also a response to, the emergence of 'crime' in Italy as a major feature of public discourse. On the other, it unfolded within a deep turmoil in the structure of the Italian political landscape, marked by the request of local powers (especially regions and cities) to play a much more decisive role in crime prevention *vis-à-vis* the central government.[5] We believe that these two aspects are closely related, because the level at which the issue of crime emerged was that of day-to-day local life.

The emergence of 'crime' in recent Italian history as a central question of public debate took place together with a crucial transition of Italian society from being strongly divided along class and political lines (or anyway so perceived and described by its members) to a society where the central sections of the working class became incorporated inside the established system of governance. The old 'straight from the Cold War' centrist Christian democratic governments went adrift on the bloodshed of the workers who fell in Reggio Emilia in July 1960. A crucial protracted transition followed. After 1962, with the centre-left coalitions, the role of the police slowly started changing, from being a public order force engaged in the control and repression of the Left and the working class, to a force that was more and more supposed to deal with 'ordinary' crime (Della Porta and Reiter 1994; Della Porta 1996; Reiter 1996).[6] After several years of social peace and reform, around 1967 the music once again started to change. Now a more powerful social and political movement, less aligned with the Soviet Union, posed a massive threat to the conservative *status quo*. It was not possible to oppose it openly in the streets because this would have meant a bloodbath and the end of democracy (even if at the time there were, in Italy, those who were in favour of this, 'like in Greece, in Argentina and in Chile'). Instead, a mixture of instruments were used, partly straightforward right-wing terrorism, partly the stupidity of left-wing terrorists, but especially, and increasingly, the mass-mediatisation of Italian society, on the North American example. Terrorisms of all colours, directions and sources came to occupy centre stage and in a sense 'replaced' direct conflicts with the police as a source of politically motivated violence. The estimated number of victims of political violence between 1969 and 1988 was 428. Later on, after the fall of the Berlin wall and the end of the Cold War, the political forces that had managed the transition, the Christian democrats and the socialists, were disposed of, buried under an avalanche of investigations for corruption and for collusion with organised crime. Now the old working class, which had always been in the opposition, could be invited into government.[7] Only at this point, the criminal enemy was not a political enemy any more but the enemy of all, a 'common' criminal, often (starting in the 1980s) a *foreign* common criminal.

What happened to 'ordinary crime' in the meanwhile? Crime, at least crime as represented in official statistics, increased dramatically, especially property crime, as shown in Figure 7.1. In Italy there have in fact been two periods showing strong increases in the recorded crime rate: the first was the 1970s and the second the early 1990s (see Figure 7.1). A rise in fear of crime and social alarm developed, however, only around the second of these. Indeed, interpretations such as those provided by a 'routine activity approach' would seem rather useful in order to address all of this, because

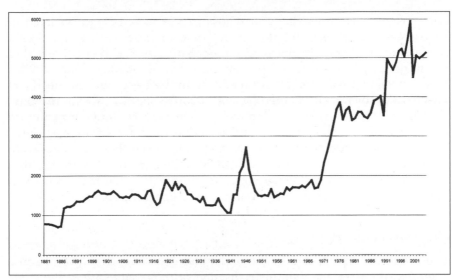

Figure 7.1 Number of crimes (*delitti*) per 100,000 inhabitants in Italy, 1881–2004

it is quite difficult to separate the increase in crime rates from the various 'economic miracles'.[8] Until after the fall of the Berlin wall and the co-optation of the Left among the 'respectable' government members, the phenomena of fear and 'moral panic' had not been particularly relevant in the public field and in political agenda. In the second half of the 1970s and in the 1980s, elected institutions, public opinion and political parties had directed their attention towards the Mafia – and other related forms of organised crime – and especially towards political terrorism. In both cases, there is no doubt that Italy experienced the outbreak of a widespread moral panic and a law and order campaign emerged, accompanied by strong law enforcement tendencies in criminal policy. In a few cases, however, Mafia and political terrorism gave rise to a community-based reaction, except for the most politicised sectors of the public opinion, especially within the Left. Even then, public opinion did not demand more punishment, the death penalty and so on. The alarm surrounding events of Mafia and terrorism neither extended to other less serious forms of crime, nor gave rise to a widespread feeling of lack of safety, such as has been experienced more recently.

If one analyses the articles that appeared in the journal that marked the appearance of a 'critical criminology' in Italy, *La Questione Criminale* (1975–81), one finds that topics of 'law and order' were very present. They were, however, never coupled with so-called 'common' crime but always with 'political repression'. This fact has often been interpreted as an instance of a certain Italian backwardness, which meant that concern about terrorism and organised crime held centre stage whereas the campaigns for law and order about street crime, of which the 'new criminologists' were writing and whose papers were being translated in *La Questione Criminale*, did not really come to exist. As we mentioned earlier, however, we did not realise that also in the UK they were rather recent developments (see the pioneering work by Stanley Cohen (1972), *Folk Devils and Moral Panics*) and that even in the USA they had been just 'discovered' by labelling theorists or theorists of the 'social reaction' (Becker, Lemert, Gusfield and others).[9] One may certainly hypothesise that the murders linked to organised crime and terrorism may have brought about a substantial social reaction. However, these murders were those of 'excellent cadavers', as Sicilians called them (Stille 1995) and, correspondingly, the following social reaction was much more one from the political and judicial elites than from the general public.

Microphysics of crime

The fast and deep change in the social and economic structure of some cities and districts, the deindustrialisation of those same areas, the crisis of a 'work ethic' and of work as a means to promote social progress and personal dignity, the disappearance of traditional urban social networks – often related to political participation – and the consequent fragmentation of social identities: all of this has created a context in which new images of disorder tended to emerge, often related to the presence of immigrants and, more rarely, of groups of homeless youth (who, rather than for committing crime, are considered responsible for a social disorder in the city, of the kind described most famously in Wilson and Kelling (1982) or Skogan (1990), a disorder perceived as opposite to the values and ideals of the former working class).[10]

In a 1997 speech in Bologna, Prime Minister Romano Prodi stated that 'the problem of the safety of the country seems to be no longer one of external safety, but an internal one: the safety of citizens in their everyday life' (Prodi 1997). In the new post-Cold War era, the issue of safety was no longer just a question of external security – or, at most, of a concept of 'public order', which was nothing more than a domestic reflection of international divisions, as it had been in fact until the 1980s. Crime, and criminals, were now our common enemy – even better if they could be described as products of a common new 'external' enemy, a 'fifth column' in our midst, the undesirable, undocumented, clandestine immigrants. Immigrant sections of the population are already in many countries the core of a new working class. In the most developed cities of Emilia-Romagna, this is already the case in many factories. The 'tough' jobs that Italians are unwilling to devote themselves to, make it such that in some factories of the city of Reggio Emilia, for instance, nine out of ten workers are not born in Italy. In such cities, the offspring of immigrant and mixed marriages are already more than one in ten, in a country where only about 5 per cent of the population are foreign. It is not difficult to foresee that here too, very soon, the 'foreign' work force will represent a very substantial section of the 'Italian' working class, exactly in the same way in which this happened to Italians, among others, in the United States, Belgium or Germany.

This complex change obviously shifted the centre of gravity of control from the national state to localities. The loss of control as a political function in a class-divided society in favour instead of a concept of police as the protection of the middle-class majority of the population from street crime, essentially moved the pivot of policing from the national state to places closer to citizens, their homes and their goods. (This also accounts, in our opinion, for the ambiguity, malaise and difficulties in which police forces find themselves still now every time the problem of control shifts back to a political/national/collective format: the issues of terrorism and organised crime in Spain or Italy; 'difficult neighbourhoods' in France and other Central European countries; soccer hooliganism in Italy; political radical groups all over, and so on.) This train of events created the conditions for the creation of a concern with crime expressed in the concepts of 'crime prevention' and 'security' or 'safety'. In this context new discourses and policies about crime prevention, and safety policies, emerged. The old centralised 'state' system was one geared to struggle against forms of organised crime, whether criminal or political – a type of 'crime', or simply of opposition, that as such had to be countered at the national level because it was directed against the very 'core' of the state, within a bitterly divided polity. The current situation is very different. So-called *microcriminalità* – as Italian media used to call street crime, maybe unwittingly echoing Michel Foucault's 'microphysics of power'[11] – cannot care less about the 'grand narrative' of the state. It has to do instead with the very local, mundane, everyday life: routine series of petty thefts, muggings, burglaries, drug-dealing, street-walking, that take place side by side with the places where 'respectable' citizens live and work. The instruments to counter *microcriminalità* can hardly be, then, the majestic ones of the state, even if governments – as well as national police forces – have a hard time in coming to deal with such undesired reduction of their 'aura'.

Why have things not really worked out that way? Why has the pioneering experience of *Città sicure* been almost ignored at the national, political level? We would submit that the 'modernisation' process implied in the *Città sicure* initiative has gone the usual way things go when we talk of 'modernisation' in the sphere of crime, deviance and security. It is one thing to be concerned with citizens' security. It is a totally different thing to go after the 'political capital' represented by citizens' fear (Simon 2007). A 'rational' approach may severely endanger that capital, a capital that politicians and political campaigners may instead be eager to exploit to their advantage.

The development of crime prevention policies in Europe and Italy

Italy, Europe, and some open questions about crime prevention

If the general social and political context of Italy is as described above, we now focus on the strategies, discourses and practices of crime prevention developed in Italy in the last 15 years. These strategies and practices are – and were – deeply influenced and shaped also by the European context and by the changes that occurred in the field of crime prevention in the past decades in many other European countries. This is the reason why we begin our analysis focusing first on some general issues about crime prevention that are part of a European discourse and have already been analysed in other comparative studies. We then enter more directly in the reconstruction of some distinctive features of Italian experience and debates about crime prevention, and describe some recent changes and tendencies occurred in recent years in this country.

Many European countries in the past decades focused on the development of discourses and practices that show clearly the 'need to shift resources and focus towards crime prevention, rather than focusing on more reactive and coercive forms of policing and criminal justice' (Stenson and Edwards 2004: 209). This emphasis and attention towards crime prevention still remains an open question, because, despite the great amount of scientific literature and efforts in explaining it, its definition is becoming increasingly vague and confused. Under the label of 'crime prevention' policies, in fact, we find a wide range of practices and measures that share the attempt to avoid the development of criminal behaviours or victimisation, or the occurrence of criminal events, or that try to reduce the recurrence of crime. The extension and, consequently, increasing vagueness of the concept of crime prevention has been the object of thoughtful analyses in socio-criminological literature in the past decades, which has stressed its novelty as a 'disparate set of practices that may be contrasted with those more traditional approaches to crime control' (Gilling 1997: xi).[12] Some of the most distinctive features of the changing concept of crime prevention are:

- The expansion of the number of actors entitled to act legitimately in crime prevention, as is well expressed by the increasing powers and responsibility of local governments in many European countries.

- As a consequence of such expansion, the fragmentation of decision-making processes and the following increasing conflicts among different actors in this field.[13]

- A further, important change is the attempt at incorporating social and community organisations in the policy-making process or in its implementation, or in both (Hughes and Edwards 2002).

• The emergence of European policies, also in the field of crime control.

Some further topics that are still open questions are: How can these changes in the concept and practices of crime prevention be explained? What is the increasing role of new actors at a local level in this field? Can the new local dimension of crime prevention represent a chance for true change in the direction of the balancing of power between national and local governments and of the development of social justice and citizens' rights, while increasing prevention and protection?

In the great amount of literature on the issue, two main and general approaches can be distinguished in trying to deal with these points. The first focuses on the shift from the 'welfare regulatory' state to the neo-liberal one and on how such shift affected cultures, polices and practices of social order and crime control (O'Malley 1992; Garland 2001; Landreville 2005). The social control policies of the post-war period were, in most European countries, led by the national state and by national agencies, and were based on an idea of crime as a social or individual deficit. Crime prevention, consequently, was to be pursued through social reforms and social policies, while penal policies were to develop through rehabilitative strategies. The shift towards a new culture and new policies of crime control, which occurred in different periods in the last decades in most European countries, on the contrary focused on individual responsibility, on the role of the victim and on different preventive strategies and punishment policies. According to some, rehabilitation and social inclusion were replaced by so-called 'actuarial penal strategies' (Feeley and Simon 1994), the attention towards criminals by the new role played by the victims, and the attention towards causes of crime by the attempts at controlling crime in a manner that would make it compatible with ordinary urban life (Garland 1997).

The emergence of new attempts to intervene in crime control policies has been understood also in a different perspective, where – without denying the dynamic previously described – so-called 'new' prevention and the local nature of safety policies are seen as the favoured approach for developing an alternative model of social order. Local policies and cities are considered, respectively, the best instrument and the best site for intervening on crime and deviance issues. In this context, so-called 'new' prevention is offered as the answer for governments (both national and local) in search of a strategy to face both 'high crime societies' (Garland 2001) and the concurrent decentralisation of mechanisms of control from national states to local governments. On both of these points, as we shall see later, Italy represents an interesting case study.

The 'two European models' of crime prevention, their overlapping and their change over time

During the 1980s, comparative studies about prevention policies showed the emergence of two different models of crime prevention, which are also partially related to the two main approaches to changes in crime control described above.[14] The United Kingdom and France are usually referred to as the two different European contexts where these models developed first and most clearly. According to this distinction, the crime prevention policies that developed in the UK, were mainly based on these principles:

- The prevalence of situational crime prevention over social crime prevention.

- The leading role of the police and, more generally, a predominance of a 'technical level' over the political one.

- The emphasis on individual responsibility and on the victim's role.

- The involvement of local communities in crime control and in surveillance tasks, as in the well-known 'neighbourhood watch' programmes.

- The focus on pragmatism, implementation, management and evaluation.

- A strategy of responsibilisation from the national state towards other actors (Garland 1996) but with the central state, however (and precisely the Home Office), keeping the leading role for what concerns priorities, resources, evaluations, and so on.

The theoretical framework of this model is to be found in theories of opportunity and also related common-sense approaches, such as the well-known and politically successful 'broken windows' theory for what concerns urban disorder. While being essentially 'British', this model largely influenced, at an early stage, some European countries, such as the Netherlands and Belgium (see Chapters 6 and 8, this volume), and later on also some other continental contexts.

Comparative literature on crime prevention policies has very often opposed this model in favour of a French – or 'Continental' – one, whose main features differ from those in the following ways.

- The prevalence of social prevention over situational prevention.

- The attempt to give elected bodies, especially at a local level, a central role.[15]

- An idea of crime as the result of social deprivation, marginality, lack of opportunities, urban decay, and so on.

- A limited responsibilisation of individuals and communities, and an attempt to involve collective organisations, social services, and other institutional actors.

Those original models were not, in fact, that distinct from each other. They shared, already in those very first years, more than what appears from their reduction to 'models' and, during the past decade, they have moved closer and closer, so that the features they share are probably more than those that separate them (Duprez and Hebberecht 2001). While maintaining some of its original features, for instance, the British model came to include – at least for a period – an involvement of local authorities in crime prevention policies and fostered the idea of community safety as a key concept to balance the police's leading role. The same occurred in the French model, where more coercive measures, or situational strategies, were often included in crime prevention policies (Roché 2004; Wyvekens, Chapter 5 this volume). As a result, most crime prevention policies are nowadays a mix of situational and social measures, although the situational approach prevails.[16]

The development of the Italian model, between the search for integration and the absence of the state

Italy is an interesting case for a better understanding of this 'mixed' model of crime prevention. The new infrastructure of crime prevention developed in the country at the beginning of the 1990s is articulated in many city-level projects, often co-ordinated by regional governments, which deliver funding and in some cases technical support. Regional laws about local safety are the true Italian peculiarity in delivering crime prevention measures. From the 1990s until a few years ago, regional governments in Italy usually behaved in a manner akin to that of national governments in other European contexts, offering a general framework for the development of local crime prevention projects. Eleven of the 20 regions enacted laws, in the past years, the aim of which was to support, in different ways, municipalities and local police forces under the label of 'local safety policies'. Hence, a new infrastructure of local governance of crime prevention has been established in the absence of the nation state.

This peculiarity reflects the institutional conflict between different levels of government and how the struggle of local authorities to acquire new competencies and responsibilities in many different sectors of public policies has been influential in shaping the Italian model of crime prevention. In this respect, the Italian context also shows clearly how contemporary crime control practices and politics are at the core of a complex and not yet solved – as we shall see better later on – process of redistribution of responsibilities among the state, the local government and the civil society (Selmini 2005: 319).

From the point of view of its content, the model[17] is characterised by a mix between traditional social measures, new measures for public reassurance (victim support, community mobilisation) and situational crime prevention (surveillance, administrative control and environmental design with defensive aims).[18] Situational crime prevention measures, which represented a true novelty, were enthusiastically adopted in many cities, and in some areas they now prevail over social prevention. Given the fact that local authorities have no competencies in penal law enforcement or in crime repression, but were nonetheless willing to extend their sphere of intervention further, cities have been in search of new instruments for controlling people and behaviours. These instruments have been found in the intensification of surveillance, mainly performed by the municipal police,[19] in the use of administrative orders and in environmental design. The administrative orders ('mayoral ordinances') are grounded in administrative powers rather than in criminal law powers. They are the prerogative of mayors who, for reasons of public hygiene or other generic risks to the well-being of citizens, have the power to enact such orders to face 'emergencies' and also to keep under routine control many different activities and groups in public spaces. By means of these administrative orders, we have witnessed substantial interventions of local police especially against street prostitution, disorder, incivilities, and nuisances related to undocumented immigrants.

A combination of the above measures allowed local authorities to develop what can be called an 'integrated approach'. This means that local crime prevention programmes try to fine-tune social inclusion and exclusion, as well as to tackle causes of crime, while at the same time managing crime symptoms. However, if 'integrated crime prevention' is a rather successful political slogan, this does not mean that 'integration' would really allow local governments to follow these two different approaches. In fact, the kind of social measures that they can implement remain at the level of a welfarist philosophy, given that intervention on structural causes of crime requires a whole range of competencies in the field of immigration, labour market and general welfare that are not fully available to local governments.

Consequently, after almost 15 years of implementation of local crime prevention schemes, we are now witnessing a failure of the primary idea based on the development of a new model of local governance of crime able to tackle 'causes' of crime while at the same time proving effective in managing crime symptoms. An analysis of more recent general programmes on local crime prevention (Selmini 2009) highlights the extent to which these programmes are more and more characterised by a situational approach and an increasing weakness of their primary social-inclusionary rationality.

Social crime prevention: decline or change?

According to the most common definition, social crime prevention includes measures that seek to eliminate or reduce structural crime factors, act on possible causes of crime through general social programmes (Robert 1991: 16), or, according to a similar definition, influence or modify the reasons that bring people to commit offences due to conditions of social disadvantage (Gilling 1997: 5). Unlike situational prevention, this strategy puts the focus back on the potential offender and her/his inclination to commit crime, considered not so much as the result of an individual pathology but rather as a deficit deriving from personal and socio-structural conditions. According to some scholars, social prevention is not just a specific prevention modality, but rather a global policy for social well-being that crosses all sectors of administrative policies (Walgrave and de Cauter 1986; Peyre 1986). Other authors focus on social development, considered as the basis of these policies. Their purpose would be to study the origin and reproduction of inequalities responsible for 'disadvantaged contexts' in order to overcome them (Hastings 1998: 117). The fields of intervention of social prevention, according to the authors of a broad review of crime prevention programmes (Graham and Bennett 1995), are urban policy, health policies, family policies, education policies, labour market policies and, finally, social integration policies generally speaking.

Our studies of the Italian context, based on a classification of social crime prevention measures derived from relevant local practitioners and responsible authorities, shows some interesting differences from the aforementioned definitions of social crime prevention, as well as some additional features:

- A 'collective dimension' and the rejection of an individualistic approach – social crime prevention is seen as addressed to social groups and not to individuals.

- Among those social groups, there are not only those at risk of becoming criminals or deviant, but also those at risk of being victimised – or those who have already been victimised – by crime; the 'potential criminal' and the 'vulnerable citizen' are both subjects of social crime measures.

- A change in the final aims, which are no longer focused on preventing crime through the amelioration of social disdvantages, but on a more limited purpose to support, through different forms of assistance, some groups 'at risk'. No longer are general crime prevention aims prioritised; more frequently the priority is a type of a 'social pacification' among different groups, through different forms of social mediation.

Interviewed about their practices of social crime prevention programmes, local politicians and officers in charge of local crime prevention programmes listed the following measures:

Social prevention addressed to subjects
Harm reduction for drug addicts and prostitution
General social help for homeless and marginalised individuals (shelters, etc.)
Services for the integration of immigrants
Services to crime victims

Social prevention for the physical environment and the community
Mediation of conflicts among social groups
Animation of public spaces (through entertainment, etc.)
Urban renewal

The instruments to implement these measures are also different. In addition to traditional social work, they include urban renewal, street repairs, administrative orders and the ever more frequent possibility that non-specialised operators adopt preventive measures too, such as the participation of common citizens in crime prevention programmes. In the Italian context, community crime prevention has been reinterpreted by those in charge of implemention as part of a social prevention strategy, based mainly on measures to foster community cohesion and ameliorate the physical environment, in order to improve the quality of life and reduce conflicts and fear of crime in some areas. Recalling the Chicago School's main assumptions, the basic idea is that crime, deviance and disorder are the result of the decline of community, conflicts between heterogeneous social groups, the abandonment of public space, and the deterioration of community relations. Consequently, interventions must act on these phenomena, using different strategies that collectively we might define as 'community crime prevention'.

In the context we described above, social prevention, while still a well-established concept, is changing radically its nature in the everyday practice of safety policies. Furthermore, it is increasingly at risk of losing its traditional features.[20] More precisely, measures of social prevention clearly show a shift of focus, from intervening radically on the causes of crime through social reform to simply offering 'humanitarian' and often short-term solutions for some social emergencies. On the one hand, situational rationality seems to permeate also those measures that were once called 'social'; on the other hand, social interventions are increasingly being used as auxiliary to situational interventions.

We are also witnessing a change in the object of social crime prevention, which is no longer seeking to deal with social groups at risk of becoming criminals, but rather is concerned to protect real and potential victims from both victimisation and feelings of insecurity. Public reassurance – a broad and vague definition that embraces different practices aimed at preventing fear of crime and unsafety or conflicts in neighbourhoods and between different social groups – is increasingly replacing traditional social crime prevention (Baillergeau 2007; Selmini 2003). This 'loss of focus' of social crime prevention – above all, when these measures are mixed with the situational ones in the local safety policies – is documented in many different contexts (Gilling 2001). It has been related to the 'conceptual ambiguity' of social crime prevention in itself that 'opens the doors to multiple and contradictory political interests, and at the end of the day, makes it vulnerable to co-optation by conventional crime control agendas' (Knepper 2007: 140).

Together with such changes in social crime prevention, a further issue, worth noting is the recent emergence – at least in Italy – of *developmental* crime prevention, as an alternative to traditional social prevention. Developmental and situational crime prevention are now presented as the new alliance able to tackle crime in its different dimensions:

> The solution (for the future) is an integrated prevention where, beside a selective penal prevention, other preventive measures are developed: the situational and the psycho-social . . . Given the fact that crime behaviour is the result of predisposition and opportunities, we need to intervene on predisposition until it is possible, and then modify opportunities. (Savona 2004: 277)

With the replacement of the social crime prevention with the early (or developmental, or risk-focused) crime prevention,[21] the process of alignment of Italian tendencies to the general European ones about crime prevention was almost completed.

Recent changes and further developments

In these last few pages, we have described the development of crime prevention policies in Italy, and how these policies were deeply rooted in the context of a peculiar form of local governance of crime. We have remarked on some local peculiarities, external influences, and finally recent convergences that are making the Italian experiences not so different from others in the European context.

The situational and the social approaches meet the needs and interests of local politicians in different ways. This is not at all different from what occurred, and is occurring, in other contexts. The success of situational crime prevention lies in its capacity to offer pragmatic and fast political responses to manage crime and disorder problems for those who are responsible of the government of ordinary urban life; that is, for the mayors and other politicians.[22] What is remarkable is the fact that in Italy this approach to crime prevention has been accepted enthusiastically without any diffusion of the kind of criminological knowledge on which it depends, namely opportunity theory and the routine activity approach. While these are part of the recent interest of some academics (Barbagli 1995; Savona 2004), they are largely unknown and unfamiliar to our scientific discourse on crime and crime prevention. This fact in itself suggests interesting reflections on the sources of criminal policy change!

A further Italian peculiarity was that the national state, during the past decade, has continued pursuing its traditional law enforcement strategies without paying much attention to the infrastructure of crime prevention that was taking shape at a local level. The whole apparatus of local governance of crime prevention has been developing for many years without any kind of formalisation, in the absence of any nation legal framework and without any support or resources from central government. Even though the development of a partnership strategy is – apparently – a complicated matter in many different European contexts (Aden 2002; Hope 2002; Le Goff 2004), in Italy we witnessed a remarkable absence of the national government in the search for institutional co-operation and in the involvement in these new practices of crime prevention. This was the result of a cultural, professional and political inadequacy of Italian national political and professional elites. It was also a consequence of the traditional backwardness and weakness of the central Italian state apparatus and of the culture and organisation of our national police forces, traditionally ill equipped to work within a preventive approach.

However, the framework described in this chapter has deeply changed because of new legislation passed by the conservative government that won the election in April 2008, although it should be noted that many of these changes were already part of a crime prevention reform on local safety issues elaborated by the previous centre-left government. Change, therefore, does not come only from the political ideology of those leading the government, but also from the office of crime control strategy within the Ministry of the Interior, whose needs and interests aligned themselves with those of the new government, strongly committed to developing a 'tough on crime' strategy on many different levels. A new law was passed in the summer of 2008. Its general strategy is to reduce local governments' powers and strengthen the role of mayors as representatives of the national government at a local level, deeply reforming the whole infrastructure of crime prevention, and undermining all efforts at delivering a strategy based on integration of different measures. The main results of this reform – the consequences of which in the everyday practice of crime prevention and its overlap with regional laws are not yet easy to foresee – are:

- The re-establishment of national sovereignty about ordinary, mundane crime at a symbolic level.

- The responsibilisation of mayors as 'executive officers' of the Ministry of the Interior and of the prefects, while apparently giving them stronger powers in the use of administrative orders in managing everyday crime in urban contexts.

- The expansion in the use of administrative instruments for the purpose of controlling behaviours and situations.

- The responsibilisation of local police in the field of crime prevention, but mainly at the orders of national representatives of the state.

- The stronger relevance of incivilities, 'urban disorder' and anti-social behaviours in the discourses about crime prevention.

In conclusion, in Italy, as probably elsewhere, the whole framework of crime prevention seems now to be traversed by contradictory, fragmentary and changing tendencies. It is, however, clear that the struggle of local governments in order to find their place in the field of crime prevention has basically failed. In its place, national administrative control of behaviours and situations has definitely become the main source of discourse and practice about crime prevention.

Notes

1 This is a revised version of papers presented by Dario Melossi and Rossella Selmini at the CRIMPREV First General Conference (Brussels, 8–10 February 2007) and by Dario Melossi at the CRIMPREV Meeting at the University of Leeds (Leeds, 7–8 June 2007).
2 It may be useful to mention Gøsta Esping-Andersen's classification of the welfare state in three types: a 'Social Democratic' one, typical of Northern European countries; a 'Conservative/Corporatist' one, typical of Continental Europe; and a 'Liberal' one, typical of the US (Esping-Andersen 1987).
3 One should compare these reflections by Mills to some of the more sociological writings by Italian poet, novelist and film-maker Pier Paolo Pasolini on the mutation of the Italian working class in the 1970s – keeping also in mind, probably, the circulation of these ideas, coming from American social sciences, among Italian intellectuals of the 1960s.
4 See especially the conclusion to *One-Dimensional Man* (Marcuse 1964: 247–57).
5 Attempts at revising Article 117 of the Italian Constitution, which defines the respective roles and competencies of the central state and the regions, have until now failed. In the early 1990s this issue was muddled by the emergence of a political force, the 'Northern League', that demanded independence for Northern Italy from the rest of the country.
6 Between 1946 and 1962, 126 citizens and 12 police officers were killed in street clashes (D'Orsi 1972). This is not counting the peasants killed by landowners'

organised gangs in the South in the period immediately after the end of the war: in Sicily in particular a conspiracy of Mafia gangsters, local (and national) reactionary forces, and 'Allied' secret services, tried to play a separatist card for the island, succeeding, however, 'only' in destroying the peasant radical movement and opening the following *de facto* government between central powers and the mafia.

7 Socio-economic change brought 'to power' the organised working class but also at the same time its nemesis, 'post-Fordism' (decline of the factory, decline of work ethics, etc.). A general process of class fragmentation ensued that marked both a deep decline in the self-understanding of large sectors of the population as 'working class', and increasing symptoms of social disorganisation especially among working-class youth (such as the sudden and huge creation of a drug culture and market after the mid 1970s).

8 Even if it is not as useful in order to understand the decline in the 1990s; furthermore there is an important demographic argument. See also Katherine Beckett's arguments in her criticisms of Garland (Beckett 2001).

9 See, *contra*, King (2003).

10 In response, 'citizen committees' were spontaneously created, often in areas that had traditionally seen a strong presence of the traditional Left parties (Selmini 1997). For example, in Milena Chiodi's (1999: 241–5) research on the specific case of a Modena neighbourhood, clearly immigrants are visible, they are perceived as not used to the rule of democratic participation, and they tend to concentrate in those areas of the city that are more vulnerable, and where communities are in search of new identities. Such 'new identities' may be found, however, as in the case studied by Chiodi, in organising the neighbourhood against the immigrants. In the words of the citizens Chiodi interviewed, they have been able to build a 'renewed unity' in their struggle to 'clean' their neighbourhood of the unwanted guests. Erickson or Matza could not have expressed the matter more clearly: the social cohesion of the 'Crocetta' neighbourhood in Modena was at least temporarily strengthened by the unity of intents and actions against 'North African drug dealers'. This episode is revealing of the contradictions and ambiguities of the processes and feelings involved. A sense of democratic participation mixes with one of parochialism, the old faith in 'the unity of the working class' with outright exclusion and racism. The traditional Left institutions and values seem to be unable to orient and direct the course of events and, in some respects, even the pioneering role of initiatives such as *Città sicure* may appear as having played more the role of 'sorcerer's apprentice' than that of the Leninist vanguard of the working class! And in fact, in some cases, when citizen and community organisations' claims have not been catered to, the backlash for this lack of attention has been significant, as in the clamorous electoral defeat of the Left in Bologna in 1999, a city that it had administered uninterruptedly since the end of the war.

11 Such is the title of a collection of Michel Foucault's essays in Italian, referring to Foucault's concept of 'micro-power' (Foucault 1977). Indeed, one could venture to suggest that Foucault's polemic against a state-centred concept of power was the way in which European culture started to question itself about the obsolescence of the old nineteenth-century European nation-states as well as the introduction of the notion of political pluralism (Melossi 1990, 2005).

12 The concept of 'new' prevention and its main features have been promoted and fully analysed, in the European context, especially by Philippe Robert (1991).

13 A dynamic that has been thoughtfully studied in the perspective of 'governance' (Crawford 1997; Garland 2001; Loader and Walker 2007).

14 On these changes in crime prevention policies in Europe and the emergence of the two models, see Robert (1991). A more recent analysis of the same issues is to be found in Duprez and Hebberecht (2001).

15 However, this emphasis on local government was, in France, more rhetoric than real, given the strong centralist nature of the French institutional framework (see Chapter 5, this volume), while it worked better in those countries with a weaker state structure, as the case of Italy.

16 The compatibility of a 'situational rationality' with a 'social justice' one and the spread of articulated models of crime prevention were analysed by O'Malley (1992).

17 This description of the Italian way to 'new' prevention is based on national research about crime prevention policies in 103 Italian cities during the last five years of the 1990s, on similar studies concerning some Italian regions (Regione Toscana 2002; Giovannetti and Maluccelli 2001), and on a partial updating of the first national research (Selmini 2003).

18 The combination of these measures represents the contemporary content of Italian security policies. Their features are a further example of the circulation of practices, which is part of the 'travelling process' in the field of criminal justice (Melossi et al. 2009). Originally, in fact, the concepts and practices of social and situational prevention arrived through academic relationships both with British 'Left Realism' and with some French sociologists and criminologists. The network of cities affiliated to the European Forum for Urban Safety also played an important role in this process of transferring policies. The relationship of Italian local governments with this association stressed the connections with the French-speaking world and other continental countries, partially balancing the Anglo-American influence and giving the Italian projects the aforementioned 'mixed' character (Selmini 2005).

19 Municipal police, which depend on the mayor, have an exclusive competency in the general field of administrative police, but also the status of a public security force. Apart from the normative definition of their competencies, their role in crime prevention has increased enormously in the past ten years.

20 A dynamic that has been defined also as the 'criminalisation of social policies', already analysed in different European context (Cartuyvels 1996; Pitch 2006).

21 About the similarities and differences among these definitions, all of them conceptually included in the main category of developmental crime prevention, see Homel (2005: 71–3) and also Farrington and Welsh (2007).

22 Among the many who have reflected upon the practical and political appeal of situational crime prevention, see above all Hope and Sparks (2000).

References

Aden, H. (2002) 'Le possibilità di riforma di un sistema di polizia semi(de)centralizzato', Dei delitti e delle pene, 1-2-3: 145–57.

Baillergeau, E. (2007) 'Intervention sociale, prévention et controle social. La prévention social d'hier à aujourd'hui', *Deviance et Société*, 32(1): 3–20.

Balibar, E. (1991) 'Es Gibt keinen Staat in Europa: *razzismo e politica nell'Europa d'oggi'*, in E. Balibar (ed.) *Le frontiere della democrazia*. Roma: Manifestolibri, pp. 117–37.

Barbagli, M. (1995) *L'occasione e l'uomo ladro. Furti e rapine in Italia*. Bologna: Il Mulino.

Beckett, K. (2001) 'Crime and Control in the Culture of Late Modernity', *Law and Society Review*, 35: 899–930.

Cartuyvels, Y. (1996) 'Insécurité et prévention en Belgique: les ambiguités d'un modèle "globale intégré" entre concertation partenariale et intégration verticale', *Deviance et Société*, 20(2): 153–71.

Chiodi, M. (1999) 'Immigrazione, devianza e percezione d'insicureza', *Dei delitti e delle pene* VI:3: 115–40.

Christie, N. (1986) 'Suitable Enemies', in H. Bianchi and R. van Swaaningen (eds) *Abolitionism: Towards a Non-Repressive Approach to Crime*. Amsterdam: Free University Press, pp. 42–54.

Cid, J. and Larrauri, E. (1998) 'Prisons and Alternatives to Prison in Spain', in V. Ruggiero, N. South and I. Taylor (eds) *The New European Criminology: Crime and Social Order in Europe*. London: Routledge, pp. 146–55.

Cohen, S. (1972) *Folk Devils and Moral Panic: The Creation of the Mods and Rockers*. New York: St Martin's Press, 2002.

Crawford, A. (1997) *The Local Governance of Crime: Appeals to Community and Partnerships*. Oxford: Clarendon Press.

D'Orsi, A. (1972) *Il potere repressivo: la polizia*. Milano: Feltrinelli.

Della Porta, D. (1996) 'Polizia e ordine pubblico', *Polis*, 10: 333–6.

Della Porta, D. and Reiter, H. (1994) 'Da "polizia del governo" a "polizia dei cittadini"? Le politiche dell'ordine pubblico in Italia', *Stato e mercato*, 48: 433–65.

Duprez, D. and Hebberecht, P. (2001) 'Sur le politiques de prévention et de sécurité en Europe: réflexions introductive sur un tournant', *Deviance et société*, 25(4): 371–6.

Durkheim, E. (1893) *The Division of Labor in Society*. New York: The Free Press, 1964.

Esping-Andersen, G. (1987) *Three World of Welfare*. Princeton: Princeton University Press.

Farrington D. P. and Welsh, B. C. (2007) *Saving Children from a Life of Crime*. Oxford: Oxford University Press.

Feeley, M. and Simon J. (1994) 'The New Penology: Notes on the Emerging New Criminal Law', in D. Nelken (ed.) *The Futures of Criminology*. London: Sage, pp. 173–201.

Foucault, M. (1977) *Microfisica del potere*. Torino: Einaudi.

Garland, D. (1996) 'The Limits of the Sovereign State: Strategies of Crime Control in Contemporary Society', *British Journal of Criminology*, 36(4): 445–71.

Garland, D. (1997) '"Governmentality" and the Problem of Crime: Foucault, Criminology and Sociology', *Theoretical Criminology*, 1(2): 173–214.

Garland, D. (2001) *The Culture of Control: Crime and Social Order in Contemporary Society*. Oxford: Oxford University Press.

Gilling, D. (1997) *Crime Prevention: Theory, Policy and Politics*. London: UCL.

Gilling, D. (2001) 'Community Safety and Social Policy', *European Journal on Criminal Policy and Research*, 9: 381–400.

Giovannetti, M. and Maluccelli, L. (2001) *Politiche di sicurezza e azioni di prevenzione nei comuni e nelle province della regione Marche,* unpublished research report.

Graham, J. and Bennett, T. (1995) *Crime Prevention Strategies in Europe and North America.* Helsinki: HEUNI.

Green, P. (2000) 'Criminal Justice and Democratisation in Turkey: The Paradox of Transition', in P. Green and A. Rutherford (eds) *Criminal Policy in Transition.* Oxford: Hart, pp. 195–220.

Hastings, R. (1998) 'La prévention du crime par le développement social: une stratégie à la recherche d'une synthèse', *Criminologie,* 31(1): 109–23.

Homel, R. (2005) 'Developmental Crime Prevention' in N. Tilley (ed.) *Handbook of Crime Prevention and Community Safety.* Cullompton: Willan Publishing, pp. 71–106.

Hope, T. (2002) 'La riduzione della criminalità, la sicurezza locale e la nuova filosofia del management pubblico', *Dei delitti e delle pene,* 1-2-3: 207–29.

Hope, T. and Sparks, R. (eds) (2000) *Crime, Risk and Insecurity.* London: Routledge.

Hughes, G. and Edwards, A. (eds) (2002) *Crime Control and Community: The New Politics of Public Safety.* Cullompton: Willan Publishing.

Jauregui Bereciartu, G. (1986) *Decline of the Nation-State.* Reno: University of Nevada Press.

King, P. (2003) 'Moral Panics and Violent Street Crime 1750–2000', in B. Godfrey, C. Emsley and G. Dunstall (eds) *Comparative Histories of Crime.* Cullompton: Willan Publishing, pp. 53–71.

Knepper, P. (2007) *Criminology and Social Policy.* London: Sage.

Landreville, P. (2005) 'Ordre social et répression pénale. Un demi-siècle de transformations', paper presented at the International Meeting *Crime et insécurité: un demi-siècle de bouleversements,* Versailles, 29 September–1 October.

Laurent, V. (1999) 'Les Renseignements Généraux à la découverte des quartiers', *Le Monde diplomatique,* 541: 26–7.

Le Goff, T. (2004) 'Réformer la sécurité par la coproduction:action or rhétorique?' in S. Roché (ed.) *Réformer la police et la sécurité. Les nouvelles tenances en Europe et aux Etats Unis.* Paris: Odile Jacob, pp. 82–104.

Loader, I. and Walker, N. (2007) *Civilizing Security.* Cambridge: Cambridge University Press.

Marcuse, H. (1964) *One-Dimensional Man.* Boston, MA: Beacon Press.

Matza, D. (1969) *Becoming Deviant.* Englewood Cliffs, NJ: Prentice-Hall.

Melossi, D. (1990) *The State of Social Control: A Sociological Study of Concepts of State and Social Control in the Making of Democracy.* Cambridge: Polity Press.

Melossi, D. (2005) 'Security, Social Control, Democracy and Migration within the "Constitution" of the EU', *European Law Journal,* 11: 5–21.

Melossi, D., Sparks, R. and Sozzo, M. (eds) (2009) *Travels of the Criminal Question: Cultural Embeddedness and Diffusion.* Oxford: Hart.

Mills, C. W. (1956) *The Power Elite.* New York: Oxford University Press.

Mills, C. W. (1959) *The Sociological Imagination.* New York: Oxford University Press.

Monjardet, D. (1999) 'Rèinventer la police urbaine', *Les Annales de la recherche urbaine,* 83/84: 15–22.

Mulcahy, A. (1999) 'Visions of Normality: Peace and the Reconstruction of Policing in Northern Ireland', *Social and Legal Studies,* 8: 277–95.

O'Malley, P. (1992) 'Risk, Power and Crime Prevention', *Economy and Society,* 21(3): 252–75.

Peyre, V. (1986) 'Introduction: Elements d'un débat sur la prévention de la délinquance', *Annales de Vaucresson*, 24(1): 9–13.

Pitch, T. (2006) *La società della prevenzione*. Roma: Carocci.

Prodi, R. (1997) Unpublished speech to the seminar 'La sicurezza in Emilia – Romagna', Bologna, 5 April.

Putnam, R. D. (1993) *Making Democracy Work: Civic Traditions in Modern Italy*. Princeton: Princeton University Press.

Regione Toscana (2002) *Relazione generale sullo stato della sicurezza in Toscana e sull'attuazione della legge regionale 16 August 2001, n. 38*. Firenze: Regione Toscana.

Reiter, H. (1996) 'Le forze di polizia e l'ordine pubblico in Italia', *Polis*, 10: 337–60.

Robert, P. (1991) 'Les chercheurs face aux politiques de prévention', in P. Robert (ed.) *Les politiques de prévention de la delinquance a l'aune de la recherche. Un bilan international*. Paris: L'Harmattan, pp. 13–27.

Roché, S. (2004) 'Réformes dans la police et formes de gouvernement', in S. Roché (ed.) *Réformer la police et la sécurité. Les nouvelles tendances en Europe et aux Etats-Units*. Paris: Odile Jacobs, pp. 7–37.

Savona, E. U. (2004) 'Ipotesi per uno scenario della prevenzione', in R. Selmini (ed.) *La sicurezza urbana*. Bologna: Il Mulino, pp. 273–84.

Selmini, R. (1997) 'Il punto di vista dei comitati di cittadini'. *Quaderni di Città sicure*, 11(a): 77–94.

Selmini, R. (2003) 'Le politiche di sicurezza: origini, sviluppo e prospettive', in M. Barbagli (ed.) *Rapporto sulla criminalità in Italia*. Bologna: Il Mulino, pp. 611–48.

Selmini, R. (2005) 'Towards *Città sicure*? Political action and institutional conflict in contemporary preventive and safety policies in Italy', *Theoretical Criminology*, 9(3): 307–23.

Selmini, R. (2009) 'Introduzione', in *Rapporto Annuale sulla sicurezza in Emilia–Romagna, Quaderni di Città sicure*, 33: 1–10.

Simon, J. (2007) *Governing through Crime: How the War on Crime Transformed American Democracy and Created a Culture of Fear*. New York: Oxford University Press.

Skogan, W. G. (1990) *Disorder and Decline: Crime and the Spiral of Decay in American Neighborhoods*. Berkeley: University of California Press.

Stenson, K. and Edwards, A. (2004) 'Policy Transfer in Local Crime Control: Beyond Naive Emulation', in T. Newburn and R. Sparks (eds) *Criminal Justice and Political Cultures: National and International Dimensions of Crime Control*. Cullompton: Willan Publishing, pp. 209–33.

Stille, A. (1995) *Excellent Cadavers*. London: Vintage.

Walgrave, L. and de Cauter, F. (1986) 'Une tentative de clarification de la notion de "prévention"', *Annales de Vaucresson*, 24(1): 31–51.

Wilson, J. Q. and Kelling G. L. (1982) 'Broken Windows: The Police and Neighborhood Safety', *The Atlantic Monthly*, March: 29–38.

Chapter 8

Crime prevention at the Belgian federal level: from a social democratic policy to a neo-liberal and authoritarian policy in a social democratic context

Patrick Hebberecht

Introduction

In this contribution I analyse the development of Belgian crime prevention policy at the national and later at the federal level, and its implementation at the local level from 1985 until 2007. For a good understanding of the evolution of crime prevention policy during this time, it will be sub-divided into three periods according to the coalition of political parties governing at the national/federal level. Following this criterion, a distinction is made between three periods: first, 1985 to 1988, during which a coalition of Christian democratic and liberal parties governed; second, 1988 to 1999, when a coalition of Christian democratic and socialist parties were in power; and third, the period 1999 to 2007, which witnessed a coalition of liberal and socialist parties (and from 1999 until 2003 also of green parties). It is important to note that since the 1970s, due to the regional conflicts of interest within Belgium almost all political formations are split, with both a Flemish and French-speaking political party, which are totally independent from each other.

In the subsequent discussion of the evolution of crime prevention policy in Belgium, the political-ideological orientation of the different phases of the crime prevention policy will be specified, as will the specific types of crime, the prevention methods and the target groups privileged in these different phases. In so doing, close attention is given to the relation between the national/federal level and the local level.

After the initial descriptive overview the chapter will analyse further some specific topics in the evolution of the prevention policy during the period from 1985 until 2007. These will include the effects of the changing institutional context and organisation of the police forces on crime prevention policy; the influence of political ideologies on the place of crime prevention policy within broader criminal policy; and the changing priorities of crime prevention policy. The influence of prevention strategies and models drawn from other European countries on the evolution of Belgian prevention policy will also be discussed. In the final section, the evolution of crime prevention policy will be placed in the context of neo-liberal economic globalisation and the crisis of the nation state.

Until 1985 the Belgian government had not developed a specific national prevention policy. The prevention of criminality was believed to derive from the general preventive effects of the police and criminal justice system as well as by way of the special preventive effects of individual criminal sanctions oriented towards the social reintegration of offenders. The prevention of juvenile delinquency was developed by the juvenile protection system. In the context of a new neo-liberal economic and political context of the mid 1980s, the Belgian government subsequently took the first initiative to set up a national prevention policy. Before considering this, first let us reconstruct the crime prevention policy elaborated by the Christian democratic and liberal governments during the period from 1985 until 1988, before going on to consider the Christian democratic and socialist governments during the period from 1988 until 1999 and finally the liberal-socialist-green government (1999–2003) and the liberal-socialist government (2003–07).

The Christian democratic and liberal prevention policy (1985–88): a new national prevention policy and structure

The marginalising social and cultural effects of the economic crisis in the 1970s, combined with the processes of economic restructuring and its impact on specific social groups, led to an increase in property crimes and vandalism as well as an increase in feelings of insecurity. Because of the increase in problems of crime and insecurity, but also due to the reduction in detection rates, a new police prevention policy was developed by the *gendarmerie* and some local police forces, most notably in Flanders (Hebberecht 1990). Potential victims were encouraged by police services to take techno-preventive measures and to adopt avoidance and security behaviours. In collaboration with other partners (such as school head teachers, parents' associations, and leaders of youth centres) preventive projects were developed by the *gendarmerie* at district levels (comparable with the judicial districts) in order to avoid deviant and delinquent behaviour of (mainly middle-class) youth (Berkmoes 1990). Some municipal police forces, Ghent for example, set up some forms of neighbourhood watch schemes (Carlier 1990).

From 1981 the government, a coalition of Christian democratic and liberal parties, tried to restructure the Belgian Keynesian welfare state according to neo-liberal prescriptions. Only when the legitimacy of the government was heavily threatened by a combination of the unsolved killings by the so-called 'Gang of Nijvel', acts of terrorism of the 'Cellules Communistes Combattantes' and the dramatic events of the football game between Juventus and Liverpool in the Brussels Heysel stadium in 1985, did the government begin to outline a security and prevention policy towards several types of crime. By means of his security plan (note that the word 'security' was used for the first time in a government plan), the Minister of Justice, the French-speaking liberal Gol, sought to strengthen and improve collaboration between the *gendarmerie*, the communal police and the judicial police in their fight against banditry and terrorism. To fight property crime and vandalism, the Minister of the Interior, the French-speaking Christian democrat Nothomb, created a new national prevention structure and policy. The new police prevention policy was the inspiration for the new national prevention policy. At that time, the institutions of the Belgian unitary state marked the structure of the prevention policy, the elaboration and implementation of which was centralised at national and provincial level. At that time Belgium had nine provinces and the provincial governors acted under the authority of the Minister of the Interior. The *gendarmerie* and the communal police forces of the larger cities were the main actors in the Belgian prevention policy at the national and provincial level. Consequently, during the period 1985 until 1988 the local administration, the mayor and welfare services were not involved in Belgian prevention policy.

Between 1985 and 1988, a neo-liberal component was developed in Belgian prevention policy. According to this neo-liberal component, property crime and vandalism came to be seen as the product of leaving properties unprotected and inadequate supervision (Clarke 1980). Belgian prevention policy focused on reducing opportunities to commit crimes and increasing informal, functional and formal control in (semi-)public places (Hauber 1999). Citizens were to be viewed as primarily and especially responsible for their own security. They were to be regarded as responsible for protecting themselves and their possessions as well as taking increased control for their surroundings. The state's role, by contrast, was to support the citizens by fulfilling its responsibilities, including the provision of security advice, support for victims and increased police surveillance on the streets.

Christian democratic and socialist prevention policy (1988–99): from prevention to security

The elaboration of a social democratic component in Belgian prevention policy (1988–92)

After years of opposition, Flemish and French-speaking socialists entered a coalition with Flemish and French-speaking Christian democratic parties. In different governmental constitutions this political coalition existed until 1999. During this period, Flemish socialists held the position of Minister of the Interior. Under their authority, the Belgian prevention policy was further developed (Cartuyvels and Hebberecht 2002). In 1988 the socialists no longer opposed the neo-liberal inspired economic and political restructuring which the Christian democratic and liberal governments had put into practice in the 1980s. The socialist parties were determined to conduct a social policy that mitigated the marginalising and social excluding effects of these neo-liberal processes of change (Meynen 2000). In so doing, they engaged in defending the social security system and commenced a fight against poverty and social exclusion. An immigration policy was shaped in the fight against discrimination and racism. As a part of this broader social policy, the prevention policy was oriented towards the effects on crime and insecurity of the neo-liberal transformations wrought during the 1980s.

Several types of theft and vandalism increased significantly according to police records. Rates of vandalism in and around schools and football stadiums also kept rising. In middle-class urban neighbourhoods and suburbs perceptions of insecurity increased. Especially under the influence of French sociological analyses of social exclusion these problems of crime and insecurity were seen as a consequence of the deterioration and disintegration of several urban neighbourhoods (Dubet 1987; Delarue 1991; Delebarre 1993).

Within the framework of what became known as the Whit Sunday Plan of 5 June 1990, a government plan to reform the police and justice system, the Minister of the Interior, the Flemish socialist Louis Tobback, reoriented the national prevention policy towards a local, administrative and integrated approach. Tobback privileged the local municipality, the city and some deteriorated neighbourhoods, bypassing the provincial level. The mayor was given key responsibility for the development, integration and execution of a prevention policy at the local level. The role of the police services and thus of their privileged situational and techno-prevention moved somewhat into the background. The government reorganised the communal police in a front-line police force and the *gendarmerie* in a secondary role. According to this new division of police tasks only the municipal police had a limited role to play in the local prevention policy. After all, the municipal police exercise their administrative competencies under the authority of the mayor. Social and welfare organisations were given an important task in preventing crimes committed by vulnerable and marginalised youth as well as in the reduction of fear of crime among vulnerable social groups. In the opinion of the Minister of the Interior the local administrative prevention policy had to integrate both situational and social approaches and a (potential) victim and (potential) perpetrator orientation. The mayor had to ensure that the various actors in the field of prevention worked together in partnership. To implement this new vision the Minister of the Interior financed 27 pilot prevention projects. To stimulate public, political and administrative support for the integrated local prevention policy, the Minister distributed to all mayors a ministerial circular OOP18 (30/01/1992) containing a model regulation for setting up a communal advisory board on prevention.

From the public pronouncements and policy documents of the Minister of the Interior, Tobback, we can deduce that a social democratic component in Belgian prevention policy was elaborated. Tobback developed a local prevention policy with a more structural, social and urban dimension (De Haan 1999). According to this social democratic component, crime and insecurity problems are connected with unequal life-chances, social deprivation and discrimination. The social question here is particularly seen as an urban issue. Crime problems and subjective feelings of unsafety are to be prevented in the first place by social prevention for the benefit of vulnerable social groups (Poulet 1995; Synergie 1995).

The transformation of the social democratic component of Belgian prevention policy in a social liberal direction (1992–95)

During the parliamentary elections of 24 November 1991, the Flemish extreme right political party (Vlaams Blok) had an electoral breakthrough in Flanders. It had conducted a campaign against immigrants and in favour of a repressive and tough crime control policy. Despite the fact that the previous coalition of Christian democrats and socialists lost almost 10 per cent of their votes, they still formed the new government. Moreover, the Flemish socialist Tobback remained at the Ministry of the Interior.

The Council of Ministers approved the 'Security of the Citizen' guideline drafted by the Interior and Justice Ministries on 19 June 1992 (Cartuyvels and Hebberecht 2002). The principle of an integrated approach to local prevention was confirmed in the shape of the security and prevention contracts that were set up. However, the desire manifested in 1990 to aim prevention work first and foremost at socially vulnerable individuals and deal with the processes of economic, social and political marginalisation that threatened them had disappeared. Communal police services were again given the most important role. Citizens were responsible for their own security, just as was the case in the 1980s. Situational control perspectives resurfaced, since the best way of preventing crime was considered to be reducing the opportunities to commit crime. So, the priority emphasis was put on various types of technical prevention measures, such as police surveillance, delegation of security tasks to private security services, housekeepers, shop personnel, transport workers. If social prevention was not forgotten, this was because acting upon the social causes of crime (through outreach youth work, for example) could help prevent crime.

These new orientations in the prevention policy were now framed within a broader security policy of the mayor and police and from the end of 1992 supported by the negotiation of security and prevention contracts with cities and municipalities. A security contract consisted of a section concerning community policing and a section covering prevention. About 75 per cent of the financing of a security contract was channelled into projects that sought to improve the quality of communal policing and were designed to bring police closer to citizens. In the section concerning prevention, projects were chosen that reflected the new preventive philosophy of the government. By the summer of 1992, security contracts had already been signed with five large Belgian towns and seven at-risk municipalities of the Brussels Region for the period covering the winter of 1992 and all of 1993. Prevention contracts consisted exclusively of preventive projects.

The creation of the role of a municipal prevention officer in charge of co-ordinating prevention policy, and the establishment of a municipal advisory board for the prevention of crime, were both made compulsory for all cities and municipalities that received financing through security and prevention contracts. Between the end of 1992 and 1995 the number of security contracts increased to 29 cities and municipalities. In 1995 another 29 cities and municipalities agreed prevention contracts. The royal decree of 12 March 1993 marked the birth of a Permanent Secretariat for Prevention Policy, which was directly accountable to the Minister of the Interior. This Secretariat was given a number of tasks that included supporting local prevention initiatives, and co-ordinating and evaluating the federal prevention policy.

The continuing transformation of Belgian prevention policy in a social liberal direction and the beginnings of an authoritarian, moral conservative component (1995–99)

Following the legislative elections of 21 May 1995 a new coalition brought the Christian democrats and socialists back to power. Johan Vande Lanotte, a Flemish socialist, was reinstated as Minister of the Interior (the position he had filled to replace Louis Tobback at the end of the previous legislature). The existing policing and prevention sections of the security contracts were expanded to incorporate a focus on drugs, justice and city guards. The section concerning drugs financed projects aimed at the prevention of drug use, and medical social projects especially targeted at homeless drug addicts. The section on justice provided financial support for the implementation and support of alternative measures. The section on city guards provided funding for long-term unemployed people with work as wardens in the exercise of control functions and supervision in streets, squares and public places. In 1996 the Minister of the Interior planned also the integration of projects of urban regeneration within the security contracts. For this reason, from 1998 security contracts were reformulated into security and society contracts.

In the second half of the 1990s inhabitants of rural areas and outer areas of small cities increasingly became victims of burglary. In Flanders this led to several citizen initiatives that organised surveillance in their own neighbourhoods. Fearing that the extreme right-wing party Vlaams Blok would benefit from the resulting discontent towards central and local government, both the *gendarmerie* and the municipal police established Neighbourhood Watch Networks, together with the inhabitants of certain neighbourhoods. In doing so, information about suspicious situations and persons was distributed to all inhabitants of these areas more quickly, so that they could take necessary preventive measures. Additionally, these initiatives facilitated a better flow of information from citizens to the police about suspicious persons and situations. These citizen initiatives were regulated through a ministerial circular of the Minister of the Interior, Vande Lanotte. The initiatives were adopted widely in Flanders; by contrast, they were unsuccessful in the Brussels and Walloon Regions.

The discovery, in August 1996, of the bodies of two murdered young girls hit Belgium like a shock wave. The subsequent public concern for what became known as the Dutroux Scandal strengthened the position within the government of the Minister of Justice, the Flemish Christian democrat Declercq. He was now able to push through reform of the justice system. These events meant that the Minister of the Interior was well aware that the total financial support for his prevention and security policy would no longer continue to increase, as had been the case since 1992. The financial, administrative and scientific evaluation of the security and prevention contracts now became a priority for the Minister of the Interior (Depovere and Ponsaers 1998; Mary 2003). The results of this evaluation made it possible to drop some unsuccessful projects from a contract and to start with some new innovative projects.

The escape of Dutroux from a police office in April 1998 led to the resignation of the Ministers of Justice and the Interior. The Flemish socialist Luc Vanden Bossche became the new Minister of the Interior. In the run-up to the elections of 1999, the 'get tough' approach on crime, advocated by the extreme right Vlaams Blok, captured a lot of public attention. In the attempt to break the right-wing monopoly of this election theme, the Flemish liberal party positioned itself as the champion of a more authoritarian repressive approach to crime. In this electoral climate, in which the social democratic/social liberal model of prevention was sidelined, the Minister of Interior, Luc Vanden Bossche, took the political initiative and introduced a new bill to provide local authorities with greater powers to advance a repressive fight against public disorder. Under certain conditions the municipal council was to be able to determine whether criminal or administrative sanctions should be used against disorderly behaviours. On 13 May 1999, immediately prior to the elections, this new law came into effect.

The federal prevention policy of the 'purple–green' government Verhofstadt I (1999–2003) and 'purple' government Verhofstadt II (2003–07): prevention policy integrated in a security policy

The federal prevention policy of the 'purple–green' government Verhofstadt I (1999–2003)

Despite the prevention and security policies adopted as well as the tougher approach to law and order taken by the Justice Department, problems of crime and insecurity did not become less serious towards the end of the twentieth century. The percentage of victims of various types of property crimes and vandalism remained high. The number of burglaries increased. Street crimes were increasingly committed with aggression. In the aftermath of the Dutroux case, sexual offences remained a preoccupation within public opinion. In addition, several types of organised crime were given widespread attention by the media. The population in general was more concerned about crime, as reflected in the continuing electoral success of the extreme right party Vlaams Blok.

With the 'purple–green' government Verhofstadt I, a coalition of liberal, socialist and green parties was formed in June 1999. For the first time, the federal and local prevention policies explicitly became part of a much broader integrated federal approach to security and criminal policy (Hebberecht 2000). This new security policy sought to ensure greater co-ordination and efficiency between all segments in the criminal justice system, from prevention to repression and sanction. It also sought to integrate governmental interventions from the local level to the international level. The Minister of Justice, the Flemish liberal Verwilghen, had responsibility for elaborating a federal integrated security plan. The Minister aimed to strengthen the neo-liberal component of the security policy by prioritising the fight against street crime and organised crime, the decriminalisation of white collar crime, the implementation of management techniques, the privatisation of several police and justice functions and the development of possibilities for greater private–public partnerships. The political will to build in a more authoritarian and moral conservative component within the integrated security policy is evidenced by the tougher approach towards street crime and juvenile delinquency adopted by the police and justice system. This new normative orientation also could be seen reflected in changes to penal law and penal procedure that allowed possibilities for more severe punishments and gave police greater powers to combat crime.

The prevention policy role within the integrated security policy became less important in the period 1999–2003. The restructuring of the Belgian police services into a federal and local police force in 2002 led to the loss of the section concerning the municipal police in the security and society contracts. Hence, the former distinction between security and society contracts and prevention contracts no longer remained. From 2002, these contracts were called security and prevention contracts and were fixed with 73 cities and municipalities. The local prevention structure, which was built up by socialists during the 1990s, was retained by the liberal Minister of the Interior, the French-speaking Antoine Duquesne. The content of the security and prevention contracts was now oriented towards the new priorities formulated in the federal security plan, namely situational and technological prevention of property crime, street violence and disorder caused by drug use and drug trafficking. No space was left in the federal prevention policy for a more social, structural and urban dimension. Consequently, the social democratic/social liberal component diminished. In 2002 a general reform of the federal departments was implemented. The tasks of the Permanent Secretariat for Prevention Policy were taken over by the 'Local Integrated Security Policy' service of the 'General Direction of the Security and Prevention Policy' of the Federal Department of the Interior.

The federal prevention policy of the 'purple' government Verhofstadt II (2003–07)

During the parliamentary elections in 2003, the Flemish liberal party did not achieve the electoral success it hoped for. On the contrary, the Flemish – and more so the French-speaking socialists – strengthened their position. The new 'purple' government Verhofstadt II was a coalition of liberal and socialist parties. In this coalition, the liberal party was less able to force its neo-liberal, authoritarian and moral conservative vision on security and prevention policy. The party retained the position of the Minister of the Interior, the Flemish liberal Patrick Dewael, but had to give up the position of the Minister of Justice in favour of the French-speaking socialists. Even more than in 1999 the new federal security plan in 2004 was a compromise between, on the one hand, a neo-liberal but also a moral conservative and authoritarian vision of the Flemish liberals, and, on the other hand, the more social and humanistic vision of the French-speaking socialists (Hebberecht 2004).

The existing security and prevention contracts were renewed for the period 2005 and 2006 and on 7 December 2006 a new Royal Decree reoriented the structure, style and content of the security and prevention contracts. The new 'strategic security and prevention plans', as they were now called, were structured by the types of crimes the city or municipality intended to prevent in the first place and by the priorities of the federal government. These last priorities were outlined in the Royal Decree and included property crimes, crimes against the person, public disorder, drug addiction and the security of certain vulnerable groups, such as the elderly and certain professionals. General and strategic objectives were formulated for the prevention of these crimes. Each city or municipality had to select from some of the general and strategic objectives outlined and to formulate operational objectives and related indicators and evaluation targets. The priorities of the city or municipality had to be based on a local diagnosis of the insecurity problems. Priorities had also to be in line with the zonal security plan of the local police. For these crimes general, strategic and operational objectives had to be formulated. It was no longer necessary (as had been required under the previous security and prevention contracts) to mention for every prioritised crime the actions, methods and financial means to reach the operational objectives. Rather, a global subsidy was given by the federal government to realise the strategic security and prevention plan over a period of four years (2007–10). However, if the objectives are not realised the city or municipality could be financially sanctioned.

Since the mid 1990s different types of wardens and watchers were created to improve the security on the streets, in social housing, on public transport, at the football stadium. The Royal Decree of 15 May 2007 created a uniform legal framework for all the security and prevention functions not belonging to the public and private police. The new function of *gemeenschapswacht* (community warden) was created.

After the parliamentary elections of June 2007 Belgium was confronted with a deep political crisis at the federal level. Because of the difficulties in forming a new federal government, the 'purple' government Verhofstadt II continued to handle the current affairs until the end of 2007. In expectation of a political compromise about a new constitutional reform a new government was constituted with five parties, the Flemish and French-speaking liberals and Christian democrats and the French-speaking socialists. Until 21 March 2008 this government was provisionally led by the Flemish liberal Verhofstadt. Since then the Christian democrat Yves Leterme became the Prime Minister. All that time the Flemish liberal Patrick Dewael stayed at the Department of the Interior. Since the elections of 2007 no new initiatives at the level of the prevention policy have been undertaken.

The role of the institutional context, organisation of the police and political ideology

The institutional context of Belgium, the organisation of the police forces and the neo-liberal, social democratic and social liberal political ideologies played a determining role in the development of Belgian prevention policy. The first governmental crime prevention policy was structured in 1985 by the institutional context of the national Belgian state. The Minister of the Interior was the competent authority for the elaboration of prevention policy. This neo-liberal oriented policy, characterised by a top-down approach, was developed independently from the criminal justice policy. The governors of the provinces were responsible for the elaboration and implementation of the national prevention policy. The main actors in the crime prevention structure were the *gendarmerie* and the communal police forces, which for the purpose of their administrative competencies were dependent upon the Minister of the Interior. National prevention policy in the 1980s was aimed at individual middle-class citizens and middle-class neighbourhoods situated around Belgium cities. These constituted the core electorate of the governing Christian democratic and liberal parties. Primarily prevention policy was targeted at preventing victimisation among these groups. Hence, technological and situational prevention methods were privileged, heralding a neo-liberal component within prevention policy.

When crime prevention policy was reoriented at the end of 1990, Belgium was no longer a nation state but was transformed in a federal state with three regions (the Flemish, Brussels and Walloon regions) and with three communities (Flemish, French and German) by the constitutional reform of 1988 (Platel 2004). The Belgian state was now composed of three levels of government. The first is the Federal government, which has the residual powers not assigned to other levels of government (notably national defence, foreign policy, the mint, social security, the justice system and the Ministry of the Interior). The second level is the Regions. Their powers are defined territorially and include, among other things, housing, transport, public workers and foreign trade. At the third level of government lies the Communities, the powers of which are linked to the language of the citizens and include education, culture, health and assistance to people (and thus youth assistance).

The reorientation of the prevention policy under the Christian democratic–socialist governments (1988–99) was first inspired by a social democratic vision which from the mid 1990s was transformed in a social liberal one. In the first half of the 1990s inhabitants of working-class neighbourhoods within the cities became the privileged group of a social democratic inspired prevention policy. Their victimisation and insecurity by crime were taken seriously. More social prevention projects were set up, aimed at crime afflicting those areas. As such, crime prevention policy became part of a broader social policy against poverty, social exclusion, discrimination and racism. A more robust social democratic component in crime prevention policy was constituted. In the second half of the 1990s more attention also went to the security demands emanating from the middle-class neighbourhood inhabitants in suburban and rural areas. The social prevention projects were now aimed less at changing the structural economic and social position of marginalised groups, and became part of a broader security policy of the mayor and police. The objective of prevention projects was no longer the improvement of the economic and social conditions of excluded persons but a decrease of crime and insecurity. The social democratic component in crime prevention policy was gradually transformed into a social liberal one.

The local level of the city or commune was privileged for the elaboration of prevention policy. Prevention policy was no longer shaped by a top-down relationship between the federal and local level. Given the formalisation of prevention policy through contracts, local administrative authorities obtained an increasingly important partnership role in co-determining the policy content. For political-ideological reasons prevention policy became more important within broader criminal policy due to the inclusion of wider policies under the auspice of prevention (such as drug policy, diversionary policies, employment policy and urban policy). Since 1992, the Brussels and Walloon regions and the French community sustained the security and prevention contracts of the Minister of the Interior by financing some social crime prevention projects. Politically they wanted to support the social democratic crime prevention policy of the socialist Ministers of the Interior. However, for political reasons this was not the case for the government of the Flemish community, where Christian democrats held a majority. The Flemish government wanted to distance itself from the federal government that took initiatives by means of a security and prevention policy deploying competencies that in fact belonged to the authority of the communities and the regions.

From the end of 1990 to the end of 1992 the communal police played only a secondary role in local prevention policy. From the end of 1992 until 1999, prevention policy became part of a wider security agenda of the police. The role of the communal police in local prevention policy was reinforced. The professional identity crisis of welfare workers employed in the frame of the security and prevention contracts was experienced differently in both parts of Belgium. In Brussels and the Walloon Region there was greater resistance than in Flanders to the fact that welfare and social work was placed in the context of prevention and security policy of the police. Consequently, social and welfare workers in the French-speaking part of Belgium have succeeded more than in the Flemish part to develop welfare dynamics from within the framework of the security and prevention policy in a way that is independent of police interventions towards the same problems (Goris 2000; Van Campenhoudt *et al*. 2000; Mary 2003).

The dominant role of the communal police in local prevention policy was terminated by the liberal Ministers of the Interior during the governments Verhofstadt I and II (1999–2007). In 2002 the three Belgian police forces – the *gendarmerie*, the communal police and the judiciary police – were reorganised into a federal and a zonal police. As a result of this reorganisation, the execution of preventive tasks of the zonal police became more independent from local prevention policy. Police prevention projects had to be incorporated into the zonal security plan rather than the security and prevention contracts. Consequently, the zonal police have become less interested in crime prevention. Many preventive tasks are now performed by civilians working in zonal police forces, such as giving information about technological preventive measures. As was already the case since 1990 for the *gendarmerie*, the federal police had no preventive competency to fulfil.

Under the governments Verhofstadt I and II prevention policy became a part of a federal integrated security plan elaborated by the Minister of Justice under the 'purple–green' government (1999–2003) and by the Prime Minister himself under the 'purple' government (2003–07). The prevention element within this security and criminal policy diminished in importance from 1999 until 2007, largely because for neo-liberal political-ideological reasons parts of other policies that were included in prevention policy during the period 1992–98 were now systematically excluded (Willekens 2006). The regions and communities became less involved in the prevention policy. While the prevention policy and security policy of the mayor and police developed by the governments Verhofstadt I and II became more integrated in a broader criminal policy, at the same time prevention policy became less integrated. As in the 1980s, the Ministers of the Interior limited their competencies to specific situational and techno-logical prevention. Since 1999, preventive initiatives have been especially oriented towards the (commercial) middle class, the professions and small and medium-sized businesses. The neo-liberal component in crime prevention policy was reinforced and for the first time a new moral conservative, authoritarian dynamic emerged.

Belgian crime prevention policy and models of crime prevention in the European Union

Since the federalisation of Belgium in the 1980s politicians and policy-makers in the Flemish part have been influenced by Anglo-Saxon and Dutch developments while those in the French-speaking part by evol-utions in France. From this perspective the development of the federal Belgian prevention policy is an interesting case of the transfer of policies from England and Wales, the Netherlands and France (Stenson and Edwards 2004). A comparative study of the crime prevention models in those countries is necessary for a good understanding of the prevention policy developments in Belgium (Hebberecht and Sack 1997; Hebberecht 2002; Hughes 2007; Crawford 2007).

The new police prevention strategy developed in the first half of the 1980s was strongly influenced by the prevention policies elaborated by the British police from the end of the 1970s (Johnston and Shapland 1997; Crawford 1997, 2002b). Many of these new British police initiatives were known to Belgian police forces via the Dutch police, who had introduced them in the Netherlands (de Savornin-Lohman 1997). Also the Belgian national prevention policy developed after 1985 was strongly influenced by both British and Dutch prevention policies, although unlike in the Netherlands, the mayor and local administration played no significant role in the Belgian prevention policy of the 1980s.

By contrast, the reorientation of the federal prevention policy at the end of 1990 towards a local, administrative and integrated prevention policy was strongly influenced by the social prevention policies elaborated since the beginning of the 1980s in France (Body-Gendrot and Duprez 2002). The important role of the mayor in the elaboration of an integrated local prevention policy was emulated from the French example, as was the institution of the local advisory prevention council.

As in England and Wales, the Netherlands and France, prevention policy took the form of a contractualisation of relations between central government and localities, notably since the end of 1990. Local prevention projects were only financed if they were consistent with the government prevention philosophy. In England and Wales, France and the Netherlands a new administrative organisation at the national level was set up to elaborate, co-ordinate and implement the national prevention policy. In Belgium this was also evident in 1993 with the establishment of a Permanent Secretariat for prevention policy. The security and prevention contracts negotiated between the Minister of the Interior and the local authorities of some cities and municipalities were a typical Belgian policy initiative which influenced the further evolution of prevention policy in France in the 1990s (De Maillard 2005). The initiative to employ long-term unemployed workers as city guards, a key element of the security contracts, was heavily inspired by the project of the Dutch city guards (Van Dijk 1990; Van Swaaningen 2002). So too, the integration of the prevention policy in a broader integrated security policy over recent years was influenced by the Dutch integrated security plans (Van Swaaningen 2005).

Contrary to the 1980s and the beginning of the 1990s, when the situational and technological prevention model of England and Wales and the Netherlands competed with a more social preventive model of France and Barcelona in Spain, the more recent integration of both models by the

New Labour government in Britain since 1997 has dominated European developments (Crawford 2002a; Hughes 2007). This is evident in other Western European countries and in the new member states of the European Union since 2004. In Belgium we can characterise the prevention policy of recent years as a neo-liberal and authoritarian policy adapted to a social democratic context in which this external influence has been present (Hebberecht 2008).

Federal crime prevention policy, neo-liberal globalisation and the crisis of the nation state

Changes in the federal crime prevention policy were not only an indirect reaction to new developments in crime and insecurity; they were also the product of political choices made by a reorganised federal state in a neo-liberal global context (Hughes 1998; Taylor 1999). Since the end of the 1980s neo-liberal economic globalisation led in the first place to urban social fragmentation, polarisation, inequality and cultural diversification (Lea 2002). By these processes certain neighbourhoods were confronted with social problems and problems of crime and insecurity. The authorities had less success in realising social integration, cohesion and cultural homogeneity while simultaneously meeting the demands of companies and enterprises. Authorities were increasingly confronted with contradictory demands for security. On the one side, (global) enterprises are less dependent on government by way of their greater mobility. Social integration and stability, realised by a social and welfare policy, are less important for them. Those (global) enterprises are also less willing to contribute financially to such a policy. Nowadays they demand more security and control of 'risk' populations that might disturb and threaten the economic process. The federal governments tried to meet those demands by enforcing a neo-liberal component in their crime prevention policy and since the end of the 1990s also by developing a more authoritarian and moral conservative approach.

On the other side, the government is still confronted, although to a lesser extent, with a demand from sections of the population to deal with problems of crime and insecurity by developing a social and welfare policy. By not meeting these demands, government can lose their legitimacy among those groups of the population. For this reason, a social democratic/social liberal component in the government crime prevention policy was elaborated in the 1990s and still exists in the local prevention policy of some cities.

In line with Garland's (2001) analysis, the federal governments have developed in their security policy a double strategy, namely a pragmatic strategy of preventive partnership and since the end of the 1990s also a strategy of a more authoritarian and punitive segregation of certain 'risk' populations. A pragmatic strategy of preventive partnership was developed in order to overcome the limitations of the functioning of the criminal justice system in the fight against property crimes. The authorities displaced responsibility for the protection of all kinds of possessions to neighbourhood watch, to the (potential) victims and to the private sector. This strategy concentrated attention on the effects of crime (the victims and fear of crime) and less on the causes of crime. Numerous partnerships between the private and public sector, set up by the governments Verhofstadt I and II, have also to be understood in the context of this strategy.

For the first time in the crime prevention policy of the last few decades a more authoritarian strategy of segregation of certain risk populations has been elaborated. The target groups of this strategy have been young people from ethnic minorities, illegal persons, prostitutes, beggars and drug addicts. This strategy of segregation was especially elaborated in the fight against public disorder. This political strategy of segregation was promoted in a radical form by the extreme right-wing Vlaams Blok/Vlaams Belang and in a milder form by the Flemish conservative liberals and Christian democrats.

Since the parliamentary elections of June 2007 Belgium has been confronted with a deep political crisis. On the Flemish side, the Christian democratic party, a democratic Flemish nationalist party and the extreme right party Vlaams Belang are demanding a more far-reaching federalisation of Belgium with more competencies for the Flemish region. By contrast, all the French-speaking parties are opposed to this proposal. At the end of 2007 a government was formed with the Christian democratic and liberal party on the Flemish side and the Christian democratic, liberal and socialist party on the French-speaking part. Until 21 March 2008 this government was provisionally led by the Flemish liberal Verhofstadt. Since then this coalition of parties has been led by the Flemish Christian democrat Yves Leterme.

The federal crime prevention policy was reoriented in 2007 by the former 'purple' government Verhofstadt II. New strategic security and prevention plans were contracted with cities and municipalities for a period of four years (2007–10). This new prevention policy is now implemented by the actual government. The strategic security and prevention plans were structured by the types of crimes the city or municipality intended to prevent in the first place and by the priorities of the federal government. The priorities of the new government are also oriented towards the situational and techno-prevention of property crimes and the authoritarian approach of public disorders. In cities and municipalities where the local political power relations are in favour of the liberal or Christian democratic party these federal priorities are also reinforced by local neo-liberal and authoritarian and moral conservative inspired priorities. This trend is more present in the Flemish part of Belgium. In other cities and municipalities, where the socialist party is politically dominant social liberal inspired priorities are still included in the strategic security and prevention plans. Undoubtedly, the results of the next federal parliamentary elections (2011) and municipal elections (2012) will be important for the further development of prevention policy in Belgium.

References

Berkmoes, H. (1990) 'Politionele preventie: een halte naar bestuurlijke preventie?', in C. Eliaerts, E. Enhus and R. Senden (eds) *Politie in beweging. Bijdrage tot de discussie over de politie van morgen*. Antwerp/Arnhem: Kluwer/Gouda Quint, pp. 111–18.

Body-Gendrot, S. and Duprez, D. (2002) 'Security and Prevention Policies in France in the 1990s', in P. Hebberecht and D. Duprez (eds) *The Prevention and Security Policies in Europe*. Brussels: VUB Press, pp. 95–132.

Carlier, F. (1990) 'De buurtobservatieactie: een politioneel preventieve reactie op de elitaire technopreventie te Gent', in C. Eliaerts, E. Enhus and R. Senden (eds) *Politie in beweging. Bijdrage tot de discussie over de politie van morgen*. Antwerp/Arnhem: Kluwer/Gouda Quint, pp. 89–110.

Cartuyvels, Y. and Hebberecht P. (2002) 'The Belgian Federal Security and Crime Prevention Policy in the 1990s', in P. Hebberecht and D. Duprez (eds) *The Prevention and Security Policies in Europe*, Brussels: VUB Press, pp. 15–50.

Clarke, R. (1980) 'Situational Crime Prevention: Theory and Practice', *British Journal of Criminology*, 20(2): 136–47.

Crawford, A. (1997) *The Local Governance of Crime: Appeals to Community and Partnerships*. Oxford: Clarendon Press.

Crawford, A. (2002a) 'The Growth of Crime Prevention in France as Contrasted with the English Experience: Some Thoughts on the Politics of Insecurity', in G. Hughes, E. McLaughlin and J. Muncie (eds) *Crime Prevention and Community Safety: New Directions*. London: Sage, pp. 214–39.

Crawford, A. (2002b) 'The Politics of Community Safety and Crime Prevention in England and Wales: New Strategies and Developments', in P. Hebberecht and D. Duprez (eds) *The Prevention and Security Policies in Europe*. Brussels: VUB Press, pp. 51–94.

Crawford, A. (2007) 'Crime Prevention and Community Safety', in M. Maguire, R. Morgan and R. Reiner (eds) *The Oxford Handbook of Criminology*, 4th edn. Oxford: Oxford University Press, pp. 866–909.

Delarue, J.-M. (1991) *La relégation*. Paris: La Documentation Française.

Delebarre, M. (1993) *Le temps des villes*. Paris : Seuil.

De Maillard, J. (2005) 'The Governance of Safety in France: Is There Anyone in Charge?', *Theoretical Criminology*, 9(3): 325–44.

Depovere, K. and Ponsaers, P. (1998) *Evaluatie preventiecontracten. Vijf jaar preventiecontracten in Vlaanderen ('93–'98)*. Ghent: Onderzoeksgroep Criminologie en Rechtssociologie.

Dubet, F. (1987) *La galère: jeunes en survie*. Paris: Fayard.

Garland, D. (2001) *The Culture of Control*. Oxford: Oxford University Press.

Goris, P. (2000) *Op zoek naar de krijtlijnen van een sociaal rechtvaardige veiligheidszorg. Analyse van relaties tussen professionele actoren in het kader van een geïntegreerde preventieve aanpak van veiligheidsproblemen in achtergestelde woonbuurten.* Leuven: KULeuven.

De Haan, W. (1999) 'Sociaal beleid als structurele criminaliteitspreventie', in E. Lissenberg, S. van Ruller and R. Van Swaaningen (eds) *Tegen de regels III. Een inleiding in de criminologie.* Nijmegen: Ars Aequi Libri, pp. 243–57.

Hauber, A. (1999) 'Situationele en individuele preventie', in E. Lissenberg, S. van Ruller and R. Van Swaaningen (eds) *Tegen de regels III. Een inleiding in de criminologie.* Nijmegen: Ars Aequi Libri, pp. 258–73.

Hebberecht, P. (1990) 'Het Belgisch politioneel preventiebeleid', in C. Eliaerts, E. Enhus and R. Senden (eds) *Politie in beweging. Bijdrage tot de discussie over de politie van morgen.* Antwerp/Arnhem: Kluwer/Gouda Quint, pp. 81–8.

Hebberecht, P. (2000) 'Het Federaal veiligheidsplan versterkt de ongelijkheid inzake veiligheid', *Panopticon,* 21(2): 101–112.

Hebberecht, P. (2002) 'On Prevention and Security Policy in Europe', in P. Hebberecht and D. Duprez (eds) (2002) *The Prevention and Security Policies in Europe,* Brussels: VUB Press, pp. 7–14.

Hebberecht, P. (2004) 'De kadernota Integrale Veiligheid van de paarse regering Verhofstadt II en het Belgisch preventiebeleid', *Panopticon,* 25(5): 1–8.

Hebberecht, P. (2008) *De 'verpaarsing' van de criminaliteitsbestrijding in België. Kritische opstellen over de misdaad en misdaadcontrole in de laatmoderniteit.* Brussels: VUB Press.

Hebberecht, P. and Sack, F. (1997) 'New Forms of Prevention in Europe', in P. Hebberecht and F. Sack (eds) *La Prévention de la Délinquance en Europe: Nouvelles Stratégies.* Paris: L'Harmattan, pp. 21–32.

Hughes, G. (1998) *Understanding Crime Prevention: Social Control, Risk and Late Modernity.* Buckingham: Open University Press.

Hughes, G. (2007) *The Politics of Crime and Community.* Basingstoke: Palgrave.

Johnston, V. and Shapland, J. (1997) 'The United Kingdom and the New Prevention', in P. Hebberecht and F. Sack (eds) *La Prévention de la Délinquance en Europe: Nouvelles Stratégies.* Paris: L'Harmattan, pp. 33–59.

Lea, J. (2002) *Crime and Modernity.* London: Sage.

Mary, P. (ed.) (2003) *Dix ans de contrats de sécurité: Evaluation et actualité.* Brussels: Bruylant.

Meynen, A. (2000) 'Economic and Social Policy since the 1950s', in E. Witte, J. Craeybeckx and A. Meynen (eds) *Political History of Belgium: From 1830 Onwards.* Antwerp/Brussels: Standaard Uitgeverij/VUB University Press, pp. 201–37.

Platel, M. (2004) *Communautaire geschiedenis van België van 1830 tot vandaag.* Leuven: Davidsfonds.

Poulet, I. (1995) *Les nouvelles politiques de prévention. Une nouvelle forme d'action publique?* Brussels: Services fédéraux des affaires scientifiques.

de Savornin-Lohman, J. (1997) 'New Forms of Crime Prevention: The Dutch Experience', in P. Hebberecht and F. Sack (eds) *La Prévention de la Délinquance en Europe: Nouvelles Stratégies.* Paris: L'Harmattan, pp. 83–100.

Stenson, K. and Edwards, A. (2004) 'Policy Transfer in Local Crime Control: Beyond Naive Emulation', in T. Newburn and R. Sparks (eds) *Criminal Justice and Political Cultures: National and International Dimensions of Crime Control.* Cullompton: Willan Publishing, pp. 209–33.

Synergie (1995) *La prévention intégrée au niveau local.* Brussels: Politeia.

Taylor, I. (1999) *Crime in Context: A Critical Criminology of Market Societies.* Cambridge: Polity Press.

Van Campenhoudt, L., Cartuyvels, Y., Digneffe, F., Kaminski, D., Mary, Ph. and Rea, A. (eds) (2000) *Réponses à l'insécurité: Des discours aux pratiques*. Brussels: Labor.

Van Dijk, J. (1990) 'Crime Prevention Policy: Current State and Prospects', in G. Kaiser and H.-J. Albrecht (eds) *Crime and Criminal Policy in Europe*. Freiburg: Max Planck Institute, pp. 205–20.

Van Swaaningen, R. (2002) 'Towards a Replacement Discourse on Community Safety: Lessons from the Netherlands', in G. Hughes, E. McLaughlin and J. Muncie (eds) *Crime Prevention and Community Safety: New Directions*. London: Sage, pp. 260–78.

Van Swaaningen, R. (2005) 'Public Safety and the Management of Fear', *Theoretical Criminology*, 9(3): 289–307.

Willekens, P. (2006) 'Beter één vogel in de hand dan tien in de lucht: integrale veiligheid', *Orde van de Dag. Criminaliteit en samenleving*, 35, 9–16.

Chapter 9

Going around in circles? Reflections on crime prevention strategies in Germany

Michael Jasch

Crime prevention has many different faces. This applies to Germany in particular because of the federal structure of the country. The German constitution provides a highly differentiated separation of powers within the wide field of criminal justice: the central government retains the legislative competence for criminal law and criminal procedure, whereas police laws and strategies are a matter for the 16 federal states. Moreover, the smallest administrative unit in Germany, the local community, is entitled to pass a broad range of regulations concerning public order and social policy that can be very influential for the implementation or development of local prevention policies. Hence, it is not surprising that such a federal structure leads to a rather patchy picture of crime prevention policies. Nevertheless, there have been and there are today some common trends and developments in Germany as a whole. The aim of this chapter is first to give a brief account of crime prevention strategies applied from the 1970s until the 1990s, before looking at recent policies since the turn of the millennium. Finally, there is a critical summary of the major developments in German crime prevention policies during the past decades.

A brief history of prevention strategies

Exploring the context: criminal justice and prevention in Germany

In Germany, crime prevention is a relatively new item on the agenda of politicians, criminologists and the police. During the first decade after

World War Two, researchers as well as practitioners were strongly focused on questions concerning the detection and repression of specific groups of offenders and offences. Criminology as an independent academic discipline was almost non-existent in those years, and crime prevention was merely a subject for books on the penal law, but not dealt with as a social phenomenon.[1] In the second half of the 1960s, public attention was directed to the student protests and riots – a rather new and irritating experience for the young democracy that was celebrating its 'economic miracle' at the same time. As a legacy of the student movement of the 1960s, Germany was confronted with the appearance of the Red Army Faction (RAF), a group of left-wing terrorists who totally dominated the national discourse on criminal justice and caused a kind of public hysteria until the end of the 1970s. During the following decade, a civil protest movement took the centre stage of public and political debates on crime and public disorder again: the rise of the peace movement and the ecological movement led to permanent – and sometimes violent – mass protests against the deployment of nuclear missiles in West Germany, against nuclear power stations and environmental pollution. After two police officers were killed in the course of violent protests against the expansion of Frankfurt airport, debates about these civil unrests became a general discourse about public order, crime and the power of the state. Compared to these 'big issues' and several spectacular cases, everyday crime and its prevention played a rather minimal role in public debates during all these years. Nevertheless, different approaches to crime prevention that have been applied in Germany in the decades before 1990 can be identified.

Technical prevention in the 1970s

Almost 40 years ago, crime prevention became visible as a distinguished subject of criminal justice policy and discourses for the first time in post-war Germany. In the 1970s, police started to praise prevention as 'the noblest task for the police' and promoted the establishment of police information centres in all cities and regions around the country. Although the first information centre had already been established in 1921 in Berlin, there was no co-ordinated network of such offices in all federal states before. To the present day, it remains the primary purpose of these centres to advise citizens how they can protect themselves from becoming a victim of crime by means of technical provisions and correct behaviour. The work of the police information centres has been accompanied by a nationwide public relations programme (*Kriminalpolizeiliches Vorbeugungsprogramm*, see Weinberger 1984), responsible for developing information campaigns on various crime prevention techniques in every day life, especially the prevention of burglary, theft and fraud. Thus, crime prevention was understood as form of 'technical prevention' in the first place, with police as security consultants for citizens who were regarded as responsible for the security of their own premises and vehicles. At the institutional level, two things are noteworthy about these early prevention activities: first, it was in the 1970s that police discovered prevention work as a subject that needed to be addressed systematically. The German federal police, the *Bundeskriminalamt* (BKA), organised an initial conference entitled 'Police and Prevention' in those years (Bundeskriminalamt 1976). Second, the development of technical prevention programmes was essentially a top-down movement, initiated by the central government and the authorities of the federal states, and subsequently administered by the police.

Already some years later, prevention programmes no longer relied merely on technical provisions. In the first half of the 1980s, Germany experienced an economic recession with an increase in the unemployment rate by more than 100 per cent between 1980 and 1983. Especially in big cities, difficult economic conditions were a major cause for the establishment of various social initiatives and youth projects by charities, local authorities and state institutions – and presumably for a shift in prevention strategies as well. Social prevention, defined as measures aimed at tackling the root causes of crime and the disposition of individuals to offend (Graham and Bennett 1997: 11), became the commanding notion of crime prevention in the 1980s. Edwin Kube, a former chief of the BKA, wrote in 1987:

> It has to be the task for (practical and scientific) crime prevention to determine the individual and social circumstances of delinquent behaviour and to develop, to realise and to evaluate practicable methods of preventing criminality ... Prevention is a complex task, because it can only become successful if it influences social policies too. (Kube 1987: 7f.)

In practice, the preventive aspects of the work of schools, youth centres and social workers were suddenly recognised.

A typical example of the new approach was the pilot project 'Prevention Programme Police/Social Workers', set up in the federal state of Lower Saxony in order to combine manpower and working skills of police officers and social workers (Schwind *et al.* 1980). Inevitably, the boundaries between police work and social services were blurring in the course of such projects. This by-product of the new inter-agency approach provoked serious critique with regard to potential net-widening effects. Several scholars argued that prevention might be a 'problematic objective for the criminal justice system' (Albrecht 1989) because the new co-operation between social services and the police would in fact amount to a concealment of the professional interests of the criminal justice agencies, still oriented towards repression and control (see the debates in Kreuzer

1981). At the institutional level, the new focus on social work automatically resulted in a partial inclusion of non-state organisations in the field of crime prevention work. Compared to the 1970s, the new trend also represented a change in relation to the main target of prevention efforts: from a notion of 'technical self-protection' to a 'strategy of proactive intervention', focused on convicted or potential offenders. By the end of the 1980s, the notion of prevention had gained ground in Germany. The phenomenon of crime, traditionally regarded as a matter to be dealt with repressively by state institutions, has increasingly come to be regarded as a field for prevention initiatives. Nevertheless, during both decades the prevention of crime was rather an implicit task to be accomplished – never at the top of the agenda, neither of politicians nor among German criminologists.

The rise of prevention in the 1990s

It was not until the early 1990s that crime prevention became a priority issue in discussions on the criminal justice system in Germany (Meier 2007: 268). The political context of the rise of a preventative ideology is obvious. The breakdown of the former Eastern bloc, the reunification of the two German states, the globalisation of the economic system and a large and sudden immigration from the East to Western Europe – a development that especially affected Germany – had dramatically reshaped the social and economic circumstances in Central Europe. Feelings of social insecurity were probably the driving force behind extremely high rates of fear of crime, especially in the Eastern federal states (Jasch and Hefendehl 2001; see Figure 9.1).

The results of surveys when people had been asked about their general assessment of public security were even more frightening. In the middle of the 1990s, 86 per cent of East Germans and about 70 per cent of the adult population in the West thought that security in public spaces would be at risk. According to empirical studies in 1993, nearly every second adult was afraid of becoming a victim of a robbery, theft or burglary (Frevel 1999: 59). In those years, we can observe two major tendencies in German prevention strategies: first, an attempt to reallocate the responsibility for the challenge of crime prevention; and second, a trend towards localisation – or perhaps better described as a municipalisation – of crime prevention. Both these features are interconnected and form what has become known as the German approach to community crime prevention (*Kommunale Kriminalprävention*).

Localisation and institutionalisation

In the first half of the 1990s, a new slogan became extremely fashionable among policy-makers and police officers. Crime prevention, they claimed, has to be a task for the whole society and, at the organisational level, for

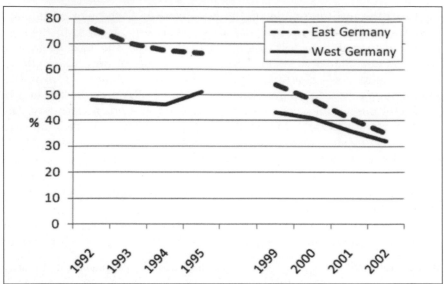

Source: *Gesellschaft sozialwissenschaftl. Infrastruktureinrichtungen.*

Note: Question: 'Do you feel threatened by crime in our country?' Shown: percentage of 'Yes'. No separate data for East/West were available for the years from 1996 to 1998. 'East Germany' refers to the five federal states on the territory of the former GDR and Berlin.

Figure 9.1   Fear of crime in East and West Germany, 1992–2002

the local community (e.g. Baier and Feltes 1994: 697; Bundesministerien 2006: 692). This axiom contains two elements that had been rather unfamiliar for Germans who were used to regarding crime exclusively as a problem for the state and not for private citizens. Furthermore, the constitutional idea of 'the state' comprises the central government and the federal states, but does not include local authorities, which are conceptualised as a self-administration of the local community (Art. 28 *Grundgesetz*). Consequently, the new approach heralded a twofold shift of responsibility for crime prevention. The state institutions traditionally concerned with crime – the government and the police – attempted to share their responsibility with the citizens and local authorities. Sound justification for the local focus derived from the established criminological finding that about 80 per cent of offences are committed by persons who live in the city where the offence takes place (Steffen 2006: 1145), but it is likely, that sharing the costs and the risk of failure of prevention activities were also strong motives for reallocating the task of crime prevention.

The cornerstone of this policy has been the establishment of local crime prevention councils all over Germany. In most federal states, the Home Offices strongly encouraged – if not to say initiated – the establishment of prevention councils at the local level. At the same time, similar organisations were set up at the federal state level to co-ordinate and support the local prevention councils. Finally, organisations were established in order to co-ordinate and support the new prevention-oriented policy at the national level. In 1993, the German Foundation for Crime Prevention and the Rehabilitation of Offenders was founded by a group consisting of academics, the Minister of Justice and a former Director of the Public Prosecution Service, and started to organise national Days of Prevention (*Deutscher Präventionstag*)[3], a conference where practitioners from prevention projects meet annually. In addition, the German Forum for Crime Prevention, set up by the Home Secretaries of the federal states in 1997, should 'initiate and co-ordinate national crime prevention strategies . . . of governmental and private institutions' (Bundesministerien 2001: 467). The establishment of these organisations has been geared to similar bodies in Denmark, Belgium and England. Thus, there is now an organisational structure in existence at all three administrative levels for the exchange of information and experiences with prevention projects. Germany might thus be clearly considered as a country with a process-focused approach, which aims – in contrast to scheme-focused strategies – at creating structures and administrative arrangements in order to deliver prevention efforts over the long term (Crawford 1998).

It is noticeable, however, that the initiative for the establishment of the entire infrastructure came from the official side – the government, local authorities, and at the local level from the police. Bearing in mind the fact that the local police forces in Germany are not independent but under the direction of the federal state government, police can be regarded as a long arm of the criminal justice strategy in each federal-state. In the state of North Rhine-Westphalia, for example, the Home Secretary formally committed all police authorities to stimulate the institutionalisation of local prevention councils (Frehsee 1998: 744). At the federal state level, it was each government that set up the prevention councils, although some academics and representatives of churches and private institutions had been invited to participate.

A central purpose of the new community councils has been to establish an inter-agency approach to crime prevention: not only the police and the justice agencies, but also social services, local authorities, sports clubs, shop owners, churches, trade unions and neighbourhoods should be concerned with crime. In many cases, these councils have achieved the networking goal where senior representatives of different authorities get to know each other and talk to each other on a regular basis. However, this kind of community prevention has failed to involve a broad range of 'ordinary citizens' and has not become well known in most local communities. Prevention councils 'German style' have been organised too much in a top-down way by the police and state authorities – and so, the state has remained the dominating and driving force behind these councils up to now. Yet, there are NGOs involved in prevention work and in some exceptional cases, the initiative came from private citizens (for example, in the city of Gießen; Schneider and Stock 1996). But in most cases, the people and organisations involved are professionally concerned with crime anyway and just reflect the local structure of power, the majority culture of the local community. With regard to the role of the state, not much has changed significantly in comparison with the implementation of prevention strategies in previous decades (see above). Thus, an inter-agency structure for police and local authorities has been implemented successfully, but the local citizens have tended to stay away from local prevention councils. It is of no surprise then that such committees raise critical questions as to the potential net-widening effects of social control within a local community (Frehsee 1998; Kreissl 1987).

In general, the topics dealt with by the local councils could be as extensive as suggested by the local situations and public perceptions of problems. In practice, however, the vast majority of councils have focused on setting up working groups on youth delinquency, graffiti and the prevention of violence. Also, inter-agency groups on the prevention of xenophobic attacks and committees concerned with drug crimes and the prevention of substance abuse are very popular among councils.[4] It has been criticised, correctly, that the council's focus on young people, who are perceived and simultaneously construed as a risk for society, may have stigmatising effects for particular parts of the community (Steffen 2004: 6; Ostendorf 2005: 8). It is noteworthy that, according to a nationwide survey (Bundesministerien 2001: 471), about 80 per cent of the local projects applied a social approach to crime prevention (primary prevention) whereas just 9 per cent reported activities in the field of situational crime prevention. However, we have to take into account the fact that the options for local authorities to improve the living conditions of particular groups are rather restricted because problems like school funding, unemployment, social benefits or immigration policies are beyond the responsibility of local authorities.

Reallocation of responsibility

As noted above, there has been a strong tendency on the part of traditional criminal justice agencies and the state to share the responsibility for crime prevention work with local communities. Some official statements made it very clear that the state could not, or did not want to, cope with the problem of crime exclusively any more. In 1995, the then Home Secretary of the federal state Baden-Württemberg argued at the opening of a conference on community prevention that 'nowadays, security can not be provided by the authorities of the state or the local government alone' (Birzle 1995: 9).[5] Today, the internet homepage of the police in Bavaria states that 'internal security requires joint responsibility, the engagement and assistance of the citizens'.[6]

In this context, sharing the task of crime prevention has not been just a theoretical concept. A distinctive feature of community crime prevention policies has been the active involvement of private citizens in the work of the police. In some federal states, different models of private policing – citizens who support the police in an organised form – were set up (Pütter and Kant 2000). The security guards project (*Sicherheitswacht*) in Bavaria, established in 1994, was the first policing initiative in the context of community prevention;[7] other federal states, like Hessen (*Freiwilliger Polizeidienst*), Brandenburg (*Sicherheitspartner*) and Sachsen followed the Bavarian example.[8] In most cases, these volunteers do not have the same powers as police officers. In particular, they are not armed (with the exception of Baden-Württemberg) and they are not entitled to use direct force except in cases of emergency or self defence. It is intended that their job is to 'have an eye open' on the streets, to call the police if necessary, to support the professional police and to be a contact partner for the community. On the beat, the volunteers are supposed to help prevent 'vandalism and street crime' and their presence is intended to 'improve security and the feeling of security of citizens'.[9]

From very different perspectives, this kind of private policing has always been a source of dispute. Some politicians and the police have argued that these voluntary citizens are not sufficiently qualified for the tasks they perform. The police unions in particular have articulated this argument, and it is obvious and plausible that police have a considerable interest in protecting their jobs[10] or even seeking to increase the number of officers rather than see some aspects of their work transferred to a group of inexpensive but superficially trained volunteers. Similar problems occur in the relationship between police and private security companies. However, this turned out not to be a major issue in Germany – probably because there are not yet so many 'quasi-public' areas in private ownership in German cities and conditions for the establishment of security firms and the training of personnel have been put on a statutory basis.[11] Such an atmosphere of competition between different groups of the 'extended police family' is well known from other European countries and may be an obstacle for the deliverance of local security (Crawford *et al.* 2005: 83). In fact, there is evidence in Germany that some volunteers are not very skilled in de-escalating situations. In April 2007 a citizen patrolman in Hessen was seriously attacked after he had stopped a car driver who was not wearing his seat belt. This incident triggered a wide public debate on the question of whether it is responsible for the state to send semi-professionals out on to the streets for the sake of public order. On the other hand, from a liberal point of view, there are claims that we simply do not need even more control of deviance and more surveillance. Especially in Germany, the involvement of ordinary citizens in police work raises awkward memories for a section of the population because of the fascist legacy from before and during World War Two and – more recently, in a different way and with other consequences – the totalitarian regime of the GDR. Both used models of private policing in order to keep the people under control.

Moreover, there are indications that citizen patrols are ineffective with regard to crime rates. According to an early study on the *Sicherheitswacht*, conducted by a group of sociologists based at Munich University, the most significant actions the guards engaged in was to tell off men urinating in public and to reproach youngsters listening to loud music at night on the streets (Hitzler 1996). Since significant reductions of crime rates could not really be expected from citizen patrols, it may well be that tackling fear of crime was a much stronger motive for the establishment of such projects from the outset.[12] In essence, the establishment of citizen patrols has been a way to show the people that someone cares about crime and public order.

Furthermore, in some regions with specific problems, involving citizens in the course of community prevention has been used as an attempt to keep the criminal justice activities of the public under the control of the state and to prevent vigilantism. That becomes apparent from the official statement of the prevention council in the eastern federal state of Brandenburg, describing its prevention concept of Security Partnerships (*Sicherheitspartnerschaft*). The establishment of local Partnership Programmes, the council writes, was 'triggered by citizens' reactions to a series of burglaries, especially committed by gangs from Eastern Europe. Because of growing feelings of insecurity, vigilante groups turned up in several communities in order to protect themselves.'[13]

The uncertain future of community prevention
Localisation and the reallocation of responsibility for crime prevention by implementing an inter-agency approach have been the main characteristics of community prevention in Germany. Beyond these features, however, quite different prevention policies have been established under the elastic umbrella term of 'community prevention' (Schreiber 2007; Lehne 2006). Whereas some states and cities have used rather traditional means of control and patrolling that reminds us of the so-called 'zero tolerance policing' in the USA, others have focused on strategies of primary prevention in the field of youth crime. After more than 15 years of community prevention, the experiences are assessed quite differently. The majority of practitioners and criminologists praise the fact that prevention has become an issue for local communities and regard the community approach as an adequate starting point for long-term prevention policies based on empirical and practical experiences (Feltes 2006: 835; Schwind 2008: §18; Heinz 1998: 47). Moreover, there is a broad consensus that much more evaluation research on preventive approaches and projects is urgently required (Walter 2002: 7; Bundesministerien 2006: 684). On the other hand, it has been argued that local prevention councils are rather symbolic means of criminal policy that have little if any positive

effects on crime or the fear of crime (Jasch 2003; Hornbostel 1998). As one research study summarised the reality of the councils work in 2004: 'The main result [of prevention councils] has been to produce concepts, papers and discussions instead of effective projects. Furthermore, most committees are lacking in manpower and necessary financial resources, they are not legitimised democratically and their resolutions and recommendations entail little commitment' (Steffen 2004: 2).

Hence, the future of community prevention in German cities with regard to their organisational form as well as their activities seems to be uncertain. It is unlikely that particular councils are going to be abolished by local authorities, but there is a risk that they might simply go to sleep – in particular because nowadays everyday crime is not the major issue for the population any more as it was in the 1990s. Some academics recommend the development of a 'collaborative crime prevention' approach based on a consensus between all groups of society without stigmatising particular sections of the population on the basis of the existing community approach in Germany (Feltes 2006: 835). Others suggest that prevention councils should secure democratic legitimacy and ensure suitable financial resources in order to establish a long-term security strategy at the local level (Steffen 2006: 10). Still others argue that prevention initiatives should become less bureaucratic and more pluralistic (Jasch 2003: 417) and that the funding of prevention activities should be dependent on research results and evaluations (Walter 2002: 7). In this context, it might turn out to be useful that crime prevention has been based on a process-focused approach with organisational structures at the national, regional and local level because this institutional framework could ensure that the issue of crime prevention is kept alive.

The new millennium

The vast majority of community projects of the 1990s are still in operation today, even though they are not making the headlines of criminal justice discourse any more. In Germany, as in most other European countries, the prevention of everyday crime has been superseded by the threat of international terrorism in the aftermath of 11 September 2001, the attacks in London (in 2005) and Madrid (in 2004) and some arrests of suspected terrorists in German cities. In the course of counter-terrorism efforts, the face of the criminal justice system has changed also in Germany and the threat of terror is dominating public debates on criminal policy. Legislation and policing policies in the first decade of the twenty-first century have been characterised by a trend towards more punitive and repressive measures. Simultaneously, the perception of crime prevention has changed towards a rediscovery of 'prevention by means of repression'. In past decades, prevention strategies consisted of measures that intended to

205

convince people not to commit a crime. Nowadays, prevention has come more and more to mean incapacitating people from committing offences.

However, I do not believe that 9/11 can be regarded as the decisive and unique turning point in German criminal policy. In fact, there was a punitive trend in existence already before September 2001 (see also Hassemer 2007). This pre-existing trend was marked by a permanent extension of police powers, especially techniques of control, an increase in the use of preventive detention and the introduction of some new criminal offences. This has simply been accelerated since 2001, and it is by no means only directed at terrorism, but also at ordinary street crimes and at people who are presumed to be 'dangerous'. The recent tendency of the criminal justice policy can be illustrated briefly by means of four examples.

(i) Justified with the goal of crime prevention, the powers available to police and prosecutors to compel people to render a DNA sample have been expanded. Some years ago, the prosecution service was entitled to gather DNA data only from offenders convicted of serious violent or sexual offences under the condition that further offences committed by him or her were likely. Since a reform of §81g StPO[14] in 2005, it is available for all types of offenders, not just serious offenders but also for graffiti-sprayers, shoplifters and fare dodgers. Only two conditions must be met to compel a minor offender to undergo a DNA test and to record the data obtained for the purpose of future, anticipated proceedings. First, the individual must be regarded as a persistent offender. Second, there must be 'reason to believe' that he or she might commit further similar offences in the future. Such a law is problematic because criminologists have not yet discovered reliable indicators that enable us to identify persons who will continue to offend persistently or who will become a multiple or serious offender in the future (e.g. Sampson and Laub 2006).

(ii) One of the most striking developments in German criminal law is the extension of preventive detention (*Sicherungsverwahrung*, §§66ff. StGB[15]), imprisonment on the grounds that a convicted offender is regarded as dangerous to the public. Usually, offenders receive a prison sentence that reflects his or her personal guilt, according to the principle of personal responsibility that governs German criminal law. In recent years, judges were given extended statutory powers to impose further preventive detention on the grounds of the prognosis that the offender may be a danger to the public in the future. The instrument of preventive detention is primarily used for sex and serious violent offenders; however, it is also used to detain persistent burglars and defrauders. Since 2004, preventive detention in cases of serious violent crimes can also be imposed years after the criminal trial if the assumed dangerousness of the offender emerges only during the offender's time in prison (§66b StGB; for details see Albrecht 2006). As a consequence of various extensions to the law, the number of persons in preventive detention has more than doubled between 1996 and 2006.[16] This is perhaps the most radical mode of prevention by means of repression one can think of.

(iii) CCTV has been expanded enormously. In public places, cameras are frequently used in order to restrain drug trafficking and vandalism. Although we know that dealers simply change sites for their business and the effect on crime rates is rather limited (Gill and Spriggs 2005), the cameras remain and provide surveillance of many city areas. In particular, CCTV has been expanded in public transport. Cameras have become a common element inside trains and buses of public transport as well as in tube and railway stations. Ever since CCTV played a crucial role in the arrest of two men with an Islamist background, who planted bombs in public trains in Cologne in 2006, police and politicians use the incident to argue in favour of surveillance cameras, although it was in fact rather an example of the *limited* preventive effects of CCTV.[17] Up to now, there are no systems of 'intelligent scene analysis' in operation in Germany because we are quite sceptical whether such an extension of surveillance complies with data protection laws and the constitution. However, there is already one railway station where a camera system that should recognise individual faces by analysing biometric data is currently running on a trial basis.

(iv) Furthermore, we can observe a development that represents the nature of prevention strategies although it does not take place in the context of criminal or public order law. It has become very attractive for the state to collect as much data on citizens as possible. For instance, since 2005 the social services and tax authorities are entitled to gather data from the bank accounts of all citizens in order to detect tax offences and fraudulent applications for social security benefits or student grants. The police and intelligence service – usually strictly separated for historical reasons – became entitled to exchange data gathered on individuals. In compliance with European law,[18] all German passports in the future will contain biometrical data as well as two computerised fingerprints. Also due to a recent European guideline,[19] a new law has introduced the storage of all telecommunication data (calls by telephone and mobiles, emails, SMS and browsing the internet) of the citizens for at least six months.

Four decades of prevention: going around in circles?

During the past 30 years, we have witnessed developments that look somewhat like going around in circles. From a merely repressive approach to crime over technical and situational prevention to a notion of social prevention in the 1980s and community strategies in the 1990s, we have returned full circle back to a dominance of repressive techniques in recent years. However, if we compare the reality of crime prevention today with the situation in the 1970s, it becomes obvious that the number of institutions, committees and councils concerned with primary prevention in Germany has increased enormously. Almost every federal state and the majority of large German cities have introduced prevention committees in order to establish an inter-agency approach to crime. Today, the central government leaves no doubt on its commitment to a process-oriented approach to crime prevention when stating that 'permanent structures are necessary' for a successful crime prevention policy (Bundesministerien 2006: 692).

However, it remains an open question whether a high number of prevention committees really constitutes a high priority given to a preventive approach to crime in criminal justice policy. Although there has been a certain rise of prevention policies at central and regional level in Germany, most academics and practitioners are rather unsatisfied with the outcomes. Wiebke Steffen, a leading sociologist with the Bavarian police, recently concluded that neither the practice of community prevention nor the police prevention schemes may be called a track record as such: 'At the local level, the insight that crime prevention has to be a task for the entire society and an overall responsibility instead of a by-product of politics is still not prevailing' (Steffen 2006: 1153). The official rhetoric relies on a twofold approach, with repressive criminal sanctions and the extension of control strategies as well as proactive and community-oriented prevention projects: 'The antagonism between prevention and repression has to be regarded as antiquated, at least since also the criminal law has chosen crime prevention as its objective', the government declared in its latest report on security (Bundesministerien 2006: 684). Such a statement shows that there is a need for future research to clarify the precise relationship between the concepts of 'prevention' and 'repression'.

The question remains, however, whether one of the two concepts will prevail in the practice of criminal policy. Whereas local community initiatives suffer from a lack of manpower, money and practical projects (see above), the expansion of police powers, preventive detention, data pools with personal data of citizens and other measures which are highly relevant for civil rights might be more sustainable. In practice, there is a highly visible tendency away from social prevention that aims at the social circumstances of persons at risk, as well as away from the presumed causes of crime and towards prevention by means of repression and surveillance. The old and well-known saying by Franz von Liszt, that the best criminal policy would be a good social policy, has today become almost out of fashion.

Yet, we have to take note of one exception to this development. Under the heading of 'Early Prevention' a new area of prevention work is emerging in academic and public discussions. An increasing number of politicians,[20] social workers and criminologists put forward the view that we should intervene at a very early stage of people's lives in order to prevent deviancy and future crime. Crime prevention, they claim, has to start in families with parents who are strained with the upbringing of their children (Galm 2005), in kindergartens and primary schools; even the prenatal period of child development has been discussed as a potential field for preventive measures (Anders-Hoepgen 2006; Beelmann *et al.* 2006; for a critical view see Ostendorf 2005). This seems to be a striking example for a general trend of modern states to abandon 'restraint towards intervention in people's private affairs' and to apply a policy of 'behaviour modification' (Furedi 2005: 146f.). Although there is no doubt that strained families do need and deserve help, it is questionable whether we really need 'crime prevention' as an objective to justify social work. We have to bear in mind that early prevention strategies might result in an early screening of marginalised and potentially 'dangerous' families and in a sort of 'social engineering' of future generations. Sooner or later, early prevention measures might resort to coercive interventions in the private life of families if the assistance offered by the state is refused. The new approach reminds us that crime prevention is an ambivalent and potentially dangerous guiding principle. With the intensity and realm of prevention, the extent of control, regulations and interventions in a society will grow. Already 20 years ago there were warnings in Germany that the society would be slowly transformed from a 'constitutional state' into a 'prevention state' (Denninger 1989). Today, the critics have gone one step further and claim that the statutes of the 'prevention state' have turned into a 'post-preventive security law' (Albrecht 2007: 6) which puts security first and nourishes the 'safety utopia' (Boutellier 2004) of modern societies.

We do not yet have much reliable knowledge about the political reasons for this shift of criminal policy. However, it appears plausible that at least three factors are at work. First, people's willingness to accept risks as an immanent condition of human life has diminished radically. Thus, we tend to regard criminals and deviants primarily as future risks, and less as fellow citizens. Second, in modern and pluralistic societies, crime has become one of the last common 'enemies', and the fight against crime carries a strong potential for moral and normative guidance. Third, a tough approach to crime might be a comfortable way for the state to prove its capacity to act. Whereas the impact of national governments on economic and environmental developments is rather limited in a globalised world with multinational concerns, crime appears to be a subject that can be tackled by politicians. Moreover, in contrast to social work for youths, the unskilled and the rising number of poor people in a society that separates more and more between 'winners' and 'losers', repressive means are supposed to be the tough approach to crime. In the long term, it would be more promising to return to a policy of social prevention, which takes the particularities of local communities into account.

Notes

1 The only exception to this narrow, merely juridical, perception of crime was Heinrich Mengs' book on the *Prophylaxis of Crime* (1948). It remained the only academic publication on crime prevention in a broader sense until the end of the 1960s.

2 The federal government of Schleswig-Holstein played a leading role in developing the organisational framework of community prevention and established the first German Prevention Council at federal state level in 1990, followed by the first local council in the city of Lübeck, a high-crime area in the same state. Up to now, eight similar councils at the federal state level and about 2,000 at the local level have been established (Schreiber 2007). Moreover, some federal states have set up permanent offices or co-ordination bureaus, which are comparable to prevention councils.

3 For more information see www.praeventionstag.de

4 A comprehensive register of local prevention projects is available on the internet homepage of the Federal Police *Bundeskriminalamt*: http://infodok.bka.de (for a recent analysis of the structure of prevention councils see Schreiber 2007).

5 Similar to the statement by Kube/Schneider/Stock (1996: 16): 'For police and ... the criminal justice system, the options for prevention activities are rather limited.'

6 www.polizei.bayern.de/wir/sicherheitswacht/index.html (accessed April 2008).

7 Independent of the new community approach, there is a voluntary police service (about 1,200 citizens in 20 cities) which has been in operation in the federal state of Baden-Württemberg since the 1960s. In Berlin, on the other hand, a coalition of social democrats and socialists abolished the voluntary police service in the capital in 2002, arguing that it would be a relict from the Cold War Period, unsuitable for contemporary security challenges.

8 In 2007, the voluntary police in Hessen consisted of 700 citizens in 90 cities and towns. In Sachsen about 600 citizens have joined this service and the Bavarian *Sicherheitswacht* counted 530 volunteers in 58 cities.

9 Quotes from the information leaflet on the Bavarian *Sicherheitswacht*.

10 According to the police union, the German states reduced the number of jobs for police officers by 10,000 and for civil employees by 7,000 between 2000 and 2006 (www.gdp.de, accessed April 2008).

11 §34a, Trade and Commerce Regulation Act (*Gewerbeordnung*).

12 Today, the central government declares clearly that 'crime prevention must also strengthen the population's feelings of security' (Bundesministerien 2006: 691).

13 www.brandenburg.de/sixcms/detail.php/59444 (accessed April 2008).

14 German Criminal Procedure Code (*Strafprozessordnung*).

15 German Penal Code (*Strafgesetzbuch*).

16 375 offenders were detained in preventive detention in 2006 (31 March), compared to 176 persons in 1996 (source: Statistisches Bundesamt Wiesbaden 2006).

17 The bombs were placed successfully by the offenders but did not explode because they were badly constructed.

18 Decree (EU) No. 2252/2004 of the European Council, 13 December 2004.
19 Guideline No. 2006/24/EG of the European Parliament and the Council, 15 March 2006.
20 In January 2008, the Green Party in the German Parliament suggested 'early prevention, education and work with parents' as a programme for the reduction of youth crime (http://www.gruene-bundestag.de/cms/jugendliche/dok/215/215379. handeln_statt_einfach_sitzen_lassen.pdf). One year before, the Liberal Democrats asked for 'early prevention measures in order to identify families at risk before a child is born and to supervise them' in order to prevent child abuse (3ÙFVhttp://dip21.bundestag.de/dip21/btd/16/044/1604415.pdf).

References

Albrecht, H.-J. (2006) 'Antworten auf Gefährlichkeit – Sicherungsverwahrung und unbestimmter Freiheitsentzug', in T. Feltes, C. Pfeiffer and G. Steinhilper (eds) *Kriminalpolitik und ihre wissenschaftlichen Grundlagen. Festschrift für Schwind.* Heidelberg: Müller, pp. 191–210.

Albrecht, P.-A. (1989) 'Prevention as a Problematic Objective in the Criminal Justice System', in P.-A. Albrecht and O. Backes (eds) *Crime Prevention and Intervention: Legal and Ethical Problems.* Berlin: de Gruyter, pp. 47–72.

Albrecht, P.-A. (2007) 'Das nach-präventive Strafrecht: Abschied vom Recht', in Institut für Kriminalwissenschaften Frankfurt a.M. (ed.) *Jenseits des rechtsstaatlichen Strafrechts.* Frankfurt a.M.: Lang, pp. 3–26.

Anders-Hoepgen, E.-J. (2006) *Auf Gewalt geschaltet. Zusammenhänge zwischen pränatalen, perinatalen und frühkindlichen Erfahrungen und späterer Gewalttätigkeit und Möglichkeiten der Frühprävention.* Marburg: Tectum.

Baier, R. and Feltes, T. (1994) 'Kommunale Kriminalprävention', *Kriminalistik,* 48(10): 693–7.

Beelmann, A., Jaursch, S., Lösel, F. and Stemmler, M. (2006) 'Frühe universelle Prävention von dissozialen Entwicklungsproblemen: Implementation und Wirksamkeit eines verhaltensorientierten Elterntrainings', *Praxis der Rechtspsychologie,* 16(1/2): 120–43.

Birzle, F. (1995) 'Kommunale Kriminalprävention in Baden-Württemberg. Von der Idee zur Umsetzung', in T. Feltes (ed.) *Kommunale Kriminalprävention in Baden-Würtemberg.* Holzkirchen: Felix, pp. 3–9.

Boutellier, H. (2004) *The Safety Utopia: Contemporary Discontent and Desire as to Crime and Punishment.* Dordrecht: Kluwer.

Bundeskriminalamt (ed.) (1976) *Polizei und Prävention.* Wiesbaden: Eigenverlag.

Bundesministerien der Justiz und des Inneren (eds) (2001) *1. Periodischer Sicherheitsbericht der Bundesregierung.* Berlin: Eigenverlag.

Bundesministerien der Justiz und des Inneren (eds) (2006) *2. Periodischer Sicherheitsbericht der Bundesregierung.* Berlin: Eigenverlag.

Crawford, A. (1998) *Crime Prevention and Community Safety: Politics, Policies and Practices.* London: Pearson Longman.

Crawford, A., Lister, S., Blackburn, S. and Burnett, J. (2005) *Plural Policing: The Mixed Economy of Visible Patrols in England and Wales.* Bristol: Policy Press.

Denninger, E. (1989) *'Der Präventionsstaat'*, *Kritische Justiz*, 21(1): 1–15.

Feltes, T. (2006) 'Kommunale Kriminalprävention gegen weltweiten Terrorismus?', in T. Feltes, C. Pfeiffer and G. Steinhilper (eds) *Kriminalpolitik und ihre wissenschaftlichen Grundlagen. Festschrift für Schwind*. Heidelberg: Müller, pp. 825–39.

Frehsee, D. (1998) 'Politische Funktionen Kommunaler Kriminalprävention', in H. J. Albrecht, F. Dünkel, F. and H.-J. Kerner (eds) *Internationale Perspektiven in Kriminologie und Strafrecht. Festschrift für Kaiser*. Berlin: Duncker & Humblot, pp. 739–63.

Frevel, B. (1999) *Kriminalität – Gefährdung für die Innere Sicherheit?* Opladen: Leske & Budrich.

Furedi, F. (2005) *Politics of Fear: Beyond Left and Right*. London: Continuum.

Galm, B. (2005) 'Frühprävention von Gewalt gegen Kinder in psychosozial belasteten Familien. Früherkennung – Frühe Hilfen', *Deutsches Jugendinstitut-Bulletin*, No. 72: 4–5.

Gill, M. and Spriggs, A. (2005) *Assessing the Impact of CCTV*, Home Office Research Study 292. London: Home Office.

Graham, J. and Bennett, T. (1997) *Strategien der Kriminalprävention in Europa und Nordamerika*. Godesberg: Forum.

Hassemer, W. (2007) 'Sicherheit durch Strafrecht', in Institut für Kriminalwissenschaften Frankfurt a.M. (ed.) *Jenseits des rechtsstaatlichen Strafrechts*. Frankfurt a.M.: Lang, pp. 99–137.

Heinz, W. (1998) 'Kriminalprävention – Anmerkungen zu einer überfälligen Kurskorrektur der Kriminalpolitik', in H.-J. Kerner, J.-M. Jehle and E. Marks (eds) *Entwicklung der Kriminalprävention in Deutschland*. Godesberg: Forum, pp. 17–59.

Hitzler, R. (1996) 'Der in die Polizeiarbeit eingebundene Bürger. Zur symbolischen Politik mit der bayerischen Sicherheitswacht', in J. Reichertz and N. Schroer (eds) *Qualitäten polizeilichen Handelns. Studien zu einer verstehenden Polizeiforschung*. Opladen: Leske & Budrich, pp. 30–47.

Hornbostel, S. (1998) 'Die Konstruktion von Unsicherheitslagen durch kommunale Präventionsräte', in R. Hitzler and H. Peters (eds) *Inszenierung. Innere Sicherheit – Daten und Diskurse*. Opladen: Leske & Budrich, pp. 93–112.

Jasch, M. (2003) 'Kommunale Kriminalprävention in der Krise?', *Monatsschrift für Kriminologie und Strafrechtsreform*, pp. 411–20.

Jasch, M. and Hefendehl, R. (2001) 'Kriminalgeografie und Furcht in ostdeutschen Städten – oder von der Notwendigkeit, auf schnelle Veränderungen forschungstechnisch zu reagieren oder diese zu ignorieren', *Monatsschrift für Kriminologie und Strafrechtsreform*, pp. 67–81.

Kreissl, R. (1987) 'Die Simulation sozialer Ordnung. Gemeindenahe Kriminalitätsbekämpfung', *Kriminologisches Journal*, pp. 269–84.

Kreuzer, A. (ed.) (1981) *Polizei und Sozialarbeit: Bestandsaufnahme theoretischer Aspekte und praktischer Erfahrungen; Tagungsbericht der Expertentagung 'Polizei und Sozialarbeit'*. Wiesbaden: Akademische Verlagsgesellschaft.

Kube, E. (1987) *Systematische Kriminalprävention*. Wiesbaden: Bundeskriminalamt.

Kube, E., Schneider, H. and Stock, J. (eds) (1996) *Vereint gegen kriminalität. Wege der kommunalen Kriminalprävention in Deutschland*. Lübeck: Schmidt-Römhild.

Lehne, W. (2006) 'Präventionsräte, Stadtteilforen, Sicherheitspartnerschaften. Die Reorganisation des Politikfeldes "Innere Sicherheit"', in T. v. Trotha (ed.)

Politischer Wandel, Gesellschaft und Kriminalitätsdiskurse. Festschrift für F. Sack. Baden-Baden: Nomos, pp. 299–319.

Meier, B.-D. (2007): *Kriminologie.* München: Beck-Verlag.

Ostendorf, H. (2005) 'Prävention um jeden Preis? Eine kritische Analyse kriminalpräventiven Handelns', in *Internet-Dokumentation der DVJJ.* Hannover: DVJJ. Online at: www.dvjj.de/download.php?id=334

Pütter, N. and Kant, M. (2000) 'Ehrenamtliche PolizeihelferInnen. Polizeidienste, Sicherheitswachten und Sicherheitspartner', *Bürgerrechte & Polizei* (CILIP) 66(2): 16–30.

Sampson, R. and Laub, J. (2006) *Developmental Criminology and its Discontents: Trajectories of Crime from Childhood to Old Age.* London: Sage.

Schneider, H. and Stock, J. (1996) 'Kriminalprävention Gießen e.V. Initiativfunktion von Seiten privater Gruppen', in E. Kube, H. Schneider and J. Stock (eds) *Vereint gegen Kriminalität. Wege der kommunalen Kriminalprävention in Deutschland.* Lübeck: Schmidt-Römhild.

Schreiber, V. (2007) *Lokale Präventionsgremien in Deutschland.* Institut für Humangeographie der J.W.Goethe-Universität, Frankfurt a.M.: Eigenverlag.

Schwind, H.-D. (2008) *Kriminologie, 18. Aufl.* Heidelberg: Kriminalistik-Verlag.

Schwind, H.-D., Steinhilper, G. and Wilhelm-Reiss, M. (1980) 'Prevention Programme Police/Social Workers (PPS): A Modelproject in the Lower Saxony Department of Justice, Hannover, Federal Republic of Germany', *Police Studies*, 3(2): 15–20.

Steffen, W. (2004) 'Gremien Kommunaler Kriminalprävention – Bestandsaufnahme und Perspektive', in H.-J. Kerner and E. Marks (eds) Deutscher Präventionstag: Hannover. Online at: www.praeventionstag.de/html/GetDokumentation.cms?XID=81

Steffen, W. (2006) 'Kriminalprävention in Deutschland: Eine Erfolgsgeschichte? Erzählt an den Beispielen Kommunale Kriminalprävention und Polizeiliche Kriminalprävention', in T. Feltes, C. Pfeiffer and G. Steinhilper (eds) *Kriminalpolitik und ihre wissenschaftlichen Grundlagen. Festschrift für Schwind.* Heidelberg: C. F. Müller, pp. 1141–54.

Walter, M. (2002) 'Kommunale Kriminalprävention – wozu wird sie führen?', *forum kriminalprävention*, 2(4): 6–7.

Weinberger, R.-P. (1984) *Polizeiliche Prävention durch Öffentlichkeitsarbeit: dargestellt am kriminalpolizeilichen Vorbeugungsprogramm in der Bundesrepublik Deutschland.* München: Florentz.

Chapter 10

Crime prevention in Hungary: why is it so hard to argue for the necessity of a community approach?

Klara Kerezsi

Hungary's history in the twentieth century – similar to that of other Eastern European countries – has been characterised by constant change, which has often meant fundamental transformations in its political, social and economic system. The free parliamentary elections in the spring of 1990 ended 40 years of socialist rule in Hungary. This had an enormous impact on all aspects of the social, political and economic life of the country, and thus on crime and crime control policies. This chapter discusses the following issues: first, the history of crime prevention, trends in crime, and the main features of Hungarian crime control policy; second, the 'stillbirth', birth, and then revival of the idea of crime prevention; and the circumstances influencing crime prevention policy over the past 18 years; and third, harmony and discordance in the Hungarian approach to crime prevention and the main features of the Community Crime Prevention Strategy.

'Zigzags' in crime control policy

Crime in Hungary became an acute political question in the early years of the transition after 1990. The first few years of this period had been chaotic, with a massive increase in social disorder and in the rate of recorded crime. The rise in the number of detections lagged far behind the increase in the number of reported offences. The involvement of young people in crime also increased to a worrying extent.

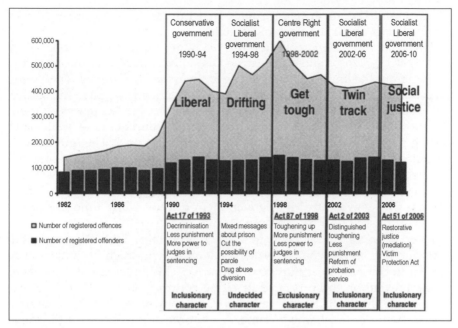

Figure 10.1 'Zigzags' in crime control policy, 1990–2010

After the change of regime, similar to the other post-Communist countries of Eastern Europe, Hungarian policy-makers faced a dual challenge of the rising crime and the parallel decline in perceptions of public safety combined with the necessity of a democratic transformation in the criminal justice system, accentuated by the needs of an increasingly open society. Figure 10.1 summarises the shifting political landscape in Hungary since 1990. During the first period of the transition, legal reforms were dominated by the requirements of so-called 'Europeanisation'. As a result, the increase in crime had practically no influence on crime control policy.

Between 1990 and 1994 the first freely elected Conservative government followed a consistent rationale and a humane approach in its criminal justice policy despite a rapidly increasing crime rate. The 1993 amendment of the Criminal Code, among other things, decriminalised prostitution, reduced the minimum term of imprisonment from three months to one day, expanded the application of non-custodial sanctions, increased flexibility in sentencing, and for the first time in Hungarian criminal law, introduced the option of treatment instead of punishment for petty drug offenders.

The subsequent Socialist Liberal government (between 1994 and 1998) initiated a debate on how to design a more effective criminal justice system, and declared its commitment to continued criminal justice reforms. Unfortunately, the desired criminal policy direction became

215

blurred, and the government sent mixed messages to the public and to professionals about the aims of its policy.

The general election campaign in 1998 demonstrated that public safety and fighting crime could be construed as salient issues, and the emphasis shifted from the limits of criminal law to the issue of efficiency. The Young Democrats' Party (FIDESZ) won the election with a 'law and order' programme, promising to introduce mandatory life sentences without parole and generally tougher punishments. The concept of the 'visible and strong police' was aimed at deterring street crime. The public was promised a 'tough on crime' stance, as well as a deterrence-oriented reform of the Penal Code. The sentencing system became stricter, and the criminal law was given an increased role in the social control of drug misuse. The new centre right government did not waste time in starting a prison construction programme.

After winning the election in 2002, the Socialist Liberal government introduced a new penal reform based on a twin-track criminal policy similar to those in most European countries. This government considered crime prevention to be part of its crime control policy, and for the first time since the transition, criminal policy showed an interest again in dealing with 'old-fashioned' crime. A comprehensive reform of the Penal Code was undertaken in 2003. Since this point, therefore, crime control policy has had two pillars in Hungary: criminal justice policy and the system of crime prevention.

After winning the election again in 2006, the Socialist Liberal government reinforced the direction it had taken in its criminal justice policy by establishing the legal and organisational framework for mediation, setting up a state-funded legal aid programme, and introducing the concept of the restraining order to support the fight against family violence.

In the course of its law enforcement and criminal justice modernisation programme, the government aimed to reduce the workload of criminal justice agencies, cut law enforcement costs, as well as help and compensate victims of crime and 'offended-against' communities. The Minister of Justice declared that community crime prevention was to be an integral part of social policy, and a core element of a coherent criminal policy. This recent approach to crime control policy is well illustrated by a quotation from an opening address by Dr József Petrétei, the former Minister of Justice:

> Social democracy as a social philosophy concept aims for full social integration. Criminal policy based on this concept is fundamentally different from the control-oriented approaches in that it is looking for means other than locks, bars and surveillance systems in an attempt to solve social problems. (Petrétei 2005)

A remarkable feature of the developments in contemporary Hungarian crime control policy is that even though the first debates concerning police

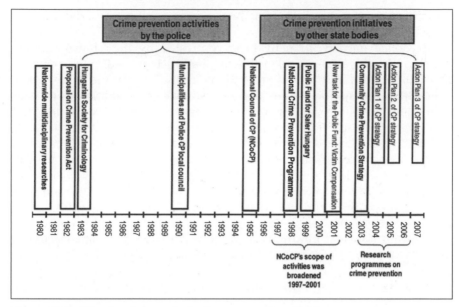

Figure 10.2   The development of crime prevention in Hungary

reform date back as far as 1988–90, the dilemmas raised in these debates on issues of decentralisation, demilitarisation and the functions, management and training of the police, *inter alia*, have still not been satisfactorily resolved. The new governmental structure does not include a Ministry of the Interior where the police had traditionally belonged. It is currently the Ministry of Justice and Law Enforcement that oversees its work.

The experience of the past few decades shows that alternating Socialist Liberal and Conservative governments have chosen different crime control principles to define directions and tools for law enforcement (see Figure 10.2). In this regard, different political directions may apply varying approaches to crime prevention too, and offer more or less restricted resources for the delivery of crime prevention programmes through setting different objectives for criminal policy.

Looking back: a short and troubled history of the prevention of crime in Hungary

The notion of crime prevention first appeared in Hungary nearly 30 years ago. The government funded a pioneering research programme on forms of deviance, from 1980 to 1985. In addition, leading criminologists and police officials initiated a proposal for a Crime Prevention Act in 1982. Although this initiative failed, crime prevention ideas gradually came to life. The Hungarian Society for Criminology was established in 1983, and the first theme in its publication series was the prevention of crime.

The police had traditionally been controlled by the Ministry of the Interior, which was also responsible for the functioning of municipalities. The Hungarian police forces are entirely central government-run, while the districts and municipalities also have some responsibilities for tasks in maintaining public order. The problem is that neither the police nor local authorities have resources dedicated for the prevention of crime. Para (1) Article 8 of the Local Governments Act (Act LXV, 1990) states that local governments have a number of tasks related to local public safety. In spite of the provision laid down in the Act, most local authorities did not set up public safety and crime prevention committees in order to improve co-operation with the police. Their attitude concerning local public safety boiled down to the slogan 'the more police the safer'. Therefore, the relationship between local governments and the police was confined to the former providing financial support for police patrols, or buying cars for local police stations.

During the first half of the 1990s the police launched a number of crime prevention initiatives. 'Community policing' was a new inspiration coming from abroad. This idea appealed to the police, because through this it could present itself as a civil organisation serving the public, and free itself of its former image of the Communist era. Besides this, local police forces opened 'crime prevention advice centres' to provide situational crime prevention advice on home security to the public. The police also launched 'DADA' programmes in schools in some of the cities and villages. This special safety programme for youngsters was based on the American DARE programme,[1] adapted to Hungarian circumstances. However, this was also the time when many police officers left the service to find jobs in the private security industry. At the turn of the 1990s, as a consequence of rising crime rates and citizens' perceptions of their lack of safety, a growing number of 'civil guard' organisations were also set up as citizens' initiatives.

The National Council of Crime Prevention (NCoCP)

A new era of crime prevention began in 1995 when the National Council of Crime Prevention (NCoCP) was set up to assist the government in its efforts to reduce crime. However, establishing this organisation did not mean that governmental efforts on crime prevention became mainstream. The first chair of the NCoCP was the director of the National Institute of Criminology with an outstanding professional achievement, but the Council itself did not have a budget. However, this special personal circumstance made it possible for the Council to develop the first National Crime Prevention Programme with the help of researchers in 1997. It became the first comprehensive governmental crime prevention programme, stating for the first time that the effectiveness of crime prevention should be ensured by implementing a complex set of community action points. Inasmuch as the Council lacked resources and co-operation from other bodies, the situation can be described as a 'Potemkin village'.[2]

The lip-service to crime prevention continued with a Governmental Decree [1075/1999] broadening the scope of NCoCP's activities with new areas of responsibility including the prevention of corruption; the co-ordination of preventative measures concerning victims; and drug prevention. In spite of these being evidently important questions, the lack of clarity in the assignment of powers remained a basic feature that characterised the NCoCP over the ensuing decade: neither its organisational form nor the expectations concerning its role were clarified. In practice, it was doubtful whose expectations the NCoCP should fulfil: the government's (which established it), or those of the Ministry of the Interior (which determined the conditions for its operation). Additionally, its tasks were not set out precisely. Some of its co-ordinating tasks clashed with those of the Victim Protection Bureau of the Ministry of the Interior, and the prevention of corruption competed with the activities of the Ministry of Justice in relation to fighting corruption. Likewise, the prevention of drugs problems in internal affairs competed with the drug prevention programme of the Ministry of Youth and Sports.

In summary, by the turn of the century it was not only impossible for the government to fulfil its responsibilities in the area of crime prevention, the administration of crime prevention activities also became confused.

Public funds for crime prevention

Hungarian crime prevention activities were akin to a badly organised beehive between 1995 and 2002. New organisations were established and old organisations were given new responsibilities, developing a certain amount of duplication in the tasks and activities. The Public Fund for a Safer Hungary was set up in 1999, with some resources to support crime prevention programmes. The members of its board consisted of criminal justice professionals, researchers, academics and higher-ranking police officers. This public funding body was also tasked with providing financial compensation for victims of serious violent crimes in 2001. Within the legal limits, the Board of Trustees decided on the level of compensation.

In the same year another public fund was established. One person was able to convince politicians about the necessity of setting up a fund in order to provide financial support to the newly established Neighbourhood Watch programmes, imported from Canada, and this person also helped launch some of the schemes in Hungary. Respect for Mr Kopácsi dated back to the Hungarian Revolution of 1956 when, as the Budapest chief of police, he changed sides and began to support the rebels. After serving a long prison sentence, he emigrated to Canada, and returned to Hungary after the change of regimes. With his help, this crime prevention initiative directly affected Hungarian practice. This public fund was also given responsibility for subsidising disaster prevention. The two public funds were subsequently amalgamated.

National strategy for community crime prevention

In October 2003 the Parliament adopted a resolution to approve the National Crime Prevention Strategy (Ministry of Justice 2003). A new National Crime Prevention Board (NCPB) was established under the auspices of the Ministry of Justice. The Board had shared chairing arrangements, with an expert chair and two co-chairs: the Minister of the Interior and the Minister of Justice. A new National Crime Prevention Centre was also set up in the Ministry of the Interior, with responsibility for the management and administrative tasks. By setting up this centre, the Minister of the Interior ensured the continuity of implementing crime prevention guidelines at ministry level.

The National Crime Prevention Strategy envisages crime prevention as a particular type of social policy that entails both professional and civic activities, and something that must be governed by state authorities. The Community Crime Prevention Strategy is designed to be accomplished through a partnership with criminal justice and law enforcement agencies.

Community crime prevention involves sets of objectives to curb the effect of the underlying causes of crime, reduce the risk of becoming a victim, increase the safety of the community as a whole, and thus improve the quality of life and the fulfilment of individual human rights. Ultimately, the Community Crime Prevention Strategy contributes to economic development, the secure operation of the market and the reduction of moral and material damage caused by crime. Expenditure on crime prevention measures must be regarded as an investment, with returns in the perceptible improvement of public safety.

During the preparation phase, a SWOT analysis[3] was used to highlight how the strategy would contribute to achieving different (and potentially conflicting) objectives and priorities. The analysis was performed in different subcategories (e.g. resources, structure, value and level of professionalism). It helped to determine crime prevention priority areas, to establish goals pertaining to these areas, and to put an action plan in place to achieve these goals. Based on the findings, a number of strengths could also be identified. These included, for instance, existing possibilities for mitigating the damage suffered by victims of violent crime; the Victim Protection Bureau, established in the Ministry of the Interior; the existence of the National Crime Prevention Council since 1995; the growing number of 'civil guard' organisations; and the efforts of the police to disseminate information on situational crime prevention. On the other hand, the analysis also revealed some significant weaknesses. These included, among many others, the shortage of finance; the lack of specialised victim services; and the underdeveloped system for measuring latent crime. The lack of an adequate sense of responsibility for local public safety by local governments was also considered to be a weakness.

An analysis of the external environment of the system was also performed from a political, economic, social and technical point of view. It revealed new opportunities for crime prevention, and first among these was the government's commitment to crime prevention, which is essential for launching any kind of new initiative. The existence of a nationwide children's welfare and child protection system, and the new drug strategy and its action plan were also considered as strengths, as was the opportunity to join the European Union Crime Prevention Network, which made it possible to adopt blueprint model programmes in crime prevention. It was obvious that any changes in the external environment might present threats to the system of crime prevention and jeopardise the fulfilment of its goals. For instance, different organisational cultures might in practice override crime prevention objectives, or the fear of crime among members of the public might not correspond with the real risk of victimisation, and new information might only exacerbate this subjective fear.

The strategy's background

The rise of crime and anti-social behaviour was a major blot on the political landscape of Central Eastern European countries undergoing transition. In the period between 1970 and 1995, the number of reported crimes increased fourfold in Hungary. Over a span of just three years, between 1989 and 1992, Hungarians faced a boom in crime that Western European countries had experienced over a lengthier period of two decades. The public was shocked by the speed of the rise in crime. However, this phenomenon was not specific to Hungary, as similar trends could be observed in all of the former socialist bloc countries. The human costs of transition in Hungary turned out to be far higher than anticipated. The loss of security and the growth in the fear of crime were closely connected with unemployment, social exclusion and the loss of a personal outlook for some age cohorts and social strata. Some social groups (for example families with children, the elderly on a low income, the unskilled and unemployed, and the Roma) paid a higher than average price for the transition. At the beginning of the new century a comparison of regional (county) crime rates and GDP *per capita* showed that where GDP was higher, the number of reported crimes was also higher (Ministry of Justice 2003: 17). Since then, this trend has become somewhat blurred. On the one hand, the Hungarian crime rate has stabilised over the last four to five

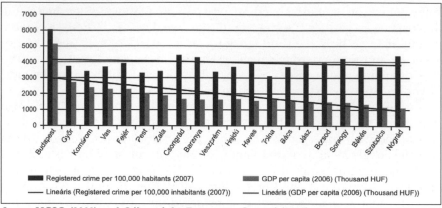

Source: HCSO (2008) and Office of the Prosecutor General (2008)

Figure 10.3   GDP *per capita*, and crime rates *per capita* by counties in Hungary

years. On the other hand, as Figure 10.3 shows, in the poorer counties where GDP *per capita* is low – especially in the north-eastern parts of the country – the crime rate *per capita* can be as high as in the more developed counties. It is noteworthy that in the poorer counties, the composition of crime shows much higher levels of violent criminality (such as hooliganism, bodily harm, vandalism) than before.

The socially and economically most disadvantaged regions (primarily the north-east of the country) are the ones that emerge as the primary regional sources of crime, where the ratio of reported offenders is higher. These areas have lower than average GDP *per capita*, whereas the unemployment rate among young people is higher, and child poverty is also more pronounced than in other parts of the country. By contrast, the capital city (Budapest) and the mid and western counties can be regarded as the primary targets of crime. These areas experience a higher number of reported crimes than the size of their population would justify, and as the amount of accumulated wealth here is larger than average, more opportunities exist for crime.

The scope and limitations of the Community Crime Prevention Strategy

The National Community Crime Prevention Strategy aimed to undertake a comprehensive task, while also attempting to take the limitations of community crime prevention into consideration. It recognised that community crime prevention could not encompass all activity types aimed at reducing crime. Community crime prevention is above all directed at reducing crime that directly harms or puts citizens and their communities at risk. In addition, in a limited way, it includes a number of activities against specific forms of crime that fall into the category of organised crime; and against certain types of crime, related to international

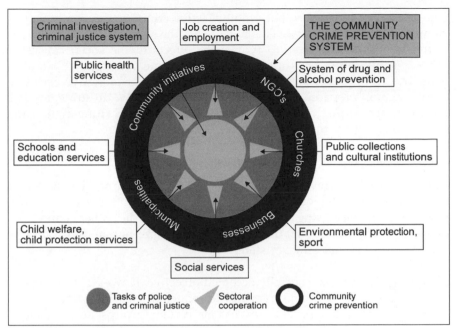

The subsystems diagram labels:
- Criminal investigation, criminal justice system
- Job creation and employment
- THE COMMUNITY CRIME PREVENTION SYSTEM
- Public health services
- System of drug and alcohol prevention
- Schools and education services
- Public collections and cultural institutions
- Child welfare, child protection services
- Environmental protection, sport
- Social services
- Community initiatives
- NGO's
- Churches
- Businesses
- Municipalities
- Tasks of police and criminal justice
- Sectoral cooperation
- Community crime prevention

Source: Ministry of Justice (2003: 42)

Figure 10.4   The subsystems of community crime prevention

migration, that can directly affect individuals, communities, NGOs and churches. Thus, community-based crime prevention is mostly effective against 'everyday' crimes that influence the public's sense of security.

In a comprehensive system of community crime prevention (see Figure 10.4), three major strands can be distinguished:

1. The various organisations that currently deal with crime prevention *ex officio*, including traditional police and criminal justice functions concerned with crime reduction.

2. Close sectoral co-operation among authorities to remove the causes of crime, reduce the number of opportunities for crime and the risk of becoming a victim of crime. All functions are included here that can be implemented via partnerships between sectors, and between government departments, as well as through necessary co-operation among the latter on an equal basis.

3. The community crime prevention system is complete with local and wider communities also assuming their responsibilities; that is, if action for attaining goals is forthcoming from people and organisations who are able and willing to improve communities' capabilities of defending themselves.

223

One of the key principles that guide effective crime prevention is that of 'simultaneous competency'. This means that the strategy can only deliver lasting results if measures to reduce the effects of the social causes of crime, victimisation and opportunities for crime are applied simultaneously. Crime prevention work at the local level is voluntary. The state administration prepares plans, different ministries draw up strategies, but their delivery at the local level is not mandatory. The Hungarian crime prevention strategy therefore lacks legal teeth.

Constitutional principles in crime prevention

Community crime prevention itself is a system of checks and balances that incorporates, on the one hand, the implementation of social control measures for increasing public safety, and on the other hand, the preservation of individual autonomy and respect for human rights. In this context, the National Strategy states:

> Combating crime is a socially accepted objective. However, measures taken to pursue this objective, and to reduce the fear of crime, have the possible side-effects of excluding certain groups and raising prejudices against juvenile delinquents, ex-prisoners, drug addicts, homeless people, poor people and Gypsies. The social crime prevention system is based on the principle of social justice. It must therefore endeavour both to avoid social exclusion and prejudice and to uphold rights of security. (Ministry of Justice 2003: 34)

In selecting the mode of prevention, the intervention must follow the principle of proportionality, and a balance must be struck between the autonomy of the individual and the exercise of community control. In pursuance of the requirements of security and the protection of human rights, the traditional system of criminal justice, with its many guarantees, must be safeguarded in such a way that it does not become subordinated to specific considerations of community crime prevention.

The Strategy's objectives and priorities

The Community Crime Prevention Strategy intends to improve the quality of life by ensuring public safety and reducing crime. It defines a system of linked objectives on different levels. In general, the strategy covers a wide range of areas, and opens the door for a large number of measures (see Figure 10.5).

The objectives form the main directions of the strategy. They define a vertical approach to the Community Crime Prevention Strategy in three major target areas: (i) the everyday life of the public; (ii) the arena of social policy concerned with crime prevention; and (iii) local and multi-sector players involved in crime prevention. This three-way division is intended

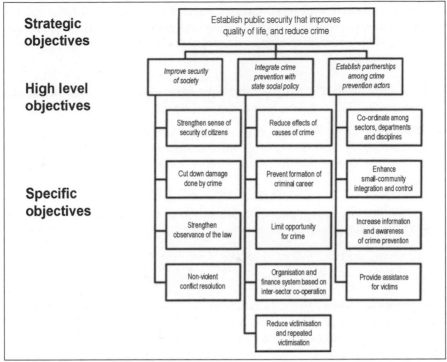

Strategic objectives	Establish public security that improves quality of life, and reduce crime		

High level objectives	Improve security of society	Integrate crime prevention with state social policy	Establish partnerships among crime prevention actors

Specific objectives:

Strengthen sense of security of citizens	Reduce effects of causes of crime	Co-ordinate among sectors, departments and disciplines
Cut down damage done by crime	Prevent formation of criminal career	Enhance small-community integration and control
Strengthen observance of the law	Limit opportunity for crime	Increase information and awareness of crime prevention
Non-violent conflict resolution	Organisation and finance system based on inter-sector co-operation	Provide assistance for victims
	Reduce victimisation and repeated victimisation	

Source: Ministry of Justice (2003: 41)

Figure 10.5   The community crime prevention strategy's system of objectives

to make the goals clear both to the public and to the organisations responsible for implementing the Strategy. Five priority areas are identi- fied: (i) the prevention and reduction of juvenile delinquency; (ii) the improvement of urban safety; (iii) the prevention of violence within the family; (iv) the prevention of victimisation and proper means to help victims of crime; and (v) the prevention of re-offending.

The management of community crime prevention in Hungary

Community crime prevention as an integral part of social policy can only be properly managed through joined-up governance by central govern- ment and ministries, joined-up public tendering for local and professional partners, as well as joined-up training for professionals (Gönczöl and Kerezsi 2004). It is the government's task to put the fundamental legislative, organisational and technical prerequisites in place for crime prevention. This requires responsible co-operation among ministries on an equal basis. It is crucial that continuous co-operation is maintained inside central government, among ministries and professional institutions, and between governmental and non-governmental organisations.

The Hungarian National Crime Prevention Board undertakes the co-ordination of community prevention on behalf of the government, and is responsible for implementing the strategy. The powers of the National Crime Prevention Board are:

- To establish long-term partnerships and fora for dialogue among partners both at horizontal and vertical levels.

- To set up such an organisation and/or partnership that which is capable of monitoring and evaluating information and recent findings from research on crime, victims and criminal justice.

- To manage regulatory and deregulatory activities defined by law.

- To periodically revise and update the action plan according to strategic goals and priorities.

- To revise and maintain a public communications strategy and an internal one for partners.

The National Crime Prevention Board is chaired by a crime prevention expert, appointed by the Prime Minister. The Secretariat of the Board is based in the Ministry of Justice and Law Enforcement. This model attempts to utilise the strengths and traditions of the earlier, more police-oriented, system of crime prevention, but also to involve new parties in the crime prevention partnership.

Effective community crime prevention means interdisciplinary co-operation in horizontal (across several ministerial departments), and vertical (between municipal and county-level local government) partnerships. It means that crime prevention is an integrated part of local public affairs, and the local action plan is an adequate response to local crime and local fear of crime. Therefore, the existence of a local partnership is an essential condition for action. Government support and public funding is granted for joint local training programmes, local surveys, programmes and monitoring.

Annual action plans

Since the initiation of the first National Crime Prevention Strategy in 2003, annual crime prevention action plans, as well as annual reports for Parliament on the implementation of the Strategy, have been prepared. The government's action plans, drawn up in accordance with the Strategy, specify tasks for the relevant ministries, national bodies and data providers, and require continuous co-operation between the relevant partners. The action plans have stimulated various new programmes each year. By way of overview, the National Crime Prevention Board has a duty to submit a biennial report to Parliament on the implementation of the Strategy. The National Crime Prevention Board also provides a conduit through which government funding for crime prevention activities is channelled. The Board announces invitations to tender every year for programmes in two categories, for 'macro' and 'micro' projects. For instance, one macro project was set up to create a compact for the protection of children in Morahalom through a wide partnership, and another to establish a probation centre as an experimental project. Examples of funded micro projects include a demonstration project for graffiti removal through community work and a project providing peer-assisted training for juveniles. However, the community crime prevention strategy and the government action plan can only become an integrated part of local social policy with the involvement of the local authorities. Municipalities must, in partnership with local police, play an active and leading role in producing plans for local community safety. The local government, as the provider of most local services and the controller of local public administration as well as the forum for local political debate, should serve to lead, stimulate and co-ordinate local crime prevention.

Conclusion

Even though the idea of crime prevention had been in existence in Hungarian criminology since the 1980s, it had no significant effect on legislation or public attitudes until the beginning of the twenty-first century. The police were active in practical crime prevention, having borrowed several ideas ranging from the community policing model to the zero tolerance approach, but local governments undertook hardly any tasks and responsibilities in this area. Despite the continuous efforts of national law enforcement and criminal justice agencies, perceptions of public safety have shown a deteriorating trend. During the last 20 years, Hungarian criminal policy has faced the dual challenge of, first, a threefold increase in the national crime rate and declining public safety, and second, the need for a democratic transformation in the criminal justice system, led by the demands of an increasingly open society. In the first period of the transition, legal changes focused on meeting the standards of a 'European criminal law'. As a result of this, the increase in crime had practically no influence on crime control policy during this time. Meanwhile, criminal policy with every new parliamentary cycle shifted either to become tougher or to take a social integration approach. Furthermore, the continuously changing organisational structure of the crime prevention system did not help to clarify crime prevention definitions and tasks.

Although a high level of inequality and multiple structural strains appeared in the course of the transition process, the political climate needed almost one and a half decades to elapse before the importance of community crime prevention became accepted. Since then, Hungarian crime control policy has been based on the two pillars of criminal justice policy and the system of crime prevention (Kerezsi and Lévay 2008).

By the end of the last century 'community' had become a central organising concept of criminal justice in the developed world. Notions of community policing, community prosecution, community justice and community corrections show that the concept of community has a strong association with criminal justice. These associations also demonstrate that close relationships have been established among the stakeholders in crime control that would have been unimaginable in previous decades. The 'reallocation' of some of the sentencing powers of the courts in the form of diversion significantly increases the role and power of prosecutors in the criminal procedure (Kerezsi 2006). However, this is only one sign of the shifting balance among the actors of criminal justice. In other ways, the sentencing guidelines (which may also be viewed as a 'straitjacket' for the courts), the obligatory minimum sanctions, the 'three strikes' laws and the subsequently withdrawn rule of a minimum prison sentences also reduce the sentencing powers of the courts.

In criminological thought the governance of safety has become associated with the preventive turn in crime control strategies in Europe that acknowledge the limits of criminal justice, invoke the direct participation of statutory as well as commercial and voluntary sector actors and, in so doing, generate new objects and places of control signified by notions of safety and security (Edwards and Hughes 2005). The zero tolerance principle applied to acts that 'spoil the quality of life' blurs the threshold between disorderly behaviour and less serious criminal offences. As Carson notes, social policy in many developed societies has generally taken on an 'increasingly communalist hue in recent years, ideas of community and social capital having come to occupy a central position in a wide variety of policy areas far beyond the purview of criminology' (2004: 193).

In Hungarian crime prevention practice too, confusingly, the term 'prevention' seems to be applied to a wide array of contradictory activities (Sansfaçon et al. 2002). The Hungarian community crime prevention strategy's main goal was to establish a sensitive balance between maintaining strong law enforcement and promoting the broader interests of society by ensuring political freedom and economic development. It is not easy to get this balance right. Too little security and the state fails to satisfy its core obligations. Too much security and it intrudes unduly and unjustly on citizens' liberties.

White (1996) elaborated three abstract crime prevention models: first, the conservative model, based on crime control and opportunity reduction; second, the liberal model, based on social problems and opportunity enhancement; and third, the radical model, based on social justice and

Table 10.1 Key distinctive features of the crime prevention strategy

Key concept	Social problem Social justice
Main strategy	Opportunity enhancement
Main crime focus	Conventional 'street' crime
Concept of criminality	Marginalisation Social alienation Market competition
Crime response	Improve opportunities Reduce inequality Enhance personal responsibility
Role of community	Auxiliary to police Community development
Limitations	Based on limited resources Narrow definition of crime

Source: Adapted from White (1996: 100)

political struggle. The Hungarian crime prevention model fits White's liberal model well, based on crime focused on social problems and opportunity enhancement (see Table 10.1).

The Hungarian National Crime Prevention Strategy considers the prevention of crime to be a particular type of social policy that entails both professional and civic activities, and something that must be governed by state authorities. As such, it adopts a top-down approach. Although the crime prevention strategy has been built on the interface between criminal and social policies, in practice there has been an apparent proliferation of situational crime prevention methods. Furthermore, the laudable aims of the strategy have been hampered by numerous setbacks in the last two decades.

First, during large-scale and rapid social changes, there is always a danger that whenever the crime rate increases, the authorities are blamed for their inability to secure public safety. Organisational changes across all levels of government, and similarly in the structure of crime prevention, have been too numerous and too frequent. Before 2003, the driving force behind crime prevention was the Ministry of the Interior, which was responsible for the police force; after 2003 it was the Ministry of Justice. Since 2006, the Ministry of Justice and Law Enforcement has been responsible for the police – thanks to another fundamental reorganisation of the structure of governance.

Second, in Hungary safety remains essentially state business, mostly police business. Although citizens do not trust the government and the police, they are willing to give up their rights in the hope of better safety (CCTV, for example), and keep relying on the state to provide this. The introduction of the rule of law is – and must be – the most fundamental achievement of the new democracies in Central and Eastern Europe. The state may still be intervening everywhere, yet at the same time it is weak in the sense that it is not able to guarantee that the rule of law will be observed. The state is also weak because it is no longer authoritarian, but public trust has not (yet) emerged. This holds true for both the trust of citizens in the state and the trust of political actors in citizens. In people's perception, and in reality, democracy is not (yet) working well. As a result, lawlessness and crime are widespread. One important manifestation of this is the considerable 'shadow' or underground economy.

Third, notwithstanding the existence of at least four crime prevention models around the world – namely social/community crime prevention, developmental crime prevention, situational/environmental crime prevention, and criminal justice system-based crime prevention – in practice only two models were recognised in Hungary during the 1990s. Moreover, there was an ongoing tug-of-war between situational and community-based crime prevention. The former was supported by the police, and the latter was held up as a model by the National Crime Prevention Board. Despite the fact that crime prevention could be interpreted in many ways, what was never well conceptualised or communicated was the intersection between the different types of prevention, and the priority crimes that the strategy should focus on. Crime prevention responsibilities were often placed on police services that could not sufficiently respond by themselves, yet few municipalities were proactively involved. Recognition of the importance of community crime prevention among local municipalities was random and slow.

Fourth, during the last two decades more and more new phenomena and demanding problems occurred that demanded solutions. Hence, the new requirements placed upon, and as a result the role, domain and measures of, crime prevention were continually changing (family violence, child victims, football hooliganism, and so on). Therefore the objectives of crime prevention practice were in a constant state of flux, while financial resources became restricted.

Fifth, the particular weaknesses of the current system are the inadequate distribution of resources, the absence of evaluation, the lack of co-operation between stakeholders, and the scarcity of training and research activities.

Sixth, while prevention programmes supported by the National Crime Prevention Board have matured in the last few years, the evaluations of these programmes have lagged behind, even though the need for an evidence-base and such evaluations has never been greater.

Seventh, the Hungarian model of crime prevention has a strong affiliation with areas outside the justice system and strikes a balance between community and situational crime prevention. However, it lacks suitable training capacity, either in the form of separate higher education courses or as part of criminology courses. Although an introductory course has been run by the police ('Crime Prevention Academy'), there is a need for municipal crime prevention managers (if they exist at all) and other field workers to be provided with many more practical skills.

The INSEC research[4] surveyed fear of crime and defensive practices among citizens, as well as local political efforts to increase public safety, in two districts of five European cities (Amsterdam, Hamburg, Vienna, Krakow and Budapest). One of the outcomes of the highest international relevance was the difference in the types of concerns raised by Western and Eastern European citizens: while the former felt distressed by the consequences of mass immigration, the latter suffered the uncertainty of living conditions brought on by transition (Barabás *et al.* 2005).

How do new criminal policy trends affect the practical application of crime prevention methods in a social environment simultaneously exposed to the processes of 'global inclusion' and 'local exclusion'? Two main processes contribute to social exclusion: first, high unemployment (especially long-term unemployment) and job insecurity for people who were previously fully integrated into mainstream society, and second, difficulty, particularly for young people, in entering the labour market and enjoying both the income and the social network associated with it. The strength of the links between the employment situation and other dimensions of life (such as family, income, housing, health, social networks) suggests that those people who are trapped in the lower segments of the labour market, or are excluded from it, suffer the risk of becoming excluded from society altogether (Council of Europe 2001: 14).

The problem of crime affects the quality of life throughout the world. The lack of public safety and ways to reduce crime has become a central issue in most countries. Although we know since Durkheim that some form and level of crime will always be with us, which requires criminal justice systems to operate, it is a community matter to decide how much money should be spent on them, and how effective their activities are in protecting the public. It is now widely recognised that traditional criminal justice responses are insufficient deterrents against acts that threaten community safety. Diverse crime reduction measures were tried, but the prevention of crime is the only kind that offers a long-lasting effect on community safety, and can help raise living standards and help people become contented.

In Hungary, safety and security as a central dilemma appears somewhat different from concerns in Western Europe. The unfavourable socio-economic conditions, low living standards and the lack of a clear value system may combine to set a person on a trajectory that may result in crime, violence and problems with alcohol and drugs. Therefore, all possible prevention policies should include the reduction of risk factors and the development of protective factors. The two basic features that all crime prevention programmes must address are social development and opportunity reduction. In this context, the promotion of social cohesion most likely to be effective will take the form of conflict resolution, reconciliation and the rebuilding of the 'social fabric' through the promotion of institutions that are sources of 'social capital'.

Notes

1 Founded in the early 1980s, Drug Abuse Resistance Education (DARE) is an education-based programme that seeks to prevent the use of illegal drugs, membership in gangs and violent behaviour.
2 The expression 'Potemkin village' refers to something that appears elaborate and impressive but in actual fact lacks substance or hides an undesirable fact or condition.
3 Identifying strengths, weaknesses, opportunities and threats.
4 Insecurities in European Cities, 'Crime Related Fears Within the Context of New Anxieties and Community-based Crime Prevention'. The research project was funded under the European Commission's Fifth Framework Programme (1998–2002).

References

Barabás, T., Irk, F. and Kovács, R. (2005) *Félelem, bünözés és bünmegelözés Európa öt nagyvárosában*. Budapest: OKRI.
Carson, W. G. (2004) 'Is Communalism Dead? Reflections on the Present and Future Practice of Crime Prevention: Part Two', *Australian and New Zealand Journal of Criminology*, 37(2): 192–210.
Council of Europe (2001) *Promoting the Policy Debate on Social Exclusion from a Comparative Perspective: Trends in Social Cohesion, No. 1*. Germany: Council of Europe. Online at: http://www.coe.int/t/dg3/socialpolicies/socialcohesion-dev/source/Trends/Trends-01_en.pdf
Edwards, A. and Hughes, G. (2005) 'Comparing the Governance of Safety in Europe: A Geo-historical Approach', *Theoretical Criminology*, 9(3): 345–63.
Gönczöl, K. and Kerezsi, K. (2004) 'The Basic Principles and the Social Background for the Hungarian Community Crime Prevention Strategy', in *Tribute to Kálmán Györgyi* [*Györgyi Kálmán ünnepi kötet*] (ed. B. Gellér) *Bibliotheca Iuridica, ELTE ÁJK*, Libri Amicorum II, pp. 265–78.
Hungarian Central Statistical Office (HCSO) (2008) *A GDP területi különbségei Magyarországon, 2006*, Statisztikai tükör. II. évf. 90. szám, Hungarian Central Statistical Office, Budapest (Hungarian). Online at: http://portal.ksh.hu/pls/ksh/docs/hun/xftp/stattukor/tergdp06.pdf

Kerezsi, K. (2006) *Control or Support: The Dilemma of Alternative Sanctions.* Budapest: Complex Kiadói Kft. English summary, pp. 287–303. Online at: http://en.okri.hu/content/view/95/9/

Kerezsi, K. and Lévay, M. (2008) 'Criminology, Crime and Criminal Justice in Hungary', *European Journal of Criminology*, 5: 239–60.

Ministry of Justice (2003) *The National Strategy for Community Crime Prevention.* Budapest: Ministry of Justice. Online at: http://bunmegelozes.easyhosting.hu/dok/national_strat_crime_prevention.pdf

Office of the Prosecutor General (2008) *Disclosure on Criminality, 2007.* Budapest: Ministry of Justice and Law Enforcement and the Office of the Prosecutor General.

Petrétei, J. (2005) Speech at the 'Crime Prevention – A Strategic Approach' Conference, 20–21 September, UK Presidency programme. Online at: www.bunmegelozes.hu/index.html?pid = 106&lang = en

Sansfaçon, D., Barchechat, O. and Oginsky, K. (2002) *Discussion Paper – From Knowledge to Policy and Practice: What Role for Evaluation?* Montreal: ICPC.

White, R. (1996) 'Situating Crime Prevention: Models, Methods and Political Perspectives', *Crime Prevention Studies*, 5: 97–113.

Chapter 11

International models of crime prevention

Margaret Shaw

Introduction

This collection of chapters provides an excellent opportunity to reflect on how far crime prevention, from a European perspective, has developed in the past 20 to 30 years, and its prospects for the future, but also to hold it up to an international mirror.[1] This chapter, for me at least, could be subtitled 'From Easingwold to Bangkok', in reference to the long distance that crime prevention has travelled – from the days of the lowly Home Office crime prevention training centre in England, which up to the early 1970s provided basic training for police officers,[2] to the crime prevention workshop that took place at the 11th UN Congress on Crime Prevention and Criminal Justice, held in Bangkok in April 2005 (Shaw and Travers 2007). The latter demonstrated how far the notion of prevention as an intervention has moved away from a narrow policing function to a much broader inter-sectoral approach, as well as expanding to countries and cities in all regions of the world.

Against the somewhat pessimistic accounts of where European crime prevention may now be going, which may be reflected in the preceding chapters in this volume, I would like to present a rather more cautiously optimistic tone. Crime prevention has been described, memorably, by Peter Homel (2006) as 'a swan swimming in the surf', going up and down time and again, yet always re-emerging. Crime prevention is not a one-time intervention. We have continually to apply, adapt, innovate, repackage and resell the underlying notions – that there are viable and long-term alternatives to repressive and reactive responses to crime and insecurity. As Stephen Lab (2005) in the USA and Janet Foster (2002) in the UK have both remarked, much of what is actually crime prevention is often called something else. There are also some emerging phenomena and approaches that challenge the models of prevention that have become so well developed and articulated in high-income western industrialised countries. These do not rely primarily on the fiats of academics and researchers about what must be done, but on acceptance of the importance of governance issues, and the limitations of context and capacity, and a realistic view about the possibilities of incremental progress.

This presentation attempts to reflect on the questions posed by the editor at the initial seminar out of which these chapters arise, regarding: how policy travels; how it is shaped by culture, context and institutions; what changes have taken place – both positive and negative – in crime prevention policies and practice; and to speculate on emerging trends and what the future might look like. This is also an opportunity to reflect, from the vantage point of a transnational perch, the International Centre for the Prevention of Crime (ICPC), on international challenges and trends, and consider what these imply for European models and their policies and strategies.

How policy travels

Much has been written about the process of policy transfer in recent years (including by a number of contributors to this volume). It is generally agreed that this takes place through a variety of processes including academic exchange (seminars, conferences, papers, journal articles), through policy and practice exchanges, often assisted by specialised regional and international networks such as CRIMPREV itself, the European Union Crime Prevention Network, the Council of Europe, the European Forum for Urban Security, ICPC, UN-HABITAT's Safer Cities Programme, FLACSO, ALTUS, or the recently established Brazilian Forum for Public Security.

Policy also travels through bilateral and multilateral exchanges. These can include professional training and practitioner study visits to examine practices, or city exchanges such as those under the URBACT project, the European Forum for Urban Security (EFUS), ICPC's city exchange programme, or through technical assistance programmes. The latter is an area where there have been significant recent policy change, exemplified in the *Paris Declaration on Aid Effectiveness* of 2005 (OECD 2005). To increase the effectiveness and sustainability of technical assistance, the Paris Declaration stresses the importance of recipient country ownership, priorities and timetables, rather than those of donor countries or organisa-tions, for example (Leeds 2007; Shaw and Dandurand 2006). Closely tied to technical assistance as a vehicle for policy transfer are funding requirements by major donors and foundations that hope to shape national and regional sensibilities and practices. These have included the World Bank, the Inter-American Development Bank, the European Union, the Department for International Development in the UK, and other regional or country aid programmes, such as CIDA (Canada), SIDA (Sweden), JICA (Japan) and GTZ (Germany).

While there has been room for criticism of donor-led interventions and requirements, there are also some very sensitive and thoughtful examples of donor project funding and evaluation that tries to advance impacts and understanding of mechanisms in violence reduction. The co-financing of a series of civil society organisations in Guatemala and Colombia by a group of Dutch donor organisations provides one example (Pearce 2007).

But policy is also influenced by international norms and standards. We now have United Nations guidelines for crime prevention, including the *Guidelines for Cooperation and Technical Assistance in Urban Crime Prevention*, adopted by ECOSOC in 1995 (Res. 1995/9), and the *Guidelines for the Prevention of Crime*, adopted in 2002 (Res. 2002/13).[4] These have provided an important standard and basis for many countries and cities. The Mexican state of Queretaro, for example, specifically modelled its crime prevention strategy on the UN Guidelines.

How policy is shaped by institutions, context or culture

'In 2000, an estimated 199,000 youth murders took place globally – equivalent to 565 children and young people aged 10–29 years dying on average each day as a result of interpersonal violence' (WHO 2002: 25). The impact of context, culture and institutions on policy is fundamental, and one of the main international lessons of the past ten years of crime prevention experimentation. The reasons for this become very clear when the broader social, political and economic context of crime prevention interventions is considered, including the very wide disparities in incomes both between and within countries, and in the range of capacities of cities, organisations, institutions and communities.

Crime problems, especially violent crime, are not evenly distributed (WHO 2008). In general, levels of victimisation from common crime (burglary, robbery, theft, assault) have declined across European Union countries in the past ten years (Van Dijk *et al.* 2007; Van Dijk 2008; ICPC 2008), as well as in North America, yet there has been a corresponding increase in violent crime and homicide in developing countries over that period. This is especially the case for Latin America and sub-Saharan Africa.

The difference that context makes is clear when we look, for example, at levels of homicide globally. As the World Health Organization (WHO 2002) has reported, some 565 children and young people globally are dying each day. They estimate the highest rates of homicide for 15 to

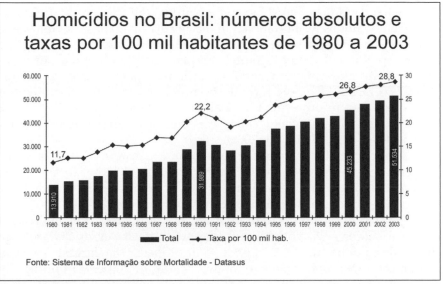

Homicídios no Brasil: números absolutos e taxas por 100 mil habitantes de 1980 a 2003

Total ◆ Taxa por 100 mil hab.

Fonte: Sistema de Informação sobre Mortalidade - Datasus

Source: S. Ramos, Center for Studies on Public Security and Citizenship,
University Candido Mendes

Figure 11.1 Homicides in Brazil: number and rate per 100,000 population,
1980–2003

17-year-olds at 37.66 per 100,000 in Latin America and the Caribbean,
compared with 5.72 in Europe and 6.37 in North America (WHO 2006).
Countries such as Guatemala and Colombia have experienced long-term
chronic violence that is intergenerational and embedded, and running
across the spectrum from war, to state, neighbourhood, school and
household violence (Pearce 2007).

In Brazil, the number of homicides rose from 13,000 in 1980 to over
55,000 a year by 2003 (see Figure 11.1), a rate of over 100 per 100,000 of
the population. Further, within Brazil extraordinary variations in risk are
evident, with far higher rates among young people, and in the most
disadvantaged areas of the major cities such as Rio de Janiero and Sao
Paulo or Recife. The Small Arms Survey (2006) calculates a rate of
firearm mortality among young men of 20–29 years in Recife, Brazil as
327 per 100,000. As the sociologist Sylvia Ramos, at the University of
Candido Mendes, Rio de Janeiro has pointed out, the overall increase in
homicides in Brazil is a stark illustration of the *age* of death (15–26),
the *gender* of death (young men), the *colour* of death (black) and the
geography of death (the *favelas* of Rio or Sao Paulo, for example) (Ramos
2006a).

There are a number of carefully demonstrated studies of the difficulties
of transplanting models developed in one country to another (Newburn
and Sparks 2004; Lau 2004; Dixon and Maher 2005). In the case of

developing, middle or low income countries, the inappropriateness of many interventions well promoted in the North is evident. After ten years, the lessons from crime prevention developments in South Africa led to the conclusion that you cannot simply transplant northern approaches without carefully assessing and adapting to local capacities and conditions (Pelser 2002). As has more recently been pointed out, if all offenders in South Africa were prosecuted, and all young offenders incarcerated, the entire justice system would collapse – it is just not feasible to build sufficient capacity (Holtmann 2008).

In such circumstances, what do European or western models of crime prevention have to offer to developing countries? How do we apply interventions such as street lighting or CCTV, or enforce the criminal law or local regulations in situations such as the following?

Fifty per cent of the population of the city of Nairobi, Kenya, lives in informal settlements, without infrastructure (roads, electricity, sewage disposal, running water or lighting). In Kibera, the largest informal settlement in Nairobi, some two million people, or 20 per cent of the city population, occupy less than 1 per cent of the city area, at a density of 3,000 persons per hectare (Biau 2007). In such circumstances, TV is often powered by car batteries or illegal hook-ups, cooking is done on open stoves, waste disposal and running water severely limited, and there are few roads to access dwellings. What is the use of CCTV cameras to deter theft or rape, or fast response times, or even fire engines, without electricity, water or access?

In the informal settlement of Nyanga in Cape Flats, South Africa, over 50 per cent of the population is below the age of 20 years and unemployed. What are the implications of enforcing local regulations and arresting all the illegal unlicensed taxi drivers or the informal traders who are performing services to their community, if this would leave them without alternative sources of income other than from crime? Nyanga does not, at present, have the social capital necessary with which to build partnerships. It does not have a community, few people know their neighbours or even speak the same language, since a high proportion are recent rural migrants, or immigrants from countries such as Somalia, Zimbabwe, Sudan or Madagascar.

In many Latin American or African countries policing systems are still patterned on the 'regime policing' associated with former state repression (Hinton 2006; Marks and Goldsmith 2006). In such countries public trust in the police is very low, and especially so in the case of young people in slums and poor areas. Police and security forces, for example, were responsible for 1,098 of the 7,000 homicides of young people in the *favelas* of Rio de Janeiro in 2005 (Ramos 2006a). In such cases, how can young people feel anything other than fear or hatred for the police? Transforming such regime policing requires major structural and organisational change. But poor state policing also arises from lack of resources and good management. Mexico City has 76,000 street police officers, and a recent study based on their views finds widespread job dissatisfaction, deplorable working conditions, equipment and uniforms (having to buy ammunition), inadequate wages, and lack of institutional and public support or respect (Azaola 2007). In such circumstances corruption is reinforced from all sides and self-image very low.

Most policing is non-state, with private police now outnumbering state police. Private security for the rich and local militia or gang 'security' for the poor seem to be a reality that is not going to go away in a hurry. In Enugu Province in Nigeria, while efforts to develop community policing have been undertaken, informal policing structures outnumber state police, and the term 'vigilante' is a positive one synonymous with guard (Stone and Miller 2005).

These are the realities of many lives in the fast-expanding urban areas in developing countries. Rapid urbanisation, especially over the past 15 years, has spurred the growth of a number of megacities of over 10 million, and of metacities of over 20 million inhabitants (UN-HABITAT 2007a). This includes the growth of informal settlements, in which some one billion slum dwellers now live in extremely deprived and difficult conditions. Thus context, and the accompanying institutions and culture, are major components of any policy that hopes to impact crime and reduce violence. In such circumstances the carefully argued notions of evidence-based crime prevention in high-income developed countries have to be recognised as themselves contextualised, and culturally and institutionally dependent. Much of the 'international exchange' in the field of crime prevention policy and research has not in fact been global, but rather bilateral, or between similar high-income western industrialised countries (cf. Farrington 2000).

Positive changes over 25 years (not always recognised!)

In looking at models of crime prevention, and the future directions they might take, it is helpful to remind ourselves of both the positive and the less positive changes that have taken place in the field in Europe and beyond. In fact, an enormous number of positive developments in the shape and practice of crime prevention have taken place (in terms of an actual focus on prevention, and not just on deterrence), over the past 20 years. These include the following.

First, there is the importance of developing strategic, planned approaches, based on good analysis of the issues, especially at the local level where the impacts of crime are primarily experienced. Although never without their problems, the role of local authorities, the police and elected officials in this regard has developed substantially since its emergence in the 1980s (Bonnemaison 1982; Ekblom et al. 1996; Shaw 2001).

Second, as suggested above, in the past ten years especially, the crucial importance of context has become apparent. There is greater awareness of what works, sometimes, and in some places, but not always, nor everywhere.

Third, the importance of implementing and sustaining projects is increasingly recognised. As 'realist criminology' has helped to demonstrate, projects do not work by themselves, people are essential, and capacity-building is an essential element of what makes them work. There has been far more attention in recent years given to the importance of governance, and sustaining prevention strategies beyond the life of one government administration. In the case of Bogota, Colombia, for example, crime has been successfully 'taken off' the political agenda and its long-term sustainability established (Bogota 2008; Velasquez 2008).

Fourth, in this respect it is now more evident that no one sector is more important than others in developing and implementing crime prevention policies – policy-makers, practitioners, researchers and academics are equally important in terms of their contributions, knowledge and capacities. Some of the lessons from the UK Crime Reduction Programme well demonstrate a failure to pay sufficient attention to all sectors, or to the implementation phases of projects (Homel *et al.* 2004; Maguire 2004).

Fifth, there is greater understanding of the importance of the role of social capital, and of the strength and capacities of communities and civil society organisations in working with institutions, whether the police or local authorities, to reduce violence (Moser and McIlwaine 2006; Shaw 2006). The role of women in this regard is especially evident in working to reduce violence and build citizenship, not only in impoverished communities, but also in situations of chronic violence (Pearce 2007).

Sixth, we now have UN Guidelines for crime prevention, establishing a series of principles and standards for crime prevention and its implementation. These basic principles (ECOSOC 2002/13) are as follows:

- Government leadership

- Socio-economic development and inclusion, co-operation and partnerships

- Sustainability, and accountability

- Knowledge base

- Human rights/rule of law/culture of lawfulness

- Interdependency

- Differentiation.

The last five years has seen an expansion of crime prevention initiatives to post-conflict countries and new democracies in all regions of the world

– supported by these norms and standards. At the 11th UN Congress on Crime Prevention and Criminal Justice held in 2005 in Bangkok, for example, programmes or projects on urban crime prevention and youth at risk from 15 countries were presented.[5] This geographical expansion is further underlined in ICPC's first *International Report on Crime Prevention and Community Safety* (2008), which also touches among other issues on the expansion of 'new' community safety professions, especially at the local level (Cherney 2004; Crawford 2006), and the increasing use of knowledge-based approaches.

More recently, there has been a shift in understanding of the centrality of basic safety and security for development, and the achievement of the Millennium Development Goals. Increasing rates of violence and crime impact on both existing or fragile democratic institutions, civil society, and economic development (Leeds 2007). In the recent past, the response has been to try to respond to crime by strengthening the criminal justice system, but not to consider prevention as a prerequisite. This shift has begun to influence the thinking of international organisations and donor countries and organisations. Development cannot be achieved if issues of crime and security are not taken into account alongside economic, employment, housing sector or justice improvements (UNODC 2005, 2007a, 2007b; Buvinic *et al.* 2005; Stone and Miller 2005; Moser and McIlwaine 2006; WHO 2008).

Less positive developments in crime prevention

There have also been some less positive developments over this period, some of them are simply the reverse of the positive developments outlined above. These include the following.

First, there has been the focus on northern models, but not on what is happening elsewhere globally. (This might be called the 'binocular view' – How are they doing over there? Why have they failed to implant community policing in Hong Kong, Sydney, or Cape Town . . .?). What this preoccupation often fails to notice are the well-adapted and functioning developments in rather different kinds of societies and cities. For example, the Koban policing system in Japan, the development of *Panchayat* police stations in the slums of Mumbai, India, or the implantation of BAC-UP policing at the local level in the Philippines (Coronel 2007; Roy *et al.* 2004).

Second, there has been comparatively little interest in what is happening elsewhere in the world in terms of the pressures of urbanisation, poverty and exclusion, guns and drugs, or trafficking and terrorism, other, perhaps, than in terms of its impact on individual developed countries.

A third pitfall has been the often intense focus on 'high-science' and 'what works' – which are perhaps too resource-rich and context-dependent, and claim too much. Such approaches assume huge capacities, funds and time, and can lead to disillusionment and disappointment by the public, practitioners and policy-makers when promises are not met and outcomes unclear. There has often been a strong emphasis on avoiding 'messy' crime prevention practices, which are not easily evaluated nor keep to strict parameters, such as multiple interventions, and social and community-based programmes. Donor funding has similarly often been tied to evaluation of impact with more regard to showing 'value for money spent' than local feasibility, or inversely dictated the use of interventions likely to demonstrate measurable impacts.

Fourth, there is the phenomenon noted by Crawford (2006) of 'defining deviancy up' with the criminalisation of incivilities, especially apparent in the UK and with the use of anti-social behaviour orders. This phenomenon has important implications for human rights, and risks being seen by some countries as an attractive policy option.

Fifth, there is also the linked issue of 'talking up' crime and insecurity (Tonry 2004; Crawford 2007; Blath 2008), to the extent that governments have fanned fear of crime, rather than reducing it. In the UK, crime is now at its lowest level for 20 years, yet levels of fear, and expectations that something should be done about it, continue to remain high. The problems associated with a major focus on fear of crime are not restricted to the UK, however. A recent victim survey in small Quebec towns, for example, found elderly women felt 'insecure' at the sight of graffiti on post boxes (UMQ 2007). This stands in considerable contrast to the insecurity that is a daily reality for South Africans, with levels of homicide and risk of robbery at levels unheard of in Europe. This has led one South African observer, Barbara Holtmann (2007), to question what it means to talk about reducing fear in such circumstances.

There are also problems stemming from the narrow focus on national, country, region-bound practice and theory, as well as the narrow 'classical' focus of much criminology. This is exemplified by recent work on, for example, youth violence and youth gangs. In part this relates to the restrictions of mainstream criminology, which has maintained a strong fixation with American theoretical and empirical approaches, and programmes that focus on young people themselves as 'the problem'. Such relatively narrow frameworks do not help in understanding, or responding to, the institutionalised nature of many gang structures found around the world.

As Hagedorn (2007b) has argued, the subject of gangs has been dominated by American criminological perspectives that do not take account of global changes or historical realities beyond the USA. This has constructed gangs as a right of passage associated with social disorganisation, immigration and industrialisation in the city. Further, much of the literature is narrow in conception because it restricts itself to studying gangs from the perspective of criminality, rather than viewing them within a broader understanding of cities and the impacts of globalisation. Even cross-cultural studies such as Malcolm Klein and colleagues' (2001) *Eurogang Paradox* can be seen as partial in this respect.

The work of the Coalition on Organized Armed Violence (COAV) and others provides a more open approach to understanding youth gangs and violence (Dowdney 2005; Hagedorn 2005, 2007a, 2007b; Leggett 2005; Standing 2003, 2005, 2006; Ward 2007). What this work suggests is that we need broader models and empirical material to help us understand the phenomenon of violence and youth groups and gangs in different countries of the world. The COAV project has examined the existence of institutionalised, embedded youth gangs in countries such as Brazil, Guatemala, Nigeria, South Africa and Northern Ireland (Dowdney 2005). Explanations are much more complex than the US theory of adolescent rebellion, and the product of social disorganisation. Such gangs often have clear historical roots, for example, in apartheid policing tactics. They often have strong ties to their local communities and receive support from them, and play both a philanthropic and a social and economic role, apart from their criminal activity associated with guns, drugs and prostitution (e.g. Standing 2003, 2005, 2006). Studies of gangs in Nicaragua and Central America similarly point to the importance of historical and contemporary factors, with the evolution of violent activities from rural areas to urban slums (Rodgers 2007), while the role of deportation policies or tough *mana duro* policing in increasing gang activities is receiving more attention (Washington Office on Latin America 2006).

Developing international models

As has been argued above, internationally, crime prevention has often had to start from a very different context and position from that of most European countries, and rarely from the luxury of an academic standpoint. Greater account tends to be taken of a wider range of factors, and more flexible, pragmatic models and wider typologies and theories are being developed. Some of this more flexible approach can be seen in work on such issues as governance, private–public policing, network nodes, club goods, which has taken a much more international and cross-disciplinary standpoint than many other areas of criminology, as well as practices around community peace-building and peace-making (Wood and Dupont 2006).

Some of the most interesting and strongest models currently impacting crime internationally, and that offer promise for the future, include integrated public health approaches, urban regeneration, and human security approaches. What is similar in each is the *methodology* of the approach, which combines interdisciplinary and multi-sector partnerships, often with strong participatory community group and NGO involvement, medium and long-term planning, and a strong focus on data collection and analysis, monitoring and evaluation. There is often focus on utilising and strengthening the role of civil society and non-government organisations, and of mainstreaming gender in crime prevention (Buvinic *et al.* 2005). In practice, elements of all three approaches are often to be found together.

Public health approaches start from the premise that violence is a public health rather than a justice issue, requiring a range of strategies to reduce and prevent it. Thus reducing all deaths in a city, whether from violence or accidents, becomes a priority. The work of the Armed Violence Prevention Programme (AVPP), which has grown out of the WHO world report on violence, exemplifies this approach (AVPP 2003), and aims to work with national and local governments, linking communities and NGOs. The AVPP programme sets out a results framework, aiming to enhance national policies and action plans on violence prevention, and develop national and civil society capacity to prevent violence using more integrated approaches. Six projects are currently being piloted. The Alexandra Township Urban Renewal Project, for example, focuses on the role of the social fabric in violence reduction, including better housing and health services, employment and sanitation (AVPP 2003).

Such an approach forms part of the 'citizen security' strategy developed in the city of Bogota, Colombia, which has seen a very marked reduction in violence and deaths since the late 1990s, under the direction of a series of mayors. It is marked by strong leadership and a comprehensive strategy that began with the application of an epidemiological analysis of violence in the city, and the establishment of a city Observatory to monitor and analyse trends. The first of these mayors, Antanas Mockus, among other innovations, has stressed the central importance of developing a culture of lawfulness and civic responsibility, with a range of very imaginative approaches, such as using clowns to model behaviour in public places to help change attitudes to public transport and traffic behaviour, or by the creation of a taxi cadre that prides itself on good service. Other major components introduced under subsequent mayors such as Enrique Penelosa have used urban regeneration and environmental design to create public parks, libraries and pedestrian streets, and dedicated safe public bus routes (the *Transmilenio*), again with a stress on citizen quality of life, rather than an modernisation for its own sake. Family police stations to tackle domestic violence, and a series of local contracts with borough mayors, to develop projects targeting specific neighbourhood problems, have also been instituted. The use of local contracts, and the development of a long-term strategy, the *Libro Blanco*, are seen as essential ingredients for ensuring the long-term sustainability of the public safety plan. As Velasquez has underlined, crime has effectively been taken out of the political party agenda (Velasquez 2008; Bogota 2008) (see Figure 11.2).

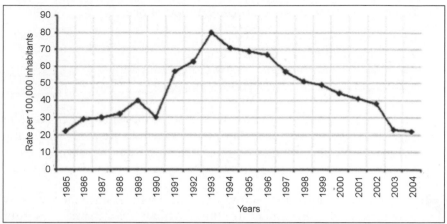

Source: Institute for Legal Medicine and Forensic Science 1985–2004, National Attorney General, Colombia, cited in Acero (2006)

Figure 11.2 Bogota, Colombia: rate of homicides per 100,000 inhabitants, 1985–2004

The case of the city of Diadema, in the metropolitan region of Sao Paulo, Brazil, provides another striking example of an approach that combines a range of strategies, including elements of public health, urban renewal, policing and enforcement changes, and social and community interventions. In 2000, Diadema had the highest rate of homicides in the metropolitan region, but by 2004 this had been reduced to the position of 18th among the municipalities. This was the result of the implementation of a ten-point crime prevention strategy, developed by Mayor Jose Filippe Junior and his council (Filippe Junior 2007).

1. The creation of a Municipal Department of Social Policies and Public Security; mapping all criminal activity.

2. The integration of all police forces in the city (Municipal, Military and Civil Regional).

3. New law enforcing the closure of all establishments selling alcohol from 11:00 p.m. to 06:00 a.m.

4. Launching the Municipal Council for the Safety and the Prevention of Crime.

5. Increasing the Municipal Police Force by 70 per cent and establishing 'The Neighbourhood Angels'.

6. Establishing 'The Young Apprentice Project'.

7. Social and environmental policies including *favela* and school projects.

8. The installation of surveillance cameras.

9. The inspections and law enforcement operations.

10. Launching three major campaigns:
    - Disarmament of Fire Arms Campaign
    - Children's Disarmament of Toy Guns Campaign
    - Drugs and Alcohol Awareness Campaign

A vibrant participatory process was also established, with regular meetings between local wards and the council to discuss needs and developing plans, and the allocation of dedicated municipal funds to be used for projects selected by residents through the participatory budgeting process.

It should also be noted that across Brazil as a whole, since the Gun Free Campaign, and the enactment of the Brazilian Disarmament Statute, which came into force in December 2003 placing restrictions on gun ownership, there has been a marked decline in firearm-related homicides, after 13 years of continual increase. Between 2003 and 2005 there was an 8.8 per cent decrease in firearm deaths, which has been estimated to have saved 12,000 lives (Macinko and de Souza 2007).[6]

The *human security approach* has also evolved from a different standpoint other than the justice system. Stemming in part from a political science standpoint, it involves the notion of *people*, rather than nation states, as the principal point of reference, and is usually associated with efforts to reduce people's vulnerability to a broad array of risks (Canadian Consortium on Human Security 2007), including:

> conflict and poverty, protecting people during violent conflict and post-conflict situations, defending people who are forced to move, overcoming economic insecurities, guaranteeing the availability and affordability of essential health care, and ensuring the elimination of illiteracy and educational deprivation and of schools that promote intolerance. (cited in UN-HABITAT 2007a: 7)

It marks a shift from the rights of the state to those of individuals, in recognition of the complexity of risks and the inability (or unwillingness) of states to ensure the security of their citizens. It underlines the expansion of roles and responsibilities beyond the state, and it recognises that the security of individuals and communities crosses borders, and cannot be ensured only from within the confines of one state. In the case of UN-HABITAT, their work has focused on security not only from crime and violence, but also from problems arising from land tenure and natural disasters, and what they term the geography of risk and vulnerability. The unequal distribution of political and social resources (Moser and McIlwaine 2006) becomes a major factor in vulnerability to violence.

Some recent examples of *urban regeneration approaches* involve considerably more than environmentally designing out crime. One outstanding example is the iTRUMP project in eThekwini (Durban), South Africa. iTRUMP is a scaling-up of the Warwick Junction Project, which began in 1997 with an effort to improve the area around the transport hub of Durban (Dobson 2007). Some of the most notable features of the Warwick Junction Project include the siting of the project office in the neighbourhood itself rather than in City Hall, a wide project spectrum that included both capital projects and human and social issues, the notion of maintaining the distinctive characteristics of an area, very creative use of existing urban structures using safety through environmental design principles, and especially extensive consultation with the users of the area. Most notably this included the informal traders selling goods brought in daily from rural and township areas, who in other scenarios might have had their goods confiscated or been thrown out in favour of a business improvement district. The herb-traders' market that has been created was the result of some 18 months of negotiation and consultation between the city, the project staff and the traders, who eventually created their own association. The traders now help to regulate and oversee the new market area. Creative solutions for other informal traders such as bovine heads and mealie sellers,[7] are similarly part of the project. Lock-ups provide overnight security for produce, and single toilets which have become overseen by nearby stallholders are now safe and clean. The impact on crime has been clear, with a reduction in incidents and violent deaths, and major health and economic gains, with a chain of some 14,000 jobs created across the municipality, as well as the creation of what has become a tourist attraction.

What these examples demonstrate is the strength of the approach and methodology – an integrated approach with the city and local government taking responsibility and providing strong leadership, and using a range of approaches based on good prior analysis. Often this involves considerable civil society participation. Using combinations of social mediation, active participation and inclusion, job creation, employment and skills training, and capacity building, such approaches provide clear examples of the importance of community engagement. They are exemplified in the participatory budgeting process used in Brazil and other Latin American countries (Cabannes 2006), the Proudly Manenburg Initiative in Cape Flats, South Africa, or the work of the Afro-Reggae Cultural Group from Rio de Janeiro in Brazil, which has actively engaged with the police to teach them their skills of dancing, music and graffiti arts, and changing mutually held stereotypes and attitudes.[8]

Where do we go from here? Are there any implications for European crime prevention?

In a sense, it can be argued that we can learn just as much about developing and implementing good crime prevention from developing countries, and from initiatives in overcrowded cities, as we can from high-income developed countries and our European neighbours, and we may have less to teach than we think.

Notwithstanding the European and northern preoccupation with whether or not partnerships are working (Dupont 2008), the arguments are that the problems confronting many regions, countries, megacities and towns around the world can be worked on using a strategic planned approach to crime prevention and community safety, and the evolving methodology and knowledge carefully developed over the past ten or more years (problem-solving, multi-sector, partnerships). What they often demonstrate are innovative responses to very unique and diverse situations. The involvement of the community often forms a major aspect of this work, but grounded in key principles such as respect for human rights and the rule of law, and inclusion and active participation. It is also a continually evolving process.

What this means is that crime prevention should pay more attention to respecting and enhancing human rights and the rule of law (Redo 2008), not infringing them; it should work to include children and young people rather than seeing them as 'yobs' or *'raccaille'*. In considering the dangers of community crime prevention, which can encourage the exclusion of strangers in the interests of neighbourhood safety, Carson has raised attention to the issue of the *obligation* to respect the rights of others (Carson 2007). As he suggests, the downward devolution of responsibilities for prevention from state to local governments and communities must also mean increased accountability, in the reverse direction, with local knowledge receiving similar attention to that given to expert knowledge. The kinds of participatory approaches developed in Latin America or India and elsewhere provide some important examples for European countries of what real, democratic, participation in governance can look like. As Carson has argued, 'it would be recognised on all sides that crime-prevention knowledge and policies are matters for genuinely dialogic processes' (Carson 2007: 720). In the same way, and following the Paris Declaration on Aid Effectiveness (OECD 2005) the movement among donor countries and organisations to develop technical assistance projects *with* recipient countries, respecting their analysis of concerns, their financial and legislative timetables, their existing capacities, rather than imposing their own, can also be seen as relevant to developed countries and their community crime prevention initiatives.

Also touched on in this chapter is the use of responses that try positively to reinforce, rather than regulate and deter in order to change behaviour, working in a sense upwards rather than downwards. Examples include the modelling of citizen behaviour in Colombia, young people changing police perceptions, or the institution of a citizen-selected police prize awarded to police who perform their job appropriately and well, rather than relying only on punishment of misbehaviour (Leeds 2007).[9]

Beyond this, models that use aspects of public health, urban regeneration or human security perspectives help to place violence and crime in a somewhat different light as part of a continuum of safety, as issues of citizen safety, and safety as a public good (EFUS 2006), rather than primarily policing matters. Difficult as it may seem, they can help to take crime out of the political agenda. They also open up consideration of the impact of individual country or city policies on other countries and regions, as in the case of gang deportation in Los Angeles, or trafficked workers in Europe. They help to enrich, and move beyond, criminology and the narrow confines of duelling categories of crime prevention or evaluation, in considering what to do, and how it can be accomplished and sustained. All this requires, as Maguire has suggested, 'a quiet iterative process over the longer term' (Maguire 2004: 214), and modest expectations of change. For European countries, some with now very considerable experience and expertise in crime prevention strategy, policy, practice and evaluation, others with developing strategies, there is much to be learnt from programmes, practices and strategies in regions around the world, including developing countries.

Notes

1 As a non-resident European, working from an international perspective, I would especially like to thank Adam Crawford, Réné Levy and the CRIMPREV initiative, for the invitation to join such a distinguished group of European scholars.
2 In the 1960s, the Crime Prevention Centre at Easingwold in the UK provided training for policemen on the importance of locks and bars and bicycle safety.
3 The Global Alliance ALTUS links together six research institutes and advocacy centres in six regions (www.altus.org). FLACSO is a consortium of Latin American research centres (www.flacso.org). The Brazilian Forum *Forum Brasileiro de Segurança Publica* was established in 2006 (see www.forum-seguranca.org.br).
4 See also the recent report to the Secretary General on the application of the guidelines *United Nations Standards and Norms in Crime Prevention and Criminal Justice*, E/CN15/2007/11.
5 A compendium of 64 promising practices from around the world was also published for the workshop (Shaw and Travers 2005, 2007), see also the ICPC (2008) report.
6 For a recent history of the firearms campaign in Brazil see www.soudapaz.org, www.vivario.org.br, www.comunidadesegura.org.

7 Both bovine heads (an aphrodisiac) and mealies (corn cobs) are traditional and very popular. They require facilities for boiling and waste disposal.
8 See Ramos (2006b) and www.proudlymanenburg.org
9 The annual Police Awards to police for doing their job well, which are presented annually by the Brazilian organisation Sou da Paz (www.soudapaz.org).

References

Acero, H. (2006) 'Bogota's Success Story', *Comunidad Segura*. Available at: www.comunidadesegura.org/?q=en/node/31203

Armed Violence Prevention Programme (AVPP) (2003) *Armed Violence Prevention Programme: Support to Community Based Violence Prevention Programmes*, Project Document. INT/03/MXX.

Azaola, E. (2007) 'The Weaknesses of Public Security Forces in Mexico City', in *Proceedings of the 7th ICPC Colloquium, Oslo, on the Role of the Police in Crime Prevention*. Montreal: ICPC.

Beato, C. (2005) *Case Study 'Fico Vivo' Homicide Control Project in Belo Horizonte*. Washington DC: International Bank for Reconstruction and Development/The World Bank.

Biau, D. (2007) 'Three Things We Should Know About Slums', *Habitat Debate*, 13(1), March.

Blath, R. (2008) 'Victimization Surveys in Comparative Perspective,' in K. Aromaa and M. Heiskanen (eds) *Victimization Surveys in Comparative Perspective. Papers from the Stockholm Symposium 2007*. Publication Series No. 56. Helsinki: HEUNI.

Bogota (2008) *Libro Blanco de la Seguridad Ciudadana y la Convivencia de Bogota*. Bogota: City of Bogota and UN-HABITAT.

Bonnemaison, G. (1982) *Rapport de la Commission des Maires sur la Sécurité*. Paris: Collection des Rapports Officiels.

Buvinic, M., Alda, E. and Lamas, J. (2005) *Emphasizing Prevention in Citizen Security. The Inter-American Development Bank's Contribution to Reducing Violence in Latin America & the Caribbean*. Washington DC: Inter-American Development Bank.

Cabannes, Y. (2006) 'Children and Young People Build Participatory Democracy in Latin American Cities', *Environment and Urbanization*, 18(1): 195–218.

Carson, W. G. (2007) 'Calamity or Catalyst: Futures for Community in 21st Century Crime Prevention', *British Journal of Criminology*, 47(5): 711–27.

Canadian Consortium on Human Security (CCHS) (2007) *Human Security for an Urban Century. Local Challenges, Global Perspectives*. Vancouver: Canadian Consortium on Human Security and Department of Foreign Affairs and International Trade. Online at: www.humansecurity-cities.org

Cherney, A. (2004) 'Contingency and Politics: The Local Government Safety Officer Role', *Criminal Justice*, 4(2): 115–28.

Coronel, M. G. (2007) 'The Philippines Strategy and Best Practice for Crime Prevention: Community-oriented Policing System', in M. Shaw and K. Travers (eds) *Strategies and Best Practices in Crime Prevention in Particular in Relation to Urban Areas and Youth at Risk*. Proceedings of the Workshop held at the 11th UN Congress on Crime Prevention and Criminal Justice, Bangkok, Thailand, 18–25 April. Montreal: ICPC. Online at www.crime-prevention-intl.org

Crawford, A. (2006) 'Fixing Broken Promises?: Neighbourhood Wardens and Social Capital', *Urban Studies*, 43(5/6): 957–76.

Crawford, A. (2007) 'Crime Prevention and Community Safety', in M. Maguire, R. Morgan, and R. Reiner (eds) *Oxford Handbook of Criminology*, 4th edn. Oxford: Oxford University Press, pp. 866–909.

Dixon, D. and Maher, L. (2005) 'Policing, Crime and Public Health: Lessons for Australia from the "New York Miracle"', *Criminal Justice*, 5(2): 115–43.

Dobson, R. (2007) 'Urban Regeneration as a Crime Prevention Strategy: The Experience of Warwick Junction, eThekwini, Durban, South Africa', in M. Shaw and K. Travers, (eds) *Strategies and Best Practices in Crime Prevention in Particular in Relation to Urban Areas and Youth at Risk*. Proceedings of the Workshop held at the 11th UN Congress on Crime Prevention and Criminal Justice, Bangkok, Thailand, 18–25 April. Montreal: ICPC, pp. 99–104.

Dowdney, L. (ed.) (2005) *Neither War nor Peace: International Comparisons of Children and Youth in Organized Armed Violence*. Rio de Janeiro: Viva Rio and Children and Youth in Organized Armed Violence.

Dupont, B. (2008) 'Crime Prevention Partnerships: Over-evaluated and Underutilized Tools', *International Report on Crime Prevention and Community Safety: Trends and Perspectives*, Montreal: ICPC, pp. 218–19.

Ekblom, P., Law, H. and Sutton, M. (1996) *Safer Cities and Domestic Burglary*. Home Office Research Study 164. London: Home Office.

European Forum for Urban Safety (EFUS) (2006) *Security, Democracy and Cities. The Zaragoza Manifesto*. Paris: European Forum for Urban Security.

Farrington, D. P. (2000) 'Explaining and Preventing Crime: The Globalization of Knowledge', *Criminology*, 38(1): 1–24.

Filippe Junior, J. (2007) 'The Experience of the City of Diadema', in M. Shaw and K. Travers (eds) *Strategies and Best Practices in Crime Prevention in Particular in Relation to Urban Areas and Youth at Risk*. Proceedings of the Workshop held at the 11th UN Congress on Crime Prevention and Criminal Justice, Bangkok, Thailand, 18–25 April. Montreal: ICPC, pp. 92–8.

Foster, J. (2002) ' "People Pieces": The Neglected but Essential Elements of Community Crime Prevention', in G. Hughes and A. Edwards (eds) *Crime Control and Community: The New Politics of Public Safety*. Cullompton: Willan Publishing, pp. 167–97.

Hagedorn, J. M. (2005) 'The Global Impact of Gangs', *Journal of Contemporary Criminal Justice*, 21(2): 153–69.

Hagedorn, J. M. (ed.) (2007a) *Gangs in the Global City. Alternatives to Traditional Criminology*. Urbana and Chicago: University of Illinois Press.

Hagedorn, J. M. (2007b) 'Gangs in Late Modernity', in J. M. Hagedorn (ed.) *Gangs in the Global City. Alternatives to Traditional Criminology*. Urbana and Chicago: University of Illinois Press, pp. 295–317.

Hinton, M. (2006) *The State of the Streets: The Police and Politics in Argentina and Brazil*. Boulder/London: Lynne Reinner Publishers.

Holtmann, B. (2007) ICPC Round Table on Cities, Lachine, Quebec (May).

Holtmann, B. (2008) Presentation at AFSSA Convention, 25–28 August. Online at: www.safesouthafrica.org.za

Homel, P. (2006) 'Annual Crime Prevention Lecture', International Centre for the Prevention of Crime, 12th September, Canberra, Australia. *Proceedings of ICPC's 6th Annual Colloquium on Crime Prevention*. Montreal: ICPC.

Homel, P., Webb, B., Tilley, N. and Nutley, S. (2004) *Investing to Deliver: Reviewing the Implementation of the UK Crime Reduction Programme*, Home Office Research Study 281. London: Home Office.

International Centre for the Prevention of Crime (ICPC) (2008) *International Report on Crime Prevention and Community Safety: Trends and Perspectives*. Montreal: ICPC.

Klein, M., Kerner, H. J., Maxon, C. L. and Weitekamp, E. (eds) (2001) *The Eurogang Paradox*. Amsterdam: Kluwer Academic.

Lab, S. (2005) *Unresolved Issues for Crime Prevention Research*. Washington DC: Office of Research and Evaluation, National Institute of Justice.

Lau, R. W. K. (2004) 'Community Policing in Hong Kong: Transplanting a Questionable Model', *Criminal Justice*, 4(1): 61–80.

Leeds, E. (2007) 'Serving States and Serving Citizens: Halting Steps Towards Police Reform in Brazil and Implications for Donor Intervention', *Policing and Society*, 17(1): 21–37.

Leggett, T. (2005) *Terugskiet: Growing up on the Street Corners of Manenburg, South Africa*. Pretoria: Institute for Security Studies.

Macinko, J. and Marinho de Souza, M. (2007) 'Reducing Firearm Injury: Lessons from Brazil', *LDI Issue Brief*, 12(7). University of Pennsylvania.

Maguire, M. (2004) 'The Crime Reduction Programme in England and Wales: Reflections on the Vision and the Reality', *Criminal Justice*, 4(3): 213–37.

Marks, M. and Goldsmith, A. (2006) 'The State, the People and Democratic Policing: The Case of South Africa', in J. Wood and B. Dupont (eds) *Democracy, Society and the Governance of Security*. Cambridge: Cambridge University Press, pp. 139–64.

Moser, C. and McIlwaine, C. (2006) 'Latin American Urban Violence as a Development Concern', *World Development*, 34(1): 89–112.

Newburn, T. and Sparks, R. (2004) *Criminal Justice and Political Cultures: National and International Dimensions of Crime Control*. Cullompton: Willan Publishing.

Organisation for Economic Co-operation and Development (OECD) (2005) *Paris Declaration on Aid Effectiveness*. High Level Forum, Paris, 28 February–2 March. Online at: www.oecd.org

Pearce, J. (2007) *Violence, Power and Participation: Building Citizenship in Contexts of Chronic Violence*, IDS Working Paper 274. Brighton: University of Sussex.

Pelser, E. (Ed.) (2002) *Crime Prevention Partnerships: Lessons from Practice*. Pretoria: Institute for Security Studies.

Ramos, S. (2006a) *Juventude e Violencia*. Presentation at the Seminario de Prevencao a Violencia e a Criminalidade, Belo Horizonte, 9–10 November.

Ramos, S. (2006b) 'Youth and the Police', in *Boletim seguranca e cidadania*, Centre for Studies on Public Security and Citizenship. Rio de Janiero: CESeC University of Candido Mendes.

Redo, S. (2008) 'Six United Nations Guiding Principles to Make Crime Prevention Work', in M. Coester and E. Marks (eds) *International Perspectives of Crime Prevention*. Mönchengladbach: Forum Verlag Godesburg, pp. 5–21.

Rodgers, D. (2007) *Slum Wars of the Twenty-First Century*, Crisis States Research Centre Working Paper 10. London: London School of Economics.

Roy, A. N., Jocklin, A. and Ahmad, J. (2004) 'Community Police Stations in Mumbai's Slums', *Environment and Urbanization*, 16(2): 135–38.

Shaw, M. (2001) *The Role of Local Government in Community Safety*. Washington DC: US Department of Justice, Bureau of Justice Assistance/Montreal: ICPC.

Shaw, M. (2006) *Communities in Action for Crime Prevention*, Background Paper for 7th ICPC Annual Colloquium, Canberra, Australia. Online at: www.crime-prevention-intl.org

Shaw, M. and Dandurand, Y. (eds) (2006) *Maximizing the Effectiveness of Technical Assistance Provided by the Fields of Crime Prevention and Criminal Justice*. Proceedings of the Workshop held by the Programme Network Institutes during the 15th Session of the UN Commission on Crime Prevention and Criminal Justice, Vienna, 24 April, Publication Series No. 49. Helsinki: HEUNI.

Shaw, M. and Travers, K. (eds) (2005) *Urban Crime and Youth at Risk: Compendium of Promising Strategies and Programme*. Montreal: ICPC. Online at: www.crime-prevention-intl.org

Shaw, M. and Travers, K. (eds) (2007) *Strategies and Best Practices in Crime Prevention in Particular in Relation to Urban Areas and Youth at Risk*, Proceedings of the Workshop held at the 11th UN Congress on Crime Prevention and Criminal Justice, Bangkok, Thailand, 18–25 April 2005. Montreal: ICPC. Online at: www.crime-prevention-intl.org

Small Arms Survey (2006) *Small Arms Survey 2006: Unfinished Business*. Geneva: Small Arms Survey and Oxford University Press.

Standing, A. (2003) *The Social Contradictions of Organized Crime on the Cape Flats*, ISS Paper 74. Pretoria: Institute for Security Studies.

Standing, A. (2005) *The Threat of Gangs and Anti-gang Policy*, ISS Paper 116. Pretoria: Institute for Security Studies.

Standing, A. (2006) *Organized Crime: A Study from the Cape Flats*. Pretoria: Institute for Security Studies.

Stone, C. and Miller, J. (2005) *Supporting Security Justice and Development: Lessons for a New Era*, Report for the UK Department of International Development and the Foreign and Commonwealth Office. New York: Vera Institute of Justice.

Tonry, M. (2004) *Punishment and Politics: Evidence and Emulation and the Making of English Crime Control Policy*. Cullompton: Willan Publishing.

UMQ (2007) *Survey*. Montreal: Union of Municipalities of Quebec.

UN-HABITAT (2007a) *Enhancing Urban Safety and Security*, Global Report on Human Settlements 2007. London: Earthscan.

UN-HABITAT (2007b) *Making Cities Safer from Crime – A Toolkit*, Safer Cities Local Crime Prevention Toolkit. Nairobi: UN-HABITAT.

UN-HABITAT (2008) *Youth and Children Championing Community Safety for a Better World*, Background Paper for the International Youth Crime Prevention and Cities Summit, 17–21 June. Durban, South Africa.

UNODC (2005) *Crime and Development in Africa*. Vienna: UNODC.

UNODC (2007a) *Crime and Development in the Caribbean*. Vienna: UNODC.

UNODC (2007b) *Crime and Development in Central America*. Vienna: UNODC.

UN Guidelines for the Prevention of Crime (2002) *Action to Promote Effective Crime Prevention*, ECOSOC Resolution 2002/13, Annex.

Van Dijk, J. (2008) *The World of Crime: Breaking the Silence of Problems of Security, Justice and Development Across the World*. Thousand Oaks: Sage.

Van Dijk, J., Manchin, R., Van Kesteren, J. and Hideg, G. (2007) *The Burden of Crime in the EU*, Research Report: A Comparative Analysis of the European Crime and Safety Survey (EU ICS) 2005. Brussels: European Commission.

Van Zyl Smit, D. and Van der Spruy, E. (2004) 'Importing Criminological Ideas in a New Democracy: Recent South African Experiences', in T. Newburn, and R. Sparks (eds) *Criminal Justice and Political Cultures: National and International Dimensions of Crime Control*. Cullompton: Willan Publishing, pp. 184–208.

Velasquez, E. (2008) 'Governance of Security in the Light of the Experience of Bogota', in *International Report on Crime Prevention and Community Safety: Trends and Perspectives*. Montreal: ICPC, pp. 214–15.

Ward, C. (2007) '*It Feels Like it's the End of the World*', *Cape Town's Youth Talk about Gangs and Community Violence*, Institute for Security Studies Monograph No. 136. Pretoria. ISS.

Washington Office on Latin America (2006) *Youth Gangs in Central America. Issues in Human Rights, Effective Policing, and Prevention*. Washington, DC: Washington Office on Latin America.

Wood, J. and Dupont, B. (eds) (2006) *Democracy, Society and the Governance of Security*. Cambridge: Cambridge University Press.

World Health Organization (2002) *World Report on Violence and Health*. Geneva: WHO.

World Health Organization (2006) *Global Estimates of Health Consequence Due to Violence Against Children*, Background Paper to the UN Secretary General's Study of Violence Against Children. Geneva: WHO.

World Health Organization (2008) *Preventing Violence and Reducing its Impact: How Development Agencies can Help*. Geneva: WHO.

Index

Added to a page number 'f' denotes a figure, 't' denotes a table and 'n' denotes notes.

Crime Prevention Policies in Comparative Perspective